# Death-related Intensifiers in the History of English

ENGLISH CORPUS LINGUISTICS

Graeme Davis / Damian Byrne (eds)

VOLUME 18

PETER LANG

Oxford - Berlin - Bruxelles - Chennai - Lausanne - New York

Zeltia Blanco-Suárez

# Death-related Intensifiers in the History of English

## Grammaticalisation and Related Phenomena

PETER LANG
Oxford - Berlin - Bruxelles - Chennai - Lausanne - New York

**Bibliographic information published by the Deutsche Nationalbibliothek.**
The German National Library lists this publication in the German National Bibliography; detailed bibliographic data is available on the Internet at http://dnb.d-nb.de.

A catalogue record for this book is available from the British Library.

Library of Congress Cataloging-in-Publication Data

Names: Blanco-Suárez, Zeltia, 1985- author.
Title: Death-related intensifiers in the history of English : grammaticalisation and related phenomena / Zeltia Blanco-Suárez.
Description: Oxford ; New York : Peter Lang, 2025. | Series: English corpus linguistics, 1610-868X ; volume no. 18 | Includes bibliographical references and index.
Identifiers: LCCN 2024051545 (print) | LCCN 2024051546 (ebook) | ISBN 9781803745145 (paperback) | ISBN 9781803745152 (ebook) | ISBN 9781803745169 (epub)
Subjects: LCSH: English language--Intensification. | English language--Grammaticalization. | Death.
Classification: LCC PE1321 .B57 2025 (print) | LCC PE1321 (ebook) | DDC 425--dc23/eng/20241210
LC record available at https://lccn.loc.gov/2024051545
LC ebook record available at https://lccn.loc.gov/2024051546

This research has received financial support from the Regional Government of Galicia (Consellería de Cultura, Educación, Formación Profesional e Universidades, grant number ED431B 2023/03).

ISSN 1610-868X
ISBN 978-1-80374-514-5 (print)
ISBN 978-1-80374-515-2 (ePDF)
ISBN 978-1-80374-516-9 (ePub)
DOI 10.3726/ b21920


Published by Peter Lang Ltd, Oxford, United Kingdom
info@peterlang.com - www.peterlang.com



This publication has been peer reviewed.

# Contents

# Figures

# Tables

# Acknowledgements

Many people have in one way or another contributed to bring this book to fruition and therefore deserve my most heartfelt thanks for all the (moral) support, positive energy and encouragement during this process. Without their support this project would surely not be successful. The monograph is based on my doctoral thesis, written and presented at the University of Santiago de Compostela under the supervision of María José López-Couso.

I am deeply indebted to my supervisor and the backbone of this piece of research, María José López-Couso, whose enthusiasm and trust in me are greatly acknowledged. I am also grateful to the three examiners who were part of my PhD viva: Hubert Cuyckens, Augusto Soares da Silva and Belén Méndez-Naya. Their most constructive and insightful comments and suggestions undoubtedly allowed me to prepare this manuscript. Likewise, I would like to thank the external reviewers for their very valuable feedback, as well as Laurel Plapp, Senior Acquisitions Editor at Peter Lang, for her help and support during the publication process. I also wish to express my deepest gratitude to my colleagues and friends at the Department of Philology of the University of Cantabria and at the Department of English of German Philology of the University of Santiago de Compostela for their support and advice during all these years, most especially to Patxi, Lidia and Noemí. In addition, I gratefully acknowledge the support of the research team *Variation, Linguistic Change* and *Grammaticalization* (VLCG) and the *English Linguistics Circle* (ELC).

For generous financial support, I am grateful to the following institutions: the Spanish Ministry of Education (AP2009-03626), the Spanish Ministry for Economy and Competitiveness (grant FFI2011-26693-C02-01), the Spanish Ministry of Science and Innovation (grants HUM2007-60706/FILO and PID2020-114604GB-100), and the Autonomous Government of Galicia (CN2011/011, CN2012/012, grants ED431D 2017/09, ED431B 2017/12 and ED431B 2023/03).

Nun plano máis persoal, quero recordar aquí o apoio recibido por moitas persoas ao longo deste percorrido, moi en especial a Soraya, Evelyn, Luisa, Elsa, Helena, Mario, Xosé, Yolanda e Yoli. Por suposto, quixera agradecer a toda a miña familia, sobre todos aos meus pais, Pili e Manolo, e a Juan, por repetirme unha e outra vez que todo o esforzo vale a pena. E como non, aos meus soles, Juan, Mariña e Catuxa, polas forzas que me dades a diario.

# Abbreviations

Corpora and electronic collections

| | |
|---|---|
| ARCHER | A Representative Corpus of Historical English Registers |
| ECF | Eighteenth Century Fiction |
| EEBOCorp 1.0 | Early English Books Online Corpus (version 1.0) |
| HC | The Helsinki Corpus of English Texts |
| NCF | Nineteenth Century Fiction |

Dictionaries

| | |
|---|---|
| MED | *Middle English Dictionary* |
| OED | *Oxford English Dictionary* |

Grammatical terms (in the Leipzig glosses)

| | |
|---|---|
| ACC | accusative |
| DAT | dative |
| DEFART | definite article |
| F | feminine |
| INF | infinitive |
| M | masculine |
| NOM | nominative |
| PL | plural |
| PRS | present |
| PST | past |

| | |
|---|---|
| PTCP | participle |
| SG | singular |
| SUP | superlative |
| 1 | first person |
| 3 | third person |

CHAPTER 1

# Introduction

Human communication consists not only in the mere exchange of propositional content, since, as claimed by Jakobson (1960) and Scheibman (2002: 9), language has functions other than the referential. One of these is the emotive or expressive function, which is focused on the speaker/writer, and which 'flavors to some extent all our utterances, on their phonic, grammatical, and lexical level' (Jakobson 1960: 354). With this function we highlight the importance of our message and add weight to our arguments, given that it implies the direct expression of the speaker's or writer's attitude towards the proposition. By way of illustration, if we want to emphasise the importance of something, we will not, in all likelihood, describe it simply as *important*. Instead, we will probably refer to it as *terribly important*, *incredibly important* or *highly important*, stressing as well, through intonation, the intensifying adverbs *terribly*, *incredibly* and *highly*. The use of expressive features such as interjections, stress and intensifying adverbs, therefore, is aimed to persuade our interlocutors and thus achieve our conversational purposes.

Humans show in fact an apparent taste for hyperbolic expressions and exaggeration (Peters 1994: 271), which is directly linked to the expressive function of language: the more we stress the relevance of our message, the more persuasive it will be. Our tendency to overstatement manifests itself in a proliferation of mechanisms of intensification in everyday language. Such linguistic devices, used to give prominence or relevance to our discourse, are known as *intensifiers* or *intensification strategies*, and include, among many others, intensifying adverbs (*bloody* and *awfully*, for instance), intensifying prefixes (e.g. *super–* and *mega–*, as in *super cute* and *mega rich*), intonation, the use of the superlative and the repetition of words (e.g. *very*,

*very important*). In the present work intensifiers are defined, along the lines of Bolinger (1972: 17), as 'any device that scales a quality, whether up or down or somewhere between the two'. They are, therefore, words and expressions which indicate a degree along a scale. Consider the examples in (1.1)–(1.4):

(1.1) *Some of the bus drivers are* ***super*** *nice, but most aren't.* (*Longman Dictionary of Contemporary English*, s.v. *super*[3] adv.)
(1.2) *That's* ***fucking*** *good coffee.* (*Longman Dictionary of Contemporary English Online*, s.v. *fucking* adj. and adv.)
(1.3) *I'm* ***dying for*** *a cup of coffee* (*MacMillan Dictionary*, s.v. *be dying for something/ to do something*)
(1.4) *That's* ***awfully*** *good of you. It's just too bad you didn't catch him.* (2003. Lisa Tucker. *The song reader: a novel.* COHA)

The intensifiers in bold in these examples reinforce the expressivity of the utterance, and are equivalent to *very nice*, *very good*, *I'm really looking forward to having a cup of coffee* and *very good*, respectively. Although *super*, *fucking*, *dying for* and *awfully* in (1.1)–(1.4) express high degree, intensifiers can also indicate low degree, as in (1.5), in which *at all* expresses the lowest degree possible ('I do not support her in any way'):

(1.5) *They don't support her* ***at all.*** (Quirk et al. 1985: 598).

The use of intensifiers or intensification strategies so as to convey the relevance of our message has, however, a downside. Over time, intensifiers may lose their initial expressive force through frequent use and may eventually be replaced by other forms fulfilling the same function. Renewal or *recycling* within the intensifier domain is highly conspicuous (Tagliamonte 2008), since these words are particularly liable to fashion, as well as highly sensitive to sociolinguistic factors. Intensifiers, therefore, offer an exceptional 'picture of fevered invention and competition that would be hard to come by elsewhere' (Bolinger 1972: 18). This susceptibility to change has placed intensifiers in the spotlight of studies on semantic change and sociolinguistic variation. However, despite all the scholarly attention which they have received, there is still room for further research on intensifiers. This monograph is therefore intended as a contribution to enhance our understanding of the origin, development and use of English intensifiers. In the remainder of this chapter, I look into the scope and aims of the study (Section 1.1) and provide the outline of this piece of research (Section 1.2).

## 1.1. Scope and aims of the study

Anthropologically speaking, the experience of death is of the most genuine concern for all cultures and societies worldwide, since it marks the most extreme limits of human existence. With such an impact on our daily routines, it comes as no surprise that death can successfully be exploited as a source of intensification in language, perhaps even cross-linguistically. As noted by Claridge (2011: 176), 'the existence of hyperbolic uses in different languages within the same semantic fields and partly with the same items is evidence for a cross-linguistic universal'.

The present study explores the use of death for intensification purposes in the English language. In particular, it aims to shed light on how certain forms from the semantic field of death, such as the ones illustrated in examples (1.6)–(1.10), came to be used as intensifiers to express high degree in Present-Day English (PDE).

(1.6) *What we've done so far is* ***dead*** *easy.* (1994. Science demonstration lesson. BYU-BNC)

(1.7) *He wasn't joking. I could tell he meant it. He was* ***deadly*** *serious and I knew it.* (1991. Malcolm Hammer. *Sudden death*. BYU-BNC)

(1.8) *'Southwest', amended the young man Martin.' "And in a* ***mortal*** *hurry by all the signs."* (1992. Ellis Peters. *The holy thief*. BYU-BNC)

(1.9) *This impression that I got or er erm* (pause) *that incident at school, played such a big part in my life after that, I was* ***mortally*** *embarrassed for the rest of my school life.* (1987. Gwynedd County Council tape 5: interview for oral history project (Leisure). BYU-BNC)

(1.10) *Four and a half thousand pounds*! [...] *She's chuffed* ***to death****. Only thing she weren't chuffed about is she couldn't cash cheque, it had to go all through bank and everything.* (1992. 25 convs rec. by 'Kathleen2' (PS1FC). BYU-BNC).

Although the use of death for intensifying or hyperbolic purposes has been explored in part by Claridge (2011: 197–207), Margerie (2011) and Blanco-Suárez (2013, 2014a, 2014b), a comprehensive diachronic corpus-based study of death-related intensifiers in English is still missing. The monograph will therefore be the first of its kind to provide a full account of the evolution of *dead(ly)*, *mortal(ly)* and *to death* from Early English to the present day, thereby filling this research gap. To this end, it will draw on data from several corpora and electronic collections of texts. The analysis conducted takes as a model the cline for the semantic development of intensifiers proposed by Sylvia Adamson (2000), which distinguishes three different types of meanings of intensifiers: descriptive > affective > intensifying. Thus, intensifiers originally show literal or descriptive meanings. Over time, these forms increase in subjectivity and come to express more affective or subjective values, before developing, at a later stage, purely intensifying meanings. Moreover, most intensifiers are argued to originate in lexical material and develop increasingly abstract or grammatical meanings over time via a grammaticalisation process (cf. Méndez-Naya 2003: 375). This is the case, for instance, of the intensifier *awfully* (e.g. *awfully glad*), which initially meant 'terribly, dreadfully' (OED, s.v. *awfully* adv. I 1). A number of initial research questions arise here:

- Is Adamson's (2000) model adequate to account for the semantic development of death-related intensifiers too?
- How well and to what extent do the forms under study here fit into the subjectivity and grammaticalisation clines proposed in the literature?
- When are the first intensifying uses of *dead(ly)*, *mortal(ly)* and *to death* attested? Do these uses coincide with Early Modern English (EModE), a most productive period for English intensifiers, according to Peters (1994)?
- In which contexts can we find these early intensifying uses? Are there any parallelisms in the collocations of the death-related intensifiers under study?

These and other questions concerning death-related intensifiers constitute the focus of the present research.

In order to study the semantic development of *dead(ly)*, *mortal(ly)* and *to death*, a number of variables were considered. The first of these concerns the actual collocation in which these intensifiers are attested, that is, the word(s) with which they co-occur. The type of meaning of the collocation (e.g. *deadly sin*, *dead sure*, *mortal scared*) is the second variable examined. For this, I have adapted the threefold distinction made by Adamson (2000) and distinguished two further intermediate levels: one between descriptive and subjective meanings and another between subjective and intensifying. The addition of these stages to the cline was intended to minimise the bias in the analysis of the data, given that assigning the examples to a particular category was not always straightforward. Thirdly, I looked at semantic prosody (cf. Stubbs 1995), that is, whether the collocate of *dead(ly)*, *mortal(ly)* and *to death* was semantically positive, negative or neutral. Finally, I also took into consideration the type of word modified by these forms, that is, whether it was a noun, an adjective, a verb, an adverb, etc. These four linguistic variables were examined in detail for each of the forms in four different historical periods, namely Middle English (ME), Early Modern English (EModE), Late Modern English (LModE) and twentieth-century English, and were statistically tested. Moreover, the actual strength of the association between the intensifier and its collocate was calculated by means of various statistical measures designed to assess the degree of collocational strength: the mutual information (*MI*) test and its cubed variant (*MI3*), the log-likelihood test and the *z*-score.

Being corpus-based, the collocational analysis conducted in this piece of research relied chiefly on corpora and electronic databases, though additional sources were used to supplement the corpus data. The *Oxford English Dictionary* (OED) and the *Middle English Dictionary* (MED) were consulted in order to obtain a preliminary overview of the origin and development of these intensifiers. The information provided by these historical dictionaries was subsequently expanded with evidence from a number of corpora and electronic collections of texts. Two classic corpora, which together cover the whole history of English, the HC (*Helsinki Corpus of English Texts*) and ARCHER (*A Representative Corpus of Historical English Registers*), were used in the hope of gaining an understanding of the overall evolution of these forms in the long diachrony, from the ME period up to PDE. The evidence from these sources, however, turned out to be insufficient and was hence complemented with larger corpora and databases for EModE and LModE. Thus, *Early English Books Online Corpus 1.0* (EEBOCorp 1.0), *Eighteenth Century Fiction* (ECF) and *Nineteenth Century Fiction* (NCF) shed light on the uses of the forms under analysis at these specific periods, providing a good number of examples of intensifying uses, which were scarce or inexistent in much smaller corpora such as the HC and ARCHER.

The novelty and strength of this study, however, lies not only in its topic. The diachronic semantic analysis presented in this piece of work is unprecedented in trying to provide a systematic analysis of a large volume of data, given the number of examples eventually examined (40,976 occurrences in total). A semantic analysis of the type conducted here posed an additional major challenge, since many of the instances involved discriminating between closely related meanings and, therefore, establishing rather fine-grained distinctions. Opting for a random sample of the data, although initially considered, was finally discarded as a result of the overall low frequency of these forms as intensifiers, which would clearly be insufficient to draw many firm conclusions on their overall diachronic development and contexts of use.

## 1.2. Outline of the study

The book consists of two clearly differentiated parts, the first one devoted to the literature review (Chapters 2, 3 and 4) and methodological issues (Chapter 5), and the second one to the case study on death-related intensifiers (Chapter 6).

Chapter 2 opens with a theoretical discussion of the role of intensification in language and how it is realised linguistically by means of various intensification strategies or intensifiers. Section 2.2 discusses intensifiers and their most distinguishing features, and presents the two major models of classification for intensifiers which have been proposed in the literature, namely degree-based models vs. semantic-based ones. Finally, some concluding remarks are provided to close the chapter in Section 2.3.

The purpose of Chapter 3 is to offer a detailed overview of grammaticalisation, the theory upon which this study hinges. After some preliminary remarks about the history of the term and its development in Section 3.1, I introduce the parameters and principles of grammaticalisation, as established by Lehmann (1985) and Hopper (1991), respectively (Section 3.2). Next, in Section 3.3, some of the phenomena typically associated with grammaticalisation are discussed, specifically unidirectionality, reanalysis and (inter)subjectification, before closing the chapter with a brief summary in Section 3.4.

Chapter 4 is intended to link the two theoretical chapters on intensification and grammaticalisation (Chapters 2 and 3) with the corpus-based study on death-related intensifiers (Chapter 6). The chapter thus includes a detailed diachronic overview of English intensifiers which have been tackled in the literature from the perspective of grammaticalisation. This review, however, is only concerned with intensifiers which scale upwards on a degree scale, expressing either maximum (the so-called maximisers, cf. Section 4.1.1) or high degree (the so-called boosters, cf. Section 4.1.2), in line with the function of *dead(ly)*, *mortal(ly)* and *to death*. Intensifiers which express low degree, therefore, have been excluded from that discussion. Finally, some concluding remarks are provided in Section 4.2.

Chapter 5 is concerned with methodological issues. As stated in Section 1.1, this research is primarily corpus-based. The chapter therefore opens with some introductory remarks on Corpus Linguistics, the framework adopted here. Next, in Section 5.2 I introduce the different sources of data consulted: dictionaries, corpora and electronic collections. Section 5.3, on the other hand, deals with the computer tool used for the analysis, Wordsmith 6.0 and its Concordance function, and with the different tests used to assess the statistical significance of the results. Finally, Section 5.4 explains the design of the database and its particulars, as well as the variables of analysis.

The actual corpus-based study is presented in Chapter 6. In the first part of the chapter (6.1) I provide an outline of the evolution of *dead(ly)*, *mortal(ly)* and *to death* in the light of the evidence provided by the OED and the MED. Next, I turn on to corpus evidence to trace the long diachrony of these intensifiers (Section 6.2), expanding the initial results from the OED and MED with empirical data from the HC, ARCHER, EEBOCorp 1.0, ECF and NCF. Therefore, the collocational study undertaken in this section allows, on the one hand, to provide the most comprehensive account of how these forms evolved over time. On the other, by considering the types of meanings expressed by these forms, in combination with their semantic prosodies and the type of words modified, the study also provides useful insights into how these intensifiers behave in each of the periods in the history of history and which of these were most productive for their intensifying function, hence allowing a much more fine-grained analysis. Lastly, Section 6.3 examines the development of the selected intensifiers in relation to the framework of grammaticalisation, hence applying all the theoretical underpinnings discussed in Chapter 3 to the data analysis.

Finally, Chapter 7 provides a summary of the main findings, together with some thoughts on potential research avenues in connection with the limitations of the current study.

CHAPTER 2

# Intensification and intensifiers in language

Chapter 2, the first theoretical chapter of the current study, addresses the notion of intensification in language and how it is linguistically expressed (cf. Section 2.1). Intensifiers, those mechanisms which are used cross-linguistically to convey intensification, are the focus of Section 2.2, which opens with some terminological issues and presents the main features of intensifiers, as well as how they are classified in the present research. Finally, Section 2.3 provides some remarks in the guise of conclusion. This chapter hence aims to contextualise the topic of intensifiers more generally, as intensifiers will also be the focus of Chapter 4, yet in this case the chapter deals specifically with the diachronic evolution of English intensifiers, mostly in the light of grammaticalisation (cf. Chapter 3), in line with the research undertaken in this work.

## 2.1. Defining and conveying intensification

In the interest of maximum communicative efficiency, speakers are constantly looking for new ways of attaining the required expressiveness, so that languages show a natural tendency towards constant innovation and the recycling of unproductive elements. The apparent human taste for hyperbolic expressions (Peters 1994: 271) fits in perfectly with this idea of a continuous updating of languages. Exaggeration and intensification are pervasive in everyday communication because they are very convenient devices for the purpose of convincing others, and persuading our interlocutor(s) is one of the basic goals of any communicative act. In fact, language is not only used for the expression of content (what

Halliday labels the *ideational* function) but can also serve an interpersonal function, by means of which the speaker intrudes on the speech event to express an opinion, persuade, etc. (Halliday 1973: 106). This intrusion on the part of the speaker to express commitment to the proposition is defined as *intensity* by Labov (1984). In this sense, intensification or intensity can be an extremely fruitful tool for emphasis and, hence, for persuasion. In Partington's words, 'the importance of intensification in the communicative process is that it is a vehicle for impressing, praising, persuading, insulting and generally influencing the listener's reception of the message' (1993: 178).

Intensity or intensification is not an exclusive property of language, as it also applies to other fields, such as Physics, Mathematics, Chemistry, Music and Geology (cf. Vermeire 1979; Flores 2004). However, the crucial question here is what is understood by intensification and how it is manifested in language. Intensification in language refers to the degree of a specific quality, and it cannot be measured objectively but is rather a 'subjective norm relative to the speaker's experience' (Vermeire 1979: 9), which implies expressing an emotional attitude towards what is being predicated (Vermeire 1979: 15). Thus, temperature can be calculated in objective terms, so that a temperature of 2,000 °C is considered to be intense heat. Nevertheless, temperature can also be subjectively perceived, since it depends on one's own experience. For instance, 40 °C is certainly not as suffocating for a person living in the desert as for a person living in Oslo. The difference in temperature, however, can also be indicated in language through different nuances: *boiling hot*, *suffocatingly hot*, *rather hot* and even *a bit hot*.

Inherent to the concept of intensification are the notions of quantity and scalarity or configuration of scales. Intensity always involves measuring a quantity. Nonetheless, while quantity is more concrete and can easily be expressed numerically (e.g. cake), intensity is more abstract and applies to abstract uncountables (e.g. happiness). Moreover, intensification is also directly linked to the recognition and formation of mental scales, a cognitive-linguistic process common to all humans. The basis for the construction of these mental scales is provided by comparison, since, as Flores (2004) argues, it is only when a situation is comparable that it will also be gradable. For instance, if we say that something is big, it is because we can contrast it with something else which we consider smaller, and it is in this way that we may place it on a continuum or scale of size. Furthermore, it seems that languages tend to create fictional boundaries even in those cases when a limit is not given. Flores (2004: 41) gives the example of *vor Neid platzen* in German ('to be green with envy', literally, 'to explode with envy'), where the explosion is obviously an unreal consequence of being envious of something; a limit or extreme is set up, that is, being envious to the extreme.

Intensification, therefore, can be broadly defined as the 'placement of a predication on a scale of intensity, or degree of realisation of the predication, reaching from extremely/very low to very/extremely high' (Claridge 2011: 9). It is thus conceived as a binary process which implies looking both upwards and downwards on a scale. In other words, it serves to express both exaggeration and depreciation (cf. Bolinger 1972: 20; van Os 1989: 1). Gradability, however, is not an exclusive property of adjectives, but can also be shown in verbs, nouns, adverbs and even prepositional phrases (cf. Bolinger 1972; van Os 1989; Flores 2004). For Bolinger (1972), for instance, in addition to degree adjectives and degree adverbs, there also exist degree nouns and degree verbs. For example, he explains that the noun *fool* admits a degree reading, as in *he is a big fool* 'he is very foolish', whereas the noun *lad* does not, which just means 'large in size' if modified by the adjective *big* (Bolinger 1972: 146). As far as verbs are concerned, he suggests that those which can be intensified accept intensifying adverbs such as *rather*, *so* or *quite* (e.g. *he quite exasperates me*), whereas those which do not accept such readings cannot be modified by these adverbs. This is the case of the verb *wait*, a non-degree verb which does not admit the adverb *so* (e.g. in a question such as **why do you wait so*?) (1972: 160).

Intensification can be linguistically fulfilled by means of various strategies or mechanisms. Linguistic elements with both a reinforcing and a weakening effect and which modify items that can be placed on a degree scale are generally known as *intensifiers* or *degree words*. Early works, such as Borst (1902) and Kirchner (1955), opted for the generic label *Gradadverbien* ('degree adverbs'), though under this term they also included forms which formally are not adverbs. In line with authors such as van Os (1989) and Bolinger (1972), in this work I will adopt the general label *intensifier* to refer to those forms which can have both a reinforcing and a downgrading function. Whenever it is necessary to highlight the different ways in which intensification is linguistically fulfilled, I will equally refer to intensifiers as *intensification/intensifying strategies* or *intensification/intensifying mechanisms.*

Two of the pioneering scholars in the academic discussion about intensification are Cornelis Stoffel and Eugene Borst, who already at the beginning of the twentieth century devoted whole monographs to degree adverbs, published in 1901 and 1902, respectively. Since then, however, studies on intensification strategies or intensifiers have succeeded. In general terms, the intensification mechanisms can be broadly classified into three types: (1) those which highlight the relevance of a given message through the use of figures of speech, such as litotes, hendiadys or hyperbole; (2) lexical and morphosyntactic devices (e.g. repetitions, the use of comparatives and superlatives, prefixes and suffixes, word order, inherently superlative forms or adverbs of degree); and (3) those where intensification is achieved by means of intonation and stress. These three types of intensification strategies are, however, beyond the scope of the present study. For further details on these intensification mechanisms, refer to Mathesius (1939), Kirchner (1955), Moreno de Oliveira (1962), Spitzbardt (1965), Biedermann (1969), Bolinger (1972), Bäcklund (1973), Cruzeiro (1973), Vermeire (1979), Suscinskij (1985), van Os (1989), Peters (1993), Renkema (1997), Lorenz (1999), Flores (2004) and Claridge (2011).

## 2.2. Intensifiers

### *2.2.1. General features*

The items examined here receive different labels in the literature on the topic, among them *intensifiers*, *degree modifiers* and *degree words.* In broad terms, these refer to 'any device that scales a quality, whether up or down or somewhere between the two' (Bolinger 1972: 17). David Crystal's *Dictionary of Linguistics and Phonetics* also goes along the same lines and defines *intensifier* as 'a class of adverbs which have a heightening or lowering effect on the meaning of another element in the sentence' (2003: 237). Nevertheless, other views further restrict this notion and consider that intensifiers only have a heightening effect (cf. Paradis 1997; Biber et al. 1999; Méndez-Naya 2003).

In this monograph, the label *intensifier* is to be taken in the broadest sense, thus allowing for indication of both upper and lower degrees on an imaginary degree scale. Given that I take intensification in Bolinger's sense (cf. Section 2.1), that is, as the expression of both high and low degrees on a scale, hence allowing for exaggeration and depreciation, I will be consistent with this position and take the term *intensifier* in this same way. However, it should be noted that the items examined here, death-related intensifiers, can only express high or extreme degree, which makes this distinction virtually unnecessary for this research. Furthermore, as understood in the present study, the category of intensifiers comprises not only the prototypical cases of intensifying adverbs modifying adjectives (*dead easy*), but also adjectives with an intensifying effect (*deadly drinker*), prepositional phrases, as in the case of *to death* in example (2.1), and even constructions such as *to be dying for something* or *to be dying to do something*, as in (2.2). For this reason, I differ from those scholars who establish a close correspondence between adverbs and intensifiers (cf., for instance, Partington (1993) or Crystal's (2003) definition above), and rather contend hereafter that elements other than adverbs can perform intensifying functions, traditionally attributed to adverbials.

(2.1) *I'm sick **to death** of you.* (*Oxford Dictionaries*: <http://www.oxforddictionaries.com/es/definicion/ingles/death>)

(2.2) *She was **dying to** ask where he'd got it.* (*Longman Dictionary of Contemporary English*, s.v. *die* v.)

Moreover, even though intensifiers are mainly associated with adverbs and they mostly function as modifiers of adjective phrases, they can also modify prepositional phrases, noun phrases and verb phrases, as in (2.3)–(2.5), respectively, taken from Paradis (1997: 14):

(2.3) *They were **much** in love with each other.*

(2.4) *It was **quite** a sight.*

(2.5) *I **totally** agree with you.*

On the other hand, the terminological confusion arises partly on account of the difficulties in keeping apart the notions of degree and quantification. This issue, however, will not be delved into in the present monograph, for the items under study are not expressive of quantification (cf., among others, Vermeire 1979).

Furthermore, intensifiers are to be distinguished from certain adverbs which can also express the speaker's attitude (cf. van Os 1989). These adverbs, the same as quantifiers, can function as intensifiers when in contact with intensifiable elements, although their main function is not that of intensification (cf. Quirk et al. 1985: 447). They express speaker stance instead and modify the whole sentence in many cases. The main difference with intensifiers, therefore, is that they can be both left and right dislocated. Quirk et al. (1985: 447 and 612–31) use the terms *emphasiser* and *disjunct* in their work. Emphasisers thus achieve a very similar effect to that of intensifiers, that is, they add to the force of the element they are modifying, although not to their degree (cf. Quirk et al. 1985: 447). When emphasisers are dislocated they are called *disjuncts*. Thus, in (2.6) *frankly* is considered to be an emphasiser, while in (2.7), where it is left dislocated, it is regarded as a disjunct in Quirkian terminology. The same applies to the German adverb *wirklich* in examples (2.8)–(2.10), taken from van Os (1989: 85). In (2.8) *wirklich* ('really') functions as an intensifier modifying the adjective *gut*, meaning 'really good', whereas in (2.9) and (2.10) *wirklich* is a sentence adverbial which expresses the speaker's commitment to the truth of what (s)he is saying, either right (2.9) or left dislocated (example (2.10)).

(2.6) *I'm **frankly** surprised at your behaviour.*

(2.7) ***Frankly**, I'm surprised at your behaviour.*

| | | | | |
|---|---|---|---|---|
| (2.8) | *Er* | *ist* | ***wirklich*** | *gut.* |
| | He | be-PRS.3SG | really | good |
| (2.9) | *Er* | *ist* | *gut,* | ***wirklich!*** |
| | He | be-PRS.3SG | good | really |
| (2.10) | ***Wirklich,*** | *er* | *ist* | *gut!* |
| | Really | he | be-PRS.3SG | good |

### 2.2.2. *Models of classification*

The models which have been proposed to categorise intensifiers can be broadly classified into two main groups: on the one hand, those classifications which consider intensifiers as markers of degree on a given degree scale and, on the other, those models which categorise them on semantic grounds. As regards the former type, many authors consider intensifiers as markers of degree and hence choose specific labels according to the number of divisions which they establish on a potential degree scale. The level of specificity varies considerably, ranging from very detailed models, such as the ones by Biedermann (1969), Bäcklund (1973), van Os (1989) or Quirk et al. (1985), to much less specific proposals of categorisation, such as those found in the grammars by Biber et al. (1999) and Huddleston and Pullum et al. (2002). The proposals by Bolinger (1972) and Quirk et al. (1985) are among the most widely used in the literature. For the purposes of the current study, however, I will follow Carita Paradis' model (1997, 2001, 2008), which largely draws on Bolinger (1972) and Quirk et al. (1985), but additionally adopts a cognitive approach to meaning. Paradis essentially distinguishes the same degree levels as Quirk et al. (1985), but discards the use of the label *intensifier* in favour of the term *degree modifier*. In her model, degree modifiers are conceived of as occupying a position on a continuum which runs from the strongly reinforcing modifiers down to the strongly attenuating ones. Moreover, the gradability which these items express can be conceived in terms of an 'either-or' relationship (totality degree modifiers) or as expressing scaling (scalar degree modifiers), as shown in Figure 2.1, adapted from Paradis (1997).

In addition, both totality and scalar modifiers can have a reinforcing or an attenuating function. Totality modifiers with a reinforcing function are called maximisers, as they express the maximum force, and include forms such as *absolutely*, *completely*, *totally*, *perfectly* and *utterly*. In turn, scalar modifiers with a reinforcing value are called boosters and consist of items like *very*, *terribly*, *extremely*, *awfully* and *jolly*, among many others. Totality modifiers with an attenuating function are named approximators and include modifiers of the type of *almost*. Finally, scalar modifiers of the attenuating type can be moderators, like *rather*, *pretty* and *fairly*, or

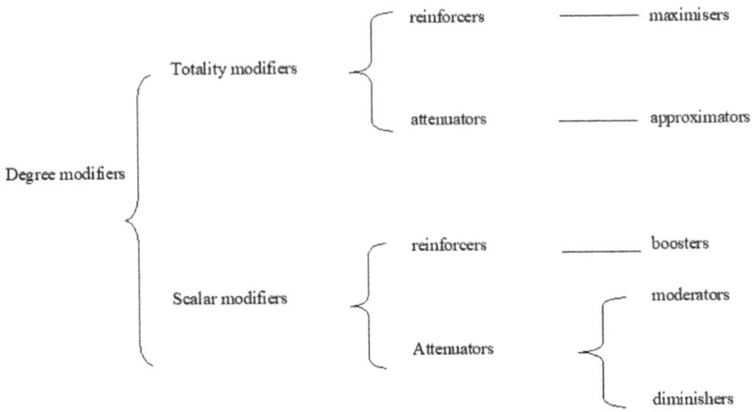


Figure 2.1. Paradis' (1997) classification of intensifiers

diminishers, such as *somewhat*, *slightly* and *a little*. Note that except for the label *moderator*, which is taken from Allerton (1987), the other terms of totality and scalar modifiers recognised by Paradis are labels used in Quirk et al.'s (1985) grammar. The death-related intensifiers under study here can either be totality or scalar modifiers and therefore always have a reinforcing function, acting as maximisers or boosters, respectively.

Paradis' proposal differs from most degree-based models, as mentioned above, since she adopts a cognitive approach to meaning and questions the widespread view that degree is associated with a given class of words. For her, degree is 'pervasive in language and can be used in combination with most word class construals' (2008: 339). In this sense, she further extends the notion of boundedness, typically associated with nouns and verbs, to adjectives. Boundedness in adjectives relates to gradability and is not a fixed property, but can rather be changed through a process called *contextual modulation* or *coercion* (Paradis 2001). On the basis of boundedness, degree modifiers can also be classified as scalar or totality modifiers: scalar modifiers are unbounded, while totality modifiers are bounded. Moreover, there exists a very close connection between a given adjective and the degree modifier it selects, as the choice of a degree modifier depends heavily on the mode of construal of the adjective, that is, on whether it accepts a totality or a scalarity reading, and, to a lesser extent, on stylistic considerations, such as the emotive force of the modifier or its degree of formality. Typically, it is gradable adjectives that are used in combination with degree modifiers. Nonetheless, non-gradable adjectives such as *British* may also take on gradable readings through *contextual modulation* or *coercion*, when referring, for instance, to someone's accent (e.g. *he sounds very British*).[1] This shows that the interaction between the content and the schematic domain is crucial to the interpretation or conceptualisation of the adjective. Likewise, gradable adjectives, that is, those which can take degree modifiers, are subdivided into three different types, and it is precisely the conceptualisation of each of these types which constrains the choice of the modifier (Paradis 2001: 51–3):

i. Scalar adjectives: these are conceived of as occupying a range on an imaginary scale and their conceptualisation calls for scalar degree modifiers, either with a reinforcing (boosters) or an attenuating function (moderators and diminishers). Scalar adjectives are mainly subjective (e.g. *interesting*, *nice*, *good*, etc.).
ii. Extreme adjectives express a superlative degree of a feature. This allows for their conceptualisation as occupying the outer parts of a mental scale (e.g. *excellent*, *huge*, *terrific*, etc.). They are strongly evaluative or subjective and require totality degree modifiers, either maximisers or approximators like *almost*.
iii. Limit adjectives are associated with some sort of limit and, for this reason, they are conceptualised in terms of 'either-or'. In contrast to extreme and scalar gradable adjectives, these are not subjective, since there is general consensus on the applicability of the adjective. One such example is *dead* in *a dead body*. In this case in particular, nobody will question whether the body is dead or not. By contrast, examples such as *an interesting book* or *an excellent film* are likely to cause difference of opinion on account of the subjective nature of the adjectives *interesting* and *excellent*. Limit adjectives, since they are associated with completeness, can only take totality modifiers, either maximisers or approximators.

1 From Huddleston and Pullum et al. (2002: 531).

In contrast to degree-based models of intensifiers, which established several divisions along a potential degree scale, semantically based classifications generally divide intensifiers or degree modifiers into those which are predominantly objective, referring to qualities such as dimensions, quantity, excess and totality (e.g. *highly*, *completely* and *abundantly*), on the one hand, and those which are predominantly subjective and indicate psychological conditions and feelings (e.g. *magnificently*, *furiously*, *horribly*). This is the case of the models proposed by Spitzbardt (1965) and Suscinskij (1985), the latter for German. Two further semantically based approaches are the ones by Renkema (1997) and Lorenz (1999). These proposals also establish several semantic subtypes, but additionally allow for the distinction of degree levels: Renkema (1997), for instance, also distinguishes between high and low intensification, and Lorenz (1999) combines the Quirkian degrees of intensification with semantic categories.

The classification which will be adopted here is the one by Paradis (1997, 2001, 2008), which is one of the most comprehensive models, since in addition to establishing the relevant degree levels, Paradis considers the intrinsic relation between the degree modifier and the item modified. For this reason, I will not delve further into all the different degree- or semantically based models in this chapter. Moreover, death-related intensifiers, the focus of this research, only have a heightening function and can therefore only be boosters or maximisers. As a consequence, I will disregard here any subdivisions of intensifiers with a downtoning effect. Unlike Paradis, however, throughout this monograph I will resort to the widely used term *intensifier*, a label which she refuses on account of its ambiguity. As mentioned in Section 2.1, I have taken *intensification* in Bolinger's (1972) sense, that is, as an indication of both exaggeration and depreciation. By the same token, *intensifier* in the present work is to be taken as expressive of both high and low degree on the scale. In all other respects, Paradis' taxonomy of intensifiers will be subsequently followed.

## 2.3. Summary

This chapter has dealt with the manifold mechanisms which are available in language to emphasise the expressivity of a given utterance, that is, to express linguistic intensification. It has been shown that these intensification strategies or intensifiers are far from being restricted to degree adverbs. As suggested in Section 2.1, intensification strategies in language range instead from adverbs or adjectives with an intensifying function to prepositional phrases, figures of speech, comparative and superlative expressions or intonation, among many other devices. This chapter has also briefly discussed the main features of intensifiers and how they differ from similar elements such as quantifiers and emphasisers (Section 2.2.1). Next, Section 2.2.2 has presented the two main types of models of classification which have been put forward in the literature to categorise intensifiers, namely those models which propose a classification based on the degree levels indicated by the different intensifiers, on the one hand, and those which rely on semantic criteria, on the other. As argued in Section 2.2, for the present purposes I will be following Paradis' model (1997, 2001, 2008), which is degree-based.

CHAPTER 3

# Grammaticalisation

## 3.1. Defining grammaticalisation

Language variation and change are consistently found in natural languages and one of the tasks of the historical linguist is to identify and describe regularities in diachronic changes and explain how these are brought about (Marchello-Nizia 2006: 13). Grammaticalisation, as a theory aiming at the description of how grammatical forms emerge, dates back to the early twentieth century, when Antoine Meillet (1912) coined this term. Nonetheless, discussions about the origin of grammatical forms are much older and can be traced back to the tenth century at least, when Chinese writers postulated a distinction between 'full' and 'empty' linguistic symbols and claimed that all empty symbols derived from formerly full ones (Heine et al. 1991: 5).

In current linguistic terminology, the label *grammaticalisation* has two different senses. On the one hand, it refers to a type of linguistic change and, on the other, to the theoretical approach which studies this type of change (cf. Hopper and Traugott 2003; Marchello-Nizia 2006, among others). As a type of change, grammaticalisation is found cross-linguistically and denotes the process whereby particular items become increasingly more grammatical in the course of time. In fact, two types of grammaticalisation are commonly distinguished in the literature, namely primary grammaticalisation and secondary grammaticalisation. Primary grammaticalisation refers to the development of lexical items into grammatical material, while secondary grammaticalisation denotes the development of already grammatical forms into more grammatical ones (cf. Traugott 2010: 40–1). Moreover, grammaticalisation, also frequently referred to as *grammaticization* (Hopper 1991; Himmelmann 2004) and *grammatization*

(Matisoff 1991), is cross-componential (McMahon 1994: 161), causing disruptions in all linguistic components. As McMahon has claimed, 'grammaticalization is not only a syntactic change, but a global change affecting also the morphology, phonology and semantics' (1994: 106).

Although grammaticalisation is generally seen as a process whereby a lexical or less grammatical item develops increasingly more grammatical meaning (cf. Kuryłowicz 1965: 69; Fischer and Rosenbach 2000: 2), recent literature on grammaticalisation regards this definition as inaccurate, inasmuch as it is not a particular lexical item that becomes grammaticalised, but rather the whole construction in which it appears (cf. Bybee 2003: 602), as proved by the developments in Construction Grammar.[1] In addition, the importance of discourse and pragmatic factors in grammaticalisation has also been pointed out over the past few years (cf., among many others, Fischer and Rosenbach 2000; Hopper and Traugott 2003; Couper-Kuhlen 2011; Degand and Vandenbergen 2011; Diewald 2011a, 2011b; Nicolle 2011; Onodera 2011; Brinton 2017).

Grammaticalisation on the whole correlates with a number of features such as semantic bleaching or erosion of meaning (desemanticisation or semantic depletion as for Lehmann 1995), loss of phonetic substance (attrition in Lehmann 1985, 1995), loss of autonomy, increasingly fixed positions in the phrase or clause, reanalysis or reformulation of the construction, decategorialisation and increase in (inter)subjectivity or (inter)

1 Construction Grammar does not establish a clear-cut distinction between syntax and lexis. Constructions are instead considered as part of a lexicon-syntax continuum (Hoffmann and Trousdale 2013: 1). Moreover, this theory presents itself as more comprehensive than that of grammaticalisation, since it does not only allow for grammatical change, but also for lexical change and, hence, for lexicalisation (cf. Brinton and Traugott 2005; see also footnote 6). As Hilpert notes (2013: 460), 'the diachronic branch of Construction Grammar is thus a broader enterprise than the study of grammaticalization [...]'. In a constructional framework, both grammaticalisation and lexicalisation are viewed as constructional changes involving entrenchment (cf., among others, Bybee 2003), though grammaticalisation involves the emergence of more schematic constructions, which are typically frequent, whereas in lexicalisation constructions are more substantive (Trousdale 2010: 53–4).

subjectification (cf. Finegan 1995; Traugott 1989, 1995, 2003, 2007, among others). These features, which have been described in terms of grammaticalisation parameters and principles, or as phenomena concomitant to grammaticalisation, are discussed in detail in Sections 3.2 and 3.3, respectively. Finally, Section 3.4 contains some concluding remarks to close this chapter.

## 3.2. Grammaticalisation: Parameters and principles

Grammaticalisation has been described in terms of a set of parameters (Lehmann 1985) and principles (Hopper 1991). These are presented in detail in this section, as they will be applied to the analysis of the death-related intensifiers under study here (cf. Chapter 6).

Christian Lehmann (1985, 1995) accounts for grammaticalisation as both a synchronic and a diachronic process and argues that the degree of grammaticalisation of an element can be measured in relation to three aspects: weight, cohesion and variability. These properties can in turn be considered both paradigmatically and syntagmatically, yielding a set of parameters, as shown in Table 3.1, adapted from Lehmann (1995: 123).

Table 3.1. Lehmann's parameters of grammaticalisation

| **Aspects** | **Paradigmatic parameters** | **Syntagmatic parameters** |
|---|---|---|
| Weight | Integrity | Scope |
| Cohesion | Paradigmaticity | Bondedness |
| Variability | Paradigmatic variability | Syntagmatic variability |

When we consider grammaticalisation from a diachronic perspective, taking into account these parameters and aspects, a number of processes come into play. These are shown in Table 3.2 (Lehmann 1985: 309).

Table 3.2. Lehmann's parameters and processes of grammaticalisation

| | Parameter | Weak grammaticalisation | Process | Strong grammaticalisation |
|---|---|---|---|---|
| **Paradigmatic** | *Integrity* | Bundle of semantic features; possibly polysyllabic | *Attrition* | Few semantic features; oligo- or monosegmental |
| | *Paradigmaticity* | Item participates loosely in semantic field | *Paradigmaticisation* | Small, tightly integrated paradigm |
| | *Paradigmatic variability* | Free choice of items according to communicative intentions | *Obligatorification* | Choice systematically constrained, use largely obligatory |
| **Syntagmatic** | *Scope* | Item relates to constituent of arbitrary complexity | *Condensation* | Item modifies word or stem |
| | *Bondedness* | Item is independently juxtaposed | *Coalescence* | Item is affix or even phonological feature of carrier |
| | *Syntagmatic variability* | Item can be shifted around freely | *Fixation* | Item occupies fixed slot |

The process by means of which a given linguistic sign loses part of its integrity, being deprived of semantic or phonological substance, is called *attrition*. Semantic attrition is also known as bleaching or desemanticisation (cf. Heine 2003, among others), while phonological attrition or loss of phonetic substance is also referred to as erosion (cf. Heine et al. 1991).

Semantic attrition or bleaching implies generalisation or weakening of semantic content. It is considered to be characteristic of grammaticalisation, given that grammaticalisation typically involves a change from lexical to grammatical and the items undergoing grammaticalisation become increasingly more general and abstract in meaning, so that they can be used in a wider range of contexts. This is due to habituation because 'a stimulus loses its impact if it occurs very frequently' (Bybee 2003: 605).

In the grammaticalisation literature, it is generally acknowledged that semantic bleaching occurs only in the late stages of the process (Hopper and Traugott 2003: 94), while the early stages of grammaticalisation are characterised rather by a shift of meaning. In the words of Hopper and Traugott (2003: 94), 'there is no doubt that, over time, meanings tend to become weakened during the process of grammaticalization. Nevertheless, all the evidence for early stages is that initially there is a redistribution or shift, not a loss, of meaning.'

In this connection, Heine (2002: 83) claims that in order to study the development of grammatical meanings, we also need to take into account the contexts which give rise to them. He suggests that there exist a number of intermediate stages before a given construction with an original or source meaning develops into a new construction with a different meaning, the so-called target meaning. Thus, he distinguishes four stages in the rise of new grammatical meanings. At the very first stage, we find a particular expression with a source meaning, which can occur in a variety of different contexts. The second stage corresponds to what Heine calls a *bridging context*, that is, a context which facilitates the interpretation of that expression with a meaning different from the source one. Nevertheless, although at this stage a new or target meaning can be inferred, the source meaning cannot be discarded. The third stage is the so-called *switch context*, implying that at this time the source meaning is ruled out and that only the target meaning is found. Finally, at the last stage the target meaning expands to new contexts and is no longer dependent on the circumstances which gave rise to it. The development of degree adverbs from originally manner adverbs involves in fact such contexts, in which the degree meaning is at first only inferred contextually. For instance, *swiþe*, the prototypical Old English (henceforth OE) intensifier, is derived from the adjective *swiþ* 'strong'. For this reason, the first intensifying uses of *swiþe* were attested with verbs harmonic with its original lexical meaning, such as *fight* (Méndez-Naya 20: 111–12). In these cases *swiþe* admitted a potential degree reading in context: 'fight very much'. The inference of this degree meaning eventually allowed *swiþe* to occur in new contexts with non-harmonic verbs (e.g. *blissian* 'rejoice'), as well as with adjectives and participles. *Dead(ly)*, *mortal(ly)* and *to death*, the death-related intensifiers at issue here, underwent a similar development (cf. Sections 6.2.2–6.2.6): at first a degree meaning could only be inferred in contexts which implied features reminiscent of death, such as paleness or quietness, hence collocations such as *mortal/deadly pale*. Later on, however, these forms expanded to contexts which were incompatible with their source meaning and which only allowed for an intensifying meaning, in collocations such as *mortally tedious* and *blush to death* (examples (6.199) and (6.231), respectively). This is, therefore, in keeping with what Hopper and Traugott (2003: 94–5) suggest for semantic bleaching and grammaticalisation, that is, that bleaching does not occur all of a sudden; rather what we find at the very initial stages of any grammaticalisation process is a switch of meaning, which becomes increasingly more general as grammaticalisation advances.

Since, as we have seen, bleaching is very closely related to grammaticalisation, the literature on grammaticalisation provides manifold instances of this change, many of which are cross-linguistically replicated. Paradigmatic examples include, among many others:

i. Causal subordinators, which are argued to derive from temporal markers. This is the case, for instance, of French *puisque* (< Latin *posteaquam* 'after, ever since') and of German *weil* (< Old High German *dia wila so* 'so long as'), both meaning 'since, because' (Heine and Kuteva 2002: 291).
ii. Concessive markers, which ultimately go back to temporal expressions, including prepositions and conjunctions. For example, English *while* and German *während* had a temporal meaning before developing the concessive reading 'although' (Heine and Kuteva 2002: 292).

iii. The indefinite article *a*(*n*), which has its roots in the numeral *one* (Heine and Kuteva 2002: 220)
iv. The PDE intensifier *very*, a form which was borrowed from Old French and ultimately derives from Latin *verus* 'true' (Breban and Davidse 2016: 229–30).
v. The PDE suffix *–ly*, which ultimately goes back to the OE noun *līc* 'body' (Kastovsky 2006).

All the aforementioned examples involve bleaching and grammaticalisation. However, the first three cases (temporal > causal; temporal > concessive; numeral > indefinite) represent examples of desemanticisation of material which is already grammatical and which becomes increasingly more grammatical (secondary grammaticalisation). By contrast, the development of *very* and that of the English suffix *–ly* constitute clear cases of grammaticalisation of lexical into grammatical material (primary grammaticalisation). In line with the aforementioned case of *very*, *dead*(*ly*), *mortal*(*ly*) and *to death* also have their roots in lexical material, representing therefore cases of primary grammaticalisation (cf. Section 6.3).

The other type of attrition discussed by Lehmann is phonological attrition or the gradual loss of phonetic substance, which is also known as erosion (cf. Heine et al. 1991). Phonological attrition takes place in a number of well-known examples of grammaticalisation, such as the *going to*-construction, which is often morphologically and phonologically reduced to *gonna* [ˈgənə] (cf. Bybee 2003, 2006), or the emerging modals *wanna* (< *want to*) and *gotta* (< *got to*), reduced to [ˈwɒnə] and [ˈgɒtə], respectively (cf. Krug 2003).

Loss of phonetic substance or erosion is not exclusively found in grammaticalisation, since it is omnipresent in linguistic change (Heine et al. 1991: 127) and can therefore occur outside grammaticalisation (e.g. the diachronic levelling and eventual loss of verbal inflections from OE to ME). Likewise, we can also find instances of grammaticalised elements with no phonological attrition. One such instance is the grammaticalisation of intensifiers, which does not usually involve phonological attrition, as is the case of the death-related forms studied here and of other intensifiers such as *very* or *terribly*.

The second process discussed by Lehmann is *paradigmaticisation*, the tendency for grammaticalised forms to be arranged into paradigms (Heine 2003: 588). Paradigmaticisation leads to increased homogeneity in a given paradigm. Thus, the French prepositions form a more homogeneous category than the Latin ones, as they come to form the paradigm of oblique cases, while in Latin they could perform further functions.

Lehmann's *obligatorification* refers to the process by means of which certain elements become obligatory in a given context. For instance, the noun *pas* is the only compulsory element in negative clauses in contemporary French so that the pre-verbal adverb *ne* is frequently elided in speech: *je* (***ne***) *parle* ***pas*** *français* 'I do not speak French'. From a historical perspective, however, the only mandatory element in the negation pattern was pre-verbal *ne*, while *pas* was simply a reinforcing particle which occurred predominantly with motion verbs (Hopper 1991: 26; Hopper and Traugott 2003: 117), yet it became increasingly frequent over time. This increase in token frequency[2] allowed it to expand to further constructions with verbs other than those of motion, eventually becoming the obligatory grammaticalised marker of negation in Present-day French.

Moving on now to the syntagmatic axis, Lehmann's process of *condensation* involves reduction of the scope of a given sign and structural simplicity: 'the more a sign is grammaticalised, the less complex become the constituents with which it can combine' (Lehmann 1985: 308). Illustrative examples of condensation are provided by the development from possessive *have* (*I have the letter written*) to perfective *have* (*I have written the letter*), which implies reduction of scope from clause to phrase level (Norde 2009: 128) and the development of the adverbs *very* or *terribly*. These were originally adjuncts of manner having the whole clause as scope; when they

2 Token or text frequency is 'the frequency of occurrence of a unit, usually a word or morpheme, in running text' (Bybee 2003: 604), although in a text we can also count the token frequency of constructions like *be going to* or *be supposed to*. Type frequency, the other type of frequency distinguished by Bybee (2003), refers to the different lexical items to which a particular pattern or construction is applicable, i.e., to its dictionary frequency (Bybee and Thompson 1997: 378). For instance, the past tense can be expressed in different ways in English, although the highest type frequency corresponds to the formation with the suffix *–ed*.

grammaticalised as intensifiers, however, their scope was reduced to the phrase level, modifying only other adjectives or adverbs (Méndez-Naya 2003: 376; cf. also Section 6.3).

*Coalescence* is defined by Lehmann (1985: 308; 1995: 148) as an increase in bondedness (Lehmann 1985: 308; 1995: 148) or the 'collapsing together of adjacent forms' (Heine 2003: 588). Examples of coalescence are the rise of the future forms in the Romance languages (e.g. French *chanterai*) from the Latin construction *habeo* + infinitive and the development of the French adverb *beaucoup* 'a lot' from the noun phrase (*un*) *beau coup* ('a strong blow/knock') (Marchello-Nizia 2006: 142–8).

The last process discussed by Lehmann is called *fixation*, which entails the loss of syntagmatic variability (Lehmann 1985: 308); in other words, grammaticalised items occupy fixed slots and do not have as much freedom as items which show incipient grammaticalisation. Thus, the adverbs ending in *–ment*(*e*) in the Romance languages are derived from the Latin noun *mente* 'mind', which could precede or follow adjectives. In the Romance languages, however, this position has become fixed and the original noun *mente* has become a suffix which thus occurs only in postposition. The adverb *clearly* is hence *clairement* in French, *chiaramente* in Italian, *claramente* in Galician, Portuguese and Spanish and *clarament* in Catalan. Likewise, the rise of intensifiers is associated with fixation, since this new function is concomitant with fixation in premodifier position (Méndez-Naya 2019: 96; cf. also Section 6.3).

Lehmann's parameters discussed in the preceding paragraphs can be complemented by Hopper's five principles of grammaticalisation, namely layering, divergence, specialisation, persistence and decategorialisation (Hopper 1991: 22–31). In Hopper's view, the main advantage of these principles is that they can be applied at early stages of grammaticalisation, while Lehmann's parameters are characteristic of rather advanced stages of the process.

Concerning *layering*, it has been claimed that while new layers develop in grammaticalisation, the older ones may coexist and even interact with them. In Hopper's words, 'when a form or set of forms emerges in a functional domain, it does not immediately (and may never) replace an already existing set of functionally equivalent forms, but rather the two set of forms co-exist' (1991: 23). These old and new layers may specialise or develop new meanings. For instance, the adverb *awfully* may be used as an intensifier ('very much') in PDE, but it may also be used literally ('in an unpleasant or bad manner'). The two meanings, therefore, coexist side by side. This is also the case with the death-related forms under study here (cf. Section 6.2). For example, *dead* can be used as an adjective in a literal sense (e.g. *a dead leaf*), but it may also occur as an intensifying adverb as in the collocation *dead easy* in example (1.6).

The principle of *divergence* (*split* in Heine and Reh 1984) is similar to that of layering, in that it also implies the coexistence of layers. In fact, it can even be understood as a case of layering, as Hopper points out (1991: 24). Nonetheless, in the case of divergence, the forms in question perform different functions, whereas layering involves the coexistence of forms performing the same function. The French word *pas*, mentioned above, illustrates the principle of divergence, since it has two distinct meanings: on the one hand, it can be a negative particle 'not'; on the other, it has a lexical meaning 'step, pace'. While the negative adverb *pas* is a grammaticalised marker in Present-day French, the noun *pas* 'step' is not and retains its lexical meaning.

The principle of *specialisation*, which corresponds roughly with Lehmann's obligatorification, applies only to advanced stages of the grammaticalisation process. Grammaticalisation thus correlates with restrictions on the array of available options, so that in the final stage the use of a particular form, with a more general and grammatical meaning, eventually becomes obligatory. Hopper exemplifies specialisation with the paradigm of French negators. This paradigm included not only the aforementioned negative particle *pas*, but also a number of forms which reinforced negation. Nevertheless, it was only *pas* that specialised as a negative marker and became the only obligatory particle in negative clauses, whereas preverbal *ne* is often elided.

*Persistence* is another of Hopper's principles, according to which 'some of the traces of earlier meanings of an item undergoing grammaticalization are likely to survive in the form of the grammatical distribution of the item concerned' (Heine 2003: 589). Thus, an auxiliary for the future such as *will* can still retain traces of its original volitional meaning in certain cases, as in *I **will** stay here* (Larreya 2009: 19). By the same token, many negative intensifiers reveal a predisposition to co-occur with negative items, as is the case of *terribly* or *dreadfully* (cf. Partington 1993: 184) and of death-related intensifiers (cf. Sections 6.2.2–6.2.6).

The last principle discussed by Hopper (1991) is *decategorialisation*, which entails the 'loss in morphosyntactic properties characteristic of the source forms' (Heine 2003: 579). Thus, forms which undergo grammaticalisation tend to lose or neutralise the prototypical features characteristic of their original class and begin to adopt traits of secondary classes (cf. Heine et al. 1991; Hopper 1991; Hopper and Traugott 2003, among others). Therefore, decategorialisation entails a shift from a 'morphologically "heavier" unit to one that is lighter, that is, from one that tends to be phonologically longer and more distinct (e.g. with stressed vowels) to one that tends to be less distinct and shorter' (Hopper and Traugott 2003: 106). This is equivalent to what Lehmann (1995: 132) labels *morphological degeneration*. Decategorialisation, therefore, involves a shift from a major category like noun or verb, that is, from lexically open classes, to a minor category like conjunction, adverb, pronoun, demonstrative or auxiliary, that is, to closed classes. This can be represented in the following cline of categoriality: major category (> intermediate category) > minor category. As a consequence, one might safely assume that diachronically all minor categories have their origin in major categories (Hopper and Traugott 2003: 107).

Examples of the shift from major to minor word classes as a result of grammaticalisation processes are manifold. For instance, the conjunction *while* (e.g. ***while** you were writing*) derives from the OE noun *hwil* ('a length of time'), a meaning which is still preserved in PDE in examples like *we were waiting for a **while*** (Hopper and Traugott 2003: 107). The shift from noun to conjunction implies that when *while* comes to function as a conjunction, it can no longer take premodifiers like articles, demonstratives, pronouns or adjectives. Moreover, as a conjunction *while* cannot function as a subject or appear in clause-initial position. However, these losses seem to be compensated by its ability to link clauses.

Lehmann's characterisation of grammaticalisation and most of the early works on this phenomenon mostly associate grammaticalisation with increased dependency and reduction at the phonological, morphological and syntactic level (see, among others, Heine et al. 1991; Haspelmath 2004). This perspective of grammaticalisation as reduction (GR in Traugott and Trousdale 2013), however, largely disregarded the role of semantics and pragmatics. Against this view, some other scholars adopted a more encompassing view of grammaticalisation, which took into account precisely semantic and pragmatic changes.[3] All these studies highlighted the role of pragmatic inferences, metonymy, metaphor and (inter)subjectivity. It is also in this light that Himmelmann (2004) proposed his model of grammaticalisation, which implies in turn semantic-pragmatic expansion, alongside syntactic expansion and host-class expansion. For Himmelmann, then, grammaticalisation implies context expansion rather than reduction (grammaticalisation as expansion, GE in Traugott and Trousdale 2013), which affects three different levels. First, the so-called host-class expansion implies widening of the collocational range of certain items. For instance, the grammaticalisation of articles from original demonstratives implies that articles may collocate with further nouns, including proper names and those which denote unique entities (e.g. *sun*). Second, syntactic expansion implies context expansion from core argument (e.g. subject or object) to more peripheral positions, such as adnominal positions. Articles are also illustrative of this kind of expansion. Thirdly and most importantly, semantic-pragmatic context expansion is also at issue in grammaticalisation. In the case of articles, for example, these may be used in broader contexts than demonstratives and with associative anaphoric uses (e.g. in the case of a house or a wedding, we may refer to *the front door* or to *the bride*, respectively, while the use of the demonstrative would be unusual in this situation).

As has just been shown, grammaticalisation may involve both reduction and expansion. Contradictory as this may seem at first sight, the two views are actually related. Thus, in relation to Lehmann's (1995) and Himmelmann's (2004) criteria for the reduction and expansion view,

3 See, in this light, Traugott (1989, 2003, 2010), Traugott and König (1991), and the numerous studies on the rise of discourse markers, such as Brinton (1996), Traugott and Dasher (2002), Waltereit (2002) and Dostie (2004).

respectively, Cuyckens (2018: 185) remarks that 'there is more correlation between the different sets of criteria than first meets the eye'.[4]

This section has dealt with grammaticalisation as typically defined in terms of a set of parameters (Lehmann 1995) and principles (Hopper 1991). Moreover, grammaticalisation was presented as involving both reduction and expansion of different types. Although, as adduced by Hopper (1991), Lehmann's parameters are more characteristic of rather advanced stages of grammaticalisation (see above), in my discussion of the diachronic evolution of death-related intensifiers I will make use of both Hopper's principles and of Lehmann's parameters, as well as of Himmelmann's criteria (cf. Section 6.3).

## 3.3. Grammaticalisation and related phenomena

### *3.3.1. Unidirectionality and grammaticalisation clines*

Examined from a diachronic perspective, grammaticalisation is thought to be unidirectional, proceeding in the same direction once it is started (cf. Heine 2003; Hopper and Traugott 2003; Haspelmath 2004, among others). The way in which this phenomenon advances gives rise to what have been called grammaticalisation clines (Hopper and Traugott 2003), grammaticalisation channels (Lehmann 1995) or grammaticalisation chains (Heine et al. 1991; Heine 1992). Such clines apply at all levels: semantic (lexical > grammatical; concrete > abstract and general meanings), syntactic (major > minor categories) and phonological (full > reduced phonological forms). Put differently, forms undergoing grammaticalisation typically move from a point at the left of the cline to the right of the cline, while the reverse movement is not frequently attested. These transitions from one stage to the other along the scale of grammaticalisation

4 For an in-depth analysis of the interconnections between the two views of grammaticalisation, namely as expansion (GE) and as reduction (GR), see Traugott and Trousdale (2013: 108–12).

are, however, not abrupt, but rather smooth changes. These clines allow us to determine the degree of grammaticalisation of a particular item or construction in relation to another. Thus, the closer a given item is to the left and, hence, to the starting grammaticalisation point, the less grammaticalised it will be, while the more distant it is from this point, the higher its degree of grammaticalisation (cf. Heine et al. 1991: 228).

As mentioned above, at a semantic level grammaticalisation seems to operate in the direction from lexis to grammar or from less grammatical to increasingly more grammatical. Representative cases of this cline include the grammaticalisation of modal auxiliaries, the development of conjunctions and prepositions from original nouns and that of intensifiers, whose origin is typically found in lexical material (see, e.g. Breban and Davidse 2016 on *very*). Directionality within the semantic domain also correlates with increased (inter)subjectivity (cf. Section 3.3.3) and a higher degree of generalisation and abstraction. Unidirectionality operates on a syntactic scale as well, as evinced in the widely attested cline major category > minor category. Thus, nouns are in many cases the source for the development of prepositions, conjunctions and pronouns, and verbs of volition and of movement are often recruited for the formation of auxiliaries. At the phonological level, it has been noted that non-grammaticalised items and constructions preserve full forms, whereas grammaticalisation very often involves phonological reduction, which is also related to the frequency of the form. Modal auxiliaries, for example, tend to be reduced, while full verbs are not reduced on such a regular basis. This is the case, for instance, of *be going to*, often reduced to *gonna* [ˈgənə] (cf. Bybee and Thompson 1997).

Although, as Hopper and Traugott (2003: 99) put it, 'the evidence for unidirectionality is systematic and cross-linguistically replicated', unidirectionality in grammaticalisation has been called into question and some examples have been adduced as evidence against the argued directionality (cf. Fischer 2000; Lass 2000; Hopper and Traugott 2003). In this context, the label *degrammaticalisation* was coined by Lehmann in 1982 for a phenomenon which was allegedly non-existent. Haspelmath is even more explicit, claiming that 'it is a fair guess to say that 99% of all shifts along the lexical/functional continuum are grammaticalizations' (1999: 1046).

Nowadays degrammaticalisation is widely accepted as a linguistic phenomenon, since 'language change is not subject to exceptionless physical laws' and exceptions to the rule can in fact be attested (Hopper and Traugott 2003: 17–18). However, the definitions of this phenomenon may vary considerably according to whether it is understood in a broad or in a narrow sense. Degrammaticalisation understood in the broadest sense would thus include conversions (for instance, of prepositions such as *up* or *down* into verbs, or of morphemes like *–ism* or *–ade* into nouns in English), the use of second person pronouns in some languages to create verbs (*tutoyer* in French or *duzen* in German, meaning 'to use the familiar form of address') and the rise of nouns from former comparative forms (English *mayor* or French *seigneur* 'sir').[5] Those who defend a narrower definition of degrammaticalisation, by contrast, claim that these are examples of lexicalisation[6] instead or standard processes of word formation, given that the changes involved are abrupt and not gradual. This is in fact Norde's view (2001, 2009), whose monograph on degrammaticalisation (2009) provides the most important and comprehensive account of the phenomenon so far. She emphasises the crucial role of context, claiming that changes into content items that are 'taken out of their context [...] will be considered lexicalization, not degrammaticalization' (2009: 9). For her, then, degrammaticalisation refers to 'a composite change whereby a gram in a specific context gains in autonomy or substance on more than one linguistic level (semantics, morphology, syntax or phonology)'

5 For an in-depth discussion of 'reversals' of grammaticalisation understood in the broadest sense, see Newmeyer (2001).

6 Lexicalisation will not be discussed in this work, given that it is not a relevant issue in my data. Briefly put, lexicalisation can be considered both synchronically and diachronically and also as a theoretical framework, just like grammaticalisation (Lightfoot 2011: 439). In general terms, lexicalisation can be broadly understood in three different ways. Firstly, as an ordinary process of word formation, including here cases of compounding, derivation, initialisms, acronyms and blends, which involve the erosion of boundaries between independent morphemes. Secondly, as a process of fusion resulting in reduced compositionality, as is the case of *handicap* < *hand in the cap*. Thirdly, lexicalisation can involve 'the emancipation of bound morphemes into free morphemes' (Norde 2009: 10), for instance, in the case of *ex* (from *ex-husband*) and *ology* 'subject of study' (cf. Brinton and Traugott 2005: 32–61).

(2009: 120). In addition, degrammaticalisation has four basic features: (i) counterdirectionality, implying any shift from right to left on the cline of grammaticality (Hopper and Traugott 2003: 7): content item > grammatical word > clitic > inflectional affix (> Ø); (ii) novelty, since the 'less grammatical uses' must be novel and not derive from 'more grammatical elements'; (iii) infrequency, as the number of grammaticalised elements clearly exceeds that of degrammaticalised ones; (iv) discontinuity, because degrammaticalisation 'entails a *single* shift from right to left on the cline of grammaticality' and therefore cannot be regarded as the complete reversal of grammaticalisation (Norde 2009: 123). Among such examples of degrammaticalisation we find the verb *wotte* 'wish' in a variety of Pennsylvania German spoken in Waterloo County, Canada (cf. Burridge 1998). *Wotte* thus arose from the preterite subjunctive of the modal *welle* 'want to', thereby involving a shift from more grammatical to more lexical. Further examples include English *ish*, developing from a suffix to a free morpheme or the Irish pronoun *muid*, originally a verbal suffix (see Willis 2007; Norde 2009).

What seems clear from the preceding discussion, then, is that although degrammaticalisation is a rather controversial topic in grammaticalisation studies and even though the definitions of this phenomenon vary considerably, it is now generally accepted as a type of linguistic change.

### *3.3.2. Reanalysis*

Another phenomenon often associated with grammaticalisation is reanalysis, which is defined by Langacker (in Heine et al. 1991: 215), as the 'change in the structure of an expression or class of expressions that does not involve any immediate or intrinsic modification of its surface manifestation'. In other words, reanalysis involves a redefinition of constituent boundaries, turning an original structure (A, B) C into a new one, reinterpreted as A (B, C). Prototypical examples cited in the literature on grammaticalisation and reanalysis include, among others, the expression of the English perfect or the future in several languages. These examples are discussed in a summary fashion in what follows.

Concerning the expression of the perfect in English, its origin is apparently found in constructions of the type shown in (3.1), involving the lexical verb *have*, followed by a direct object and a past participle inflected like an adjective, functioning as a predicative complement:

| | | | | | |
|---|---|---|---|---|---|
| (3.1) | *Ic* | ***hæbbe*** | *þone* | *fisc* | ***gefangenne*** |
| | I-NOM.SG | have-PRES.1SG | DEF.ART. ACC.M.SG | fish-ACC.M.SG | catch.PTCP. ACC.M.SG |

'I have the fish caught'

Eventually, this construction underwent a process of reanalysis: *have* came to function as an auxiliary indicating a perfective action and the participle integrated in the verb phrase, as shown in example (3.2):

| | | | | | |
|---|---|---|---|---|---|
| (3.2) | *Ic* | ***hæbbe*** | ***gefangenne*** | *þone* | *fisc* |
| | I-NOM.SG | have-PRES.1SG | catch.PTCP. ACC.M.SG | DEF.ART. ACC.M.SG | fish-ACC.M.SG |

'I have caught the fish'

The reanalysis of the construction can therefore be represented as follows:

*Ic* [*hæbbe*] [[*þone fisc*] [*gefangenne*]] > *Ic* [*hæbbe gefangen*] [*þone fisc*]

S V DO PCO S Aux V DO

A further example involving grammaticalisation and reanalysis concerns the inflectional future in the Romance languages (cf., among others, Heine et al. 1991 for Spanish and Hopper and Traugott 2003; Marchello-Nizia 2006 for French). It has been suggested that in these languages the inflectional future derived from the Latin construction which involved the verb *habeo*, a verb of possession, postposed to an infinitive, with the meaning 'have to', as in (3.3).

| | | | |
|---|---|---|---|
| (3.3) | *Haec* | ***habeo*** | ***cantare*** |
| | these | have-PRES.1SG | sing-INF |
| | 'I have these things to sing' | | |

Constructions such as the one in (3.3), with a structure of the type [[*dicere* 'say'] *habeo* 'I have'], with the main verb *hab–* and an adjacent infinitive complement, can be interpreted as obligatory or at least as future-oriented since, if asked what one can say, it might be inferred that one should say it (Hopper and Traugott 2003: 54). This future inference led to the reinterpretation of the construction as [*dicere habeo*], in which the infinitive is no longer subordinate to the main verb *habere*, but comes to be bracketed together with it. Finally, in some Romance languages, this construction became grammaticalised as a future tense marker. This is the case, for instance, of Spanish and Catalan *cantar**é***, Galician and Portuguese *cantar**ei***, French *chanter**ai*** and Italian *canter**ò***, where the bold type highlights the grammaticalised verb *have*.

Future auxiliaries illustrate another case of reanalysis, since in some languages, including English and Greek, the current auxiliaries derive from full verbs expressing volition or willingness. Thus, the OE construction which involved the verb *willan* 'want' + bare infinitive developed over time into the PDE pattern future auxiliary *will* + infinitive (Heine and Kuteva 2002: 310). Likewise, the Modern Greek future tense marker *tha* goes back to the Classical Greek volitional verb *thelo* 'want', which underwent bleaching and erosion and eventually came to be interpreted as a grammatical marker: *thelô ina* ('I wish that') > *thelô na* > *thena* > *tha* (cf. Heine 2003: 584–6; Hopper and Traugott 2003: 24).

In spite of the fact that all the examples discussed so far in this section concern both reanalysis and grammaticalisation, not all cases of reanalysis result in grammaticalisation, while grammaticalisation always involves reanalysis (Hopper and Traugott 2003: 59). These authors mention, for instance, the case of compounding, which implies a redefinition of word boundaries (e.g. *hussy* < *house* + *wife*, *fishwife* < *fish* + *wife* 'woman', *woman*

< *wif* 'woman' + *man* 'human being'), but not grammaticalisation. These are regarded as cases of lexicalisation instead.

### *3.3.3. (Inter)subjectification*

Also closely related to grammaticalisation are (inter)subjectivity, a synchronic state, and (inter)subjectification, which is considered a diachronic process (Traugott 2010: 30). After introducing these notions, some examples of these phenomena are provided for illustrative purposes, before closing the section with some comments on the relationship between grammaticalisation and (inter)subjectification.

Although traditional accounts on the functions of language (cf. Bühler [1934] 1990; Jakobson 1960) already recognised the expressive or emotive role of language, it is the referential or propositional function (*representational* in Bühler's terms) which has traditionally been considered as the most significant. Over the past decades, however, the subjective component of language and hence its expressive function has been given much more prominence, so that it is now generally acknowledged that 'language and communication are much more than the exchange of formal propositional material for purposes of conveying information' (Scheibman 2002: 9). The notion of subjectivity, however, is by no means recent, since Bréal ([1897] 2005) already recognised its importance, claiming that speakers leave their imprint in language. This involvement on the part of the speaker can be expressed grammatically by means of, among other devices, adverbials such as *sans doute* ('no doubt') or the subjunctive (*Dieu vous entende* 'may God hear you') (Bréal [1897] 2005: 164–9). Benveniste also described intersubjectivity, noting that speakers should pay attention to the needs of their interlocutors in a conversation for it to be successful (Traugott 2010: 32).

In the general literature on subjectivity, however, we can distinguish two main trends, represented by Langacker and Traugott.[7] Since Traugott's

7 For further discussions about (inter)subjectivity and (inter)subjectification, refer to Nuyts (2001), Fitzmaurice (2004), De Smet and Verstraete (2006), Athanasiadou (2007), Cuyckens et al. (2010), López-Couso (2010), Visconti (2013), Boye and Harder (2014) and Ghesquière (2014), among many others.

approach to (inter)subjectivity is the one applied to the discussion of the data in Chapter 6, I will not delve into Langacker's[8] framework here and will focus instead on Traugott's model. In line with Lyons (1982), Traugott takes subjectivity as the way in which natural languages lend themselves to the expression of 'self', whether lexically or grammatically. Subjective meanings therefore explicitly encode the speaker's or writer's point of view, beliefs and attitudes (Traugott and Dasher 2002; Traugott 2010). In turn, intersubjectivity describes 'the way in which natural languages, in their structure and their normal manner of operation, provide for the locutionary agent's expression of his or her awareness of the addressee's attitudes and beliefs, most especially their "face" or "self-image"' (Traugott 2010: 33). Intersubjective markers, then, signal the speaker's attention to the addressee's self-image and his/her face.[9]

Although Traugott is indubitably one of the chief exponents in the literature on (inter)subjectivity and on the rise of linguistic markers signalling (inter)subjectivity, other authors have also extensively dealt with this topic and recognised the need for a more formal definition of these notions. De Smet and Verstraete (2006), for instance, distinguish two major types of subjectivity:

(a) Pragmatic subjectivity 'is inherent in language and is independent of the semantics of a particular expression' (2006: 384). For example, if we describe a person as being tall, it very much depends on our conceptualisation of the world, as the average male and female height in Sweden, for instance, differs considerably from the average in Indonesia or Vietnam.

8 Langacker's framework is grounded in cognitive semantics. In this model the meaning of an expression cannot be objectively characterised, so that its semantics depends on factors such as background assumptions and the perspective taken on the scene (1990: 315). Thus, the construal is said to be objective when no reference is made to the speech event or participants, since the element itself is placed onstage as the focus of attention. Conversely, a construal is said to be subjective when the entity itself is implicit and in the offstage region (cf. also De Smet and Verstraete 2006: 369–70; López-Couso 2010: 143; Ghesquière 2014: 56–7).

9 Langacker's model is not concerned with intersubjectivity.

(b) Semantic subjectivity, by contrast, is not concerned with how the speaker uses an expression, but with the inherent meaning of that particular expression. De Smet and Verstraete (2006) distinguish between ideational and interpersonal subjectivity. Ideational subjectivity 'involves the description of a content "situated in the speaker's subjective belief-state/attitude toward the situation" ' (2006: 384). For instance, in the case of the Dutch attitudinal adjectives *leuk* ('pleasant') and *dom* ('bloody, cursed'), it is the speaker that is clearly projecting his/her view of something being pleasant or cursed, respectively. Interpersonal subjectivity, on the other hand, 'deals with the positioning of the speaker with respect to this representation and his or her interaction with the interlocutor' (2006: 385). Dutch *leuk* thus shows ideational subjectivity, expressing an evaluation on the part of the speaker, while *dom* further illustrates interpersonal subjectivity, as in *domme toeristen* ('bloody tourists'), where *dom* does not specify a type of tourists but rather the speaker's stance.

Along the lines of De Smet and Verstraete (2006), Ghesquière et al. (2014) argue for the necessity to distinguish different types of intersubjectivity, depending on the meanings coded:

(a) attitudinal intersubjectivity refers to those meanings which code the speaker's image of the hearer and the attention to his/her face needs and social self (e.g. through the use of T/V-pronouns of address or discourse markers such as *sort of* or *well* used as hedges);
(b) responsive intersubjectivity is conveyed by those items which elicit a certain (speech) act or behaviour aimed at discourse continuity or cooperation (e.g. by means of question tags or turn-taking devices such as clause-final *right* or *isn't it*?);
(c) textual intersubjectivity is evinced by those elements which 'are specifically oriented toward steering the hearer's interpretation' (2014: 137). This is the case, for instance, of certain uses of the demonstratives, which focus the hearer's attention on elements in the ongoing discourse.

Ghesquière et al.'s classification, however, is flexible and one element can in fact evince different types of intersubjective meanings. For example, *toch* in Dutch can serve as a question tag, in which case we expect a response from the hearer. This would represent responsive intersubjectivity. In addition, *toch* may convey attitudinal intersubjectivity, since it can be used to acknowledge a potentially different view of the addressee, hence expressing a counter-expectational value (Ghesquière et al. 2014: 138).

As seen in the preceding paragraphs, subjectivity is a synchronic state. The diachronic process giving rise to subjective meanings is named subjectification, 'a pragmatic-semantic process whereby meanings become increasingly based in the speaker's subjective belief state/attitude toward the proposition, in other words, towards what the speaker is talking about' (Traugott 1995: 31). Understood in this way, the phenomenon of subjectification appears to be pervasive in languages, given that speakers always want to justify the relevance of their speech acts. Nevertheless, although the persuasiveness of the speaker's message will ultimately depend on the way (s)he codes the message (cf. Traugott 1995), the collaboration of the hearer is necessary to decipher any possible inferences.

Subjectification has been pivotal in Traugott's theory of semantic change (cf. Traugott 1982, 1989), in which the following path of semantic evolution is established: propositional > textual > expressive (1989: 31), involving the gradual development of increasingly more subjective meanings. Traugott hence distinguishes three different tendencies:

- Tendency I: meanings based in the external described situation > meanings based in the internal (evaluative/perceptual/cognitive) described situation. This tendency includes semantic changes such as pejoration and amelioration, as well as metaphorical extensions from concrete to abstract meanings (1989: 34).
- Tendency II: meanings based in the external or internal described situation > meanings based in the textual and metalinguistic situation, as is the case, for instance, of the development of connectives from lexical forms (e.g. *þa while þe* 'the time that' > 'during') (1989: 35).
- Tendency III: meanings tend to become increasingly based in the speaker's subjective belief state/attitude toward the proposition (1989: 35). Within this tendency Traugott subsumes changes such

as the development of the future marker *going to*, from an original motion verb, or the rise of intensifiers such as *very*,[10] originally meaning 'true', a cognitive evaluation.

Crucial in Traugott's theory of semantic change is Tendency III, which illustrates subjectification, that is, the change from less to increasingly more subjective meanings. Subjectification is regarded as 'the major type of semantic change' (Traugott and Dasher 2002: 97), while Tendency I and Tendency II are best described in terms of metaphorical transfer and mapping from one domain to another (López-Couso 2010: 130).

Subjective meanings may in turn be used to convey the speaker's attention to the addressee, hence resulting in the codification of intersubjective meanings, a process known as intersubjectification. As stated by Traugott (2003: 128), intersubjectification refers to the 'explicit expression of the SP[eaker]/W[riter]'s attention to the "self" of addressee/reader in both an epistemic sense (paying attention to their presumed attitudes to the content of what is said) and in a more social sense (paying attention to their "face" or "image needs" associated with social stance and identity)'. Intersubjectification is crucial in languages with honorific systems, like Japanese, where morphosyntactic choices are determined by the relationship between the speaker and the addressee. This does not mean, however, that in languages with no such systems, such as English, the speaker does not take into consideration the image of the addressee. Consider, for instance, honorifics like *sir/madam* and V-pronouns in the Romance languages and in German.

The following diachronic cline of subjectivity is hence commonly observed in Traugott's theory of semantic change: non-/less subjective > subjective > intersubjective (cf. Traugott and Dasher 2002: 225; Traugott 2003: 134).[11] Examples attesting to this unidirectional cline of subjectivity

10 For a detailed account of the history of *very*, see Breban and Davidse (2016) (cf. Section 4.1.2).

11 A further step down the cline has been suggested by Fitzmaurice (2004), who maintains that intersubjective readings may give rise to interactive meanings, focusing in her case study on the discourse markers *you know*, *you see* and *you say*. Thus, from an intersubjective reading, attending to the addressee's needs, these markers come to be used to 'keep things going in a conversation' (2004: 438).

are manifold, including death-related intensifiers, as will become apparent from the data analysis presented in Chapter 6, since they have developed increasingly subjective meanings over time ('characteristic of death' > 'to a degree which I consider reminiscent of the negative aspects of death'). In what follows, a few selected examples are provided.

Margerie (2010) is concerned with the rise of the discourse marker *kind of* and its variant form *kinda*, which originated in a construction consisting of the head noun *kind*, followed by a prepositional phrase as modifier (e.g. *the **kind of** college*). This noun phrase developed an approximation reading over time (e.g. *a **kind of** reddish-brown colour*) and eventually turned into an intensifier (e.g. *I **kind of** like that sort of colour*). *Kind of* moved yet one step further, since it acquired different pragmatic meanings as a discourse marker: among other functions, it came to be used as a hedge or politeness marker, therefore showing intersubjectification (e.g. *it's **kind of** fucking important*). The development of subjective readings took place gradually, starting already in the approximative readings of *kind*, which imply an evaluation on the part of the speaker. It was these subjective readings that eventually triggered the intersubjective meanings of *kind of* and *kinda*.

The evolution of the attitudinal adjectives *leuk* and *dom* in Dutch is described in De Smet and Verstraete (2006). These had a propositional or objective meaning in origin: *leuk* meant 'neither hot nor cold' and *dom* 'dumb, unable to speak'. Over time, however, these adjectives developed an evaluative meaning, hence evincing subjectivity. *Dom* came to mean 'unintelligent' and *leuk* 'pleasant, nice', the latter via an intermediate stage in which it referred to people, denoting a calm and often slightly mocking attitude. Moreover, in Belgian Dutch *dom* developed even further, expressing a negative evaluation on the part of the speaker: 'annoying, cursed, bloody'.

Traugott (2014) presents the case study of *no doubt* and *surely*, which were borrowed from French in the fourteenth century and grammaticalised into adverbials; both underwent subjectification, *surely* being further intersubjectified, used for 'seeking uptake/corroboration by the Addressee' (2014: 18). Interestingly, Traugott's findings challenge the general hypothesis about the correlation of the left periphery with subjective meanings and of the right periphery with intersubjective meanings (Traugott 2010), since both *surely* and *no doubt* are mostly attested in the left periphery. This leads her to conclude that there might well be domains in which this tendency is more likely to occur (e.g. information-structuring), while in some other domains (e.g. discourse-management) this tendency is not as robust.

The examples mentioned above all attest to the unidirectionality of (inter)subjectification. Nonetheless, as is the case with grammaticalisation (cf. Section 3.3.1), counterexamples to the (inter)subjectification cline do exist, as detailed in López-Couso (2010: 142–3) and Ghesquière (2014: 96–7). This is also duly acknowledged by Traugott (1995: 45), who claims that although in general terms 'the hypothesis of unidirectional increase in subjectification over time is very robust' (1995: 45), some examples may run counter to the directionality chain non-subjective > subjective, especially in the early stages of the grammaticalisation process or in primary grammaticalisation (cf. Section 3.1). For instance, deictic elements such as *now* or *here*, which originally referred to the speaker or the context of speaking, gradually moved away from the speaker in what Adamson (1995) calls *de-subjectivisation*. Cornillie (2008) also presents another counterexample from Spanish, namely the semi-auxiliaries *parecer* 'seem, turn out' + infinitive and *resultar* 'result' + infinitive, which show a less-grammaticalised, intersubjective meaning over time, and which appeared earlier than *parecer* 'seem' + *que* 'that' and *resultar* 'turn out' + *que* 'that' in the historical records of Spanish.

Although, as we have seen, grammaticalisation correlates with an increase in subjectivity or 'the linguistic expression of the self' (Finegan 1995: 1), grammaticalisation and (inter)subjectification are in fact independent processes and may occur separately. Thus, the development of speech-act verb meanings in items like *agree* (originally 'be pleasing, suitable'), *insist* (from a Latin past participle meaning 'sat on') and *promise* (from a Latin past participle meaning 'sent forward'), evinces subjectification but not grammaticalisation (cf. Traugott 1995; López-Couso 2010). The same applies to processes of amelioration and pejoration. The interrelation between grammaticalisation and intersubjectification is, however, much less evident, because, as Traugott (2010: 61) notes, intersubjectification is frequently associated with politeness expressions and these very often involve lexical rather than grammatical choices.

## 3.4. Summary

This chapter has provided a very broad overview of the phenomenon of grammaticalisation, often characterised in terms of a set of parameters and principles (cf. Section 3.2). Some of the phenomena frequently associated with grammaticalisation were also discussed here, in particular unidirectionality, reanalysis and (inter)subjectification (cf. Section 3.3). The framework of grammaticalisation in general, and these notions in particular, provide the theoretical foundations for the present research and they will be resumed again and discussed in greater detail in the light of the data in Chapter 6 (cf. Section 6.3). Overall, it has been shown that grammaticalisation occurs cross-linguistically and that it is 'the cross-componential change *par excellence*' (McMahon 1994: 161), affecting semantics, phonology, morphology and syntax alike. Representative examples have been provided to illustrate how grammaticalisation affects these levels, as well as to show some of the most oft-quoted clines of grammaticalisation in the literature.

CHAPTER 4

# English intensifiers: A historical overview

A noteworthy characteristic of intensifiers is their tendency to continuous renewal by virtue of their quick loss of expressivity (cf. Lorenz 2002; Méndez-Naya 2003; Tagliamonte 2008, among others), which makes them a very fruitful topic in the study of synchronic and diachronic variation and change. Spitzbardt (1965) hence remarks that 'each period in the history of any language is characterized by its peculiar catchwords including adverbs of degree' (1965: 350). Thus, *rare*, *wondrous* and *monstrous* were in vogue in EModE and *vastly* rose in popularity in the eighteenth century. By contrast, adverbs such as *right* or *very* have been around in the intensifier system for centuries. Moreover, the loss of expressivity of a given intensifier may also result in the combination of two intensifiers. In this sense, Méndez-Naya (2017) examined the co-occurrence and iteration of intensifiers in the OE, ME and EModE periods and identified two patterns in the co-occurrence of intensifiers: on the one hand, the more grammaticalised and weakened item may appear reinforced by a new, less worn-down intensifier to its left (e.g. ***right*** *swiþe*); on the other, the oldest intensifier may appear with a newly recruited member to its right, which may be more specific and even retain semantic features of the head, as in the combination ***swiðe ungemetlice*** *mycel wind* 'such a very very strong wind', in which *ungemetlice* 'exceedingly, beyond measure' combines with another adjective of dimension: *mycel* 'strong' (Méndez-Naya 2017: 262).

Another important feature of intensifiers is that they are mostly recruited in the domain of lexis (Méndez-Naya 2003: 375) and gradually develop more general and abstract meanings, that is, they become grammaticalised in the course of time (cf. Chapter 3). The prototypical example of a fully grammaticalised intensifier which is regularly cited in the literature is that of *very* (cf. Bolinger 1972: 18; Lorenz 1999: 85; Méndez-Naya 2003: 375; Breban and Davidse 2016, among others), historically derived from the ME adjective *verray* 'true'. Nonetheless, not all intensifiers are as advanced as *very* in their grammaticalisation process. In some of them their original meaning can still be traceable. This is the case, for instance, of *terribly*, whose modern collocates reveal a predisposition to negative elements (Partington 1993: 184).

Closely related to the grammaticalisation of intensifiers are the process of subjectification (see, among others, Athanasiadou 2007; cf. Section 3.3.3) and their restrictions in mobility or fixation, in Lehmann's 1985 terms (cf. Section 3.2). Thus, the development of intensifying meanings has been associated with a continuous increase in subjectivity, as well as with a fixation of the word order options due to a reduction in their scope of modification. Adamson, in her article on the intensifier *lovely* and word order options (2000), has shown that intensifiers undergo a gradual shift from originally descriptive meanings to progressively more affective or subjective meanings (i.e. subjectification or subjectivisation), finally reaching the intensifying stage. She has also demonstrated that this increase in subjectivity correlates with a left position in the phrase. Thus, the more subjective the item is, the more likely it is to appear in the leftmost position. Conversely, objective meanings tend to appear to the right (cf. Section 4.1.2). Prior to Adamson, however, Partington had also pointed to the interdependence between syntax and semantics in regard to intensifiers. According to him, the more delexicalised or grammaticalised an intensifier is, the more syntactic restrictions it has (Partington 1993: 189–91).

Intensifiers do not only express speaker involvement and his/her commitment to the truth of the proposition (cf. Suscinskij 1985), but also function as markers of group-membership to a speech community (Peters 1992; Stenström 1999; Tagliamonte and Roberts 2005; Macaulay 2006; Barnfield and Buchstaller 2010). As Lorenz has noted (1999: 24–5), 'intensifiers are used as "shibboleths", as linguistic clues to the identity and group-membership of the speaker'. Likewise, Claridge (2011: 176), in relation to hyperbole, claims that this strategy aims to strengthen the speaker's standing and to consolidate group identity. This statement could be extended to intensifiers as well, these being typical hyperbolical devices. This consolidation of group identity is especially noticeable in the language of teenagers (Stenström 1999, 2000; Núñez-Pertejo and Palacios-Martínez 2018; Aijmer 2020), who are constantly adding new sets of expressions to the paradigm of intensifiers, as is the case of *bare* and *proper* in Multicultural London English (Núñez-Pertejo and Palacios-Martínez 2018), of *pure* in the speech of Glaswegian adolescents (Macaulay 2006) or the re-emergent use of *well* by young speakers in British English (cf. Aijmer 2021). In fact, when the intensifier which makes a speech community so distinctive spreads to other groups, the word loses its former function of identity marker and the 'linguistic trend-setters' (Peters 1994: 271) will coin a new one. In other words, intensifiers can also be regarded as 'fashion victims'.

The remainder of this chapter presents different studies in the literature on English reinforcers from the perspective of grammaticalisation, the theory which underlies the current study. This chapter thus serves to contextualise and underpin the corpus-based research undertaken here on death-related intensifiers (Chapter 6), given that the methodological and theoretical framework in these studies will serve as the basis for the current research.

## 4.1. Reinforcers from the perspective of grammaticalisation

This section reviews a number of studies which have been published on the diachronic evolution of intensifiers and reinforcers specifically in the light of the theory of grammaticalisation. Section 4.1.1 presents some case studies which have been carried out on maximisers (cf. Section 2.2.2), that is, those intensifiers which indicate maximum degree (e.g. *absolutely* or *to death*), while Section 4.1.2 turns to boosters, that is, those intensifiers which express high degree, as is the case of *very* and *right*. Section 4.2 closes the chapter.

### *4.1.1. Maximisers*

A number of PDE maximisers ultimately go back to ME, including *absolutely*, *downright* and *utterly*. Some others which originated at this period died over time, such as *throughout* or *þwert-out*. By contrast, other maximisers date to EModE, as is the case of *complete*, *to death* and *whole*.

*Absolutely*, whose most recent history is explored by McManus (2012), Núñez-Pertejo (2013) and Aijmer (2020), has a wide variety of functions in PDE other than being an intensifier, since it can also be used as verbal adjunct with scope over a verb, a clause or a sentence, as an emphatic discourse marker at the end of a clause and as a response token, in which case it expresses emphatic affirmation (Núñez-Pertejo 2013: 250). In this latter function, it is argued to be more characteristic of the spoken language and of American English (Núñez-Pertejo 2013: 269). Moreover, *absolutely* can modify a wide variety of elements as an intensifier: adjectives (e.g. ***absolutely*** *brilliant*), nouns (e.g. ***absolutely*** *shit*), adverbs (e.g. ***absolutely*** *never*), pronouns (e.g. ***absolutely*** *nothing*), determiners (***absolutely*** *no reason*), quantifying elements (***absolutely*** *everything*) and prepositional phrases (e.g. ***absolutely*** *without doubt*) (cf. Núñez-Pertejo 2013: 249–50; Aijmer 2020: 250–60). The intensifying function of *absolutely* is, however, far from new in the language, its first occurrences dating back to the fifteenth century (Núñez-Pertejo 2013: 254–5). McManus (2012: 60–70), in turn, identified the first uses of the maximiser *absolutely* slightly later, in the EModE period, yet she identified a wide variety of collocates already in LModE, including nouns and prepositions.

*Absolutely* typically collocates with non-gradable adjectives in the nineteenth- and twentieth-century British and American data examined by Núñez-Pertejo (2013), that is, with adjectives which already indicate an extreme or absolute degree (e.g. *terrifying*). The same tendency was noticed by Aijmer (2020), since its collocates in the BNC1994 and BNC2014 are in most cases extreme adjectives. Núñez-Pertejo noted 'a clear "semantic preference" towards adjectives with negative connotations' (2013: 259), a trend which was also true in the 1990s data from the BNC. In the BNC2014, however, there was hardly any difference with regard to adjective polarity (Aijmer 2020: 151). In addition to adjectival collocates, *absolutely* can be used as a noun modifier, a feature which is regarded by Núñez-Pertejo (2013) as characteristic of teenage speech, as in her twentieth-century data it is usually followed by taboo or swear words such as *fuck* or *shit*. This use, however, is far from being new, since it was already attested in the eighteenth century.

In the past few decades *absolutely* has increased in frequency in British English, in the light of Aijmer's (2020) data. This rise in token and type frequency is concomitant with a number of syntactic, semantic and pragmatic changes, therefore suggesting its ongoing grammaticalisation and increasing subjectification over time. Over time, and following the cline of directionality of other adverbials such as *in fact* or *actually*, *absolutely* evolved into a response token.

Another of the maximisers which developed its function in ME is the adverb *downright* (cf. Méndez-Naya 2008a), which was originally a spatial adjunct indicating directional path 'straight down, right down (to the ground)', hence typically collocating with verbs such as *fly* or *fall*. Moreover, in OE *right* could also appear before *down*, so that the lexicalisation of the combination *downright* was not yet complete at this stage. In ME, however, *downright* developed its degree reading: 'out-and-out, absolutely'. Thus, *downright* typically modified verbs which involved hitting somebody with a weapon, such as an axe or a sword (e.g. *hew*, *cleave*). Méndez-Naya (2008a: 272) suggests that these specific contexts were the ones which favoured an interpretation of *downright* as 'completely'. The most likely evolution of the adverb, therefore, was: to give a blow with a cutting weapon 'straight down, down to the ground' > to cut 'from top to bottom' > to cut 'completely'. *Downright* has predominantly negative semantic prosody (cf. Stubbs 1995), occurring mainly with negative collocates (e.g. *affront*, *mock*, *refuse*), though positive collocations are also marginally found (e.g. *accept*, *love*, *worship*), mainly in the eighteenth and nineteenth centuries. In addition to adverbial uses, *downright* also occurs from the sixteenth century as an adjective, therefore modifying nouns (e.g. *Papist*, *denial*). In this use, *downright* originally had a clearly directional sense: 'directed straight downwards' (e.g. ***downright** stroke*). It was not until the following century, however, that the adjective *downright* developed an intensifying reading, becoming a popular intensifier in the seventeenth and eighteenth centuries (e.g. ***downright*** *generosity*, ***downright*** *adorement*). As was the case with its adverbial counterpart, adjectival *downright* collocated predominantly with negative heads.

Like *downright*, a series of maximisers originating in the spatial domain and sharing the meaning 'out' also developed an intensifier function in ME. This is the case of *outly*, *throughout(ly)*, *þwert-out*, *outright* and *utterly*, discussed in Méndez-Naya (2014). Nonetheless, unlike other intensifiers derived from lexical elements, these adverbs originated in a more abstract source, though they have also undergone a process of grammaticalisation and metaphorical change over time. This process whereby elements meaning 'out' develop intensifying readings is by no means exclusive of English but occurs also in other languages such as Spanish (the prefix *extra–*, as in ***extraplano*** 'very flat', from Latin *extra* 'on the outside, without') or German (the prefix *ur–*, originally meaning 'out of', as in ***uralt*** 'very old').

*Utlice* or *outlice* derives from the spatial adverb *ut* 'out' by means of the suffix *–lice*. Even though *outlice* could already express maximal degree in OE, meaning 'utterly, completely', it was in fact a low-frequency item at this early stage. The intensifying function of *outlice* was continued in ME (see also McManus 2012), but the actual corpus evidence for these uses is very scarce (Méndez-Naya 2014: 248), although the maximising function is actually the most frequent in McManus' (2012) data. In PDE, however, remnants of the former intensifying uses can still be traced, though only in northern English and in Scots (Méndez-Naya 2014: 250).

*Throughout(ly)* was recorded in OE as a spatial preposition 'throughout, right through', whose meaning issues from the image schema of the CONTAINER, indicating a path and hence a motion across the enclosure of the container from side to side (Méndez-Naya 2014: 250). As was the case with *downright* (see above), *throughout* also occurred typically with verbs involving weapons, such as spears, swords, etc. (e.g. *saw*, *cut*), from which a degree reading would be inferred and foregrounded. *Throughout* could also be found as a degree modifier of adjectives and adverbs from the beginning of the thirteenth century, in which function it could also collocate with positive adjectives (e.g. *good* or *proud*). At the close of the fifteenth century, however, the intensifying function of *throughout* faded. Another rather common intensifier in ME was *þwert-out*, which could modify verbs, adjectives, adverbs and negative expressions, although its prototypical heads were adjectives. As verb modifiers, however, *throughout* and *þwert-out* collocated mainly with negative items. The change from negative to positive semantic prosody was owed, in all likelihood, to the most frequent verbal collocates of these adverbs, meaning 'abandon', which usually took complements such as sins or something which was undesirable (Méndez-Naya 2014: 258–9). Abandoning something undesirable was conceived of as something good and this inference is hypothesised to have led to the change in the semantic prosody of these intensifiers.

*Outright* dates back to the beginning of the fourteenth century. Curiously, the temporal reading of *outright* 'straightaway, immediately' was available prior to the spatial reading 'directly out', which is only attested from the fourteenth century onwards. This seems to contradict the general grammaticalisation cline by means of which temporal readings derive from spatial meanings (cf., among others, Hopper and Traugott 2003). However, Méndez-Naya acknowledges that this is due to the data which have been preserved. Verb collocates of *outright* were mostly negative and there are in fact very few examples of *outright* as a modifier of adjectives (only *wood* 'mad' and *mad*).

*Utterly*, by contrast, is much more frequent than *outright* and it was also an ME development, arising in the thirteenth century with spatial meanings ('outwardly, superficially'), and then, from the fourteenth century onwards, as an intensifier occurring mainly with negative heads, as was the case with *outright*.

As mentioned above, several maximisers developed a degree reading in EModE. *Complete*, for instance, features in the historical records from the end of the fourteenth century onwards. In its earliest descriptive meanings, it was constrained to months or periods of time and invoked 'a boundary relative to which 'completion/completeness' is assessed' (e.g. ***complet*** *the laste meridie of decembre*) (Davidse 2009: 268). The set of collocates of *complete* was expanded in the following centuries. In addition to the meaning of completion, *complete* had other senses, namely 'having all its parts or members' (e.g. *their shoulders broad for* ***complete*** *armour fit*), attested from the sixteenth century, and also 'perfect in nature or quality' (e.g. *his lawe is* ***compleet***), which is documented from the end of the fourteenth century.

It is precisely this latter meaning which eventually gave rise in the seventeenth century to the sense 'fully equipped for', collocating with nouns denoting professions (e.g. *the* ***compleatest*** *actors*). *Complete* could also occur in EModE in secondary determiner uses (e.g. *the* ***compleate*** *number of Common Counsell men*), helping to single out the referent and forming a unit with the primary determiner, and finally, as a noun intensifier (*a* ***compleat*** *villaine*). According to Davidse (2009), the noun intensifying occurrences of *complete* arose out of the former descriptive function of the adjective and did not develop, as Bolinger (1972) had claimed, from its secondary determiner uses. As a noun intensifier, *complete* appeared first with unbounded items, referring mainly to people (*knave, villain*) or to entities (*harmony*). Later on, bounded attestations emerged, first with collocates such as *victory, wreck, success,* etc., to which *complete* attributes the 'full realisation' (Davidse 2009: 278).

The maximising function of *whole* is argued to have originated in descriptive senses rather in the quantifying-identifying function of the adjective (Ghesquière and Davidse 2011: 264). This use of *whole* as a secondary determiner, making reference to the whole entity referred to by the head noun, is attested from ME, and these readings later on triggered its uses as an intensifier, recorded from EModE onwards. It is one construction in particular, *all the whole* + noun (e.g. ***all the whole*** *way*), especially common in LME and EModE, which favoured the emergence of the intensifying reading. Ghesquière and Davidse also point out that *whole* invoked originally closed intensification scales,[1] but from the end of the EModE period, it could appear with open intensification scales as well, which also entailed a widening in the range of the collocates sanctioned by *whole*.

Another of the maximisers which developed intensifying readings in EModE is *to death*. According to Margerie (2011), the earliest uses of this

1 The distinction of closed and open intensification scales drawn by the authors is based on Kennedy and McNally (2005). Open scales 'lack a minimal element, a maximal element, or both', while closed scales have 'minimal and maximal elements' (Kennedy and McNally 2005: 352).

prepositional phrase[2] occurred in resultative constructions ('X CAUSE Y TO BECOME Z') as a postmodifier of verbs of physical beating, torturing or killing (e.g. *wound*, *beat*, *stab*, *kill*, etc.). After these early prototypical uses, *to death* started to occur in a number of transitional constructions which paved the way for the later emergence of a degree reading of the phrase:

i. The first of these transitional stages is labelled by Margerie *resultative constructions with a telic verb* (e.g. *he sloh him wið a stan* ***to deaðe***). This phase is very similar in fact to the prototypical resultative one (occurring also with telic verbs such as *slay* or *wound*), though Margerie keeps them apart and claims that the two constructions are distinct. For her, the prototypical resultative construction, although construing death as an end point as is the case with the transitional pattern, represents a unitary process. Conversely, the transitional construction represents two processes and hence 'makes a DEGREE reading of *to death* significantly more likely than the prototypical construction' (Margerie 2011: 122).
ii. Constructions in which *to death* appears with verbs which do not have a literal resultative reading (e.g. *hate* or *bore*), which involve more speaker involvement towards the proposition and hence represent a case of subjectification (cf. Traugott 1995; Hopper and Traugott 2003; López-Couso 2010, among others).
iii. Constructions in which *to death* is preceded by an adjective or past participle (e.g. *sick* ***to death*** or *frozen* ***to death***), which establish a causal relationship between a state (that of being sick or frozen) and the process whereby that state may end up in death.

The final stage in the development of *to death* represents the emergence of degree readings of the intensifier, therefore suggesting semantic bleaching

2 Given that *to death* is one of death-related intensifiers discussed in this monograph, Margerie's (2011) study will also be examined in connection with my data in section 6.2.6.1.

or attrition (cf. Section 3.2). The first attested use dates to 1568 (e.g. *the which Castell the king hated* ***to the death***), although very few intensifying uses are recorded before the eighteenth century.

In PDE *to death* shows a collocational preference for negative items (e.g. *bored, worried, scared*), along the lines of other negative intensifiers like *horrifically*, although it is also recorded with elements with positive semantic prosody, such as *love* or *tickle*, therefore showing signs of ongoing grammaticalisation. Moreover, data on current uses of the language reveal occurrences of this prepositional phrase in attributive function (e.g. *pretty* ***to death*** *dress*).

In contrast to the previous studies, which focused on individual items, the research by McManus (2012) and Claridge et al. (2019) explored the category of maximisers as a whole from a diachronic perspective. McManus (2012) thus traced the long diachrony of *absolutely, completely, entirely, perfectly, quite, totally* and *utterly* in a number of diachronic corpora from ME to PDE. In view of her data, some of these maximisers developed this function already in the ME period, as is the case of *perfectly, quite* and *utterly*, whereas for others this use emerged later, in EModE, as in the case of *absolutely, completely, entirely* and *totally*. Claridge et al. (2019), who also explored this category of maximisers, focused instead on LModE, as represented by the Old Bailey Corpus (OBC). They specifically looked into the uses of *absolutely, altogether, completely, entirely, fully, perfectly, thoroughly, totally, utterly* and *wholly* over the period, so they do not discuss the origin of these forms. Their results revealed that all courtroom speakers made use of all maximisers, although *perfectly* and *entirely* were the most prototypical of LModE. In addition to an increasing use of maximisers over the period, their findings also suggest a higher incidence of these adverbs among male speakers. This could be attributed to both a formal effect of the courtroom, as well as to the fact that there was a greater proportion of well-educated males belonging to the middle or higher social ranks of society. Likewise, judges and lawyers make more recurrent use of maximisers.

To close this section, Figure 4.1 presents a timeline of the history of the forms discussed so far, showing the period at which these forms first developed an intensifying function, as well as the stage until they are attested as intensifiers. As can be gathered from the figure, most of these

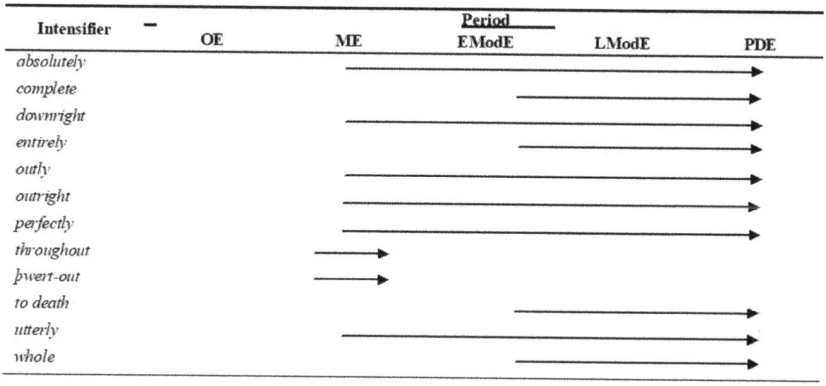


Figure 4.1. Maximisers in the history of English

forms remain as maximisers in the present day, though some of them are only marginally used in this function.

## 4.1.2. *Boosters*

Although EModE was a very fruitful period for the creation of boosters (cf. Peters 1994), some of these intensifiers developed their degree reading considerably earlier, even as early as the OE period. This is the case, among others, of *eal* 'all' (Buchstaller and Traugott 2006), *wundor* 'wonder' (Calle-Martín 2014) and *swīþe* 'very' (Méndez-Naya 2003). Moreover, although boosters are in many cases degree adverbs and these were in fact the most common intensification strategy in OE, they were by no means the only possible strategy with a boosting function in the period. Morphological devices were in fact frequently used at the time to express intensification, as shown by Méndez-Naya (2021). In her study on OE synthetic intensification devices, she focused on spatial elements, specifically on *for-* (and variants), *ofer-*, *þurh-*, *or-*, *in-*, *of-*, *forþ-* and *uþ-*. Of all these forms, only *for-*, *ofer-* and *þurh-* were found to be productive spatial formatives (e.g. in ***for**hraþe* 'very quickly', ***ofer**full* 'too full' and ***þurh**bitter* 'very bitter'). *For-* was the spatial formative with the highest type and token frequency, as well as the most advanced in the grammaticalisation process, occurring with adjectival, adverbial and verbal collocates alike. Its use continued into the ME period, though considerably more marginally and eventually becoming obsolete. The productivity of *ofer-* and *þurh-* continued in subsequent stages of the language (Méndez-Naya 2021: 14).

As mentioned above, one of the OE adverbs with a boosting function was *wundor* (e.g. ***wundor** feorr & wide* 'very far and wide'), which could occur in combination with adjectival and adverbial elements. The first attested example in Calle-Martín's (2014) data, which includes a variety of dictionaries and corpora from OE to EModE, goes back to the sixth century. At the close of the tenth century the adverb underwent collocational expansion, allowing for a number of additional adjectives and adverbs, and from the late sixteenth-century *wonder* declined dramatically. As far as collocates are concerned, *wonder* shows a clear preference for adjectives over adverbs. Moreover, the adjectival collocates of *wonder* are mostly unbounded and positive polarity elements.

Another of the boosters dating to the OE period is *eal* 'all', which could additionally be a quantifier modifying nouns or pronouns. As such it was inflected for gender, number and case. As an adverb, *eal* occurred mainly with bounded adjectives and participles, reinforcing 'the boundedness/completeness of the resultant state denoted by the participle' (Buchstaller and Traugott 2006: 353). Even though the adverb *eal* already showed a degree meaning in OE, examples of this function were rare at this stage, as noted by the authors. Further evidence for this scalar modifier function, however, is to be found in the set of compound forms derived from *eall*, in which the adverb simply boosted the quality of the adjective on a degree scale. Such OE examples include ***eal**grene* 'all green' and ***eall**mihtig* 'almighty'. Over the course of ME the adjectival collocations of *all* increased and the adverb came to occur with both bounded (e.g. ***al** dead* 'completely dead') and unbounded adjectives (***al** sad* 'very sad'). ME also witnessed an increase in fixed phrases with *all*, such as ***al** aboute(n)* 'in all directions', and in concessives such as ***al**beit* and ***al**though*.

Intensifying *all* continued through EModE. During this period, uses of this adverb as a modifier of adjectives and other adverbs became less common, although they did not die out (Buchstaller and Traugott 2006: 355). Collocations such as ***all demonyak*** ('possessed by the devil') and ***all too heavy*** are attested in their data. EModE also witnessed the development of new functions for the adverb *all*. Thus, it was in this period when *all* came to modify nouns and new compound forms with *all* developed at the time (e.g. ***all-eloquent***, ***all-heart***). It was also during EModE that the distributional difference between the adverb and quantifier *all* emerged. Thus, when *all* follows a verb, it is interpreted as an adverb, whereas when it follows an auxiliary, the most likely interpretation is that of a quantifier (Buchstaller and Traugott 2006: 356). In LModE *all* underwent further developments: for instance, *all* as a modifier of nouns expanded to denote types of people (***all** Jacobin*) and personal names (e.g ***all** Rider Haggard*) and it came to accept verbs other than *be* in copulative constructions. This expansion is continued into PDE when *all* has become increasingly common as a modifier of proper names (e.g. ***all** Rambo*). Moreover, two new functions become possible at this stage, namely its use as a quotative marker (*she's **all**, 'I didn't tell you to call him'*) and as a modifier of a wider range of verbal heads (e.g. ***all** screamed*; ***all** jumped*).

Apart from the booster *eal*, other forms dating back to the OE period were *swa* 'so', *to* 'too', *wel* 'well' and *þearle* 'very', although the most frequent intensifiers of the period, by far, were *swīþe* 'very' and *ful* 'full', which also collocate most widely (cf. Stratton 2022). In a variationist study of the OE intensification system which draws on data from the *Helsinki Corpus of English Texts* (HC), Stratton (2022) reports an increasing intensification rate over the period, which is associated with a number of factors such as position (predicative adjectives favouring intensification more than attributive ones), adjective type[3] (the semantic category DIMENSION is the preferred one with intensifiers), text type (prose works contain more intensifiers than verse texts) and text origin (translated works also show higher

3 The categories identified by Stratton (2022) are based on Dixon (1977, 2004). Dixon (2004) distinguished the following adjective types: DIMENSION (*big*, *small*), AGE (*young*), VALUE (*good*, *bad*), COLOUR (*black*), PHYSICAL PROPERTY (*hard*, *soft*), HUMAN PROPENSITY (*jealous*, *happy*), SPEED (*fast*, *quick*), DIFFICULTY (*easy*), SIMILARITY (*similar*, *unlike*), QUALIFICATION (*true*, *likely*), QUANTIFICATION (*all*, *many*), POSITION (*high*, *near*) and CARDINAL NUMBERS (*first*, *last*).

rates of intensification). In Stratton's data all forms increase in frequency over the OE period, except *to* and *well*, the only boosters with decreasing uses over time.

The most common boosters of OE were *swīþe* 'very' and *ful* 'full' (see Méndez-Naya 2003; Stratton 2022). *Swīþe* derived from the adjective *swīþ* 'strong, powerful' and the derivational suffix *–e*. The grammaticalisation from manner adverb *swīþe* 'strongly, powerfully' to intensifier *swīþe* (e.g. ***swīþe*** *coueytous* 'covetous'), therefore, must have taken place before the earliest records. Moreover, the high degree of bleaching of the adverb applies to its three different uses: as a modifier of adjectives or adverbs, as a modifier of participles and as a modifier of verbs. Nonetheless, *swīþe* appeared mostly as a modifier of adjectival or adverbial heads (cf. Méndez-Naya 2003).

Until the mid-thirteenth century, *swīþe* continued to be favoured as an intensifier. From the fourteenth century, however, it underwent a drastic reduction in its use as a modifier of adjectives and adverbs in favour of the intensifier *full*. Méndez-Naya attributes this loss of popularity to the fact that *swīþe* had been in vogue as an intensifier for centuries and had, therefore, lost its expressive force by this time. The encroachment of *full* upon the domain of *swīþe* took place in the fourteenth century according to Peters (1993), while Méndez-Naya dates this replacement already to the second half of the thirteenth century. The final demise of intensifier *swīþe* occurred in the sixteenth century and was motivated partly by the loss of its use as a verbal intensifier (Méndez-Naya 2003: 379).

The downfall of *swīþe* in the course of ME favoured the emergence of new forms in the paradigm of boosters. One such form is *right* (cf. Méndez-Naya 2006, 2007, 2008b). Drawing on data from the HC and the *Penn-Helsinki Parsed Corpus of Middle English*, second edition (PPCME2), Méndez-Naya (2006) traces the evolution of *right* as an adjunct at the phrasal and clausal levels, as a modifier of adjectives and adverbs and as a discourse marker. As an intensifier modifying other adjectives (e.g. ***right*** *fat*), *right* is an ME development. The first examples are documented in the *Ormulum*, most likely due to Scandinavian influence (Méndez-Naya 2007: 194). The collocates of *right* are mostly bounded and have positive semantic prosody, although unbounded collocates are also attested, mostly when *right* is at its height in the late fourteenth and throughout the fifteenth century. In EModE, by contrast, the frequency of *right* dropped dramatically and in this period it is only marginally found in collocations such as *right glad* and in honorifics (e.g. ***right** singular lady*), a use which has survived into PDE. The uses of *right* find a parallel in another ME booster, intensifying *most* (e.g. *a **most** effective assistant*), discussed by Méndez-Naya (2008b). Both *right* and *most* are argued to be non-prototypical boosters, because they both collocate predominantly with bounded rather than with unbounded elements. Unlike *right*, however, *most* gains ground in EModE, reaching its peak in frequency in the first half of the sixteenth century. *Most* occurs in Méndez-Naya's (2008b) data mainly in combination with positive elements, modifying, as a general rule, evaluative or subjective adjectives and with honorifics (e.g. ***Most** Honourable*), in which function it eventually replaced *right*.

Another form which entered the paradigm of boosters in late ME is *very*, which is frequently given as a prototypical instance of the grammaticalisation of intensifiers. Though it ultimately goes back to Latin *verus* ('true'), it was borrowed in the thirteenth century from Anglo-Norman. The first records in the English language appear in the context of religious collocations such as ***warrai** man and godd **warrai*** ('true man and true god'), as noted by Breban and Davidse (2016). As an intensifier, however, *very* is only documented from the late fourteenth century. In this function, it modified only nouns (e.g. *this is a **verray** sooth* ('truth')). In fact, the co-occurrence of the adjective *very* and the noun *sooth* implied semantic redundancy, which eventually triggered the reanalysis of *very* as a degree marker. This semantic redundancy also applied to *very* as an intensifier of adjectives and adverbs (e.g. *a **very** trewe evidence*). In the earliest examples, however, it is very difficult to differentiate between the original modal meaning of *very* ('truly') and its degree meaning. At the end of ME *very* developed yet another intensifying function, namely that of intensifier of postdetermining adjectives such as *same* and *self* (e.g. *the **very self** place*), adding expressive force to the whole combination.

EModE proved a crucial stage in the semantic evolution of *very*, which developed new uses and remained a popular booster over the period. Thus, it came to modify a wider set of nouns, specifically of human types (e.g.

***very** fool* or ***very** wretch*). These uses were already possible from late ME, but peaked precisely in EModE. Likewise, two further contexts were especially frequent in EModE: the modification of nouns which referred to emotional states (e.g. ***very** joy* or ***very** pity*) and the modification of nouns which denoted a beginning, an end or a middle point in space or time (e.g. *the **very** end, the **very** bottom*) (Breban and Davidse 2016: 232–3). Moreover, the uses of the intensifying adverb *very* grew exponentially in EModE, an increase which was continued in the LModE data. *Very* thus emerged as a modifier of adjectives in the superlative form (e.g. *the **very** richest* or *the **very** poorest*), of numerical ordinals (e.g. ***very** first*) and non-specific ordinals (e.g. ***very** next*), as well as of quantifiers (e.g. ***very** many*, ***very** few*).

EModE also proved a very prolific period for the emergence of boosters, as noted by Peters (1994). One of the intensifiers which developed a boosting function in this period is *really*, which dates back to the fifteenth century and was a synonym for *bodily*. The intensifying function of *really*, its main function in PDE, emerged only in the second half of the seventeenth century (cf. Defour 2012; D'Hondt and Defour 2012). In the first part of the century *really* was only recorded as an adjunct and an emphasiser (e.g. [...] *he was **really** a smith*), highlighting in the latter function the truth level rather than the objective reality of the proposition. Together with its first uses as an intensifier (e.g. *Mr. Stopwell wrongs the Court-Ladies; some of which are **really** Great Beauties*), during the second half of the seventeenth century *really* came to be used as an attitudinal disjunct in initial position (e.g. ***really** Sir, this honest freeholder speaks a great deal of truth*). By the eighteenth century *really* developed its very last function, that is, its use as a verbless question (e.g. *really*?). D'Hondt and Defour (2012) also note that the apparent late development of intensifying *really* was influenced by its relation with other competing forms: *truly*, *very* and *verily*. However, this late intensifying meaning was compensated with the rise of a new disjunct function of *really*, with pragmatic meaning, while *truly*, *very* and *verily* remained as manner adverbials.

Like *really*, *truly* also developed an intensifier reading in EModE. Though dating back to OE already, it did not have a truth-related value in Early English, but meant instead 'faithfully, loyally'. In fact, it only became an emphasiser with a truth-related value ('in a true manner') in the first half of the fourteenth century and it is also before the end of the ME period that it developed disjunct uses occurring in initial position. When placed in initial position, *truly* was ambiguous between a manner adverbial and a disjunct, most conspicuously with verbs of communication such as *tell*. This ambiguity made the transition towards disjunct uses (*I tell you truly* > (*I tell you*) *truly*), as suggested by Defour (2012). *Truly* occurred in ME mostly in biblical or religious contexts under the fixed pattern *treuli, I seye to you*. It was only from 1500 onwards that *truly* gained ground as an intensifier.

Another booster which emerged in EModE is *bloody*, which is argued to be an atypical intensifier, since in addition to being a booster, it can be an attenuator (e.g. *I'm not* ***bloody*** *surprised*). Although the adjective *bloody* dates to OE, originally meaning 'of the nature of, composed of, or like blood', it did not develop a boosting function until the seventeenth century, typically in the collocation *bloody drunk* (Biscetti 2008: 54–5). The sociohistorical context in which the phrase *bloody drunk* arose is of paramount importance in order to understand the rise of its intensifying function. Being drunk in the context of the Reformation was equivalent to being drunk with God's blood (Biscetti 2008: 60). The use of *bloody*, therefore, was not just a swearword, but could also be considered a heretic expression. The collocation *bloody drunk* denoted the cruelty and excess which ensued an inebriated state. In addition to cruelty, drunkenness became associated with moral execration, sin and something to be ashamed of. Thus, *bloody* could occur with *damn*(*ably*) and *cursed*(*ly*), hence indicating that intoxication deserved a curse. *Bloody* had, therefore, strong religious connotations. From this meaning 'worthy of extreme blame an execration for being excessively drunk', a degree meaning of excess became foregrounded ('excessively drunk'). Finally, the inherently negative semantic meaning lost weight, so that it became possible for *bloody* to occur with positive items (e.g. ***bloody*** *passionate*). Moreover, in PDE *bloody* has come to develop a new function as a focus marker (e.g. *you* ***bloody*** *now you didn't*).

Unlike the boosters discussed in the preceding paragraphs, the adjective *lovely* only came to be used with a boosting function in the nineteenth century. The development of its intensifying meaning is explored by Adamson (2000), who links it to the order of elements in the premodifying string. Thus, there is an ordering principle of premodifiers based on their inherent meaning: those adjectives which are descriptive, that is, which describe relatively objective properties of the head of the noun phrase, tend to appear closer to it. In turn, affective adjectives, that is, those which denote more subjective properties that can be a matter of opinion, generally appear to the left of the noun phrase. Position is, therefore, crucial to understand the meaning of the adjective (Adamson 2000: 45–6), as illustrated with the use of the adjective *rotten* in (4.1) and (4.2):

(4.1) *short* ***rotten*** *planks*
(4.2) ***rotten*** *short planks*

In (4.1) *rotten* is taken to be descriptive, indicating a state of decay and hence describing an objective property. Conversely, the left position of *rotten* in the noun phrase in (4.2) favours an interpretation of the adjective as affective ('worthless'), that is, as expressive of a subjective evaluation. This correlation between subjective meanings or subjectivity and the left periphery in the noun phrase is explored by Adamson in relation to the adjective *lovely*.

*Lovely* has its roots in the OE adjective *luflic* 'loving, amiable'. Its original meaning was descriptive, since it denoted a relatively objective quality. It was only in the ME period that *lovely* acquired a new affective reading ('physically beautiful') (e.g. *the lely,* ***lufely*** *to sighte*), a sense which gained ground in the course of EModE and which became dominant by the eighteenth century (Adamson 2000: 48). A further affective sense of *lovely* arose in the seventeenth century, indicating the speaker's approval (e.g. *this trout looks* ***lovely***). In this case, *lovely* could still denote the physical beauty of the trout. However, it is much more likely that in this context *lovely* refers to a comment by a fisherman, approving of the size of the trout, or by a person who is about to taste the trout (Adamson 2000: 48). The intensifying meaning of *lovely* ('very'), as in ***lovely*** *long legs*, only arose in the nineteenth century.

In the light of the evolution of *lovely*, Adamson hypothesises the following grammaticalisation cline for intensifiers (2000: 55):

descriptive adjective > affective adjective > intensifier

Adverbs of degree therefore go back to former manner adverbs which denoted objective properties but which, through a process of subjectification (cf. Section 3.3.3), came to express increasingly subjective meanings. Finally, the shift to the left of the adjective string (e.g. ***lovely*** *big party*) triggered the categorial reanalysis (cf. Section 3.3.2) from adjective to intensifier and the reinterpretation of the construction as [adv. + adj.] rather than [adj. + adj.].

Like *lovely*, *very much* also emerged as an intensifier in LModE, though the first documented uses of the form date to the mid-sixteenth century (e.g. *Judges not indifferent but* ***very much*** *affectionate against me*). It was, therefore, in LModE that it became a competitor to *much* as a booster modifying other adverbs or adjectives (González-Díaz 2008). Moreover, in the data examined by González-Díaz (2008) *very much* is also attested as an elliptical answer to a polar question, in cases in which the verb involved is gradable (e.g. *'Do you like her?' Sibyl queried. '****Very much****. She is charming.'*). In this function it behaves similarly to *indeed* and has a confirmatory meaning. This function seems to point also to a use of *very much* as a sentence modifier and, therefore, to a higher degree of grammaticalisation of the form. Moreover, the increasing sentence-adverbial status and grammaticalisation of *very much* in PDE is confirmed on the basis of data from a grammaticality judgement test conducted among students and members of staff from the University of Liverpool.

To close this section, Figure 4.2 provides a visual outline of the evolution of the English boosters described in this section.

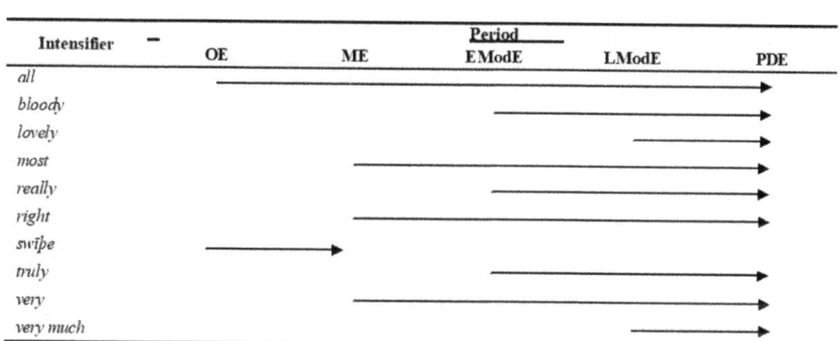


Figure 4.2. Boosters in the history of English

## 4.2. Summary

In contrast to Chapter 2, which approached intensifiers and their classification from a wider theoretical perspective, this chapter was intended to synthesise the corpus-based research carried out on English intensifiers, reviewing the most significant diachronic and synchronic contributions to the field from the framework of grammaticalisation. This chapter hence serves as a transition to the corpus-based study which will be presented in Chapter 6.

One of the distinguishing features of intensifiers is their tendency to 'recycling' (Tagliamonte 2008) or constant renewal. In fact, some members of the intensifier paradigm turn out to be quite old, as is the case of the reinforcers *all* and *swīþe*, dating to OE times. In turn, some other forms developed an intensifying reading considerably later, as is the case of the boosters *lovely* or *very much*, attested with these uses only from LModE. Section 4.1 thus reviewed the English intensifier system from OE up to PDE, paying attention to both maximisers (Section 4.1.1) and boosters (Section 4.1.2) and discussing the emergence of the intensifying function of these forms in terms of grammaticalisation.

CHAPTER 5

# Methodology

## 5.1. The research framework: Corpus Linguistics

Corpus Linguistics is generally regarded as 'the study of language based on examples of 'real life' language use' (McEnery and Wilson 2001). It therefore makes use of a *corpus* or a series of machine-readable texts considered appropriate to research a given linguistic aspect (McEnery and Hardie 2012: 1–2). While the extraction of textual data for linguistic analysis is by no means new,[1] the actual use of large collections of texts in machine-readable format is relatively more recent, dating to the compilation of the first computer corpora in the 1960s (see Svartvik 1992: 7–8; Meyer 2008: 1–2). Since then, the use of corpora has undoubtedly opened up new research fields, not only for English, but also for many other languages, and in areas as diverse as language teaching and learning, sociolinguistics, pragmatics, discourse analysis or forensic linguistics, among many others (O'Keefe and McCarthy 2010: 7). In the particular field of historical linguistics, the availability of historical corpora has not only enhanced our knowledge of the history of a given language, but it has also helped to broaden our understanding of more theoretical issues relevant to language change, including grammaticalisation (Curzan 2009; López-Couso 2016).

1 Among such early examples of research based on corpora we find biblical concordances or early grammars, such as Robert Lowth's *A Short Introduction to English Grammar* (1762), Henry Sweet's *A New English Grammar* (1891–8) or Otto Jespersen's *A Modern English Grammar on Historical Principles* (seven volumes, 1909–49). For an in-depth description of the origins of Corpus Linguistics and the history of both pre-electronic and electronic corpora, see Meyer (2008).

For the present study on the evolution of death-related intensifiers, the approach undertaken is corpus-based. Therefore, corpora feature prominently in this work, although historical dictionaries (cf. Section 5.2.1) and electronic databases (cf. Section 5.2.3) will also be used as additional sources of data. Moreover, even though the analysis from the selected materials will be inherently quantitative, given the large amount of data examined, the investigation will also be qualitative. According to an oft-quoted passage by Fillmore (1992: 35), the armchair linguist and the corpus linguist should exist in the same body. That is precisely my aim here: tracing the history of the selected death-related intensifiers by resorting to a number of diachronic sources, providing at the same time a linguistic analysis 'in the armchair style'. For, as will become apparent from the amount of data considered, 'the best machine for grinding general laws out of large collections of facts remains the same as Darwin's and Jespersen's – the human mind' (Svartvik 1992: 12).

## 5.2. Sources of evidence

### *5.2.1. Historical dictionaries*

The *Oxford English Dictionary* (OED) and the *Middle English Dictionary* (MED), the two major historical dictionaries of the English language, are two of the additional sources of evidence used in the present research for a preliminary study of the development of death-related forms.[2] As will be shown in Chapter 6, both dictionaries provide invaluable information about the diachronic evolution of death-related intensifiers, including the dates when they were firstly attested as intensifiers, their different spellings through time and relevant quotations for each of their different

2 For an overview of the history of the OED, refer to Baugh and Cable (2002: 320–5); for a detailed account of the history and compilation of the MED, see Lewis (2007: 3–7) and the MED website (<https://quod.lib.umich.edu/m/middle-english-dictionary/about>).

meanings. The OED is in fact the accepted authority on the evolution of the English language over the last millennium[3] and 'the world's most comprehensive dictionary of the English language' (Hoffmann 2004: 18). The MED dictionary, on the other hand, includes a selection of over three million citations of medieval English, on which account it has been described as 'the greatest achievement in medieval scholarship in America'.[4]

Over the past few years, both the OED and the MED have been used in the guise of corpora in diachronic research. The suitability of treating dictionary quotations as a corpus is, however, a topic of great debate.[5] The main evidence adduced against the use of these dictionaries as corpora is their limited context since the quotations therein featured are rather short and clearly insufficient. Another of the weaknesses is the high percentage of quotations from certain authors and geographical areas, as is the case of Shakespeare and England. All these limitations can however be overlooked if we take into account their numerous advantages, since each of them contains over 2.4 million quotations. Therefore, the data provided by these sources should definitely be taken into consideration in a diachronic investigation such as this one, as they prove extremely useful if we wish to obtain a preliminary overview of the changes in the meaning of *dead*(*ly*), *mortal*(*ly*) and *to death*, the death-related intensifiers at issue here.

### *5.2.2. Corpora*

As mentioned in Section 5.1, corpus work plays a pivotal role in the present study and lays the foundations for the diachronic analysis provided in Chapter 6. Although historical dictionaries (Section 5.2.1) and electronic collections (Section 5.2.3) have also been used as sources of data, the vast majority of the evidence used in this study is corpus-based. In what follows, I describe in some detail the different corpora which have been used as data sources: on the one hand, the *Helsinki Corpus of English*

3 Cf. <http://public.oed.com/about/>.

4 Cf. <http://quod.lib.umich.edu/m/med/>.

5 Cf. Fischer (1997), Hoffmann (2004), Mair (2004), Allan (2012) and Rohdenburg (2013), among others.

*Texts* (HC) and *A Representative Corpus of Historical English Registers* (ARCHER),[6] which will be used to outline the long diachrony of the selected death-related intensifiers; on the other hand, *Early English Books Online Corpus 1.0* (EEBOCorp 1.0), which has been chosen to gather data on the EModE period specifically, thus complementing the information provided by the HC and ARCHER. For the LModE period, I have used two electronic collections of texts, namely *Eighteenth Century Fiction* (ECF) and *Nineteenth Century Fiction* (NCF), which will be described in detail in Section 5.2.3.

### 5.2.2.1. *The Helsinki Corpus of English Texts* (HC)

The compilation of the *Helsinki Corpus of English Texts: Diachronic and Dialectal* (HC) started in 1984 under the directorship of Matti Rissanen and Ossi Ihalainen at the Department of English of the University of Helsinki. The project was finished in 1991. The dialectal part of the corpus contains transcripts of interviews conducted in the 1970s to speakers of British rural dialects. In turn, the historical part includes a selection of texts, covering from approximately 750 AD to 1710. This multi-genre corpus includes a selection of religious treatises, medical and legal texts, historical and biblical accounts, travelogues, sermons, letters (both private and official), diaries and fictional works. It consists of a total number of 1,572,800 words, distributed across different periods and subperiods. The excerpts included in the corpus vary in length, but generally range from 2,000 to 10,000 words, with occasional shorter texts.

The HC is available with the ICAME (International Computer Archive of Modern and Medieval English) CD-ROM, as well as through the Oxford Text Archive, and is accompanied by a manual. The *Manual to the diachronic part of the Helsinki Corpus of English Texts: Coding conventions and list of source texts* was published by Merja Kytö in 1996 (third

6 For further information on the HC and ARCHER, see the CoRD webpage <https://varieng.helsinki.fi/CoRD/>.

edition). It includes a detailed description of the coding conventions followed during the compilation of the corpus, in addition to information on its overall structure, the reference codes used in the different texts for the COCOA headers,[7] the different formats in which the corpus is available and the use of the files with different concordance software.

#### 5.2.2.2. *A Representative Corpus of Historical English Registers* (ARCHER)

ARCHER-1, originally compiled by Douglas Biber and Edward Finegan in the early 1990s, comprised a variety of British and American English texts from different genres, covering the time span 1600–999. From the time of compilation of the original corpus in 1993, a number of versions have succeeded ARCHER-1: ARCHER-2 (2005), ARCHER 3.1 (2006), ARCHER 3.2 (2013) and ARCHER 3.3 (in preparation). The versions which followed the original ARCHER-1 are a result of an international project which involves a consortium of participants from different universities around the world, namely the universities of Bamberg, Freiburg, Heidelberg, Helsinki, Lancaster, Leicester, Manchester, Michigan, Northern Arizona, Santiago de Compostela, Southern California, Trier, Uppsala and Zurich. Since 2008 ARCHER has been coordinated at the University of Manchester. ARCHER can be consulted online on the CQP website[8] or on site at the consortium universities.

The current version, ARCHER 3.2, is divided into eight fifty-year periods for the British English texts: 1600–49, 1650–99, 1700–49, 1750–99, 1800–49, 1850–99, 1900–49 and 1950–99, totalling 1,957,499 words. By contrast, the American English component is divided into five fifty-year periods, from 1750 to 1999, with a total of 1,340,581 words. ARCHER 3.2 includes twelve different genres: advertising (a), drama (d), fiction (f), sermons (h), journal (j), legal (l), medicine (m), news (n), early prose (p),

7 COCOA headers refer to the header information or information which appears at the beginning of a file, such as the name of the file, the name of the text and its author, the date of the text and the text type, etc. For further information on COCOA headers, see the manual to the HC by Kytö (1996) and Hickey (2003: 7–8).

8 <https://cqpweb.lancs.ac.uk/>

science (s), letters (l) and diaries (d). Each genre and variety features ten texts of approximately 2,000 words each. The corpus is available in both untagged and tagged formats.[9]

For the purposes of this research, only the British English component of ARCHER has been used, given that this monograph addresses the evolution of death-related intensifiers in this particular variety of the language.

### 5.2.2.3. *Early English Books Online Corpus 1.0* (EEBOCorp 1.0)

Published in 1998 by the Chadwyck-Healey publishing group, Early English Books Online (EEBO) is a database which contains over 130,000 works printed in England, Ireland, Scotland, Wales and North America, as well as English works printed elsewhere. EEBO covers the Early Modern English period, more specifically the time span 1473–700. In addition to online consultation (upon subscription),[10] transcriptions for different EEBO texts have also been developed by the Text Creation Partnership (TCP), so that it is possible to obtain some of the EEBO texts in TEI-compliant XML format. Since January 2015 EEBO (Phase I) can also be freely obtained from the TCP webpage.

Although the search interface allows to type in the desired word or combination of words in the keyword box and further restrict the search to a given period, author and/or work, EEBO searches pose some serious problems. For example, if we want to search for a particular item such as *mortally*, we obtain all the tokens for the relevant period, which can be ordered chronologically or alphabetically by author. However, in order to visualise them, it is necessary to click individually on every author or work. Moreover, we are given just one concordance line, which is clearly insufficient for the purposes of my analysis, as it normally requires further context. This entails an additional difficulty, namely that the whole text has to be downloaded. Since many of the works in EEBO contain a considerable amount of illustrations, the downloading process and the actual visualisation of the tokens are considerably delayed. Furthermore,

9 For a detailed account of ARCHER and its different versions, see Yáñez-Bouza (2011).

10 EEBO can be consulted online at <http://eebo.chadwyck.com/home>.

considering the number of occurrences yielded by this database for each of the intensifiers analysed in this work (cf. Table 5.1), it is clear that the enterprise is, to say the least, impracticable.

Table 5.1. Number of tokens for *dead, deadly, mortal, mortally* and *to death* in EEBO (Chadwyck-Healey)[11]

| EEBO-Chadwyck-Healey | Number of tokens |
|---|---|
| *dead* | 276,557 |
| *deadly* | 27,374 |
| *mortal* | 31,188 |
| *mortally* | 3,421 |
| *to death* | 64,222 |

EEBOCorp 1.0, based on EEBO, was created by Peter Petré in 2013 and contains about 525 million words. For the compilation of EEBOCorp 1.0, however, undated texts and posthumously published texts have been discarded. EEBOCorp 1.0 is, on the whole, much more advantageous and suitable for linguistic research than EEBO, since it can be used with any concordancer and hence facilitate the searches. Although it is available with its own concordancer, EEBOCorp Concordancer 1.5, developed by Peter Petré, I opted to use WordSmith with all three corpora: HC, ARCHER and EEBOCorp 1.0.

### 5.2.3. *Electronic collections*

In addition to the HC, ARCHER and EEBOCorp 1.0, two historical databases have been used for purposes of data retrieval in the present research, namely *Eighteenth Century Fiction* (ECF) and *Nineteenth*

11 These results refer exclusively to the PDE spellings of each of the five forms under analysis. If the variant spellings were considered, the figures would obviously be much higher.

*Century Fiction* (NCF). Like the OED and MED (cf. Section 5.2.1), these databases can also be used as 'historical corpora' for linguistic research even though they are not corpora strictly speaking. According to Schlüter (2013: 119–35), one of the main difficulties historical linguists have to face is the limitation in the data for certain periods of the language, and collections of this kind, which contain a vast number of words, may well serve to fill some of the gaps left by traditional corpora.

ECF and NCF are produced by Chadwyck-Healey and distributed by ProQuest, and are available in CD-ROM format or online at a rather costly yearly subscription. In addition to their high price, as Schlüter notes (2013: 123), their main disadvantage is that they contain full texts rather than balanced samples. Moreover, these texts are not offered as simple text files but are displayed through the Chadwyck-Healey search interface, which is designed mainly for literary scholarship rather than for the purposes of linguistic analysis.

ECF is a collection of ninety-six complete works of British prose writers covering the period 1700–80. The collection features celebrated authors such as Daniel Defoe, Henry Fielding, Samuel Richardson, Eliza Haywood and Jonathan Swift, and totals over 11 million words. In turn, NCF contains 250 novels from British and Irish authors from the period 1782 to 1903, including Jane Austen, Mary Shelley, Walter Scott, Charles Dickens and the Brontës, amounting to roughly 37.5 million words.

In order to look for a specific intensifier, for instance, we have to type in the word(s) we wish to search in the field *Keyword(s) in Work*. This provides us with the total number of tokens in the whole database. These results are then displayed alphabetically by author and work, since it may be the case that several works by the same author are included in the collection. We then have to click on the individual records for that work in order to visualise the relevant occurrences in their context of use. Although this procedure is rather unpractical and time-consuming, the advantages of using these databases, given the vast amount of data which they contain, clearly outnumber their drawbacks. Moreover, when several occurrences of a given headword are found in a particular text, it is possible to view all of these in one page. This is actually rather practical, as otherwise we would have to click on each of the hits individually in order to see the relevant token in context. Nonetheless, we are still faced with a crucial problem: the context may be too limited for the correct interpretation of the example and we may need to read its immediate cotext. In this regard, corpora and concordance software are clearly much more advantageous and time-saving.

Schlüter (2013: 123) mentions that Chadwyck-Healey offers the possibility of obtaining the raw data of ECF and NCF free of charge for their subsequent use with concordancing software.[12] Since these data are provided in an XML-file, one would then need to convert them to plain text for their use with a concordancer. In the present study, however, I decided to use Chadwyck-Healey's search interface in order to look for the items under examination, and these data were then stored in an Excel database (cf. Section 5.4.1) to be processed and subsequently analysed.

## 5.3. Computer and statistical tools

### *5.3.1. Wordsmith 6.0*

The software used to process the data retrieved from the three selected corpora (HC, ARCHER and EEBOCorp 1.0) is WordSmith (version 6.0), which contains three different tools: WordList, Concord and KeyWords. For the present purposes, only the Concord was used, which allowed me to trace all the tokens of a particular word or construction, in this case the death-related intensifiers, in the text(s) selected, accompanied by the immediate left and right context. This tool is therefore fundamental for the analysis of collocations.

In order to run a concordance for a particular word or string of words in a given corpus, we need to specify the search word first. In the case of the present study, in order to account for spelling variation at previous stages of the language, I have used the wildcard * to allow for the different orthographic variants of *dead(ly)*, *to death* and *mortal(ly)*, since the asterisk

12 This also holds for other Chadwyck-Healey collections not discussed here.

stands for any letter or combination of letters. *Dead* could hence be spelt as *deade*, *deede*, *deid*, *did*, *dyad*, *dyead*, *deed* and *dede*, among others; *deadly* had, among other orthographic variants, *dedli*, *dedeli*, *deadli*, *dyadlich*, *dyeadlich*, *deedli*, *dedly*, *dedely*, *deedly* and *deadlie*. The same holds for the other forms under study here, which also had a wide range of spelling variants in earlier English.

### *5.3.2. Statistical tools*

This section discusses the statistical tests which were used to assess the significance of the results. In the case of the three corpora, I have taken into account the variation in the raw frequencies from one period to another, to calculate if the increase or decrease in the number of occurrences was significant between periods, provided that one of the values in the comparison did not involve a zero value. In the HC, three different periods were compared, namely OE, ME and EModE. For EEBOCorp 1.0, I have established the following periods for comparison: period I (1470–99), period II (1500–49), period III (1550–99), period IV (1600–49) and period V (1650–99). Finally, as for ARCHER, I have considered the seventeenth, eighteenth, nineteenth and twentieth century data separately. This comparison across periods applied to the variables 'type of meaning', 'semantic prosody' and 'word category' (cf. Section 5.4.2). In this regard, two different statistical tests were applied: the chi-square test ($\chi^2$) and Fisher's exact test. The former was used when the absolute frequencies were over 5, while the latter applied in those cases in which the raw frequencies were 5 or lower, since the chi-square test is not as reliable as Fisher's exact test with low frequencies. Both tests compare the observed values, that is, the actual number of tokens of a given word or construction in a particular corpus, with the expected frequencies of a given item in a text, that is, 'those frequencies that we would expect if the only factor operating had been chance' (Cantos-Gómez 2013: 76). The greater the difference between the observed and expected frequencies, the less likely it is for chance to account for that difference. In turn, when the expected and observed frequencies are closer, the more likely it is that this difference is due to chance (cf. Cantos-Gómez 2013: 76). Moreover, the closer to 0 the probability value *p* is, the more statistically significant this difference will be; on the contrary, the closer this value is to 1, the most likely it is that this difference can be accounted for in terms of chance. The results for the observed and expected frequencies must be displayed in a contingency table, in this case a 2 × 2 contingency table. In order to calculate the chi-square value, I have used an online calculator,[13] in which the different frequencies in the contingency table were introduced and the results for the chi-square and *p*-values were automatically calculated. Moreover, for the chi-square formula, an additional factor needs to be taken into consideration, namely the number of degrees of freedom. According to Cantos-Gómez (2013: 78), the degrees of freedom are calculated as follows:

$$df = (\text{number of columns in the table} - 1) \times (\text{number of rows in the table} - 1).$$

In the present research, the number of degrees of freedom was always 1 (df = 1), as there are always two columns and two rows: (2–1) × (2–1) = 1.

By way of illustration, in the case of the descriptive uses in ARCHER in the seventeenth and eighteenth centuries, the *p*-value is very close to 1 in the case of the chi-square version without Yates's correction (0.79133678), and it is exactly 1 in the version with Yates's correction, which is applied in cases in which the table shows low counts in some cells (Cantos-Gómez 2013: 80). In both cases, however, the values are very close to 1, which implies that the difference in descriptive uses between the two centuries in ARCHER is not statistically significant.

As mentioned above, Fisher's exact test is used with token frequencies of 5 or lower than 5, as is the case of the subjective meanings of the adjective *mortal* in ARCHER in the seventeenth and eighteenth centuries (1 vs 5 occurrences, respectively). As was the case with the chi-square test described above, a contingency table is also needed. In the first row of the table we introduce the total number of attestations in the corpus, while in the second row we write the total number of words in the corpus for that specific period. The online calculator will then give us the relevant statistical

13 <http://www.quantpsy.org/chisq/chisq.htm>.

value and the level of significance.[14] In this case, the calculator indicated that the results from the test were not significant at $p < 0.01$.

The chi-square test and Fisher's exact test applied to the variables 'type of meaning', 'semantic prosody' and 'word category' (cf. Section 5.4.2). However, in order to measure the actual strength of the associations of the different death-related intensifiers analysed with their collocates, more specific tests were required, in particular the Mutual Information (*MI*) and its cubed variant (*MI3*), the log-likelihood test and the *z*-score.

The *MI* score calculates the strength of the association between a node word and its collocates. Here the node is the form (*dead(ly)*, *mortal(ly)* and *to death*) and the collocate is normally taken to be the word which occurs either immediately before or after the node. *MI* measures the joint probability of observing a word1 in combination with a word2, that is, it compares the probability of observing these two words together with the probabilities of observing them independently. If the association between w1 and w2 is strong, the *MI* score will be higher than 0. If there is not a strong association between the node and the collocate, then *MI* will be around 0. Finally, the value will be negative in those cases in which the two words shun each other (Cantos-Gómez 2013: 205). Therefore, the higher the *MI* value is, the stronger the link between the node and the collocate. A cut-off point of 3 is sometimes established as evidence of two words being collocates; this is the value which has been taken as a reference in the present work. The *MI* test, however, appears to give too much weight to low-frequency items so that a corrected version of this test has been designed, the *MI3* formula, which offers more realistic scores. This version is simply the same *MI* formula but taken to the power of 3. In the case of the *MI3* formula, the cut-off point to be considered for statistical significance is 4.75 (Cantos- Gómez 2013: 207).

The *log-likelihood* test (*LL*) is also commonly used in relation to collocations. It 'determines whether a word (w1) is a collocation of another word (w2) by taking the ratio between how often it occurs in a text/corpus compared to how often it would be expected to occur based on the model of chance (independence)' (Cantos-Gómez 2013: 208). As in the case of the *MI* values, the

14 <http://www.socscistatistics.com/tests/fisher/Default2.aspx>.

higher this score, the stronger the link between the node and the collocate. A value of 6.6 or higher is considered to be significant at $p < 0.01$.

The last test considered for collocations is the so-called *z*-score, which measures the difference between the observed frequency of a given node and its collocate, as well as their expected frequencies. For a score to be significant at $p < 0.01$, the cut-off measure should be at least 2.576.

In order to calculate all these collocational measures, I have resorted to a very functional tool designed by Brezina (2014) at the University Centre for Computer Corpus Research on Language (UCREL) from the University of Lancaster.[15] This is a web resource called 'Statistics in Corpus linguistics', which allows to use different statistical tools for free. The ones which are relevant for the current discussion are found under 'Semantics and discourse: Collocations, keywords and lockwords'. When we click on this function, it is possible to calculate all these measures by introducing the relevant figures for the number of tokens in the corpus, the frequency of the node (here the item under analysis) in that corpus, the frequency of the collocate in the same corpus (i.e. the number of occurrences of the collocate individually) and the window size. In this case, I have marked one token to the left and one token to the right. If we then click on 'Calculate associations', we obtain the results for all the relevant measures. By way of illustration, consider the collocation *adjudged to death* in EEBOCorp 1.0. EEBOCorp 1.0 comprised a total number of 525,432,293 words, and this is the value which we enter in square A ('Tokens in the corpus'). Then we have to introduce the absolute frequency of the node (*to death*), which occurs 30,531 times in the whole corpus. *Adjudged* is found 4,318 times in EEBOCorp 1.0 ('Frequency of collocate'), and the combination of the participle with the prepositional phrase is recorded 113 times ('Frequency of the collocation'). In regard to window size, I have only marked one collocate to the right and one to the left. Once we introduce all the relevant parameters, the tool calculates the observed and expected frequencies, as well as all the collocational tests discussed above: *MI*, *MI3*, log-likelihood and *z*-score. Considering the different results obtained for these tests, together with the cut-off values mentioned above, it can be concluded that the collocation *adjudged to death* is highly statistically significant.

15 <http://corpora.lancs.ac.uk/stats/toolbox.php>.

## 5.4. The database and the variables of analysis

### *5.4.1. The Excel database*

In order to process the data for analysis, I have created an Excel database. In those cases in which the results were retrieved from corpora (HC, ARCHER and EEBOCorp 1.0), the results have been exported directly from WordSmith to an Excel spreadsheet. This was in fact the most convenient and practical option since the Concord function in WordSmith offers the possibility of exporting the concordances to Excel. By contrast, the two Chadwyck-Healey databases, ECF and NCF, do not allow to export the results automatically to Excel, on which account they had to be manually saved in an Excel spreadsheet with all the relevant information for the subsequent analysis. Both linguistic and extralinguistic information have been coded for each example. The different linguistic variables considered will be discussed in detail in Section 5.4.2.

### *5.4.2. Linguistic variables*

The core of the analysis carried out in this study has been the data provided by the different corpora and collections of texts described in Sections 5.2.2 and 5.2.3. However, the OED and the MED have also been used in the hope of gaining further insights into the behaviour of the death-related intensifiers *dead(ly)*, *mortal(ly)* and *to death* over time. The analysis has focused on the different collocations of these forms, taking into account their type of meaning, on the basis of the cline for intensifiers described by Adamson (2000: 55): descriptive > affective > intensifying. As seen in Section 4.1.2, Adamson proposed this cline in relation to the adjective *lovely*, which initially denoted a human quality, being a synonym for 'loving, amiable' (e.g. *for sheo to him so* ***lovely*** *was and trewe*), and came to develop a new meaning in ME: 'physically beautiful' (e.g. *the lely,* ***lufely*** *to syghte*). *Lovely* then acquired a value meaning 'excellent' in

LModE, a process of subjectification, which later prompted an intensifying reading of *lovely*, as in ***lovely** big party* (2000: 54).

In this monograph, however, I have adapted Adamson's initial cline in two different ways. On the one hand, I have opted for the label *subjective* instead of *affective* in my classification, given that, to my mind, the former reflects better the process of subjectification, which is so fundamental for the eventual development of intensifying meanings. On the other hand, Adamson's cline has been found to be incomplete for the semantic analysis intended in this piece of research, since some examples of the relevant items in the data were ambiguous and not easily ascribed to one of Adamson's three developmental stages. On this account, I decided to use a fivefold classification based on Adamson's cline, which includes two further intermediate stages: one for those meanings which were ambiguous between descriptive and subjective (D/S), and another for those meanings which were unclear between a subjective and an intensifying (S/I) reading. The addition of these two intermediate stages to Adamson's proposal was intended as a way of minimising any possible biased interpretation of the data, since sometimes it is very difficult to classify a given example into one particular category, mainly because the context is not sufficient, not to mention the additional complexity of dealing with historical texts, for which our way of thinking does no longer hold.

In addition to the type of meaning, the semantic prosody of the collocations has also been taken into consideration (Stubbs 1995; Sinclair 1996; Louw 2000; Partington 2004; Smith and Nordquist 2012). The collocates of the forms *dead(ly)*, *mortal(ly)* and *to death* were marked as positive, neutral or negative, given that semantic prosody can be used as an indicator of their degree of grammaticalisation: death-related intensifiers are always negative in origin, but in the course of time they came to be used with elements which have positive semantic prosody, as the adjective *happy* in the collocation *dead happy*, or *chuffed* in *chuffed to death*. Positive semantic prosody, therefore, correlates with a higher degree of grammaticalisation; on the contrary, the more an intensifier occurs with elements which have negative semantic prosody, the less grammaticalised it will be. The analysis of the semantic prosody of these collocations was, however, not devoid of problems: it is sometimes difficult to categorise objectively whether an item is positive or negative, since, depending on the context, it could be interpreted in either way. By way of illustration, consider the adjective *proud*. *Proud* has positive semantic prosody in contexts in which, for example, we are proud of our family or of our work. However, we can also say that a person is very proud, hence implying that it is a negative quality, perhaps suggesting that (s)he is haughty and arrogant. Needless to say, this difficulty is even more conspicuous with historical data. On this account, the label *neutral semantic prosody* subsumes two different types of scenarios in this research. On the one hand, I have labelled as *neutral* those elements modified by one of the forms under analysis which are in actual fact neutral, as is the case, for example, of the noun *body* in the collocation *mortal body*; since a body cannot be positive or negative, it is hence considered as neutral. On the other hand, I have also characterised as neutral those elements which are contextually dependent and would thus allow either a positive or a negative reading, as is the case of the aforementioned adjective *proud*. In view of the vast amount of examples analysed, considering the individual context for each of the hits would not only be time-consuming, but in many cases, the context would also be clearly insufficient to decipher the specific meaning of the word.

Furthermore, the word category modified by the items under analysis here has also been tagged. Although intensifiers have traditionally been associated with adverbs (Quirk et al. 1985: 590), the category itself is much more complex and heterogeneous than previously assumed (cf. Section 2.2), as suggested, for example, by Margerie (2011) for the prepositional phrase *to death* (cf. Section 4.1.1). Therefore, the type of word modified by the forms at issue (e.g. noun, adjective, participial item, prepositional phrase, etc.) has also been considered in order to understand better their behaviour and collocational patterns. This could help to explain the potential preference of these forms for one specific word class and trace recurrent patterns in their development. Concerning participial collocates, an explanatory note seems in order here. All the participial collocates of the forms at issue have been marked in the Excel database as *participial forms* (P), regardless of whether they are verbal participles (e.g. *wounded*) or participial adjectives (e.g. *tired*). Given the volume of data eventually considered for analysis and the ambiguity of many early examples, it would be unmanageable to consistently categorise these forms as either verbal or adjectival on the basis of the tests which are often considered in the literature for the categorisation of adjectives and participles (cf., e.g. Quirk et al. 1985: 713–16). The application of these tests to my data is clearly out of the scope of the present work. Moreover, although they may be applicable in many contexts, for many examples further contextualisation is required, and even so our bias towards the data would be inevitable.

Finally, concerning extralinguistic variables, the corpus-based analysis provided in Chapter 6 has taken into account the period. This is particularly relevant in a diachronic analysis such as the one intended here, since it allows us to record the specific stage at which the forms under analysis develop more subjective meanings and are hence on their way towards subsequent intensifying uses. The file name in the case of corpora and the work in the case of electronic collections have also been noted. This was useful to go back to the individual examples, given that on many occasions it was necessary to consult further context to understand the meaning of a given item. I have also included the field 'Comments', in which I noted down not only comments about a particular spelling but also remarks about the meaning of a given word or about the position of the form in question.

CHAPTER 6

# A corpus-based analysis of death-related intensifiers in English

As suggested in Chapter 5, devoted to the methodology, the approach adopted in the present study is corpus-based. On this account, I rely heavily on corpus materials for the retrieval of data and subsequent analysis. In addition to the corpora and electronic collections presented in the previous chapter for the different stages of the language, however, supplementary data will be obtained from the two major historical dictionaries, the MED and the OED. It is thus hoped that the combination of these resources will serve to provide a comprehensive account of the diachronic development of death-related intensifiers over time.

Section 6.1 presents the evidence from the MED and the OED, thereby offering an initial overview of the evolution of the intensifiers *dead*(*ly*), *mortal*(*ly*) and *to death*. The section opens with the discussion of *dead* and *deadly*, the native OE forms, followed by *mortal* and *mortally*, their Anglo-Norman counterpart. The prepositional phrase *to death* is the last of the forms examined. Section 6.2 is aimed to corroborate and expand the information initially yielded by the two historical dictionaries on the basis of data from several corpora and databases, which will provide valuable insights into the collocational patterns and development of these forms across time. These sources will thus serve to trace the whole history or long diachrony of these intensifiers, from their earliest uses until the most recent twentieth-century data. Finally, in Section 6.3 I set out the evolution and the collocational behaviour of these death-related intensifiers through time in connection with grammaticalisation.

## 6.1. Preliminary remarks: Evidence from the dictionaries

### *6.1.1.* Dead

The form *dead* can be an adjective, an adverb and a noun. In what follows I concentrate exclusively on the adjectival and adverbial forms, given that these are the ones which will eventually develop intensifying uses. I therefore discard nominal occurrences of *dead* such as (6.1):

(6.1) *Vysyte þe seke. And bere þe* ***ded.***
visit the sick and bury the dead
(c. 1426. OED, s.v. *dead* n. B1b)

The adjectival form *dead*, originally participial, is a common Germanic adjective, and as such it is recorded already in the OE period, as in example (6.2), taken from *Beowulf*, with the same literal meaning as in PDE, that is, 'that has ceased to live; deprived of life'. This loss of life was not necessarily physical, but could also be spiritual, as recorded already from the ME period (example (6.3)).

(6.2) *þa wæs Heregar* ***dead,*** *min yldra mæg*
then be-PST-SG Heregar dead my older kinsman
(c. 1100. OED, s.v. *dead* adj. I 1a)

(6.3) *Whanne ȝe weren* ***deede*** *in ȝoure giltis and synnes.*
When you be-PST-PL dead in your gilt-PL and sin-PL
(1382. OED, s.v. *dead* adj. I 4)

Furthermore, adjectival *dead* could also apply to parts of the body, implying that these were benumbed or insensible, as in example (6.4), and to the state when somebody is in a swoon, or in a *dead sleep*, as in (6.5).

(6.4) *The messenger of so vnhappie newes, Would faine haue dyde:* ***dead*** *was his hart within.* (1590. OED, s.v. *dead* adj. I 2a)

(6.5) *þe* ***dede*** *slep him ouer-eode* ['overpowered']. (c.1300. MED, s.v. *ded* adj. 4e)

A number of readings of *dead* which moved away from these literal meanings towards more metaphorical uses of the adjective arose also in the ME period. *Dead* could thus be used to refer to the complexion and its colour, for instance, implying that it was wan and pallid (6.6), or to a period of time in which there was no activity or sound (6.7), hence often collocating with nouns such as *calm* or *silence*, as in (6.8) and (6.9). In a metaphorical sense, it could also allude to a deadly or mortal hate for someone (see (6.10)). In all these cases, the adjective does no longer imply a physical or spiritual death, but it denotes qualities or properties which rather suggest or are reminiscent of death, such as paleness, stillness or lack of movement or activity. In the case of the collocation *dead hate*, it is implied that when we bear such an antipathy to a person, we wish his/her death. Therefore, death is still in the background and can still be easily evoked in such instances.

(6.6) *He can not but sobbe & wepe..with a* ***ded*** *visage.* (c. 1425. MED, s.v. *ded* adj. 3a)
(6.7) *It was in the* ***deadist*** *time of winter.* (1573. OED, s.v. *dead* adj. I 18a)
(6.8) *That we may not be tossed with boisterous Winds, nor overtaken by a sudden* ***dead*** *Calm.* (1673. OED, s.v. *dead* adj. I 26).
(6.9) *A* ***dead*** *silence on the subject seems to have prevailed.* (1783. OED, s.v. *dead* adj. I 26).
(6.10) *He come to þe kyng in a kene* ['fierce'] *yre, Dang* ['beat'] *hym derffly* ['fiercely'] *in a* ***ded*** *hate.* (c. 1540. MED, s.v. *ded* adj. 6)

According to the OED, from the second half of the seventeenth century *dead* came to develop intensifying meanings (cf. (6.11)–(6.12)). The original literal reading was cancelled and, therefore, no longer possible in these cases. In (6.11), for instance, the seed is fully grown and ripe, and in this case *dead* is a synonym of *complete* or *absolute*. Likewise, in (6.12) we are informed that the articles which were bought were very cheap, and *dead* here could also be paraphrased as *complete, absolute, downright*. It is then no longer possible to call to mind death-related properties in this case, such as paleness, quietness, stillness, etc., as in examples (6.6) – (6.10).

(6.11) *Till the seed..be come to a full and* ***dead*** *ripenesse.* (1660. OED, s.v. *dead* adj. I 31a)
(6.12) *I had them a* ***dead*** *bargain.* (1766. OED, s.v. *dead* adj. I 31a)

The development of the adverb *dead* is comparable to that of its adjectival homonym, although the adverbial form could already occur with transferred uses from its early history, as is reflected in the meanings given for this word in both the MED and the OED: 'as if dead' and 'in a manner, or to a degree, characteristic of or suggesting death', respectively. The earliest example recorded in the dictionaries is from Gower's *Confessio Amantis*, and dates from approximately 1393:[1]

(6.13) *Sche swounede in his hond, And, as who seith, lay* ***ded*** *oppressed.* (a. 1393. MED, s.v. *ded* adv. a)

In this case, *dead* modifies the participle form *oppressed* 'overcome', and hence both literal and more figurative readings of the adverb are possible. Since a person has fainted, apparently overcome with a particular feeling (*ded oppressed*), we might conjecture that the person has actually died, possibly as a consequence of a fall or of a heart attack. On the other hand, we might think that she has lost consciousness, but is not actually dead. If we read on, we realise that a literal interpretation is not plausible, since the character, Lucretia, commits suicide later on, after her rape. The MED gives further examples of such ambiguous readings of *dead* without further contextual information, in which it is not clear whether the person is dead or actually alive, given that the state of losing consciousness is, both symbolically and physiologically, close to death.

In addition to these unclear contexts, the MED provides another example in which *dead* is used to refer to somebody's eyes (6.14). Interestingly, the eyes of the person in question cannot be literally dead, since (s)he has not passed away. What is assumed here is that the eyes of cowards hardly move (they are *of febill mevynge*) and are not as vivid as those of brave people. Therefore, in this quote from a medical treatise, *dead* shows incipient subjectivity (cf. Section 3.3.3), given that the writer, in characterising the eyes as *dede lokynge*, and this as a feature of a cowardly person, is expressing at the same time a negative appreciation of the situation.

(6.14) *Lytill eighyn* ***dede*** *lokynge, lytille of stature and lowe, and of febill mevynge* ['motion']; *thes bene the tokenys of cowardy.* (a. 1500. MED, s.v. *ded* adv. a)

1 Example (6.13) is recorded in both the MED and the OED.

The early quotations of adverbial *dead* in the OED also reveal interesting parallels with the homonymous adjectival form, and in actual fact the collocates of the adjective and those of the adverb are very similar, hence collocations such as *dead slow* or *dead calm*, which were also possible for the adjective:

(6.15) *Leaden-footed griefe, Who neuer goes but with a* ***dead****-slowe pace.* (1596. OED, s.v. *dead* C adv. 1a)
(6.16) *In a few minutes it fell* ***dead*** *calm.* (1840. OED, s.v. *dead* C adv. 1a)

Finally, *dead* came to acquire intensifying meanings over time. The very first attestations of the adverb *dead* in this function date to the end of the sixteenth century, somewhat earlier than intensifying uses of the adjective *dead* (see above). The earliest example attested in the OED is given under (6.17), and additional examples are shown in (6.18)–(6.20). As in (6.11)–(6.12) for adjectival *dead*, in these cases it is not possible either to assign death-related properties to the collocates of the adverb *dead*. In turn, *dead* is used here as a synonym for *utterly*, *entirely*, *absolutely*, and implies an outmost degree. It is, therefore, semantically bleached (cf. Section 3.2) and does no longer admit a literal reading. In the examples below, it could be paraphrased as *completely sure*, *fully ripe*, *extremely lame* and *absolutely right*, respectively.

(6.17) *Oh he is olde dogge at expounding, and* ***deade*** *sure at a Catechisme.* (1589. OED, s.v. dead C adv. 2a)
(6.18) *Before the rice is '****dead*** *ripe'.* (1857. OED, s.v. *dead* C adv. 2a)
(6.19) *Only one horse..which soon became* ***dead*** *lame.* (1860. OED, s.v. *dead* C adv. 2a)
(6.20) *You're* ***dead*** *right in saying he's too young.* (1895. OED, s.v. *dead* C adv. 2a)

### *6.1.2.* Deadly

As is the case with *dead*, *deadly* can be an adjective and an adverb, both forms having their roots in the OE period, as the MED and OED seem to suggest.

The adjective *deadly* originally meant 'subject to death, mortal', as evinced in collocations such as *deadly man* ((6.21)) or *deadly body* ((6.22)).

(6.21)

| | | | | | | | |
|---|---|---|---|---|---|---|---|
| *Ðæt* | *an* | ***deadlic*** | *man* | *mihte* | *ealne* | *middaneard* | *oferseon.* |
| that | a | deadly | man | might | all | world | observe |

(c.1000. OED, s.v. *deadly* adj. 1a)

(6.22)

| | | | | | | |
|---|---|---|---|---|---|---|
| *Se* | *lichame* | *is* | ***deadlic*** | *þurh* | *Adames* | *gylt* |
| the | body | be-PRS-SG | deadly | through | Adam-G-SG | gilt |

(a. 1225. MED,, s.v. *dedli* adj. 1a)

From its very earliest records, *deadly* could also apply to anything which could cause death and hence be mortal, as is the case of the wound in example (6.23). Similarly, *deadly* could also be applied to those sins which resulted in the spiritual death of the individual (6.24), as opposed to venial sins, which could be forgiven. In all these cases, then, *deadly* has a literal meaning.

(6.23) *Non of hem had **dedeli** wounde.* (c. 1330. MED, s.v. *dedli* adj. 2a)
(6.24) *Lecherie..is on of þe zeuen **dyadliches** zennes,* (1340. MED, s.v. *dedli* adj. 3a)

From the ME period onwards, *deadly* could equally occur with non-literal and more metaphorical uses, in very similar contexts to those for adjectival and adverbial *dead*. It could thus apply to the countenance, suggesting extreme paleness, like that of a corpse (example (6.25)). Darkness, gloom, dullness or silence, which are figuratively associated with death, could also be qualified as deadly. Example (6.26), for instance, depicts an atmosphere of gloom and darkness; the terrifying roar of the waves breaking on the cliff in (6.27) could easily be taken as a presage of doom. Finally, in (6.28) the silence is also interpreted negatively and as a sign of a possible terrible fate. In all these cases, therefore, the adjective conveys negative affect, that is, the speaker's negative appreciation of the situation, and *deadly* hence shows incipient subjectivity (cf. Section 3.3.3).

(6.25) *His coloure gan to chaunge in-to a **dedely** hewe.* (c.1400. OED, s.v. *deadly* adj. 7a)
(6.26) *þe folk in **dedeli** mirknes* ['darkness'] *stadd.* (a. 1400. MED, s.v. *dedli* adj. 4a)

(6.27) *Ther were a fewe welles Came rennynge fro the clyves adoun, That made a* ***dedly****, slepynge soun.* (c.1450. MED, s.v. *dedli* adj. 4a)
(6.28) *There was such a* ***deadlie*** *silence in the porte.* (1600. OED, s.v. *deadly* adj. 7c)

From the second half of the seventeenth century *deadly* developed intensifying meanings ('terrible', 'awful'), as in (6.29)–(6.30), for which a literal reading is more obscure. (6.29) describes a heavy drinker, and although drinking in excess can in actual fact have a fatal outcome, what is meant here is simply that this person drinks to excess, so the meaning of *deadly* in this case is much closer to that of an intensifier. This idea of excess is also present in (6.30), since the speaker criticises those who thirst for money and are in a terrible haste to become rich. Nonetheless, in none of these examples are death-related properties evoked, unlike in (6.25)-(6.28), which alluded to paleness, gloom, darkness, etc. *Deadly* in this case is semantically bleached (cf. Section 3.2) and has therefore a more general meaning.

(6.29) *A* ***deadly*** *drinker he is, and grown exceeding fat.* (1660. OED, s.v. *deadly* adj. 8a)
(6.30) *Why such* ***deadly*** *haste to make money?* (1843. OED, s.v. *deadly* adj. 8a)

The adverb *deadly*, which is also recorded in OE, developed intensifying readings considerably earlier than its adjectival counterpart, since the intensifying adverb arose already in the fifteenth century (cf. (6.35)), while the first recorded uses of the intensifying adjective date to the second half of the seventeenth century (cf. (6.29)). In origin, the adverb *deadly* was synonymous with *fatally*, *mortally* (6.31)–(6.32), and, as was the case with the adjective, it also developed non-literal, metaphorical readings over time ((6.33)–(6.34)), eventually becoming an intensifier, as in (6.35)–(6.36). (6.31) and (6.32) thus show literal or descriptive uses of the adverb: *deadliche idoruen feondes* 'deadly wounded enemies' suggests that these people had mortal wounds and on this account they started to cry. In (6.32) the reader is prevented against shaving the beard, since that itself is a deadly sin, and hence results in spiritual death. By contrast, in (6.33) and (6.34) the adverb is no longer taken literally, though certain death-related aspects can still be called to mind: hating somebody so much might imply wishing that person's death, and a *deadly pale face* is a face which is as colourless as a corpse. These examples, which show incipient subjectivity, count as subjective readings of the adverb (cf. Section 3.3.3). Finally, in (6.35) and (6.36) *deadly* does not admit a literal interpretation either, nor can death-related values be evoked. Instead, *deadly* here functions as a mere equivalent of *absolutely*, *extremely*: 'extremely foolish' and 'extremely dear', respectively. Thus, the quality of stupidity or foolishness is considered to be extreme in (6.35) and in (6.36) the cups are claimed to be pretty, yet very precious.

(6.31) *þe feondes* ['fiends'], *þe þer weren* ***deadliche*** *idoruen* ['wounded'], *fengen to ȝeien* ['cry']. (1220. MED, s.v. *dedli* adv. 1a)
(6.32) *Þei seye þat wee synne* ***dedly*** [F mortelement] *in schauynge* ['shaving'] *oure berdes* ['beards']. (c.1425. MED, s.v. *dedli* adv. 2).
(6.33) ***Dedliche*** *þat Jeu I hate.* (c. 1390. MED, s.v. *dedli* adv. 1a)
(6.34) *Custaunce, with a* ***dedly*** *pale face..toward hir ship she wente.* (c. 1390. MED, s.v. *dedli* adv. 3)
(6.35) *I þat es sa* ***dedli*** *dill* ['foolish, stupid']. (a.1400. OED, s.v. *deadly* adv. 4)
(6.36) *These Cups are pretty, but they're* ***deadly*** *dear.* (a.1703. OED, s.v. *deadly* adv. 4)

### *6.1.3.* Mortal

The adjective *mortal* is a borrowing from Anglo-Norman and Middle French *mortel*, the very first records of which date to the late fourteenth century. Unlike *dead* and *deadly*, however, which developed increasingly subjectivised meanings over time (cf. Sections 6.1.1 and 6.1.2), *mortal* was adopted into the English language already with both literal and subjective meanings. Intensifying readings of *mortal* arose only later, in the eighteenth century.

With regard to the literal or descriptive meanings of *mortal*, this adjective was used as opposed to *divine*, hence applying to humans, to human life, the human body, etc. (cf. (6.37)), in which the body, once feeble and sick, is said to be immortal in Heaven. It could also apply to anything which could cause death, such as an illness, a wound, a poison, an armed conflict or a weapon (cf. (6.38)). Finally, example (6.39) shows that, as was the case for the uses of *dead* and *deadly* (Sections 6.1.1 and 6.1.2), death need not necessarily be physical, but could also refer to the soul, especially after having committed a mortal or deadly sin.

(6.37) *Ther as the body, that whilom* ['once'] *was syk, freele* ['feeble'] *and feble and* ***mortal*** [vrr. mortell; dedely], *is inmortal.* (c. 1390. MED, s.v. *mortal* adj. 1a)

(6.38) *Thus gan encrece* ['increase'] *the fame & the renoun Of Iulius conquest on se* ['sea'] & *eek on londe, Whos* ***mortal*** *suerd* ['sword'] *ther myht non withstonde.* (a. 1439. MED, s.v. *mortal* adj. 2b)

(6.39) *Dedly synne..ycallyd ys* ***mortal*** *Be-cause hys hurtys ffynally Ben in effect verray dedly.* (a.1480. OED, s.v. *mortal* adj. 6a)

Parallel to these literal or descriptive meanings of the adjective, *mortal* had already in origin a number of non-literal readings showing some degree of subjectivity (cf. Section 3.3.3), which referred to semantic fields such as hatred, enmity, fear or paleness, as was the case with *dead* and *deadly*. Hence, being a mortal foe or enemy of somebody implies wishing that person's death, as in the case of Palamon, who fights with his cousin Arcite and tells him that he is his deadly enemy in (6.40). A mortal face in (6.41) also suggests another feature which might recall death, namely paleness.

(6.40) *For I am Palamon thy* ***mortal*** [v.r. mortel] *foo.* (c. 1385. OED, s.v. *mortal* adj. A 1a).

(6.41) *But or she died she caste for to write..With pale face and a* ***mortal*** *cheere* ['face']. (a.1439. MED, s.v. *mortal* adj. 5)

According to the OED, intensifying *mortal* was firstly attested in the eighteenth century. These intensifying meanings, illustrated in (6.43)–(6.44), are most likely related to its prior use as an emphatic expletive, which is recorded from the early seventeenth century (6.42), and which might have favoured the inference of extreme degree. In (6.42), for instance, the expletive *mortal* could be paraphrased as *by no means at all* or *by no earthly means*. In (6.43) *mortal* expresses extreme degree, implying that Lord Nottingham and the Duchess of Roxburgh made an enormous effort to persuade the Princess, and so does in (6.44), in which *a mortal hurry* can be substituted by *a terrible hurry*.

(6.42) *Shall I goe fetch the ladies to the catastrophe?..Dav. By no* ***mortall*** *meanes.* (1616. OED, s.v. *mortal* adj. 7a)

(6.43) *Lord Nottingham and the Duchess of Roxburgh take* ***mortal*** *pains to make the Princess think well of the Tories.* (1716. OED, s.v. *mortal* adj. 7a)

(6.44) *Well, it ain't that I'm in a* ***mortal*** *hurry.* (1864. OED, s.v. *mortal* adj. 7a)

The development of the adverb *mortal*, synonymous with its suffixed counterpart *mortally* (cf. Section 6.1.4), is similar to that of the adjective *mortal*, since it also developed intensifying meanings in the eighteenth century, though there are virtually no records for this adverb in the dictionaries. Thus, the battle in (6.45) is said to be *mortal fierce*, that is, it was very bloody and there were many casualties, which implies a literal reading of the adverb. By contrast, examples (6.46) and (6.47) illustrate intensifying uses of *mortal*, meaning 'extremely'.

(6.45) *The batayll was there* ***mortall*** *fyers & doubtous for bothe partyes*. (c.1500. OED, s.v. *mortal* b adv.)
(6.46) *St. John's well, after the name of a* ***mortal*** *cold bath in Nottinghamshire*. (1753. OED, s.v. *mortal* b adv.)
(6.47) *She is* ***mortal*** *fond of the book, and has got it by heart*. (1778. OED, s.v. *mortal* b adv.)

### *6.1.4.* Mortally

The adverb *mortally* is formed on the adjective *mortal*, to which the suffix *–ly* is added. Its first records date to the late fourteenth century (6.48). *Mortally* also had a literal meaning in origin ('fatally; in such a manner that death ensues'), referring to anything that could result in death, which could be physical (6.48) or spiritual (6.49). In (6.48), for instance, an example which was also recorded in the MED and OED entries for *mortal*, the sultaness has planned to kill the guests who have been invited to his son's wedding, and on this account she is characterised as a scorpion with a deadly sting. Likewise, in (6.49) the protagonist confesses to have sinned deadly or mortally, for which reason his soul will be condemned.

(6.48) *Mortall* [v.r. mortaill; *Heng: But this scorpion..The Sowdanesse..Caste vnder this ful* ***mortally*** *to stynge*]. (c.1390. OED, s.v. *mortally* adv. 1)
(6.49) *I graunt my selfe therin to have..offended* ***mortally****, commyttynge deedly synne and dampnable*. (1526. OED, s.v. *mortally* adv. 1)

Conversely, (6.50)–(6.51) show subjective readings of *mortally*, which were also present from the very early history of the adverb. In (6.50) the adverb collocates with the verb *hate*, and as we have seen for *dead(ly)* and *mortal* in the previous sections, death can be easily evoked in this particular context. *Mortally irous* in (6.51) is analogous to *haten mortally* in (6.50). In this context, the adjective *irous* might be ambiguous between 'wrathful, enraged' and 'fierce, cruel', given that it refers to king Thelamon, who bore a mortal hatred to king Philomene, whom he attacks with a spear.[2]

(6.50) *Ne telleth neuere no man in youre lyf How that another man hath dight* ['have sexual intercourse with'] *his wyf; He wol yow haten* ***mortally*** [vr. mortelly], *certeyn*. (c. 1390. MED, s.v. *mortally* adv. b)

(6.51) *He to hym was* ***mortally*** *Irous*. (c. 1425. MED, s.v. *mortally* adv. b)

According to the OED, intensifying readings of *mortally* arose in the eighteenth century, as illustrated in (6.52)–(6.53), in which the adverb simply maximises the degree of a given quality, such as ugliness and dwarfism in (6.52) and the passion for fishing in (6.53):

(6.52) *The people are in general* ***mortally*** *ugly and dwarfish*. (1789. OED, s.v. *mortally* adv. 5)

(6.53) *I* ***mortally*** *love to fish—just any kind of fishin'*. (1975. OED, s.v. *mortally* adv. 5)

## *6.1.5.* To death

The prepositional phrase *to death* is attested with a literal meaning from the OE period, while its first intensifying uses emerged centuries later. Thus, *to death* modified at first verbs which expressed a violent action, including those which already meant 'to kill', such as stoning somebody to death (cf. example (6.54)) or slaying somebody. Likewise, it could also modify verbs which expressed legal punishment, such as *condemn*, *sentence* or *deem* ('give or pronounce judgement'), as in (6.55):

(6.54) *He sloh* ['slew'] *him wið a stan* ***to deaðe***. (c. 1225. OED, s.v. *death* n. phrases P1a)

| (6.55) | *Hig* | *genyþeriað* | *hyne* | ***to*** | ***deaþe*** |
|---|---|---|---|---|---|
| | they | condemn-PRES-PL | he-ACC.M.SG | to | death |

(OE. OED, s.v. *death* n. phrases P1b)

2 *Ful proudly cam hym [for] to reskewe, And after sore gan for to purswe With a spere vp-on Philomene, And from his horse he leide hym on þe grene* ['field, grassy place, ground'], *Maugre* ['in spite of'] *his force, þe story telleþ þus, For he to hym was* ***mortally*** *Irous*. <http://xtf.lib.virginia.edu/xtf/view?docId=chadwyck_ep/uvaGenText/tei/chep_1.0284.xml;chunk.id=d3;toc.depth=10 0;brand=default>

*To death* could also appear with adjectives or participles indicating sickness or injury, as a synonym for *mortally* (example (6.56)), as well as in the context of a battle, war, duel, etc., in which it implied that this was fought until the end of one's life (example (6.57)):

(6.56) ***To the deth** he wownded was*. (a. 1450. MED, s.v. *deth* n. 3c)
(6.57) *In greate sufferaunce of persecusyon euen* ***to the death***. (1546. OED, s.v. *death* n. phrases P2c)

However, *to death* could also occur from its very earliest records with non-literal and metaphorical uses, collocating with verbs or adjectives expressing fears, hate or sorrow, as in examples (6.58)–(6.60), in which it shows traces of incipient subjectivity (cf. Section 3.3.3).

(6.58) *Þa* [...] *hig wæron swyðe gedrefede and* ***to deaðe*** *afærede* ['Then they were very disturbed and afraid to death']. (OE. OED, s.v. *death* n. phrases 1b)
(6.59) *Herodias him hated* ***to ded.*** (a. 1400. OED, s.v. *death* n. phrases P1b)
(6.60) *My soule is sorowful til* ***to the deth***. (c. 1384. OED, s.v. *death* n. phrases P2b)

It is in the course of the sixteenth century that *to death* appeared to show its first uses as an intensifier meaning 'extremely', as in (6.61)–(6.63):

(6.61) *Clodius is inamoured* ***to dead*** *of a certaine yong woman*. (1583. OED, s.v. *death* n. phrases P1(C)b)
(6.62) *Some almost laugh'd themselves* ***to dead.*** (1806. OED, s.v. *death* n. phrases P1(C)b)
(6.63) *I'm sorry*! *I'm fucking sorry* ***to death***! *Okay*? (1997. OED, s.v. *death* n. phrases P1(C)b)

In the light of the dictionary data presented above for the different intensifiers examined, it seems that *dead*(*ly*), *mortal*(*ly*) and *to death* show different degrees of grammaticalisation in PDE, even though they can all be used with intensifying uses. The cline suggested in the literature for the development of intensifying meanings, namely descriptive > affective > intensifying (cf. Adamson 2000: 55 and Section 4.1.2), must be examined more closely considering corpus data, which will hopefully throw light on the rise of these different readings and on how these might be related.

## 6.2. Tracing the history of intensifiers: The long diachrony

### *6.2.1. Preliminary considerations*

In order to offer a full picture of the history of *dead(ly)*, *mortal(ly)* and *to death* across time and with a view to expanding the preliminary evolution provided by the historical dictionaries (cf. Section 6.1), I have resorted to a variety of corpora and electronic collections, in particular the HC, ARCHER, EEBOCorp 1.0, ECF and NCF.[3] The HC and ARCHER specifically seem especially suitable to track the long diachrony of these death-related forms, as they cover a wide time span. EEBOCorp 1.0, ECF and NCF are used here with the aim of expanding the evidence for these forms and zooming in on their usage in the EModE and LModE periods specifically, which are especially relevant in the history of these forms, given that it was precisely at this time when their intensifying readings were firstly attested. The remainder of Section 6.2 thus discusses the data from these sources for each of the intensifiers individually, with some initial remarks on the search results.

Given that most of the materials consulted cover a time span characterised by substantial spelling variation, the search for these intensifiers was carried out using the wildcard *, hence allowing for a number of orthographic variants of the items, among many others *deadlican*, *deedli*, *mourtal* or *to deathe*. The asterisk sign has the obvious advantage that one simple search yields all forms of the matching words, but the main drawback is perhaps that this can leave us with many tokens to prune manually. This is in fact the case of *dead*. Searching for *d*d** in the corpora would actually allow for potential spellings of the form such as *deide* or *deade*, but it would also result in a high number of false positives to be discarded. For this reason, for *dead* in particular I have consulted its different spellings in the OED and then searched for each of them individually. Furthermore, it should be noted that I have disregarded the OE period in the HC material in the search

3 For a detailed description of each of these sources, see Sections 5.2.2 and 5.2.3 in Chapter 5.

for this item. Therefore, the searches for *dead* in this corpus correspond exclusively to ME and EModE. In fact, looking at the different spellings of this word in OE returned many hits of *dead* in predicative position as well as of the noun phrase *the dead*. As a result, the number of relevant tokens for analysis turned out to be very low. Moreover, the intensifying function of *dead(ly)*, *mortal(ly)* and *to death* did not arise at least until ME (cf. Section 6.1), so excluding the OE period in this case seemed justified.

Searching for the form *dead* in EEBOCorp 1.0 was not without problems either. Given the high token frequency of this adjectival and adverbial form in the corpus, with over 146,834 occurrences, I chose a 1,000-token random sample. Analysing the total number of tokens in the EModE data would clearly not only be unmanageable, but it would also result in a high number of instances which would have to be eventually discarded, as the aforementioned cases of *dead* in predicative position or of the noun phrase *the dead*, which were also frequently found in EEBOCorp 1.0. Moreover, the 1,000 tokens in the random sample had to be manually pruned, which left a total of 201 analysable instances: 199 tokens (99%) corresponded to the adjective *dead* and just 2 tokens (1%) represented the adverb *dead* (cf. Table 6.1). In contrast to the procedure followed for the form *dead* in EEBOCorp 1.0, all the examples of *deadly*, *mortal(ly)* and *to death* in the materials consulted were included.

In sum, I have only disregarded in the data those cases in which the item in question appeared in predicative position (example (6.64)), was part of a set phrase (e.g. *put to death*) or proper noun (e.g. *the Dead Sea*) or corresponded to nominal uses (e.g. *a mortal* or *the dead*), as in examples (6.65)–(6.67). I have additionally excluded duplicates in the data.

(6.64) *No, it is but a Venial Sinne; if it be any, it is not* ***deadly***. (HC. 1554. *The trial of Sir Nicholas Throckmorton Knight, in the guildhall of London, for high treason*)

(6.65) *Little though we may like it, he meant what he said, and the tradition of the Church has insisted that he and the other disciples were in fact put* ***to death***, [...] (ARCHER. 1977. Enoch Powell. *Wrestling with the angel*)

(6.66) *The discovery of this 'pocket war' was made during a tour of Israeli-occupied Jordan, a large tract of land west of the Jordan River and the* ***Dead*** *Sea*. (ARCHER. 1967. *The Sunday Times* 18/06/1967)

(6.67) *Verily, verily, I say vnto you, The houre is coming, & now is, when the* ***dead*** *shall heare the voice of the Sonne of God: and they that heare, shall liue.* (HC. 1570–1640. *The Holy Bible*)

Finally, searching for the intensifiers under analysis using the wildcard * in the materials consulted also yields a considerable number of instances which do not correspond to the relevant forms, but to completely unrelated words. This is the case of (6.68) and (6.69), featuring the adverbs *designedly* and *deservedly*. These forms were obviously discarded.

(6.68) *The next day, Trefry ask'd Caesar to walk when the heat was allay'd, and* ***designedly*** *carry'd him by the cottage of the fair slave*; [...] (HC. 1640–1710. Aphra Ben. *Oroonoko*)

(6.69) [...] *for Parma and Placencia, whiche was not theyrs: whiche afterward was the cause & that* ***deseruedly****, of his sonne Peter Aloysius death.* (EEBOCorp 1.0. 1552. Matthias Flacius Illyricus. *Wonderfull newes of the death of Paule the. iii. last byshop of Rome*)

In conclusion, I have only taken into account those cases in which *dead(ly)*, *mortal(ly)* and *to death* were modifying an adjacent form, such as a noun, adjective, participial element, adverb or verb.

Before actually delving into the collocational behaviour of each of the intensifiers at issue in the different materials consulted, and, hence, into their long-term development, the overall figures for *dead(ly)*, *mortal(ly)* and *to death* are provided in Table 6.1.

Table 6.1 gives the raw figures or potential number of tokens for these items individually, in addition to the total number of tokens finally considered for analysis. As can be gathered from this table, the figures for each of the intensifiers are considerably much higher in EEBOCorp 1.0, ECF and NCF, which constitute invaluable sources of information that can provide important insights into the usage and behaviour of these items during the EModE and LModE periods. In the remainder of section 6.2, I will discuss each of the forms in chronological order in the light of the data provided by these sources, thereby accounting for their long diachrony.

Table 6.1. Raw figures and total number of examples analysed in the HC, ARCHER, EEBOCorp 1.0, ECF and NCF

| | | **Raw figures** | **Total analysed** |
|---|---|---|---|
| **HC** | *dead* | 691 | 45 (adj.) |
| | | | 0 (adv.) |
| | *deadly* | 101 | 34 (adj.) |
| | | | 3 (adv.) |
| | *mortal* | 22 | 20 (adj.) |
| | | | 0 (adv.) |
| | *mortally* | 3 | 3 |
| | *to death* | 19 | 6 |
| **ARCHER** | *dead* | 389 | 77 (adj.) |
| | | | 1 (adv.) |
| | *deadly* | 59 | 18 (adj.) |
| | | | 3 (adv.) |
| | *mortal* | 56 | 33 (adj.) |
| | | | 1 (adv.) |
| | *mortally* | 6 | 6 |
| | *to death* | 33 | 18 |
| **EEBOCorp 1.0** | *dead* | 146,834 (1,000 (random sample)) | 199 (adj.) |
| | | | 2 (adv.) |
| | *deadly* | 14,515 | 8,062 (adj.) |
| | | | 920 (adv.) |
| | *mortal* | 31,146 | 20,697 (adj.) |
| | | | 6 (adv.) |
| | *mortally* | 1,680 | 1,414 |
| | *to death* | 30,865 | 4,355 |

Table 6.1. Continued

| | | Raw figures | Total analysed |
|---|---|---|---|
| **ECF** | *dead* | 1,777 | 290 (adj.) |
| | | | 16 (adv.) |
| | *deadly* | 51 | 39 (adj.) |
| | | | 8 (adv.) |
| | *mortal* | 567 | 286 (adj.) |
| | | | 7 (adv.) |
| | *mortally* | 74 | 73 |
| | *to death* | 378 | 249 |
| **NCF** | *dead* | 5,709 | 2,074 (adj.) |
| | | | 185 (adv.) |
| | *deadly* | 661 | 479 (adj.) |
| | | | 153 (adv.) |
| | *mortal* | 1,200 | 1,009 (adj.) |
| | | | 41 (adv.) |
| | *mortally* | 123 | 122 |
| | *to death* | 866 | 536 |

### *6.2.2. The long diachrony of* dead

As indicated in Table 6.1, the HC yielded a total of 45 examples of true positives of *dead*, all of which correspond to the adjectival form. In the 45 examples analysed, *dead* occurs in combination with nouns in a total of ten different collocations, as illustrated in Table 6.2 and Table 6.3 for the ME and EModE periods, respectively. Note that the majority of the attestations of *dead* date to the ME period (41 tokens; 91.11%), while only four of the occurrences of the adjective correspond to EModE (8.89%). This dramatic drop in the use of the adjective *dead* from the ME to EModE is also highly statistically significant (Fisher's exact test = 0; $p < 0.01$). Nonetheless, if we consider the decrease in the absolute frequencies of the collocations which are attested in both ME and EModE, in particular *dead body* and *dead man*, this difference is, in turn, not statistically significant (Fisher's exact test = 0.128235; $p < 0.01$ in the case of *dead body* and Fisher's exact test = 0.0616; $p < 0.01$ in the case of *dead man*).

Table 6.2. The collocations of *dead* (adj.) in ME

| **Collocation** | **Abs. Freq.** | **%** | **NF**[4] | **Total in HC** |
|---|---|---|---|---|
| *dead body* | 6 | 85.71 | 9.86 | 7 |
| *dead brother* | 1 | 100.00 | 1.64 | 1 |
| *dead caitiff* | 1 | 100.00 | 1.64 | 1 |
| *dead corpse* | 3 | 100.00 | 4.93 | 3 |
| *dead fermour* | 2 | 100.00 | 3.29 | 2 |
| *dead flesh* | 9 | 100.00 | 14.79 | 9 |
| *dead knight* | 2 | 100.00 | 3.29 | 2 |
| *dead lichame* | 1 | 100.00 | 1.64 | 1 |
| *dead man* | 11 | 78.57 | 18.08 | 14 |
| *dead thing* | 5 | 100.00 | 8.22 | 5 |
| **Total** | **41** | **91.11** | **67.37** | **45** |

Table 6.3. The collocations of *dead* (adj.) in EModE

| **Collocation** | **Abs. Freq.** | **%** | **NF** | **Total in HC** |
|---|---|---|---|---|
| *dead body* | 1 | 14.29 | 1.81 | 7 |
| *dead man* | 3 | 21.43 | 5.44 | 14 |
| **Total** | **4** | **8.88** | **7.26** | **45** |

4 Normalised frequencies in Sections 6.2 and 6.3 are provided per million words (NF pmw).

Moreover, from the list of collocations of *dead* in Tables 6.2 and 6.3, it becomes apparent that it functioned exclusively as a noun modifier in the two periods analysed, which is only natural if we bear in mind that the only form attested in the corpus is the adjective. Regarding the types of meanings, *dead* had only descriptive or literal meanings in both ME and EModE. The adjective *dead* was thus used to modify a noun referent which was said to be no longer alive, such as a bailiff (*fermour*), a knight, a corpse or flesh. In all these examples *dead* has a literal meaning: 'lifeless, showing no sign of life', as shown in example (6.70), in which it modifies the noun *caitiff* 'prisoner, slave':

(6.70) *And there laye reynart the foxe doun on the grounde lyke a* ***dede*** *keytyf* (CMREYNAR. 1420–1500. William Caxton. *The history of Reynard the fox*)

As mentioned in Section 5.3.2, in my collocational analysis I will use a number of statistical tests to measure the degree of collocational strength of the different intensifiers and their collocates. In order to avoid possible hapax legomena and unusual word combinations, I have set a minimum threshold frequency of 3 for both the collocate, that is, the word which combines with the intensifier, and the collocation (the combination of the node, in this case *dead*, and its collocates). Moreover, I have considerably narrowed the collocation window, which has been reduced to one collocate to the right, and zero collocates to the left. In other words, I am interested exclusively in the word which appears immediately after the node *dead*. As shown in Tables 6.2 and 6.3, adjectival *dead* occurred in the HC in a total of ten different collocations: *dead body*, *dead brother*, *dead caitiff*, *dead corpse*, *dead fermour*, *dead flesh*, *dead knight*, *dead lichame*, *dead man* and *dead thing*. However, only five of these collocations are attested three times or more, the minimum collocation cut-off point. These collocations are *dead body*, *dead corpse*, *dead flesh*, *dead man* and *dead thing*. If we consider the results from the relevant statistical tests, shown in Table 6.4, we notice that these five collocations are all statistically significant, except for *dead thing*.

Thus, in regard to the first measure, the so-called *z*-score, this value should be at least 2.576 for a collocation to be counted as statistically significant (Cantos-Gómez 2013: 204) and this is actually the case for all these collocations but for *dead thing*. The mutual information values (*MI*), as Brezina et al. (2015: 159) point out, tend to emphasise rare combinations in a given corpus and this explains why this formula is

Table 6.4. Standardised scores for *dead* (adj.) in the HC

| Collocation | *z*-score | *MI* | *MI3* | *LL*-value |
|---|---|---|---|---|
| *dead body* | 6.096 | 2.842 | 8.456 | 15.576 |
| *dead brother* | 0.551 | 0.785 | 0.785 | 0.249 |
| *dead caitiff* | 13.896 | 7.608 | 7.608 | 8.828 |
| *dead corpse* | 29.528 | 8.193 | 11.363 | 29.386 |
| *dead fermour* | 22.721 | 8.023 | 10.023 | 19.011 |
| *dead flesh* | 13.437 | 4.460 | 10.800 | 38.703 |
| *dead knight* | 0.959 | 0.960 | 2.960 | 0.720 |
| *dead lichame* | 3.697 | 3.964 | 3.964 | 3.641 |
| *dead man* | 7.054 | 2.424 | 10.039 | 24.334 |
| *dead thing* | 1.360 | 0.864 | 5.508 | 1.487 |

typically accompanied by the *MI3* formula. *MI3* is actually the *MI* formula taken to the power of 3, which also gives more weight to frequent events (Cantos-Gómez 2013: 207). The collocations *dead caitiff* and *dead fermour*, which occurred once and twice in the corpus, respectively, have a high *MI* score (7.6 and 8.0) despite their low frequency. Moreover, if we consider the isolated frequencies of these collocates of *dead*, we see that neither *fermour* nor *caitiff* are particularly common words in the HC, occurring only six and four times, respectively. Even so, the different statistical measures indicate that the occurrence of these words in combination is to be considered as statistically significant. If we consider now the *MI* scores for the relevant collocations, only *dead corpse* and *dead flesh* reach the cut-off value of 3. *Dead body*, *dead man* and *dead thing* have all lower scores and are not considered statistically significant according to this test. The reason for this is that these collocates alone have a much higher token frequency. However, if we turn to the *MI3* formula, it appears that all the five collocations, including *dead thing*, are statistically significant, since they all reach the threshold level of 4.75. The last statistical test used to measure the collocational strength was the log-likelihood test (*LL*), whose cut-off point is 3.8 for a collocation to be considered statistically significant at the level of $p < 0.05$ and 6.6 or higher at the level of $p < 0.01$. In the light of the data, then, it seems that the only collocation which is not regarded as significant is *dead thing*.

Regarding semantic prosody, there are only two collocations which are negative, namely *dead corpse* and *dead caitiff*. A corpse, by nature, is always associated with death, and, hence, negative in meaning. Being a caitiff ('prisoner, slave') is also negative, since it implies that one's freedom is restricted, which is regarded as a bad and an unfortunate circumstance. The remaining eight collocations in the corpus (*dead body*, *dead brother*, *dead fermour*, *dead flesh*, *dead knight*, *dead lichame*, *dead man* and *dead thing*) have neutral semantic prosody, as shown in Table 6.5.

Table 6.5. The semantic prosody of *dead* (adj.) in the HC

| Period | | Neg | | | Neu | | Total |
|---|---|---|---|---|---|---|---|
| | Abs. Freq. | % | NF | Abs. Freq. | % | NF | |
| ME | 4 | 9.76 | 6.57 | 37 | 90.24 | 60.80 | 41 |
| EModE | 0 | 0.00 | 0 | 4 | 100.00 | 7.26 | 4 |

In the light of the data discussed above, it appears then that in the HC *dead* is only attested as an adjective functioning as a modifier of nouns, with predominantly neutral semantic prosody (in 91% of the occurrences). Moreover, in all the cases studied here *dead* is found with descriptive or literal meanings only, subjective and intensifying readings not being yet recorded in the HC data corresponding to the ME and the EModE periods.

The other corpus consulted for the long diachrony, ARCHER, yields a total of seventy-six tokens of the adjective *dead*, which occurs in forty-two different collocations, as illustrated in Tables 6.6–6.9. If we examine the occurrences of the adjective in the four different subperiods, we see that the number of instances is larger in the seventeenth and eighteenth centuries (30.26% and 26.32% of the total, respectively) than in the nineteenth and twentieth centuries (22.37% and 21.05% of the total of examples). The

Table 6.6. *Dead* (adj.) in ARCHER in the 17th c.

| Collocation | Abs. Freq. | % | NF | Total in ARCHER |
|---|---|---|---|---|
| *dead body* | 1 | 12.50 | 2.87 | 8 |
| *dead brother* | 1 | 100.00 | 2.87 | 1 |
| *dead child* | 2 | 33.33 | 5.74 | 6 |
| *dead corpse* | 2 | 100.00 | 5.74 | 2 |
| *dead dog* | 1 | 100.00 | 2.87 | 1 |
| *dead father* | 1 | 100.00 | 2.87 | 1 |
| *dead friend* | 1 | 100.00 | 2.87 | 1 |
| *dead kinsman* | 1 | 100.00 | 2.87 | 1 |
| *dead lord* | 2 | 100.00 | 6 | 2 |
| *dead man* | 6 | 50.00 | 17.22 | 12 |
| *dead mother* | 1 | 100.00 | 2.87 | 1 |
| *dead palsy* | 1 | 100.00 | 2.87 | 1 |
| *dead person* | 1 | 33.33 | 2.87 | 3 |
| *dead thing* | 1 | 100.00 | 2.87 | 1 |
| *dead work* | 1 | 100.00 | 2.87 | 1 |
| **Total** | **23** | **30.26** | **66.02** | **76** |

normalised frequencies for each of the periods seem to confirm a drastic reduction in frequency from the seventeenth to the eighteenth century (roughly, from sixty-six to thirty-seven points), a tendency which continues in the twentieth century (thirty-one and thirty points in the nineteenth and twentieth centuries, respectively). This drop in the number of attestations of the adjective from the seventeenth to the eighteenth century is, however, not statistically significant. The same applies to the transition from the eighteenth to the nineteenth century and from the nineteenth to the twentieth century.[5]

5 **17th > 18th c.**: $\chi^2$ (1) = 3.008; $p$ = 0.08285446; **18th > 19th c.**: $\chi^2$ (1) = 0.135; $p$ = 0.71330317; **19th c. > 20th c.**: $\chi^2$ (1) = 0.004; $p$ = 0.94957097.

Table 6.7. *Dead* (adj.) in ARCHER in the 18th c.

| Collocation | Abs. Freq. | % | NF | Total in ARCHER |
|---|---|---|---|---|
| *dead bough* | 1 | 100.00 | 1.87 | 1 |
| *dead branch* | 1 | 100.00 | 1.87 | 1 |
| *dead child* | 4 | 66.67 | 7.47 | 6 |
| *dead complexion* | 1 | 100.00 | 1.87 | 1 |
| *dead daughter* | 1 | 100.00 | 1.87 | 1 |
| *dead flesh* | 1 | 100.00 | 1.87 | 1 |
| *dead hog* | 1 | 100.00 | 1.87 | 1 |
| *dead language* | 3 | 100.00 | 5.60 | 3 |
| *dead man* | 2 | 16.67 | 3.73 | 12 |
| *dead melancholy* | 1 | 100.00 | 1.87 | 1 |
| *dead person* | 2 | 66.67 | 3.73 | 3 |
| *dead specimen* | 2 | 100.00 | 3.73 | 2 |
| **Total** | **20** | **26.32** | **37.33** | **76** |

Table 6.8. *Dead* (adj.) in ARCHER in the 19th c.

| Collocation | Abs. Freq. | % | NF | Total in ARCHER |
|---|---|---|---|---|
| *dead body* | 6 | 75.00 | 11.06 | 8 |
| *dead figure* | 1 | 100.00 | 1.84 | 1 |
| *dead horse* | 1 | 50.00 | 1.84 | 2 |
| *dead lady* | 2 | 100.00 | 3.69 | 2 |
| *dead man* | 1 | 8.33 | 1.84 | 12 |
| *dead Russian* | 1 | 100.00 | 1.84 | 1 |
| *dead silence* | 1 | 100.00 | 1.84 | 1 |
| *dead sister* | 1 | 50.00 | 1.84 | 2 |
| *dead skin* | 1 | 100.00 | 1.84 | 1 |
| *dead stand* | 1 | 100.00 | 1.84 | 1 |
| *dead standstill* | 1 | 100.00 | 1.84 | 1 |
| **Total** | **17** | **22.37** | **31.33** | **76** |

Table 6.9. *Dead* (adj.) in ARCHER in the 20th c.

| Collocation | Abs. Freq. | % | NF | Total in ARCHER |
|---|---|---|---|---|
| *dead body* | 1 | 12.5 | 1.88 | 8 |
| *dead elephant* | 1 | 100.00 | 1.88 | 1 |
| *dead German* | 1 | 100.00 | 1.88 | 1 |
| *dead horse* | 1 | 50,00 | 1.88 | 2 |
| *dead lover* | 1 | 100.00 | 1.88 | 1 |
| *dead man* | 3 | 25.00 | 5.65 | 12 |
| *dead mayfly* | 1 | 100.00 | 1.88 | 1 |
| *dead pain* | 1 | 100.00 | 1.88 | 1 |
| *dead product* | 1 | 100.00 | 1.88 | 1 |
| *dead seagull* | 1 | 100.00 | 1.88 | 1 |
| *dead sister* | 1 | 50.00 | 1.8 | 2 |
| *dead tree* | 2 | 100.00 | 3.77 | 2 |
| *dead wood* | 1 | 100 | 1.88 | 1 |
| **Total** | **16** | **21.05** | **30.01** | **76** |

As far as the collocations of *dead* are concerned, only five of its collocates occur at least three times in the corpus data, namely *body* (eight tokens), *child* (6 tokens), *language* (three tokens), *man* (twelve tokens) and *person* (three tokens). The remaining collocations are attested less than three times in ARCHER, hence the wide variety of collocations of the adjective. If we consider the different statistical tests to measure the degree of collocational strength between *dead* and its collocates (cf. Table 6.10), it turns out that these five collocations are statistically significant and hence we can say that the co-occurrence of *dead* and these nouns is not due to chance. In the case of *deadly person*, however, the scores for the *MI* and the *LL* tests are slightly below the threshold values.

With regard to the types of meaning (cf. Table 6.11), descriptive readings prevail in the corpus, accounting for 92.2% of the total, followed by subjective meanings (3.9%), and then by those examples which are ambiguous

Table 6.10. Standardised scores for *dead* (adj.) in ARCHER

| **Collocation** | ***z*-score** | ***MI*** | ***MI3*** | ***LL*-value** |
|---|---|---|---|---|
| *dead body* | 19.435 | 5.620 | 11.620 | 46.734 |
| *dead child* | 13.083 | 4.931 | 10.100 | 29.439 |
| *dead language* | 14.771 | 6.223 | 9.393 | 20.006 |
| *dead man* | 12.766 | 3.956 | 11.126 | 43.386 |
| *dead person* | 3.929 | 2.808 | 5.978 | 6.537 |

Table 6.11. Meaning types for *dead* (adj.) in ARCHER

| | | **D** | **D/S** | **S** | **S/I** | **Total** |
|---|---|---|---|---|---|---|
| **17th c.** | # | 23 | 0 | 0 | 0 | 23 |
| | % | 32.86 | 0.00 | 0.00 | 0.00 | 30.25 |
| | **NF** | 66.02 | 0 | 0 | 0 | 66.02 |
| **18th c.** | # | 18 | 0 | 2 | 0 | 20 |
| | % | 25.71 | 0.00 | 66.67 | 0.00 | 26.35 |
| | **NF** | 33.60 | 0 | 3.73 | 0 | 37.33 |
| **19th c.** | # | 14 | 0 | 1 | 2 | 17 |
| | % | 20.00 | 0.00 | 33.33 | 100.00 | 22.36 |
| | **NF** | 25.81 | 0 | 1.84 | 3.69 | 31.33 |
| **20th c.** | # | 15 | 1 | 0 | 0 | 16 |
| | % | 21.43 | 100.00 | 0.00 | 0.00 | 21.04 |
| | **NF** | 28.26 | 1.88 | 0 | 0 | 30.14 |
| **Total (#)** | | 70 | **1** | **3** | **2** | **76** |

between subjective and intensifying (2.6%), on the one hand, or between descriptive and subjective (1.3%), on the other hand. The ARCHER data thus contrast with the results from the HC, since the types of meanings of the adjective are more varied in the former, although descriptive meanings still prevail.[6] As will be seen in Section 6.3, ambiguous readings are critical for the ultimate development of unequivocal subjective and intensifying meanings of the adjective, for they open up the possibility of inferencing a non-literal and a degree reading, respectively.

If we compare the normalised frequencies, it appears that descriptive meanings decrease considerably from the seventeenth to the eighteenth century (66.02 to 33.60). Although descriptive meanings are, on average, more frequent in the seventeenth than in the eighteenth century, this difference is not considered to be statistically significant ($\chi^2(1) = 4.112; p = 0.04257998$). If we contrast the eighteenth and nineteenth centuries, this difference is not statistically significant either ($\chi^2$ (1) = 0.32; p = 0.57160764) and the same applies to the difference between the nineteenth and twentieth centuries ($\chi^2$ (1) = 0.003; p = 0.9563199). In the case of subjective meanings, although there is also a decrease from the eighteenth to the nineteenth century in terms both of absolute frequencies (two tokens vs one token) and normalised frequencies (3.73 vs 1.84), the difference in the two periods is not statistically significant (Fisher's exact test = 0.622663). The ambiguous readings of *dead* are only attested at individual periods: in the twentieth (D/S) and in the nineteenth century (S/I), for which reason we cannot compare these results across time.

Illustrations of the different types of meanings are provided in (6.71)–(6.74).

(6.71) *We'll dispatch him, fear not; A* ***dead*** *dog never bites.* (1626mass_d1b.1626. Philip Massinger. *The selected plays of Philip Massinger*)

(6.72) *The keen agony may gradually pass into a dull,* ***dead*** *pain; and after a time, the sensibility of the soul may seem to be wholly lost;* (18xxdale_h6b. 1850–1899. Robert W. Dale. '*The argument from experience*')

(6.73) *Started at 4 a.m. but shortly after, thro' the forgetfulness of the Engineers, she came to a* ***dead*** *standstill, for there was no steam* – (1853hall_j6b. 1853. William King Hall. *The Diaries of William King Hall*)

(6.74) *'Michel Mandrin died last night; his mother and all the children are very ill. Pray for us.'* […] *A* ***dead*** *silence followed this communication.* (1848kava_f5b. 1848. Madeleine: *A Tale of Auvergne*)

6 In the HC, however, only descriptive meanings were attested.

In (6.71) *dead* has clearly a descriptive meaning, referring to a dog which is no longer alive and, hence, can no longer bite anyone. Conversely, the meaning of *dead* in (6.72) is ambiguous. The example is taken from a sermon by Robert William Dale, where he relates the perils of sins, which, in his view, can effectively inflict serious injuries and terrible pain on our souls. It is not clear, then, if the pain is so sharp and powerful as to devastate the soul or if it is more metaphorical. Given the vague meaning of the adjective here, in this case I have decided to classify it as indeterminate between a descriptive and a subjective reading. In a similar vein, *dead* in (6.73) can also be contextually read as ambiguous between a subjective and an intensifying meaning. *Dead* is referring here to a steamboat, which has come to a stop (*dead standstill*), that is, it is no longer navigating. Lack of movement and restfulness are states which can clearly call death to mind, even though in this particular example *dead standstill* can also be taken to be synonymous with 'complete stop' and would therefore allow for a degree interpretation. To minimise the risk of a biased analysis of the data given the lack of formal, objective criteria for the semantic classification of this form, I have decided to categorise the meaning of *dead* here as ambiguous between subjective and intensifying (S/I). Example (6.74), by contrast, is taken to be subjective, since silence, much like restfulness and lack of movement, is another state that is easily associated with death. The atmosphere described in the situation presented in (6.74) is glum and mournful, for a certain M. Dubois has just read a letter in which he informs the other people in the same room that Michel Mandrin, another character, has recently passed away.

As far as semantic prosody is concerned, the overwhelming majority of the occurrences of the adjective *dead* in ARCHER have neutral semantic prosody (93.4%), while the remaining examples have negative semantic prosody (6.6%). There are, therefore, no attestations of the adjective in the corpus as a modifier of nouns with positive semantic prosody (cf. Table 6.12). Moreover, the differences concerning the negative and the neutral semantic prosody among the four different centuries were not found to be statistically significant, according to Fisher's exact test and the chi-square test.[7]

7 *Negative semantic prosody*: Fisher's exact test = 0.307224 (17th c. > 18th c.); *neutral semantic prosody*: $\chi^2$ (1) = 1.834; $p$ = 0.17565582 (17th c. > 18th c.); $\chi^2$ (1) = 0.042; $p$ = 0.83761977 (18th c. > 19th c.); $\chi^2$ (1) = 0.013; $p$ = 0.90922389 (19th c. > 20th c.).

Table 6.12. The semantic prosody of *dead* (adj.) in ARCHER

| | | Neg | Neu | Total |
|---|---|---|---|---|
| **17th c.** | # | 3 | 20 | 23 |
| | % | 60.00 | 28.17 | 30.26 |
| | **NF** | 8.61 | 57.41 | 66.02 |
| **18th c.** | # | 1 | 19 | 20 |
| | % | 20.00 | 26.76 | 26.32 |
| | **NF** | 1.87 | 35.46 | 37.33 |
| **19th c.** | # | 0 | 17 | 17 |
| | % | 0.00 | 23.94 | 22.37 |
| | **NF** | 0 | 31.33 | 31.33 |
| **20th c.** | # | 1 | 15 | 16 |
| | % | 20.00 | 21.13 | 21.05 |
| | **NF** | 1.88 | 28.26 | 30.14 |
| **Total (#)** | | **5** | **71** | **76** |

Among those nouns which have negative semantic prosody in ARCHER we find *melancholy*, *palsy*, *pain* and *corpse*, while the collocations of *dead* with the nouns *child*, *silence*, *stand*, *person*, *dog*, *body* or *tree*, for instance, have neutral semantic prosody. Although in principle we could consider that the nouns *corpse* and *body* behave much alike, their semantic prosody is, to my mind, different: while *body* is clearly neutral, a *corpse*, denoting a dead body, is always connected with death and, hence, negative in meaning.

Concerning the categories which are modified by adjectival *dead*, given that it is formally an adjective and since adjectives typically denote attributes of nouns, all the words modified by *dead* are nouns, as shown in Table 6.13.

In regard to the adverb *dead* and unlike the HC, which contained no examples of the form, ARCHER yields one token in the twentieth century. This is example (6.75), which has clearly an intensifying meaning, for *dead serious* in this particular case is equivalent to being absolutely serious. As it is only attested in the very last period, it is impossible to track the

Table 6.13. Categories modified by *dead* (adj.) in ARCHER

| Period | N | | |
|---|---|---|---|
| | **Abs. Freq.** | % | **NF** |
| **17th c.** | 23 | 30.26 | 66.02 |
| **18th c.** | 20 | 26.32 | 37.33 |
| **19th c.** | 17 | 22.37 | 31.33 |
| **20th c.** | 16 | 21.05 | 30.14 |
| **Total** | **76** | 100.00 | **38.83** |

evolution of this adverb over time, and thus discover the earliest subjective and intensifying uses and whether the former are actually attested earlier than the latter. The corpus data are therefore very limited, and it can only be concluded that adverbial *dead* functions in ARCHER as an adjective modifier and has neutral semantic prosody. Being serious or grim is, in principle, neither positive nor negative, which explains why the collocation *dead serious* has been tagged as illustrative of neutral semantic prosody.

(6.75) *I'm* ***d-d-dead*** *serious. I've got to get to Glasgow by nine to-morrow.* (1934brid_d7b. 1934. James Bridie. *A sleeping clergyman and other plays*)

The next corpus examined was EEBOCorp 1.0, which looks into the EModE period. Tables 6.14 and 6.15 show the distribution of the different types of meanings for the adjective and adverb *dead* in the corpus, respectively. As seen here, descriptive readings account for almost 95% of the occurrences of the adjective *dead* in EEBOCorp 1.0, while subjective interpretations barely amount to 5%. No instances of intensifying *dead* were attested in the random sample.

Table 6.14. Meaning types for *dead* (adj.) in EEBOCorp 1.0

| | **Abs. Freq.** | % |
|---|---|---|
| **D** | 189 | 94.97 |
| **S** | 10 | 5.03 |
| **Total** | **199** | 100.00 |

Table 6.15. Meaning types for *dead* (adv.) in EEBOCorp 1.0

| | **Abs. Freq.** | **%** |
|---|---|---|
| **S** | 2 | 100.00 |
| **Total** | 2 | 100.00 |

Example (6.76), featuring the collocation *dead lion*, shows a literal or descriptive meaning of the adjective. In turn, the collocation *dead paleness* in (6.77) is taken to be subjective, since a pallid skin is often associated with corpses and, by extension, with death in general terms. The subjective use of the adverb *dead*, which is only recorded in the collocation *dead drunk* in the random sample, is illustrated in (6.78). *Dead drunk* is here considered to be subjective: when one is under the intoxicating effects of alcohol, though not dead, our condition can certainly be reminiscent of that of a dead person, and death can therefore be easily evoked.

(6.76) *Surelye whosoeuer is ioyned to all the liuing, there is hope: for it is better to a liuing dog, then to a* ***dead*** *lyon*. (D00000998565350000. 1561. William Whittingham. *The Bible and Holy Scriptures*)

(6.77) *If now (said she) my Lord my Heart deceives, This Stone will by* ***dead*** *paleness make me look Pale as the Snowy skin of Lilly Leaves*. (D00000129517360000. 1651. William D'Avenant. *Gondibert an heroick poem*)

(6.78) [...] *yet at last recovering, after she hath made a small Speech to the People, her Companions lead her into the Temple, where she drinks her self* ***dead*** *Drunk*; (D00000112834340000. 1671. Arnoldus Montanus. *Atlas Chinensis*)

In addition to the 1,000-word random sample, I also selected a number of collocations to be searched for specifically in the EEBOCorp 1.0 data, on the basis of the quotations found in the OED entry for *dead* (adjective and adverb) (cf. Section 6.1.1) and on other collocations attested in more recent corpora of English, such as the *British National Corpus* (BNC). This search intends to complement the scarce evidence provided by the random sample, and to allow to go further into the semantic development of the adjective and adverb. The selected collocates of *dead* are given in Table 6.16.

The information provided by this selection of collocations suggests that both subjective and intensifying meanings of *dead* are already attested early in the data, which is in keeping with the preliminary evidence

Table 6.16. Selection of collocates for *dead* (adj. and adv.) in EEBOCorp 1.0

| ***dead*** **(adj.)** | | ***dead*** **(adv.)** | |
|---|---|---|---|
| **Collocate** | **Abs. Freq.** | **Collocate** | **Abs. Freq.** |
| *calm* (n.) | 38 | *beat* | - |
| *flat* (n.) | 1 | *broke* | - |
| *pale* | 4 | *calm* (adj.) | 3 |
| | | *certain* | - |
| | | *cold* (adj.) | 8 |
| | | *drunk* | 143 |
| | | *dull* | - |
| | | *easy* | - |
| | | *handsome* | - |
| | | *pale* (adj.) | 1 |
| | | *pretty* | - |
| | | *quiet* | - |
| | | *right* | 2 |
| | | *scared* | - |
| | | *serious* | - |
| | | *set* | - |
| | | *sick* | 10 |
| | | *simple* | - |
| | | *slow* | 2 |
| | | *sober* | 1 |
| | | *still* | 1 |
| | | *straight* | - |
| | | *sure* | 21 |
| | | *tired* | - |
| | | *white* | - |
| | | *wrong* | - |

provided by the OED and the MED (cf. Section 6.1.1). Collocations such as *dead calm*, *dead cold*, *dead pale* and *dead drunk* in (6.79)–(6.82) evince subjective readings of *dead*. Thus, calmness or tranquillity, coldness and paleness are all qualities which can be metaphorically related to death and are therefore counted here as subjective. The case of the collocation *dead drunk* in (6.82) is slightly different. Although in many cases in the corpus the use of *dead* in this particular collocation emphasises the inebriated condition of a person and could therefore be graded as an intensifier meaning 'very, extremely', death-related properties can still be very present. When suffering the after-effects of alcohol, our state might be reminiscent of that of a dead person and alcohol poisoning might be very close to death itself. On this account, the collocation *dead drunk* was considered as subjective rather than intensifying in the data.

(6.79) *When a Ship being at Sea, doth take in all her Sails* [...] *she is said to lye a Hull* [...] *and this is done, sometimes in* ***dead*** *Calms, to preserve the Sails* [...]; (D00000122443940000. 1685. Nathaniel Boteler. *Six dialogues about sea-services*)

(6.80) *He is stark and* ***dead*** *cold who is not set on fire by the burning and shining flames of such a charity*. (D00000132989100000. 1667. Jeremy Taylor. *The worthy communicant*).

(6.81) *And with that worde, the head beganne to shrincke, The face* ***dead*** *pale, and hollow grew the eies*: (D00000998404920000. 1592. Nicholas Breton. *The pilgrimage to paradise*).

(6.82) *At his owne weapon of Vpsie freeze will they dare him, and beat him with wine-pots till hée be* ***dead*** *drunke*. (D00000998409720000. 1608. Thomas Dekker. *The dead tearme*)

Instances of the intensifying adjective *dead* are also present in the corpus data. Example (6.83) illustrates one such intensifying reading with the collocation *dead flat*. In this case the author is describing a part of the Netherlands called the Beemster, which is characterised by a very rich soil and very flat lands.

(6.83) *This makes that part of the Countrey called the Bemster, being now the richest Soil of the Province, lying upon a* ***dead*** *flat*, [...] *which make the pleasantest Summer-Landschip of any Countrey I have seen of that sort*. (D00000117669300000. 1673. Sir William Temple. *Observations upon the United Provinces of the Netherlands*)

Intensifying meanings of the adverb are shown in (6.84)–(6.86):

(6.84) *That done, take with your Compas the first fift part of that second circle* [...] *and there make a pricke: at which prick, lay the one end of your Ruler* [...] *and so draw a* ***dead*** *right line* [...] (D00000998526600000. 1602. Thomas Blundeville. *The theoriques of the seuen planets*)

(6.85) *And for that all things in your seruice shall be fulfilled in more ample manner, I will that the noble Brandimardo go with me in my companie, for that your defence shall bée the more certain. And although the attainment be neuer so difficult; yet hauing him in my companye, I hope to make all things* ***dead*** *sure.* (D00000998488560000. 1583. Pedro de la Sierra. *The second part of the Myrror of knighthood*)

(6.86) *I knowe it is taken (as they say) to be* ***dead*** *sure that the party is a witch, if sundry such shewes of matters do concurre.* (D00000998414160000. 1593. George Gifford. *A dialogue concerning witches and witchcraftes*)

Example (6.84) is taken from an astronomy book by Blundeville, who in this excerpt informs the reader about how to calculate the latitude of any place and how, in order to do that, one needs to draw a completely straight line. The only interpretation possible here for *dead* is therefore the intensifying reading: 'completely, totally'. (6.85) and (6.86) give two examples of the collocation *dead sure*, the very first collocation documented in the OED. In fact, example (6.85) even antedates the first OED record of the collocation (cf. (6.17)), dated 1589, and which is also found in EEBOCorp 1.0. Moreover, the example is taken from a romance of chivalry, originally written in Spanish and first printed in 1580. Although the translator could have chosen another form to render the Spanish adverb *muy* 'very' into English, he used the adverb *dead* instead. In (6.86) the author mentions that the only way to be absolutely sure that a group of people are witches is when certain signs concur. In this case *dead* does not admit a literal reading either, but can only be a synonym for *completely, totally*.

In sum, the overall picture provided by the random sample and the selection of collocations suggests that both the adjective and the adverb *dead* could already occur with intensifying meanings in EModE. The number of tokens for the adverb in the random sample was very limited, but the collocational search showed that this adverb is indeed attested in the corpus. More conspicuously, some of the examples of the intensifying adverb date to the late sixteenth century, precisely the time when *dead* is first recorded as an intensifier in the OED.

The eighteenth-century evidence from ECF yields a total of 290 analysable tokens of the adjective *dead*, in a total of 77 different collocations. The number of collocations is relatively high considering the number of examples of *dead*, which owes to the fact that many collocates of the adjective are recorded only once. Table 6.17 presents the individual frequencies for the most common collocations in the data (those occurring at least five times in ECF). As shown in this table, all the collocates of *dead* are nouns, so that adjectival *dead* behaves in this regard in exactly the same way as other adjectives like *mortal* or *deadly*. Table 6.18 shows the standardised scores for the most frequent collocates of *dead*. The results indicate that in many cases there is a significant correlation between the adjective and these collocates and that their co-occurrence cannot be attributed to chance. This is the case of the collocations *dead body*, *dead dog*, *dead husband*, *dead language*, *dead man*, *dead rat* and *dead silence*, which are highly significant, and of *dead child*, which is also statistically significant. However, the collocations *dead father*, *dead friend*, *dead lord* and *dead woman* were not found to be statistically significant. In these cases, therefore, there is not a strong link between the node and the collocate.

Table 6.17. Absolute and normalised frequencies for the most frequent collocations of *dead* (adj.) in ECF

| **Collocation** | **Abs. Freq.** | **NF** |
|---|---|---|
| *dead body* | 74 | 7.63 |
| *dead child* | 7 | 0.72 |
| *dead dog* | 6 | 0.62 |
| *dead father* | 5 | 0.52 |
| *dead friend* | 6 | 0.62 |
| *dead husband* | 8 | 0.82 |
| *dead language* | 8 | 0.82 |
| *dead lord* | 6 | 0.62 |
| *dead man* | 51 | 5.26 |
| *dead rat* | 8 | 0.82 |
| *dead silence* | 6 | 0.62 |
| *dead woman* | 5 | 0.52 |

Table 6.18. Standardised scores for *dead* (adj.) in ECF

| Collocation | *z*-score | *MI* | *MI3* | *LL*-value |
|---|---|---|---|---|
| *dead body* | 48.696 | 5.088 | 17.507 | 379.199 ($p < 0.0001$) |
| *dead child* | 2.756 | 1.442 | 7.057 | 5.148 ($p < 0.05$) |
| *dead dog* | 10.612 | 4.373 | 9.543 | 24.995 ($p < 0.0001$) |
| *dead father* | 0.366 | 0.236 | 4.879 | 0.126 ($p > 0.05$) |
| *dead friend* | 0.602 | 0.354 | 5.524 | 0.333 ($p > 0.05$) |
| *dead husband* | 4.625 | 2.153 | 8.153 | 11.486 ($p < 0.001$) |
| *dead language* | 10.683 | 4.018 | 10.018 | 29.595 ($p < 0.0001$) |
| *dead lord* | 1.148 | 0.670 | 5.840 | 1.116 ($p > 0.05$) |
| *dead man* | 11.770 | 2.168 | 13.513 | 74.024 ($p < 0.0001$) |
| *dead rat* | 53.115 | 8.470 | 14.470 | 79.076 ($p < 0.0001$) |
| *dead silence* | 8.523 | 3.811 | 8.981 | 20.581 ($p < 0.0001$) |
| *dead woman* | 0.116 | 0.075 | 4.718 | 0.013 ($p > 0.05$) |

With regard to the types of meanings (cf. Table 6.19), the adjective *dead* shows a preference for descriptive or literal meanings in the eighteenth-century data. These represent 90.00% of the total, subjective meanings amount to 7.59%, while intensifying meanings of *dead* are the least frequent, making up 2.41%.

Examples (6.87)–(6.91) illustrate the different types of meanings of the adjective in the data. Example (6.87) shows a descriptive meaning, in particular the combination of the adjective with the noun *language*, which refers to a language which has not survived and has no speakers

Table 6.19. Meaning types for *dead* (adj.) in ECF

| | Abs. Freq. | % | NF |
|---|---|---|---|
| **D** | 261 | 90.00 | 26.90 |
| **S** | 22 | 7.59 | 2.27 |
| **I** | 7 | 2.41 | 0.72 |
| **Total** | **290** | **100.00** | **29.89** |

alive. Examples (6.88) and (6.89), by contrast, illustrate subjective meanings of *dead*, in combination with the nouns *pale* and *calm*. A pallid or wan colour may recall the paleness of a corpse, as in (6.88), in which the narrator describes a certain Richmond, sick with a fatal disease and with a very livid face. Peacefulness or tranquillity, as in (6.89), may also signal or be related to death. Conversely, the collocations *dead loss* in (6.90) and *dead bargain* in (6.91) are no longer associated with death and instead the adjective is simply boosting the noun in question. These collocations can be paraphrased as *complete, pure loss* and *complete, pure bargain*, respectively, and are hence considered as intensifying.

(6.87) *In all ancient or* ***dead*** *Languages we have no Term, any way adequate, whereby we may express it.* (1765–1770. Henry Brooke. *The Fool of Quality*)

(6.88) *His countenance, you observe, is Hippocratical, the very image of death: his face a* ***dead*** *pale,* [...] *and his whole body thin like a skeleton.* (1756–1766. Thomas Amory. *John Buncle*)

(6.89) *Your happiness, child, is in the still life. I love not a* ***dead*** *calm: Now a tempest, now a refreshing breeze, I shall know how to enjoy the difference---* (1754. Samuel Richardson. *Sir Charles Grandison*)

(6.90) *O! says he, I shou'd not been tir'd of you; but besides having the Satisfaction of your Company, it had sav'd me that unlucky Blow at Paris, which was a* ***dead*** *Loss to me, of above 8000 Pistoles,* [...] (1724. Daniel Defoe. *Roxana*)

(6.91) *I had them a* ***dead*** *bargain, or I should not have bought them.* (1766. Oliver Goldsmith. *The Vicar of Wakefield*)

As far as semantic prosody is concerned (see Table 6.20), the adjective *dead* occurs predominantly with neutral semantic prosody in the data (97.58%), while negative semantic prosody accounts only for 2.42% of the cases. There are no instances of the adjective as a modifier of nouns which are inherently positive in ECF. By way of illustration, nouns which

Table 6.20. Semantic prosody for *dead* (adj.) in ECF

| | **Abs. Freq.** | **%** | **NF** |
|---|---|---|---|
| **neg** | 7 | 2.42 | 0.72 |
| **neu** | 283 | 97.58 | 29.17 |
| **Total** | **290** | **100.00** | **29.89** |

are considered neutral include *body*, *bone*, *child*, *creature*, *friend*, *husband*, *lord*, *matter*, *mother*, *person* and *substance*. As for nouns modified by *dead* which have negative connotations, consider *loss*, *insensibility*, *slave* or *palsy*.

As regards the adverbial form, ECF returned only sixteen occurrences of *dead* (adv.) in four different collocations, specifically *dead asleep*, *dead coloured*, *dead drunk* and *dead still*, as shown in Table 6.21. Given that *dead coloured* and *dead still* are attested only once in the corpus, these collocations were not considered for statistical testing. For the other two collocations, *dead asleep* and *dead drunk*, the scores from the different tests indicate that the association of the adverb and the collocates *sleep* and *drunk* is strong and not random (cf. Table 6.22).

As far as the types of meanings are concerned, it is remarkable that the adverb *dead* is only attested with subjective meanings in the data, no descriptive or intensifying readings of the adverb being recorded in ECF. Two such instances are given in (6.92) and (6.93), corresponding to the collocations *dead asleep* and *dead drunk*, respectively. These collocations have been tagged as subjective because, although not literal, their meaning can still be relatively attached to the original. When asleep or under the effects of alcohol, our state, position and general condition may somehow

Table 6.21. Absolute and normalised frequencies for the most frequent collocates of *dead* (adv.) in ECF

| **Collocation** | **Abs. Freq.** | **NF** |
|---|---|---|
| *dead asleep* | 5 | 0.52 |
| *dead coloured* | 1 | 0.10 |
| *dead drunk* | 9 | 0.93 |
| *dead still* | 1 | 0.10 |

Table 6.22. Standardised scores for *dead* (adv.) in ECF

| **Collocation** | ***z*-score** | ***MI*** | ***MI3*** | ***LL*-value** |
|---|---|---|---|---|
| *dead asleep* | 13.518 | 5.268 | 9.911 | 26.840 ($p < 0.0001$) |
| *dead drunk* | 39.186 | 7.431 | 13.771 | 75.403 ($p < 0.0001$) |

resemble that of a dead person; since death can be recalled metaphorically, these collocations are not regarded as properly intensifying yet.

(6.92) *I was so* ***dead*** *asleep at first, being fatigu'd with Rowing, or Paddling, as it is call'd* [...] (1719. Daniel Defoe. *Robinson Crusoe*)

(6.93) *But when Lord Albertus and his Friends found they were out of Danger of the Infidels, they smiled upon one another; and Night coming on, and Mustapha* ***dead*** *drunk with Wine, they secured him on a Bed.* (1739. Penelope Aubin. *Count Albertus*)

As shown in Table 6.23, the adverb *dead* is preferred with elements which have negative semantic prosody (56.25% of the total), such as *dead drunk*. Neutral semantic prosody, as in *dead asleep*, *dead coloured* and *dead still*, accounts for the remaining 43.75%, and there are no occurrences of the adverb combined with positive polarity items.

Finally, *dead* is found in the database as both a modifier of adjectives and of participial forms (cf. Table 6.24), showing a stronger preference for the latter items (62.50%) over the former (37.50%).

The last of the sources consulted was NCF, which recorded a considerably higher number of occurrences of *dead* (adj.): a total of 2,074 tokens in 360 collocations (cf. Table 6.25). In fact, many of these collocations are recorded less than three times in the database, hence the wide

Table 6.23. Semantic prosody for *dead* (adv.) in ECF

| | **Abs. Freq.** | **%** | **NF** |
|---|---|---|---|
| **neg** | 9 | 56.25 | 0.93 |
| **neu** | 7 | 43.75 | 0.72 |
| **Total** | **16** | **100.00** | **1.65** |

Table 6.24. Categories modified by *dead* (adv.) in ECF

| | **Abs. Freq.** | **%** | **NF** |
|---|---|---|---|
| **Adj.** | 6 | 37.50 | 0.62 |
| **Part.** | 10 | 62.50 | 1.03 |
| **Total** | **16** | **100.00** | **1.65** |

Table 6.25. Absolute and normalised frequencies for the most frequent collocations of *dead* (adj.) in NCF

| Collocation | Abs. Freq. | NF |
|---|---|---|
| *dead body* | 201 | 5.35 |
| *dead boy* | 12 | 0.32 |
| *dead branch* | 11 | 0.29 |
| *dead brother* | 15 | 0.40 |
| *dead calm* | 34 | 0.90 |
| *dead certainty* | 13 | 0.35 |
| *dead child* | 36 | 0.96 |
| *dead corpse* | 11 | 0.29 |
| *dead dog* | 18 | 0.48 |
| *dead face* | 32 | 0.85 |
| *dead father* | 44 | 1.17 |
| *dead friend* | 40 | 1.06 |
| *dead hand* | 18 | 0.48 |
| *dead horse* | 14 | 0.37 |
| *dead hour* | 18 | 0.48 |
| *dead husband* | 19 | 0.51 |
| *dead language* | 21 | 0.56 |
| *dead leaf* | 78 | 2.08 |
| *dead lock* | 22 | 0.59 |
| *dead loss* | 12 | 0.32 |
| *dead love* | 11 | 0.29 |
| *dead man* | 376 | 10.00 |
| *dead mother* | 32 | 0.85 |
| *dead parent* | 11 | 0.29 |
| *dead pause* | 23 | 0.61 |
| *dead people* | 13 | 0.35 |
| *dead shot* | 11 | 0.29 |

(*continued*)

Table 6.25. Continued

| Collocation | Abs. Freq. | NF |
|---|---|---|
| *dead silence* | 181 | 4.82 |
| *dead son* | 12 | 0.32 |
| *dead stick* | 10 | 0.27 |
| *dead stop* | 22 | 0.59 |
| *dead thing* | 16 | 0.43 |
| *dead wife* | 14 | 0.37 |
| *dead woman* | 31 | 0.82 |

variety of collocations. Being an adjective, *dead* is only found as a modifier of nouns. Table 6.25 presents the most frequent collocations *dead* (adj.) in the data, while Table 6.26 shows the standardised scores for the most frequent collocations, that is, those which were attested at least ten times. The individual standardised scores for these combinations (cf. Table 6.26) show that only certain collocations can be considered as highly statistically significant: *dead body*, *dead branch*, *dead calm*, *dead certainty*, *dead corpse*, *dead dog*, *dead language*, *dead leaf*, *dead lock*, *dead pause*, *dead shot*, *dead silence*, *dead stick* and *dead stop*.

The most prominent collocations of *dead* in the data are the ones mentioned above, in the light of the measures from the *z*-score, the Mutual Information (*MI*) and its version to the power of three (*MI3*) and the log-likelihood tests. In turn, the association of *dead* with other collocates was not found to be so strong. In the case of *dead boy*, *dead hand*, *dead love*, *dead people* and *dead son*, for instance, only the *MI3* value reached the cut-off point, while the other statistical tests gave negative results. For the remaining collocations, the results also seemed contradictory. For *dead brother*, for example, the log-likelihood test is significant only at $p < 0.05$, and the *MI* value indicates that it is not a significant collocation. *MI* is also the only value which differs from the other three in regard to the collocations *dead child*, *dead face*, *dead father*, *dead friend*, *dead horse*, *dead husband*, *dead loss*, *dead man*, *dead mother*, *dead parent* and *dead woman*, as this score suggests a non-significant correlation between the node and the

Table 6.26. Standardised scores for *dead* (adj.) in NCF

| Collocation | *z*-score | *MI* | *MI3* | *LL*-value |
|---|---|---|---|---|
| *dead body* | 94.857 | 5.547 | 20.849 | 1,156.583 ($p < 0.0001$) |
| *dead boy* | 1.185 | 0.491 | 7.661 | 1.245 ($p > 0.05$) |
| *dead branch* | 11.106 | 3.716 | 10.634 | 36.395 ($p < 0.0001$) |
| *dead brother* | 2.901 | 1.057 | 8.871 | 6.400 ($p < 0.05$) |
| *dead calm* | 26.184 | 4.467 | 14.642 | 145.967 ($p < 0.0001$) |
| *dead certainty* | 16.849 | 4.573 | 11.973 | 57.638 ($p < 0.0001$) |
| *dead child* | 7.546 | 1.671 | 12.167 | 35.924 ($p < 0.0001$) |
| *dead corpse* | 18.180 | 5.001 | 11.920 | 55.105 ($p < 0.0001$) |
| *dead dog* | 10.165 | 2.928 | 11.268 | 41.837 ($p < 0.0001$) |
| *dead face* | 4.566 | 1.135 | 11.135 | 15.503 ($p < 0.0001$) |
| *dead father* | 6.281 | 1.320 | 12.238 | 27.767 ($p < 0.0001$) |
| *dead friend* | 4.860 | 1.083 | 11.727 | 17.830 ($p < 0.0001$) |
| *dead hand* | -1.575 | -0.532 | 7.807 | 2.784 ($p > 0.05$) |
| *dead horse* | 3.083 | 1.157 | 8.772 | 7.021 ($p < 0.01$) |
| *dead hour* | 2.403 | 0.807 | 9.147 | 4.713 ($p < 0.05$) |
| *dead husband* | 5.217 | 1.637 | 10.133 | 17.355 ($p < 0.0001$) |
| *dead language* | 13.985 | 3.489 | 12.273 | 63.396 ($p < 0.0001$) |
| *dead leaf* | 128.065 | 7.730 | 20.300 | 688.840 ($p < 0.0001$) |
| *dead lock* | 20.590 | 4.408 | 13.326 | 92.704 ($p < 0.0001$) |
| *dead loss* | 8.128 | 2.882 | 10.052 | 27.226 ($p < 0.0001$) |
| *dead love* | -0.641 | -0.278 | 6.640 | 0.438 ($p > 0.05$) |
| *dead man* | 45.860 | 2.899 | 20.008 | 860.957 ($p < 0.0001$) |
| *dead mother* | 4.915 | 1.217 | 11.217 | 17.532 ($p < 0.0001$) |
| *dead parent* | 7.669 | 2.850 | 9.769 | 24.537 ($p < 0.0001$) |
| *dead pause* | 16.569 | 3.793 | 12.840 | 78.399 ($p < 0.0001$) |
| *dead people* | 0.788 | 0.315 | 7.716 | 0.576 ($p > 0.05$) |
| *dead shot* | 8.650 | 3.119 | 10.038 | 28.131 ($p < 0.0001$) |
| *dead silence* | 89.025 | 5.516 | 20.516 | 1,033.918 ($p < 0.0001$) |

(*continued*)

Table 6.26. Continued

| Collocation | *z*-score | *MI* | *MI3* | *LL*-value |
|---|---|---|---|---|
| *dead son* | 1.674 | 0.690 | 7.860 | 2.359 (p > 0.05) |
| *dead stick* | 8.052 | 3.064 | 9.708 | 24.903 (p < 0.0001) |
| *dead stop* | 13.869 | 3.413 | 12.331 | 64.306 (p < 0.0001) |
| *dead thing* | -1.082 | -0.389 | 7.611 | 1.277 (p > 0.05) |
| *dead wife* | 1.219 | 0.468 | 8.083 | 1.326 (p > 0.05) |
| *dead woman* | 3.581 | 0.913 | 10.821 | 10.160 (p < 0.01) |

collocate. The discrepancies between these four values owe to the weight that each of them attributes to individual frequencies. Thus, as suggested in Section 5.3.2, the main drawback of the *MI* test is that it tends to give too much weight to low-frequency items. In the case of the current data, the highest *MI* score (*dead leaf*) coincides with the collocate of *dead* with the lowest token frequency, the noun *leaf*, which occurs 754 times in NCF. In turn, the lowest *MI* scores coincide with nouns such as *hand* or *friend*, which have high token frequencies (53,459 and 38,742 occurrences in NCF, respectively). In this respect, the *MI3* test is regarded as a more reliable test in a collocational analysis.

As for the types of meanings of the adjective *dead* in the database (cf. Table 6.27), descriptive readings account for the overwhelming majority of the examples (76.23%), followed by subjective (16.49%) and intensifying meanings (7.28%).

Table 6.27. Meaning types for *dead* (adj.) in NCF

| | **Abs. Freq.** | **%** | **NF** |
|---|---|---|---|
| **D** | 1,581 | 76.23 | 42.06 |
| **S** | 342 | 16.49 | 9.10 |
| **I** | 151 | 7.28 | 4.02 |
| **Total** | **2,074** | **100.00** | **55.17** |

A selection of these different meanings is given in (6.94)–(6.99). *Dead coral* in (6.94) illustrates a descriptive or literal reading of the adjective, since it describes the state of corals, which die over time and eventually give way to coral sand.

(6.94) *Again, in other spots the ceaseless lashing of the sea had broken the* ***dead*** *coral in pieces, and cast it up in the form of sand.* (1858. Robert Michael Ballantyne. *The coral island*)

Conversely, the meanings in (6.95)–(6.96) are subjective. The town described in (6.95) is said to be dead, that is, it is a town which is not prosperous, lacks business activities and is uninteresting and uneventful. A literal meaning is not entirely appropriate in this case, for the place in question may still be inhabited. However, the absence of activity or the very scarce commercial life in the town may remind of death-related properties. On this account, this specific collocation was marked as subjective, for it somehow implies the speaker's negative affect. Death-related features, specifically tranquillity and peacefulness, may also be attributed to the example in (6.96). It is said here that the storm broke as soon as Rowland helmed the boat, as before that moment the sea conditions had not been choppy at all.

(6.95) *It has been a* ***dead*** *town for twenty year, and twenty to the end o't.* (1901. George Douglas Brown. *The House with the Green Shutters*)

(6.96) *During the foregoing occurrences a* ***dead*** *calm prevailed. But as Rowland sprang to the helm, [...] a roar like a volley of ordnance was heard aloft,* (1839–1840. William Harrison Ainsworth. *Jack Sheppard. A romance*)

Examples (6.97)–(6.99), by contrast, show intensifying meanings, in which *dead* is understood as expressive of high or maximum degree. *Dead certainty*, *dead stop* and *dead flat* are hence equivalent to 'complete certainty', 'complete stop' and 'complete flatness'.

(6.97) *The host of the Saracen's Head opportunely appeared at this moment, [...] to back his entreaties with a variety of dismal conjectures regarding the state of the roads, [...] the* ***dead*** *certainty of its raining all night, [...] and other topics of inducement familiar to innkeepers.* (1837. Charles Dickens. *The Posthumous Papers of the Pickwick Club*)

(6.98) *'No,' said Ralph, coming to a* ***dead*** *stop, and clasping his hands more tightly behind him. 'I can't say it.'* (1839. Charles Dickens. *The Life and Adventures of Nicholas Nickleby*)

(6.99) *The house is situated on a* ***dead*** *flat, and seems to be shut in---almost suffocated, to my north-country notions, by trees.* (1860. Wilkie Collins. *The woman in white*)

In what concerns semantic prosody (see Table 6.28), *dead* is recorded as a modifier of nouns with neutral semantic prosody in the vast majority of its attestations in the data (96.43%), while negative and positive semantic prosody are scarce, amounting only to 2.61% and 0.96%, respectively. Collocations with neutral semantic prosody include, for instance, *dead calm, dead hand, dead machine, dead animal, dead face, dead leaf* and *dead stop*. *Dead obstinacy, dead palsy, dead faint, dead loss, dead malefactor* and *dead knave* have been marked as showing negative semantic prosody, while the nouns *glory, love, passion, hero* and *majesty* were classified as illustrative of positive semantic prosody.

In contrast to the adjective, adverbial *dead* is far less frequent in the nineteenth-century data, with 185 examples in 37 different collocations. Many of these, in fact, occur less than three times in the data. For this reason, and for convenience purposes, Table 6.29 displays exclusively those collocations of the adverb which occur at least five times, and Table 6.30 gives the standardised scores for these collocations.[8] As suggested by these

Table 6.28. Semantic prosody for *dead* (adj.) in NCF

| | **Abs. Freq.** | **%** | **NF** |
|---|---|---|---|
| **neg** | 54 | 2.61 | 1.44 |
| **neu** | 2,000 | 96.43 | 53.02 |
| **pos** | 20 | 0.96 | 0.72 |
| **Total** | **2,074** | **100.00** | **55.17** |

8 The collocation *dead still*, which also occurred five times in NCF, was not counted for statistical purposes, given that the collocate *still* can also be an adverb, in addition to an adjective, the relevant function of *still* here. As a consequence, the absolute frequency for the collocation *dead still* is very high in the data (31,640 occurrences) and it is beyond the scope of the present research to separate the adverbial from the adjectival uses of *still*.

Table 6.29. Absolute and normalised frequencies for the most frequent collocations of *dead* (adv.) in NCF

| **Collocation** | **Abs. Freq.** | **NF** |
|---|---|---|
| *dead against* | 48 | 1.28 |
| *dead asleep* | 9 | 0.24 |
| *dead beat* | 26 | 0.69 |
| *dead drunk* | 16 | 0.43 |
| *dead lame* | 5 | 0.13 |
| *dead sick* | 8 | 0.21 |
| *dead silent* | 8 | 0.21 |
| *dead sleepy* | 6 | 0.16 |
| *dead tired* | 13 | 0.35 |

Table 6.30. Standardised scores for *dead* (adv.) in NCF

| **Collocation** | ***z*-score** | ***MI*** | ***MI3*** | ***LL*-value** |
|---|---|---|---|---|
| *dead against* | 11.836 | 2.234 | 13.404 | 73.154 ($p < 0.0001$) |
| *dead asleep* | 7.358 | 2.980 | 9.320 | 21.485 ($p < 0.0001$) |
| *dead beat* | 24.358 | 4.631 | 14.032 | 117.308 ($p < 0.0001$) |
| *dead drunk* | 20.818 | 4.861 | 12.861 | 77.125 ($p < 0.0001$) |
| *dead lame* | 11.622 | 4.857 | 9.501 | 24.078 ($p < 0.0001$) |
| *dead sick* | 5.983 | 2.659 | 8.659 | 16.040 ($p < 0.0001$) |
| *dead silent* | 2.707 | 1.333 | 7.333 | 5.136 ($p < 0.05$) |
| *dead sleepy* | 13.705 | 5.056 | 10.226 | 30.510 ($p < 0.0001$) |
| *dead tired* | 10.020 | 3.266 | 10.667 | 35.610 ($p < 0.0001$) |

results, *dead beat*, *dead drunk*, *dead lame*, *dead sleepy* and *dead tired* are all highly statistically significant according to the four values. For *dead silent*, however, the log-likelihood test indicates that the collocation is statistically significant, though at $p < 0.05$, and the *MI* test shows a non-significant value. The *MI* also differs from the other scores in the case of the collocations *dead against*, *dead asleep* and *dead sick*, for which it yields a low level of significance (slightly lower than the cut-off point, 3).

As shown in Table 6.31, the adverb *dead* occurs predominantly with subjective and intensifying meanings, while those which are ambiguous between descriptive and subjective amount only to about 1%.

An illustrative selection of these meanings types is provided in examples (6.100)–(6.104). *Dead sick* in (6.100) was marked as ambiguous between descriptive and subjective, for it is unclear whether the character fell ill afterwards or was only momentarily indisposed. By contrast, in *dead tired* (6.101) the original meaning of the adverb can still be traced. Being dead tired, although not necessarily leading to one's death, may certainly recall states close to death, which explains why this collocation was labelled as subjective. The collocation *dead sick* in (6.102) clearly differs from that in (6.100). The persons referred to here are not feeling unwell, but rather tired of each other. In other words, husband and wife have had enough of each other and they split up. Therefore, a literal meaning of *dead sick* in this case is not possible. Instead *dead* functions in this instance as an intensifier with a more general meaning: 'very, extremely tired of him'. The same reading applies to the adverb in (6.103) and (6.104), in which *dead against* could be read as 'completely opposed to' and *dead trivial* as 'extremely, very trivial'.

(6.100) *But Grimsby had much skill and little scruple, and whether he took advantage of the other's trembling, blinded eagerness to deal unfairly by him, I cannot undertake to say; but Lowborough lost again, and fell* ***dead*** *sick.* (1848. Anne Brontë. *The Tenant of Wildfell Hall*)

Table 6.31. Meaning types for *dead* (adv.) in NCF

| | Abs. Freq. | % | NF |
|---|---|---|---|
| D/S | 2 | 1.08 | 0.05 |
| S | 98 | 52.97 | 2.61 |
| I | 85 | 45.95 | 2.26 |
| **Total** | **185** | **100.00** | **4.92** |

(6.101) *I am **dead** tired. I shall sleep now; and perhaps never waken. But this letter, at all events, will reach you.* (1887. William Francis Barry. *The New Antigone*)

(6.102) *She had got **dead** sick of me, and I had got of her. It never did seem natural like.* (1894. George Moore. *Esther Waters*)

(6.103) *But I know Mr. Brock. If I can't satisfy him about her family when I write to tell him of this (which of course I must do), he will be **dead** against the whole thing.* (1866. Wilkie Collins. *Armadale*)

(6.104) *He was an honest fellow enough; but not perfect; he would not go to bed, and would sit on the edge of it [...] laughing and crying at the same circumstances, which were [...] only **dead** trivial.* (1861. Charles Hearth. *The Cloister and the Hearth*)

In the light of the nineteenth-century data, the adverb *dead* is preferred with neutral and negative semantic prosody (55.68% and 41.08%, respectively), although it is also found as a modifier of inherently positive elements (3.24%) (cf. Table 6.32). *Cold, asleep, still, silent* and *set* feature among the collocates with neutral semantic prosody, whereas the collocations *dead drunk, dead tired, dead beat, dead trivial* and *dead sick* were counted as illustrative of negative semantic prosody. Finally, only the collocates *good* and *lame* were considered positive in NCF.

In what concerns the categories modified by *dead* (see Table 6.33), the results show that the adverb can modify a wide variety of elements, including adjectives, other adverbs (*dead astern, dead aback*), participial elements (*dead drunk*) and even prepositions (*dead against*) and prepositional phrases (*dead in earnest, dead on end*).

Table 6.32. Semantic prosody for *dead* (adv.) in NCF

| | **Abs. Freq.** | **%** | **NF** |
|---|---|---|---|
| **neg** | 76 | 41.08 | 2.02 |
| **neu** | 103 | 55.68 | 2.74 |
| **pos** | 6 | 3.24 | 0.16 |
| **Total** | **185** | **100.00** | **4.92** |

Table 6.33. Categories modified by *dead* (adv.) in NCF

| | Abs. Freq. | % | NF |
|---|---|---|---|
| **Adj.** | 71 | 38.38 | 1.89 |
| **Adv.** | 6 | 3.24 | 0.16 |
| **Part.** | 60 | 32.43 | 1.60 |
| **Prep.** | 48 | 25.95 | 1.28 |
| **Total** | **185** | **100.00** | **4.92** |

### 6.2.2.1. *Dead* (adj. and adv.) across time

In Section 6.2.2, I discussed the corpus results for the adjective and adverb *dead* for the different periods individually. In turn, this section summarises the results for each of the variables (type of meaning and semantic prosody) in the different materials, with the aim of providing a comprehensive picture of the evolution of *dead* across time.[9] In order to trace the diachronic timeline for this form, each of the corpora and sources consulted was taken as representative of a given period: the ME component of the HC was considered to be illustrative of ME; EEBOCorp 1.0 was selected for EModE; ECF and NCF were used for LModE, in particular for the eighteenth and nineteenth centuries, respectively; finally, the twentieth-century British data from ARCHER served to illustrate the behaviour of the forms under analysis in PDE.

It should be recalled at this point that the analysis of the adjective and the adverb *dead* in the EModE data from EEBOCorp 1.0 differed methodologically from the study of the remaining forms in the other periods: due to its high token frequency (146,834 occurrences), a random sample was required for the analysis of *dead* in EModE, which was completed with an additional search of specific collocations (cf. Section 6.2.2). For this reason, in this section I merely give a summary of the main results for the adjective and adverb *dead* in the different materials consulted and the data

9 The variable 'types of words' modified by the adjective, however, will not be discussed here, since *dead* (adj.) always modify nouns and in that regard there is no variation across time.

will not be subject to statistical testing, as is done for the other forms in Sections 6.2.3.1 to 6.2.6.1.

The preliminary evidence from the OED and MED discussed in Section 6.1.1 suggested that the adjective *dead* had in origin descriptive or literal meanings ('that has ceased to live; deprived of life'). This sense did not only apply to living organisms, but since ME could also refer to the soul, as in example (6.3). It is also from this period onwards that *dead* showed incipient subjectivity (cf. Section 3.3.3), with more metaphorical uses, for which a literal interpretation was no longer possible. In these early subjective occurrences, the adjective *dead* was typically found in contexts describing a pale complexion, quiet or still settings or hatred towards someone. In such cases, therefore, *dead* did not have a literal meaning, but expressed instead death-reminiscent values (cf. examples (6.6)–(6.10)). In the light of the dictionary data, intensifying meanings of the adjective did not emerge until the second half of the seventeenth century, as in the collocation *dead ripeness* in (6.11).

In view of the initial information provided by the OED and MED, therefore, the semantic development of the adjective *dead* seems to conform to Adamson's (2000: 55) cline of evolution for intensifiers (descriptive > affective/subjective > intensifying) (cf. Section 4.1.2), growing in subjectivity in the ME period and becoming reanalysed as an intensifier in the seventeenth century. The data from the other materials consulted for the adjective *dead* (cf. Table 6.34) corroborate this diachronic evolution only in part, as there are no subjective uses of the adjective *dead* in the earliest data from the HC and subjective *dead* only amounts to 5% of the total in the random sample from EEBOCorp 1.0 (10 occurrences). Furthermore, even though there are no intensifying occurrences in the random sample from EEBOCorp 1.0, this corpus provides one early instance of intensifying *dead*, its use in combination with the noun *flat*. This is example (6.83), in which *dead* does no longer admit a literal interpretation and is used instead to describe a region in the Netherlands which has very flat lands, being a synonym of *complete, absolute*.

Like its adjectival counterpart, the adverb *dead* seems to have followed a similar path of evolution in the light of the dictionary evidence (cf. Section 6.1.1), originating in descriptive or literal senses, developing increasingly

Table 6.34. Types of meanings for *dead* (adj.) in the data (absolute frequencies)

| | HC | EEBOCorp 1.0 | ECF | NCF | ARCHER |
|---|---|---|---|---|---|
| D | 45 | 189 | 261 | 1,581 | 70 |
| D/S | 0 | 0 | 0 | 0 | 1 |
| S | 0 | 10 | 22 | 342 | 3 |
| S/I | 0 | 0 | 0 | 0 | 2 |
| I | 0 | 0 | 7 | 151 | 0 |

subjectified uses over time, and becoming grammaticalised as a marker of degree in the late sixteenth century. The different corpora and electronic collections consulted to trace the diachrony of the adverb, however, provide limited evidence and, therefore, confirm this semantic cline of evolution only partially. As shown by the raw frequencies in Table 6.35, there are no occurrences of the adverb in the early data from the HC, and the results from the random sample from EEBOCorp 1.0 gave only two tokens of the collocation *dead drunk*, with a subjective meaning. The process of subjectification of *dead* over time, therefore, cannot be fully supported with these scanty data. However, the additional search of collocations carried out in EEBOCorp 1.0 revealed some early uses of intensifying *dead*, as proved by the collocations *dead right* and *dead sure*, in examples (6.84)–(6.86). Interestingly, one of such instances is dated earlier than the first alleged occurrence given by the OED. This is example (6.85), in which *dead sure* can be paraphrased as *completely sure* or *very sure*.

Table 6.35. Types of meanings for *dead* (adv.) in the data (absolute frequencies)

| | HC | EEBOCorp 1.0 | ECF | NCF | ARCHER |
|---|---|---|---|---|---|
| D | 0 | 0 | 0 | 0 | 0 |
| D/S | 0 | 0 | 0 | 2 | 0 |
| S | 0 | 2 | 16 | 98 | 0 |
| S/I | 0 | 0 | 0 | 0 | 0 |
| I | 0 | 0 | 0 | 85 | 1 |

In the eighteenth-century data from ECF, *dead* only shows subjective uses (e.g. in collocations such as *dead drunk*, *dead coloured* and *dead still*), while in NCF subjective uses of *dead* amount to 52.97% and intensifying *dead* represents 45.95% of the total. The data from ARCHER is extremely scarce, with just one occurrence of the collocation *dead serious*. All in all, in spite of the limited amount of examples yielded by the different materials, these have provided clear evidence of the grammaticalised status of the adverb *dead* (cf. Section 3.1), as shown by its use in collocations such as *dead astern*, *dead aback*, *dead trivial*, *dead against*, *dead sure* or *dead right*, among others, for which a literal interpretation is utterly discarded.

### *6.2.3. The long diachrony of* deadly

The HC records a total of thirty-four occurrences of the adjective *deadly*, of which 26.5% correspond to OE (9 instances, NF 21.78), 50% to ME (17 tokens, NF27.93) and 23.5% to EModE (8 examples, NF 14.52). The normalised frequencies per period thus evince a rise in the use of *deadly* from OE to ME, and then a decline during the EModE period. The difference in the number of tokens between these periods is not statistically significant ($\chi^2$ (1) = 0.165; p = 0.68459424 between OE and ME, and $\chi^2$ (1) =1.832; p = 0.1758915 between ME and EModE).

Within this set of thirty-four examples, there are a total of twelve different collocations, namely *deadly enemy*, *deadly feud*, *deadly flesh*, *deadly foe*, *deadly grief*, *deadly lichama* ('body'), *deadly life*, *deadly lust*, *deadly man*, *deadly sin*, *deadly weapon* and *deadly world*, as shown in Table 6.36, which shows the individual frequencies for each of the collocations of the adjective *deadly* in the different periods.

As we can see in this table, there are certain collocates which seem to be specific to a given period, as is the case of *lichama* ('body'), *lust* and *world* in OE, of *foe* in ME, and of *feud*, *grief* and *weapon*, which are only recorded in EModE. However, there are other collocations which are documented across the different periods. Thus, *deadly flesh*, *deadly life* and *deadly man* appeared in both OE and ME, but are no longer recorded in EModE, while *deadly enemy* and *deadly sin* are first reported in ME in this corpus. The

Table 6.36. The collocations of *deadly* (adj.) in OE, ME and EModE

| | Collocation | Abs. Freq. | % | NF | Total in HC |
|---|---|---|---|---|---|
| OE | *deadly flesh* | 1 | 50.00 | 2.42 | 2 |
| | *deadly lichama* | 3 | 100.00 | 7.26 | 3 |
| | *deadly life* | 2 | 50.00 | 4.84 | 4 |
| | *deadly lust* | 1 | 100.00 | 2.42 | 1 |
| | *deadly man* | 1 | 50.00 | 2.42 | 2 |
| | *deadly world* | 1 | 100.00 | 2.42 | 1 |
| | **Total** | **9** | **26.47** | **21.78** | **34** |
| ME | *deadly enemy* | 1 | 33.33 | 1.64 | 3 |
| | *deadly flesh* | 1 | 50.00 | 1.64 | 2 |
| | *deadly foe* | 2 | 100.00 | 3.29 | 2 |
| | *deadly life* | 2 | 50.00 | 3.29 | 4 |
| | *deadly man* | 1 | 50.00 | 1.64 | 2 |
| | *deadly sin* | 10 | 76.92 | 16.43 | 13 |
| | **Total** | **17** | **50.00** | **27.93** | **34** |
| EModE | *deadly enemy* | 2 | 66.67 | 3.63 | 3 |
| | *deadly feud* | 1 | 100.00 | 1.81 | 1 |
| | *deadly grief* | 1 | 100.00 | 1.81 | 1 |
| | *deadly sin* | 3 | 23.08 | 5.44 | 13 |
| | *deadly weapon* | 1 | 100.00 | 1.81 | 1 |
| | **Total** | **8** | **23.53** | **14.52** | **34** |

difference for the two collocations between ME and EModE is, however, not statistically significant (for *deadly enemy*, Fisher's exact test = 0.607352; $p < 0.01$, and for *deadly sin* Fisher's exact test = 0.09745; $p < 0.01$).

As in the case of *dead* above (cf. Section 6.2.2), I have also run several statistical tests in order to measure the collocational strength of *deadly* and its collocates. I have only considered those collocations which were found in the corpus at least three times. Hence, the only collocations which could be subject to statistical testing were *deadly enemy* (three tokens), *deadly lichama* (three tokens), *deadly life* (four tokens) and *deadly sin* (thirteen

Table 6.37. Standardised scores for *deadly* (adj.) in the HC

| Collocation | *z*-score | *MI* | *MI3* | *LL*-value |
|---|---|---|---|---|
| *deadly enemy* | 46.838 | 9.518 | 12.688 | 33.656 |
| *deadly lichama* | 44.684 | 9.383 | 12.553 | 33.091 |
| *deadly life* | 22.360 | 6.988 | 10.988 | 30.830 |
| *deadly sin* | 91.785 | 9.344 | 16.745 | 142.685 |

tokens). In all four cases, the combination of the node *deadly* and its collocates was found to be highly statistically significant (cf. Table 6.37).

As far as meanings are concerned, the data from the HC seem to corroborate the evidence from the OED (cf. Section 6.1.2), given that subjective readings of *deadly* (adj.) are also recorded for the first time in the ME period, although the percentage is still relatively low, amounting to barely 17% (see Table 6.38). This percentage increases 33% from ME to EModE (from roughly 17% to 50%), which is also reflected in the normalised frequencies, with a difference of 2.33 points. Descriptive meanings prevail in the three periods. These are in fact the only meanings available in OE, and they account for about 82% of the meanings in ME. Their percentage drops to 50% in EModE, which implies a difference of fifteen points between ME and EModE. Intensifying readings for the adjective *deadly*, however, are not attested in the HC, even though, it must be recalled, they have been documented in the language from the seventeenth century, as the OED suggests (see Section 6.1.2). The only difference which is statistically

Table 6.38. Meaning types for *deadly* (adj.) in the HC

| Period | D | | | S | | | I | | | Total | NF |
|---|---|---|---|---|---|---|---|---|---|---|---|
| | Abs. Freq. | % | NF | Abs. Freq. | % | NF | Abs. Freq. | % | NF | | |
| OE | 9 | 100.00 | 21.78 | 0 | 0.00 | 0 | 0 | 0.00 | 0 | 9 | 21.78 |
| ME | 14 | 82.35 | 23 | 3 | 17.65 | 4.93 | 0 | 0.00 | 0 | 17 | 27.93 |
| EModE | 4 | 50.00 | 7.26 | 4 | 50.00 | 7.26 | 0 | 0.00 | 0 | 8 | 14.52 |

significant is that concerning descriptive uses in ME and EModE, though at $p < 0.05$ (Fisher's exact test = 0.034533).

Example (6.105) shows a descriptive meaning of the adjective: lust is a sin and hence ruins the soul, being of a mortal nature, so the adjective *deadly* is to be taken literally here. Examples (6.106) and (6.107) illustrate, by contrast, subjective meanings of the adjective. *Deadly foe* in (6.106) refers to one's own enemy or adversary, that is, to somebody who seeks to do us wrong and perhaps wishes our own death. Example (6.107) is taken from a letter which Thomas More wrote to his daughter Margaret Roper, telling her that for him it is much more afflicting to see her and his son-in-law in a dangerous situation than to hear of his own death. Examples (6.106)–(6.107) can therefore not be taken in a literal sense, since hating somebody so much to the point of wishing his/her death does not imply killing him/her, and being overcome with intense sorrow does not necessarily entail someone's death either. Instead, death is construed here metaphorically, and so these meanings imply a stage further ahead than descriptive meanings in the cline towards the full grammaticalisation of *deadly*.

(6.105) *Ic was synna georn ond in* ***deaðlicum*** *listum.* (COMARTYR. 950–1050. *Martyrology*)

(6.106) *Hwa durste slepen hwil his* ***deadliche*** *fa heolde an itohe sweord up on his heaued?* (CMANCRE. 1150–1250. *Ancrene Wisse*)

(6.107) *A* ***deadly*** *grief vnto me, and moch more deadly than to here of mine owne death,* [...] *is that I perceiue my good sonne your husband, and you my good doughter* [...] *in great displeasure and daunger of great harme therby.* (CEPRIV1. 1500–1570. Elizabeth Beaumont. *Beaumont papers*)

Regarding the functions of the adjective *deadly*, the data from the HC also show that it has exclusively functioned as a noun modifier across time, as might be expected from an adjective (cf. Table 6.39).

Further to the semantic prosody of the adjective (cf. Table 6.40), it seems that *deadly* developed predominantly negative semantic prosody at the close of the OE period. In fact, in this early period *deadly* occurred primarily in combination with elements which had neutral semantic prosody, as is the case of the nouns *man*, *life*, *lichama* ('body') and *world*. However, it was also attested in the data with the noun *lust*, which is inherently negative, and with the noun *flesh*, which although it has been classified as

Table 6.39. Categories modified by *deadly* (adj.) in the HC

| Period | N | | Total | NF |
|---|---|---|---|---|
| | Abs. Freq. | NF | | |
| OE | 9 | 21.78 | 9 | 21.78 |
| ME | 17 | 27.93 | 17 | 27.93 |
| EModE | 8 | 14.52 | 8 | 14.52 |

neutral, in the context of religion we tend to contrast the soul, which is good, with the flesh, which represents evil and sin, and is hence immoral. Nonetheless, *deadly* occurs with neutral items in almost 90% of the cases in the OE data. It is only in ME and EModE that this adjective starts to collocate with nouns which have negative polarity, such as *sin*, *enemy*, *foe*, *feud* and *grief*. Moreover, the increase in the absolute frequencies for negative semantic prosody from the OE to the ME period turns out to be statistically significant at $p < 0.05$ (Fisher's exact test = 0.011749). The drop in the number of tokens from ME to EModE is, by contrast, not statistically significant, and neither is this difference statistically significant if we compare OE with ME and ME with EModE in regard to neutral semantic prosody.

As regards the adverbial form, the HC hardly yields any evidence of *deadly* (adv.): there are no examples dating to OE, and there are a total of three instances in the remaining periods (cf. Table 6.41), one in ME (33.33%, NF 1.64) and two in EModE (66.67%, NF 3.63). This slight increase in the

Table 6.40. Semantic prosody of *deadly* (adj.) in the HC

| Period | Neg | | | Pos | | | Neu | | | Total | NF |
|---|---|---|---|---|---|---|---|---|---|---|---|
| | Abs. Freq. | % | NF | Abs. Freq. | % | NF | Abs. Freq. | % | NF | | |
| OE | 1 | 11.11 | 2.42 | 0 | 0.00 | 0 | 8 | 88.89 | 19.36 | 9 | 21.78 |
| ME | 13 | 76.47 | 21.36 | 0 | 0.00 | 0 | 4 | 23.53 | 6.57 | 17 | 27.93 |
| EModE | 7 | 87.5 | 12.70 | 0 | 0.00 | 0 | 1 | 12.5 | 0 | 8 | 14.52 |

Table 6.41. Absolute frequencies, percentages and normalised frequencies of *deadly* (adv.) in the HC

| Period | Abs. Freq. | % | NF |
|---|---|---|---|
| ME | 1 | 33.33 | 1.64 |
| EModE | 2 | 66.67 | 3.63 |

use of *deadly* from ME to EModE, however, is not statistically significant (Fisher's exact test = 0.607352).

The three examples recorded in the corpus show a different collocation each, namely the combination of the adverb with the participial forms *idoruen* ('hurt') and *wounded* and the verb *wound*.

The occurrences in this corpus indicate descriptive readings, that is, meanings which are to be taken literally, as in (6.108)–(6.109). Example (6.108), for instance, describes a situation in which the Earl of Kent was severely wounded in the head, dying shortly after as a result of this injury. In (6.109) we are told that some elephants fight with each other, and, as a consequence, some members of the herd die. In the corpus data, therefore, there is no evidence of subjective or intensifying readings of the adverb, although it should be reminded here that by the early fifteenth century the adverb *deadly* had already developed intensifying meanings, and therefore subjective meanings as well, according to the OED (cf. Section 6.1.2).

(6.108) *But in the wynnynge therof he was so* ***deedly*** *wounded with an arowe in ye heed that he dyed shortly after* (CEHIST1B. Robert Fabyan. 1500–1570. *The new chronicles of England and France*)

(6.109) *Elephants royall* [...] *some fight one with another, wounding one another very* ***deadly***, (CETRAV2B. Robert Coverte. 1612. *A true and almost incredible report of an Englishman*)

Concerning the semantic prosody of the adverb (Table 6.42), and despite the scarcity of data, adverbial *deadly* occurs in the corpus only with elements which have negative semantic prosody: the verb *wound* and the derived participial *wounded* are inherently negative, and this is also the case of the ME participle *idoruen*, which also meant 'hurt, wounded'. Finally, the three examples in this corpus also suggest the greater variability of adverbs in comparison with adjectives. Thus, adverbial *deadly* is found as a modifier

Table 6.42. The semantic prosody of *deadly* (adv.) in the HC

| Period | Neg | | | Pos | | | Neu | | | Total |
|---|---|---|---|---|---|---|---|---|---|---|
| | Abs. Freq. | % | NF | Abs. Freq. | % | NF | Abs. Freq. | % | NF | |
| ME | 1 | 33.33 | 1.64 | 0 | 0.00 | 0 | 0 | 0.00 | 0 | 1 |
| EModE | 2 | 66.67 | 3.63 | 0 | 0.00 | 0 | 0 | 0.00 | 0 | 2 |

of participial forms and verbs in the corpus (cf. Table 6.43), whereas the adjective *deadly* could only modify nouns.

In view of the data presented in this section, it appears that the adjective *deadly* was much more frequent than the homonymous adverbial form in the HC, although the results only partially confirm the evidence provided by the historical dictionaries. The corpus data bear out the preliminary picture provided by the MED and OED, in the sense that subjective readings for the adjective *deadly* are recorded from the outset of the ME period, while in OE the only available meanings were descriptive. Nonetheless, and despite the valuable information provided by the HC, there are no examples in the corpus which admit a possible reading of the adjective as an intensifier, while according to the OED the intensifying function of the adjective dates back at least to the seventeenth century. The evidence for the adverbial form *deadly* in the corpus is very scarce, with only three tokens, which hardly allows to draw any corpus-based conclusion about its uses in the periods examined. In the light of the dictionary evidence the adverb *deadly* had developed intensifying readings considerably earlier than its adjectival homonym, since it could occur as an intensifier already

Table 6.43. Categories modified by *deadly* (adv.) in the HC

| Period | P | | | V | | | Total | NF |
|---|---|---|---|---|---|---|---|---|
| | Abs. Freq. | % | NF | Abs. Freq. | % | NF | | |
| ME | 1 | 33.33 | 1.64 | 0 | 0.00 | 0 | 1 | 1.64 |
| EModE | 1 | 33.33 | 1.81 | 1 | 33.33 | 1.81 | 2 | 3.63 |

in the fourteenth century (cf. example (6.35)). However, the HC only gives evidence of descriptive readings for *deadly*.

As far as the data from ARCHER is concerned, there are a total of eighteen tokens of the adjective *deadly*, distributed along the seventeenth, eighteenth and nineteenth centuries; no occurrences of *deadly* (adj.) have been attested in the twentieth-century material in the corpus. As shown in Table 6.44, over half of the occurrences of *deadly* are found in the nineteenth century (about 67%), while the remaining examples are evenly distributed between the seventeenth and eighteenth centuries

Table 6.44. The collocations of *deadly* (adj.) in the 17th, 18th and 19th c. in ARCHER

| | **Collocation** | **Abs. Freq.** | % | **NF** | **Total in ARCHER** |
|---|---|---|---|---|---|
| **17th c.** | *deadly burden* | 1 | 100.00 | 2.87 | **1** |
| | *deadly feud* | 1 | 100.00 | 2.87 | **1** |
| | *deadly sin* | 1 | 100.00 | 2.87 | **1** |
| | **Total** | **3** | **16.67** | **8.61** | **18** |
| **18th c.** | *deadly thing* | 1 | 100.00 | 1.87 | 1 |
| | *deadly wound* | 2 | 100.00 | 3.73 | 2 |
| | **Total** | **3** | **16.67** | **5.60** | **18** |
| **19th c.** | *deadly character* | 1 | 100.00 | 1.84 | 1 |
| | *deadly conflict* | 1 | 100.00 | 1.84 | 1 |
| | *deadly expression* | 1 | 100.00 | 1.84 | 1 |
| | *deadly fear* | 2 | 100.00 | 3.69 | 2 |
| | *deadly grapple* | 1 | 100.00 | 1.84 | 1 |
| | *deadly nature* | 1 | 100.00 | 1.84 | 1 |
| | *deadly pen* | 1 | 100.00 | 1.84 | 1 |
| | *deadly poison* | 2 | 100.00 | 3.69 | 2 |
| | *deadly vapour* | 1 | 100.00 | 1.84 | 1 |
| | *deadly weakeness* | 1 | 100.00 | 1.84 | 1 |
| | **Total** | **12** | **66.67** | **22.12** | **18** |

(16% each). In the light of the data presented in these tables, it also appears that the frequency of *deadly* has increased exponentially from the eighteenth to the nineteenth century, in terms of both absolute (from three to twelve tokens) and normalised frequencies (5.60 vs 22.12). This difference is in fact statistically significant at $p < 0.05$ (Fisher's exact test = 0.035208). Moreover, there is not a clear pattern in the evolution of each of the collocates of the adjective *deadly* in the corpus, since the token frequency for all of them is actually very low, and they are only found at individual periods. By way of exemplification, *deadly burden* is only attested in the seventeenth century, *deadly thing* in the eighteenth century, and the collocations *deadly fear* and *deadly poison* only appear in the nineteenth century. Furthermore, since none of the collocations of *deadly* is attested a minimum of three times in the corpus, I have decided not to apply any of the statistical tests, given that some of these tests, such as the simple mutual information score (*MI*), would give too much weight to some of these low-frequency collocations.

Table 6.45 shows the distribution of the different types of meanings of the adjective across time.

Table 6.45. Meaning types for *deadly* (adj.) in ARCHER

| | | D | D/S | S | Total |
|---|---|---|---|---|---|
| **17th c.** | # | 1 | 0 | 2 | 3 |
| | % | 10.00 | 0.00 | 28.57 | 16.67 |
| | **NF** | 2.87 | 0 | 5.74 | 8.61 |
| **18th c.** | # | 3 | 0 | 0 | 3 |
| | % | 30.00 | 0.00 | 0.00 | 16.67 |
| | **NF** | 5.60 | 0 | 0 | 5.60 |
| **19th c.** | # | 6 | 1 | 5 | 12 |
| | % | 60.00 | 100.00 | 71.43 | 66.66 |
| | **NF** | 11.06 | 1.84 | 9.22 | 22.12 |
| **Total (#)** | | **10** | **1** | **7** | **18** |

The results show that about 55% of the occurrences of *deadly* (adj.) show descriptive or literal readings (cf. example (6.110)) and roughly 39% are subjective, as in (6.111).

(6.110) *The* ***deadliest*** *poisons are those for which no test is known: there are poisons so destructive that a single drop insinuated into the veins produces death in three seconds,* [...] (1850robe_h6b. 1850. Frederick Robertson. *Sermons*)

(6.111) *I heard the remark I heard you make was something about the oddity of an individual going about London in* ***deadly*** *fear of a young man with spectacles?'* (1895mach_f6b. Arthur Machen. *The Three Imposters*)

Thus, the poison referred to in (6.110) is of a lethal nature and hence this collocation has been labelled as descriptive or literal. By contrast, example (6.111) is said to be subjective, since fear is not itself fatal. Moreover, there is also one instance (5.55%) which has been classified as ambiguous between descriptive and subjective, given here as (6.112).

(6.112) *Tisdal rasped the ponderous brass candlestick, and hurled it at the head of his treacherous entertainer. Deveril, by quickly stooping, escaped the missile* [...] *and in the next moment the two companions were locked together in desperate and* ***deadly*** *conflict.* (1847lefa_f5b. 1847. Joseph Le Fanu. *The Fortunes of Colonel Torlogh O'Brien*)

This example relates a fight between two characters, Tisdal and Deveril, in which the former violently throws a brass candlestick to the latter. In this example, therefore, the noun *conflict* is equivalent to a fight; so, considering Tisdal's reaction, it would be no surprise if the final outcome of the struggle was fatal. If we read on to find out what happened next, we discover that none of the two characters is dead. However, the meaning of *deadly* here is ambiguous, because a fight can effectively end up in someone being killed as a result, even though this is not the case in the end. In other words, although it is true that we do have a struggle between two characters and that the violence is real, the fight has no further consequences. In view of this, I have opted for marking this particular example as indeterminate between a descriptive or literal meaning and a more subjective meaning. Unlike the adjective *dead*, which was attested with meanings which were very close to those of intensifiers, and unlike the adverb *dead*, which occurred once in ARCHER with an intensifying meaning (cf. Section 6.2.2), adjectival *deadly* does not show borderline or properly intensifying meanings in the corpus. Even so, it should be noted that the percentage of subjective meanings of the adjective *deadly* in comparison with that of its zero counterpart *dead* in the same corpus is considerably higher: while in the case of *dead* the percentage of subjective readings amounted to roughly 4%, for *deadly* this percentage increases up to approximately 39%. Moreover, the difference between the three centuries in regard to both descriptive and subjective meanings is not statistically significant, according to the Fisher exact test values.[10]

In regard to the categories modified by the adjective *deadly* (cf. Table 6.46), all its collocates are nouns, as one would expect from any adjective in general.

The last variable considered is semantic prosody (cf. Table 6.47). As shown here, about 67% of the collocations of *deadly* in ARCHER have negative semantic prosody, while in the remaining 33% of the cases *deadly*, in combination with its collocates, shows neutral semantic prosody. Collocations such as *deadly conflict*, *deadly fear*, *deadly weakness* or *deadly wound* have been tagged as illustrative of negative semantic prosody. By contrast, collocations such as *deadly nature*, *deadly thing*, *deadly character* or *deadly expression* are said to represent neutral semantic prosody. Moreover, although there is an increase in the absolute frequency of both the negative and the neutral semantic prosody of the adjective over time, most

Table 6.46. Categories modified by *deadly* (adj.) in ARCHER

| **Period** | **N** | | **NF** |
|---|---|---|---|
| | **Abs. Freq.** | % | |
| **17th c.** | 3 | 16.67 | 8.61 |
| **18th c.** | 3 | 16.67 | 5.60 |
| **19th c.** | 12 | 66.66 | 22.12 |
| **Total** | **18** | **100.00** | **9.20** |

10 *Descriptive meanings*: Fisher's exact test = 1 (17th c. > 18th c.) and Fisher's exact test = 0.507888 (18th c. > 19th c.); *subjective meanings*: Fisher's exact test = 0.712204 (17th c. > 19th c.).

Table 6.47. The semantic prosody of *deadly* (adj.) in ARCHER

| | | Neg | Neu | Total |
|---|---|---|---|---|
| **17th c.** | # | 3 | 0 | 3 |
| | % | 25.00 | 0.00 | 16.67 |
| | **NF** | 8.61 | 0 | 8.61 |
| **18th c.** | # | 2 | 1 | 3 |
| | % | 16.67 | 16.67 | 16.67 |
| | **NF** | 3.73 | 1.87 | 5.60 |
| **19th c.** | # | 7 | 5 | 12 |
| | % | 58.33 | 83.33 | 66.67 |
| | **NF** | 12.9 | 9.22 | 22.12 |
| **Total (#)** | | **12** | **6** | **18** |

prominently from the eighteenth to the nineteenth century, this difference is not statistically significant, as proved by Fisher's exact test values.[11]

In line with its zero counterpart *dead* (cf. Section 6.2.2), the adverb *deadly* in ARCHER is not very frequent either, occurring only three times in the corpus, specifically in the collocations *deadly weary*, *deadly pale* and *deadly dull*, given in (6.113)–(6.115). In the three collocations, *deadly* functions as a modifier of adjectives.

(6.113) *Had our men not been so* ***deadly*** *weary, there was no reason we should not have taken Achi Baba from the Turks, who put up hardly any fight at all.* (1915hami_j7b. 1915. Ian Hamilton. *Gallipoli diary*)

(6.114) *'Well, I believe I am rather faint,' replied M. Bignon, whose features were* ***deadly*** *pale*; (1848kava_f5b. 1848. Julia Kavanagh. *A tale of Auvergne*)

(6.115) *Dined at Locke's. A very handsome dinner, but* ***deadly*** *dull company*; (1819moor_y5b.1819. Thomas Moore. *Diary of Thomas Moore*)

As far as the types of meanings are concerned (cf. Table 6.48), two of the occurrences have a subjective meaning (66.67%), namely (6.113) and (6.114),

11 *Negative semantic prosody*: Fisher's exact test = 0.388876 (17th c. > 18th c.), 0.179763 (18th c.> 19th c.); *neutral semantic prosody*: 0.218804 (18th c. > 19th c.).

Table 6.48. Meaning types for *deadly* (adv.) in ARCHER

| | | S | I | Total |
|---|---|---|---|---|
| **19th c.** | # | 1 | 1 | 2 |
| | % | 50.00 | 100.00 | 66.67 |
| | **NF** | 1.84 | 1.84 | 3.69 |
| **20th c.** | # | 1 | 0 | 1 |
| | % | 50.00 | 0.00 | 33.33 |
| | **NF** | 1.88 | 0 | 1.88 |
| **Total (#)** | | **2** | **1** | **3** |

while (6.115) has an intensifying meaning (33.33%). Thus, when one experiences tiredness or fatigue, (s)he can be in such a weak condition that (s)he can feel in a state close to death, as if (s)he was about to die. Pallor is also a state which is easily associated with a corpse and with death in general, and given the close ties between these conditions and death, I have marked the collocations in (6.113) and (6.114) as subjective. On the other hand, *deadly dull* has been classified as intensifying, for there is no connection between death and something being dull. *Dull* here means simply that the company is very boring. *Deadly*, therefore, functions as a general intensifier such as *very* or *extremely* and has lost its original literal meaning in this particular example.

In regard to semantic prosody (cf. Table 6.49), *deadly* is attested in ARCHER mainly with negative semantic prosody (two tokens, *deadly dull* and *deadly weary*, amounting to 66.67% of the total). The other example (33% of the total), showing the collocation *deadly pale*, shows neutral semantic prosody.

As regards the EModE data for *deadly* (adj.), EEBOCorp 1.0 returned 8,062 instances of the adjective and 485 different collocations. Table 6.50 shows the distribution of the adjective over the different periods in the corpus. The absolute frequencies indicate a sharp increase in the use of the adjective, especially in the transition from the second to the third period, and from the third to the fourth period, and then a drop in its use which

Table 6.49. The semantic prosody of *deadly* (adv.) in ARCHER

| | | Neg | Neu | Total |
|---|---|---|---|---|
| **19th c.** | # | 1 | 1 | 2 |
| | % | 50.00 | 100.00 | 66.67 |
| | NF | 1.84 | 1.84 | 3.69 |
| **20th c.** | # | 1 | 0 | 1 |
| | % | 50.00 | 0.00 | 33.33 |
| | NF | 1.88 | 0 | 1.88 |
| **Total (#)** | | **2** | **1** | **3** |

Table 6.50. *Deadly* (adj.) in EEBOCorp 1.0

| **Period** | **Abs. Freq.** | % | **NF (/1,000,000 words)** | **Total** |
|---|---|---|---|---|
| **I (1470s–1490s)** | 224 | 2.78 | 76.53 | 8,062 |
| **II (1500s–1540s)** | 320 | 3.97 | 31.25 | |
| **III (1550s–1590s)** | 1,859 | 23.06 | 25.35 | |
| **IV (1600s–1640s)** | 3,125 | 38.76 | 20.62 | |
| **V (1650s–1690s)** | 2,534 | 31.43 | 8.82 | |

coincides with the second half of the seventeenth century. The difference in use between the different periods is also statistically significant.[12]

Given the vast number of collocations, 485 in total, and for the sake of convenience, I will not display each of these on a table. Instead, I will give only those collocates of *deadly* with a minimum of 100 occurrences in the corpus. This list of collocates is provided in Table 6.51.

As shown here, in all the occurrences in the data *deadly* is found as a modifier of nouns, which is only natural taking into account that it is an adjective.

12 **P. I > P. II** $\chi^2$ (1) = 111.864; $p$ =0; **P. II > P. III** $\chi^2$ (1) = 11.787; $p$ = 0.00059646; **P. III > P. IV** $\chi^2$ (1) = 49.61; $p$ =0; **P. IV > P. V** $\chi^2$ (1) = 1071.016; $p$ = 0.

Table 6.51. Absolute and normalised frequencies for the most frequent collocates of *deadly* (adj.) in EEBOCorp 1.0

| **Collocate** | **Abs. Freq.** | **NF (/1,000,000 words)** |
|---|---|---|
| *deadly blow* | 252 | 0.48 |
| *deadly disease* | 134 | 0.26 |
| *deadly enemy* | 775 | 1.47 |
| *deadly feud* | 212 | 0.40 |
| *deadly foe* | 176 | 0.33 |
| *deadly hate* | 114 | 0.22 |
| *deadly hatred* | 274 | 0.52 |
| *deadly poison* | 659 | 1.25 |
| *deadly sin* | 1,452 | 2.76 |
| *deadly thing* | 109 | 0.21 |
| *deadly war* | 100 | 0.19 |
| *deadly wound* | 818 | 1.56 |

In order to know if the co-occurrence of *deadly* with these collocates is statistically significant and not to be attributed to chance, we need to obtain the standardised values (the *z*-score, the Mutual Information, the *MI3* and the Log-likelihood values), given here in Table 6.52, as was done above for the different forms in the HC and ARCHER.

Calculating these standardised values, however, implies a major drawback in the case of EEBOCorp 1.0, since in order to obtain them we need to know not only the token frequency of *deadly* in the corpus, but also the raw frequencies for each of its collocates. Computing the raw frequencies for any of the collocates of *deadly* should not be a problem with any concordancer and might seem, at first sight, rather straightforward, but this is, however, not the case here. *Blow*, *disease*, *hate*, *poison*, *sin*, *war* and *wound* can also be verbs. Therefore, we would have to filter these raw frequencies and separate the verbal forms from the nominal counterparts. By way of illustration, *blow* (including alternative spellings and plural forms) occurs over 27,000 times in EEBOCorp 1.0; *disease* is found over 57,000 times; there are over 175,000 tokens of *enemy* (and variants) in the corpus,

Table 6.52. Standardised scores for *deadly* (adj.) in EEBOCorp 1.0

| Collocation | *z*-score | *MI* | *MI3* | *LL*-value |
|---|---|---|---|---|
| *deadly blow* | 208.222 | 7.443 | 23.398 | 2,101.486 ($p < 0.0001$) |
| *deadly disease* | 75.066 | 5.460 | 19.593 | 752.726 ($p < 0.0001$) |
| *deadly enemy* | 251.083 | 6.381 | 25.577 | 5,327.355 ($p < 0.0001$) |
| *deadly feud* | 1,384.891 | 13.144 | 28.599 | 3,561.997 ($p < 0.0001$) |
| *deadly foe* | 157.556 | 7.160 | 22.079 | 1,398.791 ($p < 0.0001$) |
| *deadly hate* | 84.629 | 6.018 | 19.684 | 726.990 ($p < 0.0001$) |
| *deadly hatred* | 244.981 | 7.788 | 23.984 | 2,415.935 ($p < 0.0001$) |
| *deadly poison* | 1,085.205 | 10.805 | 29.533 | 8,618.170 ($p < 0.0001$) |
| *deadly sin* | 469.068 | 7.262 | 28.270 | 11,744.935 ($p < 0.0001$) |
| *deadly thing* | 17.116 | 2.158 | 15.695 | 156.976 ($p < 0.0001$) |
| *deadly war* | 30.003 | 3.448 | 16.735 | 296.314 ($p < 0.0001$) |
| *deadly wound* | 524.372 | 8.401 | 27.753 | 7,910.653 ($p < 0.0001$) |

over 178,000 of *sin* and its variants and over 45,000 of *wound* and variants. In the absence of a tagged version of the corpus, the only possible option would be to filter the results manually, which would be not only unfeasible, but also beyond the scope of the present research. For this reason, the standardised values offered (cf. Table 6.52) must be taken very cautiously and always bearing this problem in mind. What can be gathered from these inexact statistics is that the association of *deadly* with these collocates is not to be attributed to chance, for the standardised scores seem to indicate that these values are in fact statistically significant, and if we were to count only the nominal collocates of *deadly* the resulting picture would, in all probability, not differ much from the values given in Table 6.52.

As for the types of meanings, the number of tokens for each of these clearly increases over time and it is always in the course of the fourth to the very final period that the number of occurrences decreases. Despite the conspicuous growth in the absolute figures (cf. Table 6.53) in relation to the four different types of meanings established here, the results are only

Table 6.53. Meaning types for *deadly* (adj.) in EEBOCorp 1.0

| | | D | D/S | S | S/I | Total |
|---|---|---|---|---|---|---|
| **1470–99** | # | 199 | 0 | 25 | 0 | 224 |
| | % | 3.81 | 0.00 | 1.12 | 0.00 | 2.78 |
| | NF | 67.99 | 0 | 8.54 | 0 | 76.53 |
| **1500–49** | # | 276 | 8 | 36 | 0 | 320 |
| | % | 5.28 | 1.34 | 1.61 | 0.00 | 3.97 |
| | NF | 26.95 | 0.78 | 3.52 | 0 | 31.25 |
| **1550–99** | # | 1,104 | 146 | 609 | 0 | 1,859 |
| | % | 21.13 | 24.46 | 27.24 | 0.00 | 23.06 |
| | NF | 15.05 | 1.99 | 8.30 | 0 | 23.35 |
| **1600–49** | # | 1,920 | 265 | 936 | 4 | 3,125 |
| | % | 36.75 | 44.38 | 41.86 | 80.00 | 38.76 |
| | NF | 12.67 | 1.75 | 6.18 | 0.03 | 20.62 |
| **1650–99** | # | 1,725 | 178 | 630 | 1 | 2,534 |
| | % | 33.03 | 29,82 | 28.17 | 20.00 | 31.43 |
| | NF | 6.00 | 0.62 | 2.19 | 0.00 | 8.82 |
| **Total (#)** | | **5,224** | **597** | **2,236** | **5** | **8,062** |

statistically significant for all the periods as far as descriptive meanings are concerned.[13]

In regard to those meanings which are halfway between descriptive and subjective, the difference turns out to be statistically significant only in the last period ($\chi^2(1) = 124.23$; $p = 0$). In relation to subjective meanings, the second half of the seventeenth century was also found to be statistically significant ($\chi^2 (1) = 440.25$; $p = 0$). Finally, the results from the chi-square test indicate that the values corresponding to those meanings of *deadly* which are ambiguous between subjective and the purely intensifying ones are not statistically significant.

13 **P. I > P. II** $\chi^2$ (1) = 105.12; $p = 0$; **P. II > P. III** $\chi^2$ (1) = 76.36; $p = 0$; **P. III > P. IV** $\chi^2$ (1) = 20.71; $p = 0.000005353942$;**P. IV > P. V** $\chi^2$ (1) = 530.14; $p = 0$.

Examples (6.116)–(6.120) offer a selection of the different types of readings for the adjective *deadly* in the corpus. The collocation *deadly charms* in (6.116) corresponds to a descriptive use of the adjective, in which it is equivalent to *mortal*, that is, these charms will eventually disappear. The collocation *deadly pain* in (6.117) is considered ambiguous between descriptive and subjective: although on many occasions a very sharp pain is concomitant with a major disease, in many of these examples this pain is not clearly associated to a fatal disease, and it is hence unclear if the person will pass away. In turn, *deadly anguish* in (6.18) is regarded as subjective, since mental distress and sorrow might lead to a situation of hopelessness and disheartenment, which might also be accompanied by physical discomfort, although, in general terms, this condition is not itself fatal. Similarly, *deadly rancour* in (6.119) is also taken to be subjective: bearing deep resentment towards someone does not entail a power to kill or harm that person, though it might lead one to plan to murder him/her. By contrast, example (6.120) shows the collocation *deadly envy*, whose meaning is ambiguous between subjective and intensifying. The intention of injuring or damaging somebody is less clear when someone feels a twinge of envy for another person; therefore, it could also be argued that *deadly envy* could be paraphrased here as *pure envy* and hence function as an intensifier. However, in the context of this example, it is said that Anabaptists tend to persecute other religious groups; since the intention of harming others is still present, it could still be argued to be a subjective reading of the adjective. For this reason, this collocation was marked as ambiguous between subjective and intensifying.

(6.116) *And twixt the~ streams of streaming blod swift running With bloudles trunks, lop'd heads, legs, thighs, and armes, Vpon the riuer like dead fishes swimming; Ere Sol with Neptune sleeped, slept their harmes; All beeing shooke with deaths all* ***deadly*** *charmes*. (D00000998378270000. 1600. Cyril Tourneur. *The transformed metamorphosis*)

(6.117) *Ere whyle to whom the people would, Hir Fathers antique court restore, And Brothers wedlock once againe, Now wéeping, wringing hands poore wretch, Unto hir cruell,* ***deadly*** *paine*, (D00000998463890000. 1566. *Octauia*)

(6.118) *What shuld I speake of Helise, Hieremy and Hieu, to be short of ye greatest part of gods prophets, which were euer wrapped in wo, and* ***deadly*** *anguishe the worlde seldome or neuer ministringe any cause of gladnes, comforte, or solace*. (D00000998451290000. 1546. William Hugh. *The troubled mans medicine*)

(6.119) *Your Words a specious Mildness only bear, I fear the* ***deadly*** *Rancour hid within.* (D00000118052650000. 1698. Richard Hakluyt. *Phaeton, or, The fatal divorce a tragedy*)

(6.120) *we cannot herein but take notice of the persecuting Spirit, implacable and* ***deadly*** *Envy that is in some of these Anabaptists, tending to Persecution in the highest.* (D00000162047460000. 1674. William Penn. *The Christian-Quaker and his divine testimony*)

If we consider semantic prosody (cf. Table 6.54), *deadly* is attested with negative semantic prosody in the overwhelming majority of the examples in EEBOCorp 1.0 (86.91%), while neutral and positive semantic prosody amount to 12.99% and 0.10%, respectively. Despite the rise in the absolute frequencies for each of the semantic prosodies of the adjective, mainly in what concerns negative and neutral semantic prosody, this increase is only considered statistically significant for all the periods in regard to negative

Table 6.54. Semantic prosody for *deadly* (adj.) in EEBOCorp 1.0

| | | Neg | Neu | Pos | Total |
|---|---|---|---|---|---|
| 1470–99 | # | 208 | 16 | 0 | 224 |
| | % | 2.97 | 1.53 | 0.00 | 2.78 |
| | NF | 71.07 | 5.47 | 0 | 76.53 |
| 1500–49 | # | 299 | 21 | 0 | 320 |
| | % | 4.27 | 2.01 | 0.00 | 3.97 |
| | NF | 29.20 | 2.05 | 0 | 31.25 |
| 1550–99 | # | 1,627 | 230 | 2 | 1,859 |
| | % | 23.22 | 21.97 | 25.00 | 23.06 |
| | NF | 22.18 | 3.14 | 0.03 | 23.35 |
| 1600–49 | # | 2,741 | 380 | 4 | 3,125 |
| | % | 39.12 | 36.29 | 50.00 | 38.76 |
| | NF | 18.09 | 2.51 | 0.03 | 20.62 |
| 1650–99 | # | 2,132 | 400 | 2 | 2,534 |
| | % | 30.42 | 38.20 | 25.00 | 31.43 |
| | NF | 7.42 | 1.39 | 0.01 | 8.82 |
| **Total (#)** | | **7,007** | **1,047** | **8** | **8,062** |

semantic prosody and also in the course of the fourth to the fifth period for neutral semantic prosody.[14] Collocations showing negative semantic prosody include *deadly pain*, *deadly anguish*, *deadly rancour* and *deadly envy* in (6.117)–(6.120), while *deadly charm* in (6.116) is positive in meaning. Finally, examples of collocates which have been labelled as neutral in the data include *knight*, *thing*, *man*, *life* and *sign*, among others.

The EModE data from EEBOCorp 1.0 also returned a considerable number of examples for the adverb *deadly*, 920 in total, distributed in 131 different collocations. Table 6.55 shows the distribution of the adverb across the different periods in the corpus. As these results indicate, there is a gradual increase in the number of occurrences of the adverb from one period to the next, except for the transition from P. IV to P. V. The results are, however, not significant for all periods: it is only the increase from P. II to P. III (from 78 to 238 occurrences) and the decrease in the number of tokens from P. IV to P. V (from 414 to 162 occurrences) that is considered as highly statistically significant ($\chi^2$ (1) = 44.284; p = 0, and ($\chi^2$ (1) = 353.73; p = 0, respectively).

Table 6.56 summarises the results for the collocations which are attested at least ten times in EEBOCorp 1.0 in the five different periods: 1470s–90s, 1500s–40s, 1550s–90s, 1600s–40s and 1650s–90s.

Table 6.55. *Deadly* (adv.) in EEBOCorp 1.0

| **Period** | **Abs. Freq.** | % | **NF (/1,000,000 words)** | **Total** |
|---|---|---|---|---|
| **I (1470s–90s)** | 28 | 3.04 | 9.57 | 920 |
| **II (1500s–40s)** | 78 | 8.48 | 7.62 | |
| **III (1550s–90s)** | 238 | 25.87 | 3.25 | |
| **IV (1600s–40s)** | 414 | 45.00 | 2.73 | |
| **V (1650s–90s)** | 162 | 17.61 | 0.56 | |

14 *Negative semantic prosody*: P. I > P. II $\chi^2$ (1) = 102.52; $p = 0$; P. II > P. III $\chi^2$ (1) = 18.89; $p = 0.0000138345$; P. III> P. IV $\chi^2$ (1) = 42.51; $p = 0$; P. IV > P. V $\chi^2$ (1) = 1015.98; $p = 0$; *neutral semantic prosody*: P. IV > P. V $\chi^2$ (1) = 68.84; $p = 0$.

Table 6.56. The collocates of *deadly* (adv.) in EEBOCorp 1.0

| | Collocation | Abs. Freq. | % | NF | Total |
|---|---|---|---|---|---|
| 1470s–90s | *deadly sin* | 20 | 15.04 | 6.83 | 133 |
| 1500s–40s | *deadly sin* | 61 | 45.86 | 5.96 | 133 |
| 1550s–90s | *deadly hate* | 76 | 32.76 | 1.04 | 232 |
| | *deadly sin* | 33 | 24.81 | 0.45 | 133 |
| | *deadly wound* | 16 | 32.00 | 0.22 | 50 |
| | *deadly wounded* | 30 | 21.43 | 0.41 | 140 |
| 1600s–40s | *deadly hate* | 127 | 54.74 | 0.84 | 232 |
| | *deadly sick* | 41 | 49.40 | 0.27 | 83 |
| | *deadly sin* | 15 | 11.28 | 0.10 | 133 |
| | *deadly sting* | 11 | 57.89 | 0.07 | 19 |
| | *deadly wound* | 25 | 50.00 | 0.16 | 50 |
| | *deadly wounded* | 80 | 57.14 | 0.53 | 140 |
| 1650s–90s | *deadly hate* | 21 | 9.05 | 0.07 | 232 |
| | *deadly sick* | 33 | 39.76 | 0.11 | 83 |
| | *deadly wounded* | 26 | 18.57 | 0.09 | 140 |

In order to know if the association of the adverb *deadly* with these collocates is not random, we need to obtain the standardised values. However, as happened with the adjective *deadly* in EEBOCorp 1.0, this is not without problems (cf. supra). Thus, in order to retrieve these values, we need to obtain the raw frequencies for each of the collocates, in addition to those of *deadly*. Given the high token frequency of the collocates in the corpus, a statistical analysis would not be reliable unless we clearly separated the nominal collocates from the verbal ones. Though acknowledging this problem, I have still decided to include these values here (cf. Table 6.57), which indicate the close connection between *deadly* and these collocates.

In regard to the meaning types of the adverb (cf. Table 6.58), 56.74% of the occurrences correspond to descriptive meanings, followed by subjective meanings, which account for 35.43% of the cases. Intensifying readings of

Table 6.57. Standardised scores for *deadly* (adv.) in EEBOCorp 1.0

| Collocation | *z*-score | *MI* | *MI3* | *LL*-value |
|---|---|---|---|---|
| *deadly hate* | 84.629 | 6.018 | 19.684 | 726.990 (p < 0.0001) |
| *deadly sick* | 54.551 | 5.241 | 17.991 | 441.629 (p < 0.0001) |
| *deadly sin* | 469.068 | 7.262 | 28.270 | 11,744.935 (p < 0.0001) |
| *deadly sting* | 29.624 | 5.388 | 14.307 | 121.415 (p < 0.0001) |
| *deadly wound* | 524.372 | 8.401 | 27.753 | 7,910.653 (p < 0.0001) |
| *deadly wounded* | 129.411 | 6.926 | 21.185 | 1,067.432 (p < 0.0001) |

Table 6.58. Meaning types for *deadly* (adv.) in EEBOCorp 1.0

| | | D | D/S | S | S/I | I | Total |
|---|---|---|---|---|---|---|---|
| **1470–99** | # | 22 | 0 | 6 | 0 | 0 | 28 |
| | % | 4.21 | 0.00 | 1.84 | 0.00 | 0.00 | 3.04 |
| | NF | 7.52 | 0 | 2.05 | 0 | 0 | 9.57 |
| **1500–49** | # | 73 | 0 | 4 | 1 | 0 | 78 |
| | % | 13.98 | 0.00 | 1.23 | 20.00 | 0.00 | 8.48 |
| | NF | 7.13 | 0 | 0.39 | 0.10 | 0 | 7.62 |
| **1550–99** | # | 120 | 16 | 100 | 0 | 2 | 238 |
| | % | 22.99 | 48.49 | 30.67 | 0.00 | 5.88 | 25.87 |
| | NF | 1.64 | 0.22 | 1.36 | 0 | 0.03 | 3.25 |
| **1600–49** | # | 218 | 12 | 167 | 4 | 13 | 414 |
| | % | 41.77 | 36.36 | 51.23 | 80.00 | 38.24 | 45.00 |
| | NF | 1.44 | 0.08 | 1.10 | 0.03 | 0.09 | 2.73 |
| **1650–99** | # | 89 | 5 | 49 | 0 | 19 | 162 |
| | % | 17.05 | 15.15 | 15.03 | 0.00 | 55.88 | 17.61 |
| | NF | 0.31 | 0.02 | 0.17 | 0 | 0.07 | 0.56 |
| **Total (#)** | | **522** | **33** | **326** | **5** | **34** | **920** |

*deadly* amount to 3.70%, while those examples which are ambiguous between descriptive and subjective and between subjective and intensifying represent 3.59% and 0.54%, respectively. Descriptive occurrences of *deadly* increase over time and only decrease in the second half of the seventeenth century. The variation in the absolute frequencies is, however, only significant in the transition from P. II to P. III ($\chi^2$ (1) = 115.04; $p$ = 0) and from P. IV to P. V ($\chi^2$ (1) = 179.13; $p$ = 0). Those meanings which can be classified either as descriptive or subjective are first recorded in the sixteenth century, though their frequency gradually decreases over time. The difference in the number of tokens was not found to be statistically significant, with the exception of the transition from P. IV to P. V, which is significant at $p < 0.05$ (Fisher's exact test = 0.00339). Subjective meanings of the adverb *deadly* also increase conspicuously in the second half of the sixteenth century and early seventeenth century, to decrease again at the turn of this century. However, only the transition from P. II to P. III (Fisher's exact test = 0.006342) and that from P. IV to P. V are statistically significant ($\chi^2$ (1) = 173.03; $p$ = 0). By contrast, the variation in the number of tokens for intensifying meanings is not statistically significant.

Examples (6.121)–(6.128) present a selection of the different readings of *deadly* (adv.) in the corpus. Example (6.121) shows the adverb in combination with the participial form *slain*, a descriptive or literal sense, since it is mentioned that some men-at-arms are carrying a dead knight in a coffin. The collocation *deadly dangerous* in (6.122) is considered indeterminate between descriptive and subjective: on the one hand, being dangerous does not entail any mortal circumstances. On the other, the referents here are the bow and the arrows, which do have a lethal power. *Deadly dismayed* in (6.123) is a subjective collocation: being horrified or appalled by a particular event or circumstance is not fatal either, but one may be overwhelmed with fear and feel in a state close to death, for example, with heart pounding or a cold sweat. Examples (6.124) and (6.125), in turn, are ambiguous between subjective and intensifying. To displease somebody deadly may be interpreted, on the one hand, as to annoy or upset somebody terrifically, so that *deadly* could hence be argued to function as an intensifier. On the other hand, it could be claimed that when someone is annoyed, in this example God, (s)he may take physical revenge. For this reason, the collocation *displease deadly* was marked as ambiguous between subjective and intensifying. The same ambiguity is present in the collocation *envy deadly*; on the one hand, it could be equivalent to *envy greatly*, and hence function as an intensifier. On the other hand, it could be argued that bearing a grudge against someone implies taking revenge on that person, and hence the possibility of harming him/her is still in the background. A subjective reading, therefore, would also be possible. Finally, examples (6.126)–(6.128) present intensifying meanings of the adverb, in combination with the adjectives *unwelcome*, *lazy* and *long*. In these cases, *deadly* does not admit a literal interpretation, allowing for any type of damage whatsoever. Instead, the adverb functions here purely as a degree form, similar to *extremely* or *very*. In (6.126), the use of the intensifier is further reinforced by the presence of the superlative adverb *most*, which clearly supports the idea of high or extreme degree: 'very unwelcome', 'very lazy' and 'very long', respectively.

(6.121) *and he mette in a valey about a twenty men of armes whiche bare in a bere* ['bier, coffin'] *a knyghte* ***dedely*** *slayne* (D0000022102180000O. 1485. Sir Thomas Malory. *Le morte darthur*)

(6.122) *And in his hand a bended bow was seene, And many arrowes vnder his right side, All* ***deadly*** *daungerous,* (D0000099852958000O. 1596. Edmund Spenser. *The faerie qveene*)

(6.123) ***Deadly*** *dismayd, with horror of that dint Pyrrhochles was, and grieued eke entyre;* (D0000038160618000O. 1590. Edmund Spenser. *The faerie qveene*)

(6.124) *they wyll rather forbere the pleasours of theyr lyfe / and also rather dye then* ***dedely*** *to dysplease hym, by the doynge of any suche thynge* [...]. (D0000099840012000O. 1533. Sir Thomas More. *The second parte of the co[n]futacion of Tyndals answere*).

(6.125) *verely he* ***deadly*** *enuieth at your honour and felicitie, and grudgeth in his heart, that you should set downe the lawes of peace and warre in HVNGARIE:* (D0000099848134000O. 1603. Richard Knolles. *The generall historie of the Turkes*)

(6.126) *lest that which we heare, strike and wound vs at the heart, when wee looke for no such thing, but shall find it most* ***deadly*** *vnwelcome vnto vs.* (D0000099851570000O. 1615. Richard Rogers. *A commentary vpon the vvhole booke of Iudges*)

(6.127) *Misoponos was put to a Trade, but a* ***deadly*** *lazy Boy he was, very dull at learning,* (D0000011273116000O. 1669. Richard Brathwaite. *The history of moderation*)

(6.128) *Here I want our Authors Accuracy, or must complain of a Fallacy; for methinks it's a **deadly** long stride, to step from Adam to after-Ages, without the Bridge of some Neat Transition*; (D000001618746800000. 1676. Vincent Alsop. *Anti-sozzo*)

Concerning the variable semantic prosody, *deadly* collocates with elements which are inherently negative in 94.78% of the examples in EEBOCorp 1.0, followed by neutral semantic prosody in 4.67% of the cases and positive semantic prosody in just 0.55% of the attestations in the corpus. The absolute, relative and normalised frequencies for each of the semantic prosodies of the adverb in each period are given in Table 6.59. The variation in the total number of tokens per period is only significant in what concerns negative semantic prosody and even so, it is only significant in the transition from P. II to P. III ($\chi^2$ (1) = 47.76; $p$ = 0) and in the transition from P. IV to P. V ($\chi^2$ (1) = 358.52; $p$ = 0).

Table 6.59. Semantic prosody for *deadly* (adv.) in EEBOCorp 1.0

| | | **Neg** | **Neu** | **Pos** | **Total** |
|---|---|---|---|---|---|
| **1470–99** | # | 28 | 0 | 0 | 28 |
| | % | 3.21 | 0.00 | 0.00 | 3.04 |
| | **NF** | 9.57 | 0 | 0 | 9.57 |
| **1500–49** | # | 78 | 0 | 0 | 78 |
| | % | 8.94 | 0.00 | 0.00 | 8.48 |
| | **NF** | 7.62 | 0 | 0 | 7.62 |
| **1550–99** | # | 230 | 7 | 1 | 238 |
| | % | 26.39 | 16.28 | 20.00 | 25.87 |
| | **NF** | 3.14 | 0.10 | 0.01 | 3.25 |
| **1600–49** | # | 394 | 20 | 0 | 414 |
| | % | 45.18 | 46.51 | 0.00 | 45.00 |
| | **NF** | 2.60 | 0.13 | 0 | 2.73 |
| **1650–99** | # | 142 | 16 | 4 | 162 |
| | % | 16.28 | 37.21 | 80.00 | 17.61 |
| | **NF** | 0.49 | 0.06 | 0.01 | 0.56 |
| **Total (#)** | | **872** | **43** | **5** | **920** |

Being an adverb, *deadly* admits different types of collocates. In the EEBOCorp 1.0 data in particular, it is found predominantly as a modifier of verbs (55.54%), but also of participial forms (23.8%), adjectives (20.55%) and adverbs (0.11%), as shown in Table 6.60. The absolute frequencies generally increase over time for each of these categories, even though these figures are not statistically significant in all cases. As a modifier of verbs, the rise in the number of tokens of the adverb is not significant in the transition from P. I to P. II, but this change was found to be statistically significant in the remaining periods.[15] As a modifier of participial items, only the decrease in the number of tokens from P. IV to P. V can be regarded as statistically

Table 6.60. Categories modified by *deadly* (adv.) in EEBOCorp 1.0

| | | Adj | Adv | Part | Vb | Total |
|---|---|---|---|---|---|---|
| **1470–99** | # | 0 | 0 | 1 | 27 | 28 |
| | % | 0.00 | 0.00 | 0.46 | 5.28 | 3.04 |
| | **NF** | 0 | 0 | 0.34 | 9.22 | 9.57 |
| **1500–49** | # | 1 | 0 | 11 | 66 | 78 |
| | % | 0.53 | 0.00 | 5.02 | 12.92 | 8.48 |
| | **NF** | 0.10 | 0 | 1.07 | 6.45 | 7.62 |
| **1550–99** | # | 27 | 0 | 53 | 158 | 238 |
| | % | 14.29 | 0.00 | 24.20 | 30.92 | 25.87 |
| | **NF** | 0.37 | 0 | 0.72 | 2.15 | 3.25 |
| **1600–49** | # | 79 | 1 | 116 | 218 | 414 |
| | % | 41.80 | 100.00 | 52.97 | 42.66 | 45.00 |
| | **NF** | 0.52 | 0.01 | 0.77 | 1.44 | 2.73 |
| **1650–99** | # | 82 | 0 | 38 | 42 | 162 |
| | % | 43.38 | 0.00 | 17.35 | 8.22 | 17.61 |
| | **NF** | 0.29 | 0 | 0.13 | 0.15 | 0.56 |
| **Total (#)** | | **189** | **1** | **219** | **511** | **920** |

15 P. II > P. III ($\chi^2$ (1) = 60.147; $p$ = 0; P. III > P. IV $\chi^2$ (1) = 14.722; $p$ = 0.00009946; P. IV > P. V $\chi^2$ (1) = 277.56; $p$ =0.

significant ($\chi^2$ (1) = 111.582; $p$ = 0). The variation in the frequencies of *deadly* as a modifier of adjectives is only statistically significant when we compare P. IV and P. V.[16]

In the eighteenth-century data from ECF the adjective *deadly* was attested in thirty-nine examples, with thirty-three different collocations. Naturally, all the collocates of *deadly* (adj.) were nouns, given its adjectival nature. Table 6.61 thus shows the absolute and normalised frequencies for all the collocations. A statistical collocational analysis, however, was discarded in these cases, in view of the low frequency of the collocations, with only one or two occurrences each.

As shown in Table 6.62, *deadly* is found in the data mostly with subjective meanings, which represent over half of the total (56.42%), and also with descriptive meanings, amounting to a third of the examples (33.33%). Intensifying readings of the adjective are far less numerous (7.69%) and there is also one instance (see (6.130)) which has been classified as ambiguous between descriptive and subjective (2.56% of the total number of occurrences).

The instances in (6.129)–(6.132) exemplify the different types of meanings of the adjective in the data. A deadly contagion in (6.129) refers to a contagious disease, which eventually results in someone's death, representing, therefore, a literal or descriptive meaning of the adjective *deadly*. By contrast, in (6.130) the collocation *deadly malice* was marked as ambiguous between descriptive and subjective, for being spiteful or malicious does not automatically imply hurting or killing somebody, and, therefore, the malice is not necessarily taken literally. In turn, *deadly horror* in (6.131) describes a quality which in some way recalls death, namely terror and dread. Therefore, due to the semantic closeness of this collocate with death itself, the collocation has been classified as subjective. Finally, (6.132) evinces a meaning which is in no way related to the original sense of the adjective, and which can only be read as expressing a high degree. Having a deadly determination is equivalent to having a strong resolution or will power,

16 **Adjectives:** P. II > P. III Fisher's exact test = 0.246141; P. III > P. IV $\chi^2$ (1) = 2.145; $p$ = 0.14303504; P. IV > P. V $\chi^2$ (1) = 14.42; $p$ =0.00014624.

Table 6.61. Absolute and normalised frequencies for the collocates of *deadly* (adj.) in ECF

| Collocation | Abs. Freq. | NF |
|---|---|---|
| *deadly anxiety* | 1 | 0.10 |
| *deadly aspect* | 1 | 0.10 |
| *deadly bitter* | 1 | 0.10 |
| *deadly cold* | 1 | 0.10 |
| *deadly composition* | 2 | 0.21 |
| *deadly consequence* | 1 | 0.10 |
| *deadly consultation* | 1 | 0.10 |
| *deadly contagion* | 1 | 0.10 |
| *deadly content* | 1 | 0.10 |
| *deadly crisis* | 1 | 0.10 |
| *deadly determination* | 1 | 0.10 |
| *deadly despair* | 1 | 0.10 |
| *deadly enemy* | 1 | 0.10 |
| *deadly enmity* | 1 | 0.10 |
| *deadly fear* | 1 | 0.10 |
| *deadly gum* | 1 | 0.10 |
| *deadly hole* | 1 | 0.10 |
| *deadly horror* | 1 | 0.10 |
| *deadly instrument* | 1 | 0.10 |
| *deadly malice* | 1 | 0.10 |
| *deadly melancholy* | 1 | 0.10 |
| *deadly oath* | 2 | 0.21 |
| *deadly odd* | 1 | 0.10 |
| *deadly paleness* | 1 | 0.10 |
| *deadly pang* | 1 | 0.10 |
| *deadly passion* | 2 | 0.21 |
| *deadly poison* | 2 | 0.21 |
| *deadly potion* | 1 | 0.10 |

Table 6.61. Continued

| Collocation | Abs. Freq. | NF |
|---|---|---|
| *deadly schism* | 1 | 0.10 |
| *deadly sigh* | 1 | 0.10 |
| *deadly sin* | 2 | 0.21 |
| *deadly slap* | 2 | 0.21 |
| *deadly sound* | 1 | 0.10 |
| **Total** | **39** | **4.02** |

Table 6.62. Meaning types for *deadly* (adj.) in ECF

| | Abs. Freq. | % | NF |
|---|---|---|---|
| **D** | 13 | 33.33 | 1.34 |
| **D/S** | 1 | 2.56 | 0.10 |
| **S** | 22 | 56.42 | 2.27 |
| **I** | 3 | 7.69 | 0.31 |
| **Total** | **39** | **100.00** | **4.02** |

and, for this reason, the collocation *deadly determination* was counted as intensifying.

(6.129) *These are the Men of whom Solomon says, they go like an Ox to the slaughter, till a Dart strikes through their Liver; an admirable Description, by the way, of the foul Disease, which is a poisonous* **deadly** *Contagion mingling with the Blood, whose Center or Fountain is in the Liver;* (1722. Daniel Defoe. *Moll Flanders*)

(6.130) *But, dear Lucy, have you any spite in you? Are you capable of malice---* **deadly** *malice?* (1754. Samuel Richarson. *Sir Charles Grandison*)

(6.131) *Sometimes, despairing, chill'd with* **deadly** *Horror, I fancy you regardless of my Woe, and easy under this Restraint*! (Eliza Fowler Haywood. *The British recluse*)

(6.132) *With this* **deadly** *Determination, I went Post, from Paris to Flanders, and traced the Colonel from Place to Place, till I found him in a Village, on the Road to Amsterdam.* (1765–1770. Henry Brooke. *The Fool of Quality*)

A look at the list of collocates provided in Table 6.61 suggests that the adjective *deadly* is found in the data predominantly with elements which have negative semantic prosody (56.41%), such as *poison*, *pang* and *anxiety*, but it is also attested with neutral (35.90%) (e.g. *consequence*, *instrument* and *sound*) and positive nouns (7.69%) (e.g. *passion* and *determination*). Table 6.63 summarises the distribution of the instances according to semantic prosody.

As regards the adverbial form, only eight occurrences have been identified in ECF, in a total of five different collocations. As was the case for the adjective in the eighteenth-century data, the token frequency of the collocations in the database is very low, so they have been excluded from a statistical collocational analysis. Nonetheless, Table 6.64 gives the overall frequencies for each of these collocations of the adverb. As shown in this table, unlike the adverbs *mortal* and *mortally* in EEBOCorp 1.0 (cf. Sections

Table 6.63. Semantic prosody for *deadly* (adj.) in ECF

| | **Abs. Freq.** | **%** | **NF** |
|---|---|---|---|
| **neg** | 22 | 56.41 | 2.27 |
| **neu** | 14 | 35.90 | 1.44 |
| **pos** | 3 | 7.69 | 0.31 |
| **Total** | **39** | **100.00** | **4.02** |

Table 6.64. Absolute and normalised frequencies for the collocates of *deadly* (adv.) in ECF

| **Collocation** | **Abs. Freq.** | **NF** |
|---|---|---|
| *deadly comfortable* | 1 | 0.10 |
| *deadly fierce* | 2 | 0.21 |
| *deadly sick* | 1 | 0.10 |
| *deadly sore* | 2 | 0.21 |
| *deadly strong* | 2 | 0.21 |
| **Total** | **8** | **0.82** |

Table 6.65. Meaning types for *deadly* (adv.) in ECF

| | **Abs. Freq.** | **%** | **NF** |
|---|---|---|---|
| **D/S** | 1 | 12.50 | 0.10 |
| **S** | 2 | 25.00 | 0.21 |
| **I** | 5 | 62.50 | 0.52 |
| **Total** | **8** | **100.00** | **0.82** |

6.2.4 and 6.2.5), which modify a wider variety of word types, *deadly* in ECF modifies adjectives exclusively.

Concerning the types of meanings (cf. Table 6.65), and in contrast to *deadly* (adj.) (cf. supra), the data records primarily intensifying readings (62.50%), followed by subjective *deadly* (25.00%), and one isolated instance (see (6.133)) of a meaning which is ambiguous between descriptive and subjective (12.50% of the total).

Examples (6.133)–(6.136) are provided here in order to illustrate the three types of meanings found in the database. The collocation *deadly sick* in (6.133) differs from other examples of the same collocation in EModE, when it actually had a literal meaning (cf. supra). In this passage, taken from *Tristram Shandy*, Tristram feels indisposed and as if he was going to die, although he is just suffering from seasickness and nausea. As it is not a fatal disease and it is just short-term discomfort, the collocation *deadly sick* was marked here as ambiguous between descriptive and subjective. By contrast, *deadly sore* in (6.134) is considered as subjective, since in this passage there are no signs of any problems which may lead to a fatal outcome: here Pamela, the protagonist, simply feels fatigued and exhausted after a long journey. The remaining two examples, (6.135) and (6.136), show intensifying readings of the adverb, which can be paraphrased as 'extremely strong' and 'extremely comfortable', respectively. A literal interpretation of the adverb *deadly*, as something or somebody endowed with a lethal power, is not plausible in this case; rather, an intensifying or degree reading of *deadly* seems the most likely.

(6.133) *O I am **deadly** sick!---reach me that thing, boy--- 'tis the most discomfiting sickness ---I wish I was at the bottom---* (1760. Laurence Sterne. *Tristram Shandy*)

(6.134) *I am **deadly** sore all over, as if I had been soundly beaten.* (1742. Samuel Richardson. *Pamela*)

(6.135) *I dare say she drinks: She has a hoarse, man-like Voice, and is as thick as she's long; and yet looks so **deadly** strong, that I am afraid she would dash me at her Foot in an Instant,* (1742. Samuel Richardson. *Pamela*)

(6.136) *This name inflamed the husband's choler anew, and* [...] *he replied with a rancorous grin, 'Add rabbit him! I doubt not but you found his admonitions **deadly** comfortable!'* (1751. Tobias Smollett. *Peregrine Pickle*)

As for its semantic prosody (cf. Table 6.66), negative collocates are no longer the preferred company of *deadly* (adv.), as was the case with the adjective. Half of the occurrences of the adverb correspond in fact to neutral semantic prosody (50.00%), while negative semantic prosody represents 37.50% of the total, and positive collocates of *deadly* (adv.) represent 12.50%. The collocations with negative semantic prosody in the data are *deadly sore* and *deadly sick*; *deadly strong* and *deadly fierce* were marked as neutral, since they can be interpreted both positively and negatively depending on the context; finally, *deadly comfortable* was considered as positive.

The last of the sources examined was NCF. In this database the adjective *deadly* occurred in a total of 479 examples and in combination with 192 collocations. Logically, in all these cases *deadly* modifies nouns. Table 6.67 shows the most frequent collocations in the data, in this particular case those tokens with a minimum of five occurrences, while Table 6.68 provides the standardised scores for the corresponding collocations. As indicated by the four measures here, all the collocations are highly statistically significant.

Table 6.66. Semantic prosody for *deadly* (adv.) in ECF

| | **Abs. Freq.** | **%** | **NF** |
|---|---|---|---|
| **neg** | 3 | 37.50 | 0.31 |
| **neu** | 4 | 50.00 | 0.41 |
| **pos** | 1 | 12.50 | 0.10 |
| **Total** | **8** | **100.00** | **0.82** |

Table 6.67. Absolute and normalised frequencies for the most frequent collocations of *deadly* (adj.) in NCF

| **Collocation** | **Abs. Freq.** | **NF** |
|---|---|---|
| *deadly blow* | 13 | 0.35 |
| *deadly chill* | 7 | 0.19 |
| *deadly earnest* | 5 | 0.13 |
| *deadly enemy* | 14 | 0.37 |
| *deadly faintness* | 6 | 0.16 |
| *deadly fear* | 10 | 0.27 |
| *deadly feud* | 21 | 0.56 |
| *deadly hatred* | 16 | 0.43 |
| *deadly hue* | 5 | 0.13 |
| *deadly paleness* | 14 | 0.37 |
| *deadly pallor* | 6 | 0.16 |
| *deadly peril* | 8 | 0.21 |
| *deadly poison* | 10 | 0.27 |
| *deadly purpose* | 5 | 0.13 |
| *deadly sickness* | 10 | 0.27 |
| *deadly sin* | 27 | 0.72 |
| *deadly struggle* | 8 | 0.21 |
| *deadly vengeance* | 5 | 0.13 |
| *deadly venom* | 5 | 0.13 |
| *deadly weapon* | 9 | 0.24 |
| *deadly whiteness* | 5 | 0.13 |
| *deadly wound* | 11 | 0.29 |

In addition to descriptive (29.65%), subjective (50.31%) and intensifying meanings (4.59%), *deadly* is also attested in NCF with readings which range between descriptive and subjective (15.24%) and between subjective and intensifying (0.21%) (cf. Table 6.69).

Thus, *deadly* in (6.137) has a descriptive or literal meaning, for a person is said to be ill with a fatal disease. The fatal outcome is, nevertheless, doubtful

Table 6.68. Standardised scores for *deadly* (adj.) in NCF

| **Collocation** | ***z*-score** | ***MI*** | ***MI3*** | ***LL*-value** |
|---|---|---|---|---|
| *deadly blow* | 37.468 | 6.781 | 14.182 | 96.504 ($p < 0.0001$) |
| *deadly chill* | 40.897 | 7.913 | 13.527 | 62.914 ($p < 0.0001$) |
| *deadly earnest* | 14.686 | 5.495 | 10.139 | 28.323 ($p < 0.0001$) |
| *deadly enemy* | 28.051 | 5.966 | 13.367 | 81.968 ($p < 0.0001$) |
| *deadly faintness* | 71.726 | 9.747 | 14.917 | 69.315 ($p < 0.0001$) |
| *deadly fear* | 14.277 | 4.481 | 11.125 | 43.030 ($p < 0.0001$) |
| *deadly feud* | 197.603 | 10.932 | 19.576 | 264.876 ($p < 0.0001$) |
| *deadly hatred* | 68.778 | 8.310 | 16.124 | 143.101 ($p < 0.0001$) |
| *deadly hue* | 25.668 | 7.064 | 11.707 | 39.064 ($p < 0.0001$) |
| *deadly paleness* | 127.401 | 10.182 | 17.796 | 170.346 ($p < 0.0001$) |
| *deadly pallor* | 74.315 | 9.849 | 15.019 | 70.180 ($p < 0.0001$) |
| *deadly peril* | 35.919 | 7.351 | 13.351 | 65.680 ($p < 0.0001$) |
| *deadly poison* | 51.530 | 8.064 | 14.707 | 91.975 ($p < 0.0001$) |
| *deadly purpose* | 7.821 | 3.824 | 8.468 | 17.214 ($p < 0.0001$) |
| *deadly sickness* | 58.897 | 8.447 | 15.090 | 97.303 ($p < 0.0001$) |
| *deadly sin* | 78.610 | 7.851 | 17.361 | 240.363 ($p < 0.0001$) |
| *deadly struggle* | 23.270 | 6.122 | 12.122 | 52.154 ($p < 0.0001$) |
| *deadly vengeance* | 20.863 | 6.476 | 11.120 | 35.022 ($p < 0.0001$) |
| *deadly venom* | 68.671 | 9.884 | 14.528 | 58.731 ($p < 0.0001$) |
| *deadly weapon* | 38.331 | 7.368 | 13.708 | 74.107 ($p < 0.0001$) |
| *deadly whiteness* | 48.506 | 8.884 | 13.528 | 51.706 ($p < 0.0001$) |
| *deadly wound* | 32.179 | 6.587 | 13.506 | 78.718 ($p < 0.0001$) |

in (6.138), which describes a scene in which there has been an attack with a knife and a subsequent struggle. For this reason, the collocation *deadly assault* was classified as ambiguous between descriptive and subjective here.

(6.137) *Some real emotion---perhaps the fear which healthy young people experience at the sight of* ***deadly*** *disease---made Harry touch her arm with the softness of a child's touch*. (1861. George Meredith. *Evan Harrington*)

Table 6.69. Meaning types for *deadly* (adj.) in NCF

| | Abs. Freq. | % | NF |
|---|---|---|---|
| D | 142 | 29.65 | 3.78 |
| D/S | 73 | 15.24 | 1.94 |
| S | 241 | 50.31 | 6.41 |
| S/I | 1 | 0.21 | 0.03 |
| I | 22 | 4.59 | 0.59 |
| **Total** | **479** | **100.00** | **12.74** |

(6.138) *Aroused to a sense of the possibility of escape, Jack, who had viewed the* ***deadly*** *assault with savage satisfaction, burst from his captors and made for the door.* (1839–1840. William Harrison Ainsworth. *Jack Sheppard. A romance*)

(6.139), in turn, presents a subjective meaning, since Mrs. Milroy feels terrified at the thought of another character having discovered the contents of a letter. This dread and concern is, however, not going to kill her eventually, although it can consume and harm her, both psychologically and physically. By contrast, the collocation *deadly jealousy* in (6.140) is ambiguous between subjective and intensifying. This example narrates the rivalry between the two wives of a man, and apparently the quarrels between them in the zenana.[17] This jealousy can then be understood as an extreme and intense jealousy so that *deadly* here would function as an intensifier. However, the situation could also invite a subjective reading, since given this context, harm and damage between the two characters is not to be ruled out.

(6.139) *There were plain signs of disturbance and distress in her daughter's face. A* ***deadly*** *thrill of terror ran through Mrs. Milroy on the instant.* (1866. Wilkie Collins. *Armadale*)

(6.140) *He proposes marriage; it is accepted; the bride comes home, and a* ***deadly*** *jealousy ensues between the rival wives.* (1839. Captain Meadows Taylor. *Confessions of a thug*)

17 'In Islamic South Asia and Iran: that part of a dwelling-house in which the women of a family are secluded; a harem' (OED, s.v. *zenana*, n. 1).

Table 6.70. Semantic prosody for *deadly* (adj.) in NCF

| | Abs. Freq. | % | NF |
|---|---|---|---|
| **neg** | 311 | 64.93 | 8.27 |
| **neu** | 163 | 34.03 | 4.34 |
| **pos** | 5 | 1.04 | 0.13 |
| **Total** | **479** | **100.00** | **12.74** |

Conversely, in (6.141) and (6.142) *deadly* can only have an intensifying or degree reading: 'complete/total accuracy' and 'complete/total commonplace'. Since there is no way in which something being accurate or ordinary is fatal, *deadly* is hence considered as an intensifier in such instances.

(6.141) *Yes, then, his coldness was desireable; it encouraged an ideal of him. It suggested and seemed to propose to Clara's mind the divineness of separation instead of the* ***deadly*** *accuracy of an intimate perusal.* (1879. George Meredith. *The egoist*)

(6.142) *It's* ***deadly*** *commonplace, but, after all, the commonplaces are the great poetic truths.* (1896. Robert Louis Stevenson. *Weir of Hermiston*)

As for semantic prosody, *deadly* occurs in NCF mostly with negative elements (64.93%), but it is also found as a modifier of neutral (34.03%) and positive items (1.04%), as Table 6.70 shows. *Assault, disease, sin, struggle, animosity* and *wound*, for instance, were counted as negative collocates; *purpose, pallor, night, weapon* and *look* were marked as neutral; finally, *determination, passion, vantage* and *joy* were considered as positive collocates of *deadly* in the NCF material.

NCF also provided ample evidence of the adverbial form *deadly*, with 153 examples and 21 different collocations (see Table 6.71). Table 6.72 provides the different standardised scores for the most frequent collocations, in this case those occurring a minimum of five times in the data. The strongest association between the node and the collocate is shown by the collocation *deadly pale*, but in fact all the collocations in this table are statistically significant.

Concerning the types of meaning (cf. Table 6.73), *deadly* (adv.) is found with subjective readings in the overwhelming majority of the cases

Table 6.71. Absolute and normalised frequencies for the collocations of *deadly* (adv.) in NCF

| Collocation | Abs. Freq. | NF |
|---|---|---|
| *deadly black* | 1 | 0.03 |
| *deadly calm* | 2 | 0.05 |
| *deadly cold* | 5 | 0.13 |
| *deadly conservative* | 1 | 0.03 |
| *deadly curious* | 1 | 0.03 |
| *deadly economical* | 1 | 0.03 |
| *deadly faint* | 1 | 0.03 |
| *deadly frightened* | 1 | 0.03 |
| *deadly hate* | 1 | 0.03 |
| *deadly ill* | 1 | 0.03 |
| *deadly long* | 1 | 0.03 |
| *deadly natural* | 1 | 0.03 |
| *deadly necessary* | 1 | 0.03 |
| *deadly pale* | 106 | 2.82 |
| *deadly patient* | 1 | 0.03 |
| *deadly quiet* | 2 | 0.05 |
| *deadly sad* | 1 | 0.03 |
| *deadly sick* | 5 | 0.13 |
| *deadly still* | 1 | 0.11 |
| *deadly tired* | 1 | 0.03 |
| *deadly white* | 14 | 0.37 |

Table 6.72. Standardised scores for *deadly* (adv.) in NCF

| Collocation | *z*-score | *MI* | *MI3* | *LL*-value |
|---|---|---|---|---|
| *deadly cold* | 8.324 | 3.981 | 8.625 | 18.232 ($p < 0.0001$) |
| *deadly pale* | 225.687 | 8.956 | 22.329 | 1,075.406 ($p < 0.0001$) |
| *deadly sick* | 14.558 | 5.471 | 10.115 | 28.159 ($p < 0.0001$) |
| *deadly white* | 22.837 | 5.199 | 13.013 | 78.956 ($p < 0.0001$) |

Table 6.73. Meaning types for *deadly* (adv.) in NCF

| | **Abs. Freq.** | **%** | **NF** |
|---|---|---|---|
| **D** | 1 | 0.65 | 0.03 |
| **D/S** | 5 | 3.27 | 0.13 |
| **S** | 139 | 90.85 | 3.70 |
| **I** | 8 | 5.23 | 0.21 |
| **Total** | **153** | **100.00** | **4.07** |

(90.85%), although it is also attested with intensifying meanings (5.23%) and with meanings which are intermediate between descriptive and subjective (3.27%), in addition to one isolated instance which was marked as descriptive, corresponding to the collocation *deadly ill* (0.65% of the total).

*Deadly sick*, as in (6.143), is ambiguous between descriptive and subjective, for in this example, as in many instances of this collocation in the data, the context does not make it clear whether the person is critically ill or not. The prevalence of subjective meanings in the data owes to the fact that the collocation *deadly pale* alone already accounts for 69.28% of the total of examples (106 out of 153 tokens). (6.144) is one of such instances. The paleness of the character is accompanied in this case by a dishevelled and untidy appearance, since he is additionally covered in blood, which reinforces the negative atmosphere. With the use of the adverb *deadly*, therefore, the narrator evokes negative affect or his negative appreciation of the situation, given that the circumstances are not fatal at any moment to be taken literally. *Deadly* in examples (6.145)–(6.147), by contrast, is clearly intensifying. Though *deadly tired* could also be taken to be a subjective reading when applied to a person, in (6.145) it is used to refer to a scholarly lecture, which is said to be extremely boring and tires the character in excess. Likewise, *deadly* in *deadly curious* and *deadly conservative* can be paraphrased as *extremely*, *excessively*, and as such only admits a degree or intensifying interpretation.

(6.143) *This morning, when I came down, about half-an-hour before noon, Mr. Earnshaw was sitting by the fire,* ***deadly*** *sick; his evil genius almost as guant and ghastly, leant against the chimney.* (1847. Emily Brontë. *Wuthering heights*)

(6.144) *He was **deadly** pale, and his hair, which hung in dishevelled locks over his face, was clotted with blood.* (1858. Robert Michael Ballantyne. *The coral island*).

(6.145) *He looked at young Hexam as if he were waiting for a scholar to go on with a lesson that he knew by heart and was **deadly** tired of. But he had said his last word to him.* (1865. Charles Dickens. *Our mutual friend*)

(6.146) *But I can't for my life make out why you don't take to one or t'other of them, and put yourself at your ease. I'm **deadly** curious to know what keeps you from coming to a finish.* (1814. Fanny Burney. *The wanderer*)

(6.147) *As it was, she had no cause. Her father's political views were very mild. Lady Macleod's were **deadly** conservative.* (1864. Anthony Trollope. *Can you forgive her*)

In regard to the variable semantic prosody (cf. Table 6.74), most of the collocates of *deadly* (adv.) are neutral. This owes to the fact that the collocation *deadly pale* already makes up almost 70% of the total of examples, and this collocation is considered to represent neutral semantic prosody, for paleness can admit both a positive and a negative reading, being highly contextually dependent. Further neutral collocates of the adverb in the data are *white*, *curious*, *cold*, *economical*, *long* and *conservative*. NCF also provides examples of *deadly* as a modifier of elements with negative semantic prosody (consider the collocations *deadly sick*, *deadly tired* and *deadly sad*) and even one instance in which it modifies an inherently positive adjective: *patient*.

Unlike its zero counterpart *dead* (cf. Section 6.2.2), which could also modify other adverbs and even prepositions, the adverb *deadly* clearly shows a strong preference for adjectives in the nineteenth-century data, as shown in Table 6.75. However, there are also examples in which *deadly* modifies participial elements and one verb, namely *to hate*.

Table 6.74. Semantic prosody for *deadly* (adv.) in NCF

| | **Abs. Freq.** | **%** | **NF** |
|---|---|---|---|
| **neg** | 9 | 5.88 | 0.24 |
| **neu** | 143 | 93.46 | 3.80 |
| **pos** | 1 | 0.65 | 0.03 |
| **Total** | **153** | **100.00** | **4.07** |

Table 6.75. Categories modified by *deadly* (adv.) in NCF

| | Abs. Freq. | % | NF |
|---|---|---|---|
| **Adj.** | 149 | 97.39 | 3.96 |
| **Part.** | 3 | 1.96 | 0.08 |
| **Vb.** | 1 | 0.65 | 0.03 |
| **Total** | **153** | **100.00** | **4.07** |

### 6.2.3.1. *Deadly* (adj. and adv.) across time

Section 6.2.3 provided a detailed account of the usage and incidence of the adjective and adverb *deadly* in each of the different periods on the basis of the corpora and electronic collections consulted. In turn, this section summarises the results for each of the variables analysed (type of meaning, semantic prosody and word category) in the different materials, with the aim of providing a comprehensive picture of the evolution of this form across time. Figure 6.1 thus illustrates the evolution of the different types of meanings for the adjective *deadly* over time.[18] Table 6.76, in turn, provides both the absolute and normalised frequencies for this form in the different corpora and electronic collections.[19]

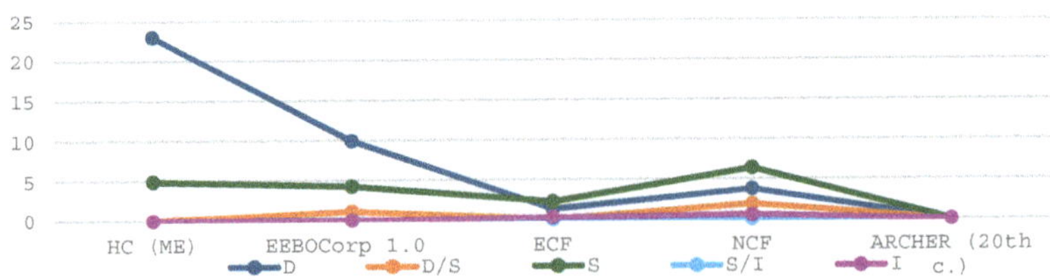


Figure 6.1. Types of meanings for *deadly* (adj.)

18 All the figures in this section provide normalised frequencies per one million words (NF pmw).

19 As in the case of *dead* in Section 6.2.2.1 and as will also be done for the other forms under analysis here (see Sections 6.2.4.1, 6.2.5.1 and 6.2.6.1 for *mortal*, *mortally* and

Table 6.76. Types of meanings for *deadly* (adj.) in the data (absolute/normalised frequencies)[20]

| | HC (ME) | EEBOCorp 1.0 | ECF | NCF | ARCHER (20th c.) |
|---|---|---|---|---|---|
| D | 14/23.00 | 5,224/9.94 | 13/1.34 | 141/3.75 | 0 |
| D/S | 0 | 597/1.14 | 1/0.10 | 70/1.86 | 0 |
| S | 3/4.93 | 2,236/4.26 | 22/2.27 | 238/6.33 | 0 |
| S/I | 0 | 5/0.01 | 0 | 1/0.03 | 0 |
| I | 0 | 0 | 3/0.31 | 22/0.59 | 0 |
| N. of words | 608,570 | 525,432,293 | 9,702,699 | 37,589,837 | 530,832 |

The normalised figures evince a sharp decrease in the use of descriptive meanings from the ME period to the start of the eighteenth century, a point in time when these uses slightly increase, to fall again from the nineteenth century onwards. Moreover, the variation in the absolute frequencies for descriptive uses in the different periods was found to be statistically significant, except if we compare the HC and EEBOCorp 1.0.[21] Those readings which are ambiguous between descriptive and subjective

*to death*, respectively), in order to trace the diachronic timeline for *deadly* (adj. and adv.) the materials consulted were considered as representative of a given period: the ME component of the HC was considered to be represent ME; EEBOCorp 1.0 was used for EModE and ECF and NCF for LModE; finally, only the twentieth-century British data from ARCHER was selected here as illustrative of the behaviour of these forms in PDE.

20 Note that Fisher's exact test and the chi-square test, the two statistical tests applied in this section, are based on absolute frequencies (cf. Section 5.3.2). Even though I shall be referring to normalised frequencies for comparative uses of the forms under analysis across the different materials, the values which are required to verify the statistical significance of the results are the token or absolute frequencies. Moreover, statistical testing cannot be considered in those cases in which there is a zero value in one of the periods, as is the case, for example, of the readings which are ambiguous between subjective and intensifying in the HC, ECF and ARCHER.

21 **HC (ME) > EEBOCorp 1.0:** $\chi^2$ (1) = 9.146; $p$ = 0.002249262; **EEBOCorp 1.0 > ECF:** $\chi^2$ (1) = 71.163; $p$ = 0; **ECF > NCF:** $\chi^2$ (1) = 13.038; $p$ = 0.00030523.

are less numerous in all the sources, as shown in Table 6.76. The first attestations date to EModE (597 exx.; NF pmw 1.14). One isolated occurrence is found in the eighteenth-century material analysed, and then the token frequency of such ambiguous examples increases again in the nineteenth century (70 exx.; NF pmw 1.86). As was the case with the HC, there are no attestations in the twentieth-century data from ARCHER. The difference in the number of tokens over the different periods for these ambiguous readings is statistically significant.[22] As far as subjective meanings are concerned, the normalised figures remain rather constant throughout ME and EModE (4.93 and 4.26, respectively), this frequency being reduced to about a half in the transition to the eighteenth century (2.27). None of these changes, however, is statistically significant.[23] By contrast, the rise in subjective uses from the eighteenth to the nineteenth century (NF pmw 6.33) is statistically significant.[24] Finally, the increase in the number of occurrences of intensifying uses from the eighteenth to the nineteenth century, both in terms of absolute and of normalised frequencies (ECF: 3 exx.; NF pmw 0.31 > NCF: 22 exx.; NF pmw 0.59), is not statistically significant at $p < 0.01$ (Fisher's value = 0.455646).

With regard to semantic prosody (see Figure 6.2), the data reveal a clear preference of the adjective *deadly* to combine with elements with negative prosody (cf. Table 6.77).

The normalised frequencies show that the use of *deadly* with negative collocates decreases dramatically from ME to the eighteenth century (from 21.36 to 2.27), to rise again at the turn of the nineteenth century (8.27). These figures, however, were not found to be statistically significant.[25] The collocates of *deadly* which have neutral semantic prosody behave similarly to their negative counterparts: the normalised figures are reduced from ME to the eighteenth century (from 6.57 to 1.44) and also increase slightly in

22 **EEBOCorp 1.0 > ECF:** Fisher's value = 0.000542 (significant at $p < 0.01$); **ECF > NCF:** Fisher's value = 0.000002 (significant at $p < 0.01$).

23 **HC > EEBOCorp 1.0:** Fisher's exact test = 0.748302; **EEBOCorp 1.0 > ECF:** $\chi^2$ (1) = 8.459; $p = 0.00363242$.

24 **ECF > NCF:** $\chi^2$ (1) = 22.436; $p = 0.00000217$.

25 **HC > EEBOCorp 1.0:** $\chi^2$ (1) = 2.363; $p = 0.12424305$; **EEBOCorp 1.0 > ECF:** $\chi^2$ (1) = 88.013; $p = 0.12424305$; **ECF > NCF:** $\chi^2$ (1) =36.369; $p = 0.12424305$.

Table 6.77. Semantic prosody for *deadly* (adj.) in the data (absolute/normalised frequencies)

| | **HC (ME)** | **EEBOCorp 1.0** | **ECF** | **NCF** | **ARCHER (20th c.)** |
|---|---|---|---|---|---|
| **neg** | 13/21.36 | 7,007/13.34 | 22/2.27 | 301/8.27 | 0 |
| **neu** | 4/6.57 | 1,047/1.99 | 14/1.44 | 166/4.34 | 0 |
| **pos** | 0 | 8/0.02 | 3/0.31 | 5/0.13 | 0 |
| **N. of words** | 608,570 | 525,432,293 | 9,702,699 | 37,589,837 | 530,832 |

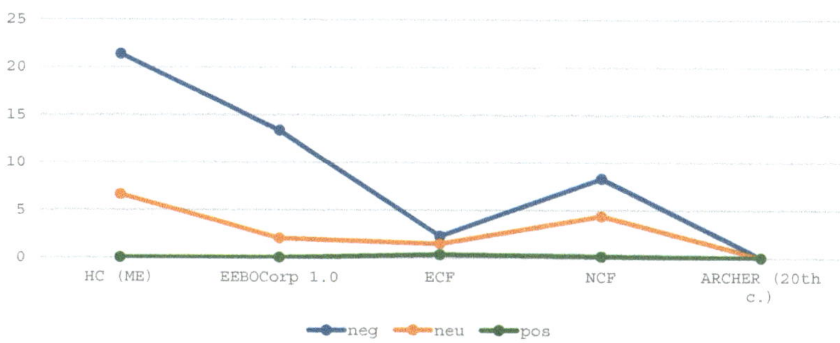


Figure 6.2. Semantic prosody for *deadly* (adj.)

the nineteenth century (4.34). Nevertheless, the difference in the number of attestations over the periods is statistically significant only in what concerns the eighteenth and nineteenth centuries.[26] Combinations of *deadly* with nouns with positive semantic prosody are relatively infrequent in the data, as shown in Table 6.162, and the normalised figures remain low in all periods. The variation in the number of occurrences was found to be statistically significant only for the EModE and eighteenth-century data.[27]

26 **HC > EEBOCorp 1.0:** Fisher's exact test = 0.035072 (not significant at $p < 0.01$); **EEBOCorp 1.0 > ECF:** $\chi^2$ (1) = 1.188; $p = 0.27573335$; **ECF > NCF:** $\chi^2$ (1) =17.139; $p = 0.00003474$.

27 **EEBOCorp 1.0 > ECF:** Fisher's exact test = 0.000882 (significant at $p < 0.01$); **ECF > NCF:** Fisher's exact test = 0.21456 (not significant at $p < 0.01$).

In view of the diachronic data from the different corpora and electronic collections discussed above, the adjective *deadly* seems to be relatively attached to its original negative meaning. As suggested by the OED (cf. Section 6.1.2), *deadly* first developed intensifying meanings in the seventeenth century, in collocations such as *deadly drinker* ('a terrible drinker'). The first instances of intensifying *deadly* in my data are attested in the ECF material. However, some earlier occurrences admit both a subjective and an intensifying interpretation. This is the case of the collocation *deadly envy* in (6.120). As explained in Section 6.2.3, for this particular example I claim two possible readings: on the one hand, *deadly envy* can be reworded as *pure envy*, in which case *deadly* would function as an intensifier. On the other, a subjective meaning would also be acceptable in this context, given that Anabaptists are said to persecute other religious groups and, therefore, there is still an implicit intention of hurting others. Further examples admitting both a subjective and an intensifying reading were also attested in EEBOCorp 1.0, in particular in the combinations of the adjective *deadly* with the nouns *jealousy*, *contempt* and *displeasure*. Example (6.148) illustrates another of such instances, featuring the collocation *deadly displeasure*.

(6.148) *when she had stripped her selfe out of her clothes, ready to go to bed, Gyges sheweth himselfe to her: whom when she had espied, and perceived the treachery, she was in a great agony, and conceived a* ***deadly*** *displeasure against the king her husband.* (D00000998366120000. 1631. Sir Richard Barckley. *The felicitie of man*)

This episode relates the moment in which the Lydian king Candaules convinces his bodyguard Gyges to stand secretly behind a cloth in the queen's chamber in order to fully admire her beauty, as Candaules considered his wife the most beautiful woman on earth. Gyges obeyed the king and spied the queen, but right after that he showed himself to her and informed her of her husband's proposal. The queen, offended by the shameful behaviour of her spouse, called Gyges secretly and informed him of her intent: either he should kill the king, marry her and become king himself, or he would die. *Displeasure* in this case means a disagreement or unfriendly relation (OED, s.v. *displeasure* n. 4) and, therefore, *deadly displeasure* can be interpreted here as a serious disagreement between the couple, which allows a degree reading of the adjective. However, a subjective interpretation is also highly likely, since we are told that the queen is ready to wreak vengeance on the king, her husband.

Meanings such as the ones illustrated in examples (6.120) and (6.148), which allow a contextualised degree reading, may well have favoured a generalised degree interpretation for the adjective *deadly*, in collocations such as *deadly drinker*, given by the OED (cf. Section 6.1.2) but also in the collocations *deadly accuracy*, *deadly commonplace* and *deadly determination*, sporadically attested in ECF and NCF (cf. Section 6.2.3).

Another unmistakable sign of the bond between *deadly* and its original death-related meaning is semantic prosody. Despite the low frequency of the adjective *deadly* as an intensifier in the material analysed (twenty-five examples in all, most of them from NCF), the data clearly indicate that, in line with its earliest sense ('mortal, fatal'), in most cases *deadly* modifies inherently negative nouns, such as *sin*, *poison*, *assault* and *animosity*. Nonetheless, nouns with positive semantic prosody are also attested as collocates of *deadly*, which in the most recent materials correlate with intensifying meanings, as is the case of the collocations *deadly joy* and *deadly determination*.

Considering the variables type of meaning and semantic prosody, it can therefore be concluded that over time the adjective *deadly* progressively developed more subjective meanings, which later evolved into intensifying readings, possibly favoured by some ambiguous contexts that allowed a double interpretation as both subjective and intensifying, as in (6.120) and (6.148). The cline of semantic evolution for intensifiers suggested by Adamson (2000) is therefore fully supported by the data analysed for the adjective *deadly* in the present piece of research. From its original meaning 'subject to death, mortal', *deadly* first underwent a process of subjectification (cf. Section 3.3.3), the earliest attestations of subjective meanings tracing back to the ME period. Once subjectified, it was further semantically bleached and reanalysed as an intensifier from the seventeenth century onwards (cf. Sections 3.2 and 3.3.2). Intensifying uses of *deadly* coexist side by side with both literal and subjective uses of the adjective, as predicted by Hopper's principles of layering and divergence (see Section 3.2). Moreover, the fact that *deadly* is attested by and large with inherently negative collocates is in keeping with another of Hopper's principles, namely persistence.

In view of all this, the degree of grammaticalisation of the adjective is not very advanced.

Like the adjective, *deadly* (adv.) also occurs mostly with descriptive and subjective uses in the data. The timeline for the different types of meanings is given in Figure 6.3, while Table 6.78 additionally provides the absolute and normalised frequencies for each of the readings over time in the different sources.

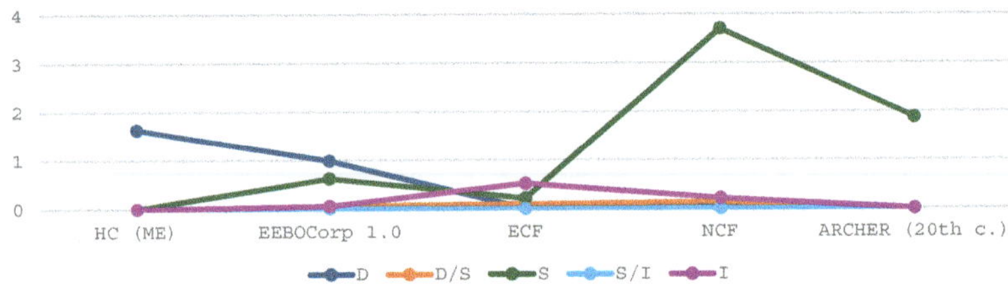


Figure 6.3. Types of meanings for *deadly* (adv.)

Table 6.78. Types of meanings for *deadly* (adv.) in the data (absolute/normalised frequencies)

| | HC (ME) | EEBOCorp 1.0 | ECF | NCF | ARCHER (20th c.) |
|---|---|---|---|---|---|
| D | 1/1.64 | 522/0.99 | 0 | 0 | 0 |
| D/S | 0 | 33/0.06 | 1/0.10 | 5/0.13 | 0 |
| S | 0 | 326/0.62 | 2/0.21 | 136/3.62 | 1/1.88 |
| S/I | 0 | 5/0.01 | 0 | 0 | 0 |
| I | 0 | 34/0.06 | 5/0.52 | 7/0.19 | 0 |
| N. of words | 608,570 | 525,432,293 | 9,702,699 | 37,589,837 | 530,832 |

As can be gathered from the figures in Table 6.78, most of the occurrences of the adverb *deadly* date to EModE. The normalised frequencies for the five meanings attested in the data remain low over time. Thus, there is only a slight decrease in regard to descriptive meanings from ME to EModE, but this is not statistically significant at $p < 0.01$ (Fisher's exact test = 0.454148). The normalised frequencies for those readings of *deadly* which are indeterminate between descriptive and subjective remain relatively stable over time and the variation among the different periods in regard to these uses is not statistically significant either.[28] Subjective occurrences of *deadly* are reduced in the transition from EEBOCorp 1.0 to ECF, but this reduction cannot be considered as statistically significant (Fisher's exact test = 0.141176). By contrast, if we compare the figures obtained for the eighteenth century with the nineteenth-century data, we witness a considerable increase, which is highly statistically significant at $p < 0.01$ (Fisher's exact test = 0). The comparison of the data from NCF and ARCHER reveals that subjective readings of *deadly* clearly drop in terms of both absolute and normalised figures. This difference is, however, not statistically significant (Fisher's exact test = 1). Finally, the very first occurrences of intensifying uses of the adverb are dated to the 1580s. Given the overall low token frequencies of intensifier *deadly*, the normalised figures for this use of the adverb remain rather low over time, and the statistical tests indicate that it is only the difference from EEBOCorp 1.0 to ECF that is to be considered as statistically significant at $p < 0.01$ (Fisher's exact test = 0.000675). On the contrary, the comparison of the eighteenth-century data with those from the nineteenth century reveal a negative result at the $p < 0.01$ level (Fisher's exact test = 0.079616).

As far as semantic prosody is concerned and in line with its adjectival counterpart (cf. supra), the adverb *deadly* tends to occur with items which are inherently negative (cf. Table 6.79 and Figure 6.4).

The normalised figures indicate that the values for negative semantic prosody remain fairly constant from ME to EModE (1.64 and 1.66), and then drop considerably at the close of EModE and the beginning of the eighteenth century (1.66 and 0.31). It is only this reduction in the number of attestations which is regarded as statistically significant at $p < 0.01$ (Fisher's exact test = 0.000189), while the comparison of the HC data with that from EEBOCorp 1.0 is not statistically significant (Fisher's exact test = 1.000002). Moreover, the comparison of the ECF results with those

28 **EEBOCorp 1.0 > ECF**: Fisher's exact test = 0.463196 (not significant at $p < 0.01$); **ECF > NCF**: Fisher's exact test = 1 (not significant at $p < 0.01$).

Table 6.79. Semantic prosody for *deadly* (adv.) in the data (absolute/normalised frequencies)

| | HC (ME) | EEBOCorp 1.0 | ECF | NCF | ARCHER (20th c.) |
|---|---|---|---|---|---|
| **neg** | 1/1.64 | 872/1.66 | 3/0.31 | 7/0.19 | 1/1.88 |
| **neu** | 0 | 43/0.08 | 4/0.41 | 141/3.75 | 0 |
| **pos** | 0 | 5/0.01 | 1/0.10 | 0 | 0 |
| **N. of words** | 608,570 | 525,432,293 | 9,702,699 | 37,589,837 | 530,832 |

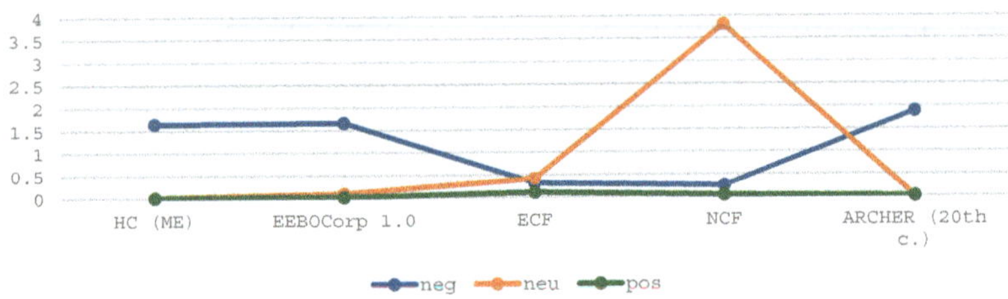


Figure 6.4. Semantic prosody for *deadly* (adv.)

from NCF, on the one hand, and of NCF and ARCHER, on the other, also yields non-significant values.[29] The values for neutral semantic prosody of the collocates of *deadly* also indicate a slight increase from EModE to the eighteenth century, if we compare the normalised frequencies (from 0.08 to 0.41), an increment which is not statistically significant at $p < 0.01$ (Fisher's exact test = 0.010372). However, from the eighteenth to the nineteenth century, we witness a dramatic increase in the uses of *deadly* with neutral semantic prosody, both in terms of the absolute and the normalised frequencies (NF pmw 3.75). This increase is, by contrast, highly statistically significant (Fisher's exact test = 0). As for positive semantic prosody, though hardly attested, the results suggest that the difference between

29 **ECF > NCF**: Fisher's exact test = 0.438482 (not significant at $p < 0.01$); **NCF > ARCHER**: Fisher's exact test = 0.10612 (not significant at $p < 0.01$).

EModE and the eighteenth century is not statistically significant at $p < 0.01$ (Fisher's exact test = 0.103974).

The last variable considered is the type of word modified by the adverb *deadly*, whose results are summarised in Table 6.80 and Figure 6.5.

The findings indicate that *deadly* functions predominantly as a modifier of verbs, participial elements and adjectives, although there is also one occurrence in the data in which *deadly* modifies another adverb (*deadly near*). As a modifier of adjectives, the normalised frequencies evince a progressive rise in frequency of the adverb over time, an increase which is most conspicuous in the transition from the eighteenth to the nineteenth century (from 0.82 to 3.86), followed by a decline from the nineteenth to the twentieth century (from 3.86 to 1.88). The statistical tests suggest that the difference in the number of occurrences from EEBOCorp 1.0 to ECF

Table 6.80. Categories modified by *deadly* (adv.) in the data (absolute/normalised frequencies)

| | HC (ME) | EEBOCorp 1.0 | ECF | NCF | ARCHER (20th c.) |
|---|---|---|---|---|---|
| **Adj.** | 0 | 192/0.36 | 8/0.82 | 145/3.86 | 1/1.88 |
| **Adv.** | 0 | 1/0.001 | 0 | 0 | 0 |
| **Part.** | 1/1.64 | 216/0.41 | 0 | 3/0.08 | 0 |
| **Vb.** | 0 | 511/0.97 | 0 | 0 | 0 |
| **N. of words** | 608,570 | 525,432,293 | 9,702,699 | 37,589,837 | 530,832 |

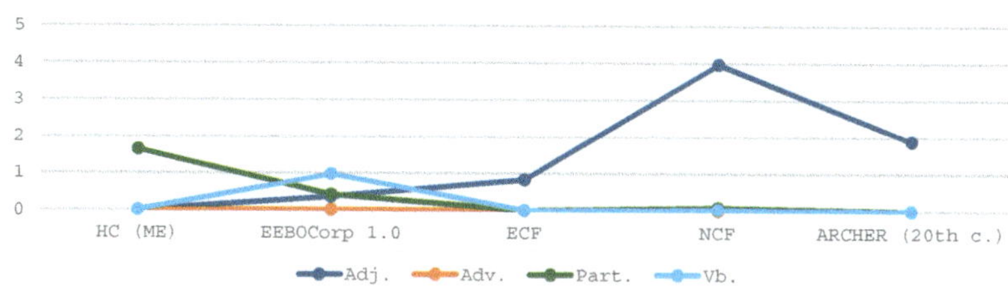


Figure 6.5. Categories modified by *deadly* (adv.)

and from NCF to ARCHER is not statistically significant ($\chi^2$ (1) = 4.215; $p$ = 0.04006807 and Fisher's exact test = 0.727532, respectively). The comparison between ECF and NCF is, by contrast, statistically significant ($\chi^2$ (1) = 21; $p$ = 0.00000459). Finally, if we compare the ME results with the EModE ones for those examples in which *deadly* is a modifier of participial elements, even though there is an actual increase of its token frequency (from 1 to 216 occurrences), the normalised figures evince an actual decrease in frequency (from 1.64 to 0.41), which is not statistically significant at $p < 0.01$ either (Fisher's exact test = 0.222126).

In the light of the variables type of meaning and semantic prosody, the adverb *deadly* behaves similarly to its homonymous adjective (cf. supra). Although the adverb is more frequently attested with intensifying meanings than the adjective *deadly* (4.27% vs 0.29% of the total of occurrences in all the sources), these are clearly marginal. Despite the dearth of intensifying examples in the data (46 in all) and even though they appear for the first time in the 1580s, it should be recalled that the adverb was already found with an unambiguous degree meaning in the fifteenth century (cf. Section 6.1.2). As was the case with the adjective *deadly*, the material analysed also contains some examples which admit a double interpretation, as subjective or as intensifying, in virtually the same context. This was the case of examples (6.124) and (6.125), involving the collocations *displease deadly* and *envy deadly*: displeasing someone deadly is equivalent to infuriating somebody to the extreme. At the same time, when someone is terribly annoyed, an actual revenge cannot be discarded, on which account a subjective interpretation is also likely here. Likewise, a degree reading of *deadly* is possible for *envy deadly* ('envy greatly'). However, the character is argued to bear a grudge in his heart and for this reason he may decide to take some form of vengeance, and hence a subjective meaning is also admitted.

These examples could in principle be considered as bridging contexts (cf. Section 3.2) towards clearly intensifying readings of the adverb, those which were found in the data in collocations such as *deadly conservative*, *deadly curious*, *deadly unwelcome*, *deadly handsome* and *deadly long*, among others. Nevertheless, most of the instances which are marked as ambiguous between subjective and intensifying in EEBOCorp 1.0 (5 in total) date from the same period as intensifying *deadly*, that is, the first half of the seventeenth century. The only exception is *deadly displease* in (6.124), which is dated 1533, while the first intensifying collocation in the corpus goes back to the 1580s. The influence of such potential bridging contexts on the rise of intensifying *deadly*, though tempting, cannot therefore be taken for granted here in the light of such limited evidence.

If semantic prosody is taken into account, the behaviour of *deadly* (adv.) is pretty similar to that of its adjectival counterpart, since the combinations of *deadly* with positive collocates amount to less than 1% of the total. In this regard, *deadly* is still very closely attached to its original negative meaning, even though positive collocates are sporadically found, such as *love*, *handsome*, *patient* and *comfortable*. Most interestingly, these collocates are associated with intensifying meanings in all the sources consulted.

Considering the types of meanings and semantic prosody, therefore, the adverb *deadly* is not very advanced in the grammaticalisation cline (see Section 3.3.1) and is, on the contrary, still fairly attached to its original, death-related meaning. Nonetheless, in view of the data analysed, it can also be argued that the adverb has undergone a process of subjectification (cf. Section 3.3.3) over time. Subjectification is more conspicuous in the case of the adverb than in that of the adjective (cf. supra), since subjective readings of the adverb amount to 43.14%, while those of the adjective represent 29.09% of the total. In addition to increased subjectivity, the adverb *deadly* has also been semantically bleached in the course of time, progressively developing a more abstract and general meaning ('very, extremely'), hence its use in combinations such as *deadly patient* or *deadly comfortable*, for which the original death-related meaning of the adverb is no longer possible. The adverb was then semantically reanalysed as an intensifier expressing a degree value. Therefore, the semantic cline proposed by Adamson (2000) for intensifiers (descriptive > affective/subjective > intensifying) is also relevant to the development of the adverb *deadly*. Adamson suggests that the semantic evolution of *lovely* as an intensifier correlates with different syntactic positions (cf. Section 4.1.2): when conveying a literal or descriptive meaning, the adjective is placed closer to the head noun because it describes inherent properties of that noun (e.g. *long* lovely *legs*). Conversely, when used as an intensifier, *lovely* occupies the leftmost position in the noun phrase (e.g. lovely *long legs*). Interestingly, some of the examples analysed in the data for the adverb *deadly* would apparently illustrate the correlation of function and syntactic position. This is the case of (6.127) and (6.128), which showed the strings *deadly lazy boy* and *deadly long stride*. Here, the most inherent qualities of the nouns *boy* and *stride* are lazy and long, whereas *deadly* is simply boosting that specific property. Therefore, the function of *deadly* as an intensifier could, in principle, be linked here to the leftmost position, as Adamson claimed for *lovely*. However, the development of the adverb *deadly* is independent from that of its adjectival counterpart, as in fact the adverb developed an intensifying function centuries earlier than its adjectival counterpart, as suggested by the dictionary evidence in Section 6.1.2. The development of the intensifying adverb *lovely*, in turn, is argued to have risen after an initial subjectification process and a syntactic reordering to the leftmost position, which provided the necessary conditions for the reanalysis of the adjective *lovely* as an intensifier.

Much alike the adjective (cf. supra), the adverb *deadly* also meets some of Hopper's principles (cf. Section 3.2), specifically those of layering, divergence, persistence and fixation. Thus, in EModE, for instance, intensifying *deadly* (adv.) coexists, side by side, with the other four types of meanings identified, which are independent of each other: descriptive, descriptive/subjective, subjective and subjective/intensifying. This represents a case of layering and divergence. At the same time, it was shown that *deadly* collocates mainly with negative items, which is in keeping with its original meaning, thus serving to illustrate Hopper's principle of persistence.

### 6.2.4. *The long diachrony of* mortal

It should be remembered at this point that the form *mortal*, borrowed in ME, could be a noun, an adjective and an adverb, functioning as the zero counterpart of the *–ly* form *mortally* (cf. Section 6.1.3). Like the form *dead*, which could also be a noun as in the phrase *the dead*, all the nominal occurrences of *mortal* in the corpus were discarded, given that these would not eventually develop an intensifying function. Therefore, I have only searched for the adverbial and adjectival forms, as explained in Section 6.2.1.

The HC recorded a total number of twenty occurrences of *mortal*, all of which correspond to the adjective. Eleven of these tokens date to the ME period (55%, NF 18.08) and nine to EModE (45%, NF 16.33). The difference in the number of examples between ME and EModE is, however, not statistically significant ($\chi^2$ (1) = 0; $p$ = 1). In total, *mortal* is attested in nine different collocations (cf. Table 6.81).

Some of the collocations of *mortal* are in fact specific to a given period. Thus, *mortal hatred* and *mortal prince* appear for the first time in the EModE data, and three other collocations, namely *mortal folk*, *mortal nature* and *mortal violence*, are only recorded in ME. The remaining four collocations (*mortal enemy*, *mortal life*, *mortal man* and *mortal thing*) are attested in both ME and EModE. *Mortal enemy*, for example, increased in frequency from ME to EModE, as indicated by the normalised figures, with a difference of 3.8 points between both periods. Conversely, *mortal life* and *mortal man*

Table 6.81. The collocations of *mortal* (adj.) in ME and EModE

| | Collocation | Abs. Freq. | % | NF | Total in HC |
|---|---|---|---|---|---|
| **ME** | *mortal enemy* | 1 | 25.00 | 1.64 | 4 |
| | *mortal folk* | 1 | 100.00 | 1.64 | 1 |
| | *mortal life* | 2 | 66.66 | 3.29 | 3 |
| | *mortal man* | 3 | 75.00 | 4.93 | 4 |
| | *mortal nature* | 1 | 100.00 | 1.64 | 1 |
| | *mortal thing* | 2 | 50.00 | 3.29 | 4 |
| | *mortal violence* | 1 | 100.00 | 1.64 | 1 |
| | **Total** | **11** | **55.00** | **18.08** | **20** |
| **EModE** | *mortal enemy* | 3 | 75.00 | 5.44 | 4 |
| | *mortal hatred* | 1 | 100.00 | 1.81 | 1 |
| | *mortal life* | 1 | 33.33 | 1.81 | 3 |
| | *mortal man* | 1 | 25.00 | 1.81 | 4 |
| | *mortal prince* | 1 | 100.00 | 1.81 | 1 |
| | *mortal thing* | 2 | 50.00 | 3.63 | 4 |
| | **Total** | **9** | **45.00** | **16.33** | **20** |

Table 6.82. Standardised scores for *mortal* (adj.) in the HC

| Collocation | *z*-score | *MI* | *MI3* | *LL*-value |
|---|---|---|---|---|
| *mortal enemy* | 76.742 | 10.526 | 14.526 | 50.486 |
| *mortal life* | 25.515 | 7.775 | 10.945 | 26.374 |
| *mortal man* | 14.609 | 5.790 | 9.790 | 25.006 |
| *mortal thing* | 19.730 | 6.634 | 10.634 | 28.874 |

had become less frequent by EModE. The former, for instance, has only one token less in EModE than in ME, but the normalised frequencies indicate a drop of 1.48 points; the same holds for *mortal man*, documented three times in the ME data and only once in EModE, but the normalised frequencies indicate a difference of 3.12 points. The only collocation which seems to remain stable over time in the corpus data is *mortal thing*, with two occurrences in both periods and a difference of 0.34 points. The difference in the use of these collocations in both ME and EModE is not considered statistically significant, according to Fisher's exact test values. Moreover, the association between the adjective *deadly* and its collocates *enemy*, *life*, *man* and *thing* was found to be statistically significant, as indicated by the different standardised scores for *mortal* (adj.), displayed in Table 6.82.

As far as meaning is concerned, three quarters of the meanings of *mortal* in the HC are descriptive (75%, fifteen tokens), while only 25% of them (five tokens) are subjective, as shown in Table 6.83. As becomes apparent from the data, descriptive meanings are reduced in about 33% from ME to EModE, with a difference of over seven points. In turn, subjective meanings grow exponentially in EModE, as there was just one occurrence in ME which was counted as subjective, represented by the collocation *deadly enemy*. The difference in subjective meanings between ME and EModE is of 5.62 points, that is, 60%. However, the variation in the number of descriptive and subjective uses of *mortal* (adj.) in the two periods is not statistically significant.[30] As was the case with the adjective and the adverb

30 Fisher's exact test = 0.310747 for descriptive uses and 0.197826 for subjective uses.

*deadly*, however, the corpus data does not provide any evidence for intensifying readings of *mortal*.

Examples (6.149)–(6.151) exemplify the types of meaning of the adjective in the corpus. Example (6.149) counts as a descriptive reading of *mortal*, whereas in (6.150) and (6.151) *mortal* is taken to be subjective. In the first example *mortal* thus opposes the divine, that is, the person in question is a human prince and not a god, and as a human he is subject to death. In turn, (6.150) describes a scene in which Mrs. Sullen tells Archer, a beau, that she will hate him unless he obeys her orders. Bearing an implacable or intense hatred for someone does not by definition imply that one wishes his/her death, or, let alone, that any intention whatsoever of killing that person is manifested. However, in this particular collocation *mortal* is still relatively attached to its original meaning: we might not know the impact of this feeling of loathing for someone, but we may as well interpret that its intensity can certainly harm the other person, though only metaphorically. Finally, example (6.151) narrates Richard Torkington's pilgrimage to Jerusalem in 1517. This passage in particular relates an event in which the tempest was so strong that he and his crew were unable to hold the course of the boat and feared that they would end up in Barbaria, the land inhabited by the Turks, the Mamluks and the Saracens, as he quotes. Similarly to *mortal hatred* in (6.150), a *mortal enemy* here does not imply that the enemy has the intrinsic ability or faculty of killing, in the same way as a mortal disease would do, for example. This explains why the meaning of *mortal* is not taken as literal or descriptive, but as subjective instead. The enemy is hence described as mortal because battles were fought to death. Moreover, this specific example must be read in its sociohistorical context. The Middle Ages were the time of the Crusades, the military campaigns which Christians led against Muslims, who were considered to be the enemy.

(6.149) *Whan this* ***mortall*** *Prynce was thus dede and grauen* ['buried'] *Kynge Henry was in quyet possessyon of the Realme* [...] (CEHIST1B. 1516. Robert Fabyan. *The new chronicles of England and France*)

(6.150) *Hold, Sir, For my most* ***mortal*** *hatred follows if you disobey what I command you now* (CEPLAY3B. 1707. George Farquhar. *The beaux stratagem*)

(6.151) *And sore we war offeryd to be dryff in to Barbaria, where Dwellyth ower* ***Mortall*** *Enimys*, (CETRAV1B. 1500- 1570. Richard Torkington. *Ye oldest diarie of Englysshe travell*)

Table 6.83. Meaning types for *mortal* (adj.) in the HC

| Period | D | | | S | | | I | | | Total | NF |
|---|---|---|---|---|---|---|---|---|---|---|---|
| | Abs. Freq. | % | NF | Abs. Freq. | % | NF | Abs. Freq. | % | NF | | |
| ME | 10 | 66.67 | 16.43 | 1 | 20.00 | 1.64 | 0 | 0.00 | 0 | 11 | 18.08 |
| EModE | 5 | 33.33 | 9.07 | 4 | 80.00 | 7.26 | 0 | 0.00 | 0 | 9 | 16.33 |

As mentioned above, *mortal* occurs in the data only as an adjective, on which account it is only attested as a noun modifier in the corpus across all periods, as shown in Table 6.84.

The semantic prosody of *mortal* is similar to that of *deadly*, since there are no examples in the data in which it shows positive polarity. Instead, in all its occurrences in the HC, *mortal* seems to appear in combination with elements which have either negative or neutral semantic prosody (cf. Table 6.85). The differences between ME and EModE are hence conspicuous: there has been an increase of about 26% in the occurrence of *mortal* with negative elements over time (3.97 points), and, in turn, the percentage of neutral elements combining with *mortal* has decreased in about 26% (NF 5.72). Nevertheless, this difference is not statistically significant, in the light of Fisher's exact test values (0.432851 for the negative semantic prosody and 0.432034 for the neutral semantic prosody). If we examine the semantic prosody more closely in combination with the collocations, then it becomes apparent that this growth in negative semantic prosody coincides with two subjective collocations which are inherently negative, namely *mortal enemy* and *mortal hatred*.

Table 6.84. Categories modified by *mortal* (adj.) in the HC

| Period | N | | Total | NF |
|---|---|---|---|---|
| | Abs. Freq. | NF | | |
| ME | 11 | 18.08 | 11 | 18.08 |
| EModE | 9 | 16.33 | 9 | 16.33 |

Table 6.85. The semantic prosody of *mortal* (adj.) in the HC

| Period | Neg | | | Pos | | | Neu | | | Total | NF |
|---|---|---|---|---|---|---|---|---|---|---|---|
| | Abs. Freq. | % | NF | Abs. Freq. | % | NF | Abs. Freq. | % | NF | | |
| ME | 2 | 18.18 | 3.29 | 0 | 0.00 | 0 | 9 | 81.82 | 14.79 | 11 | 6.99 |
| EModE | 4 | 44.44 | 7.26 | 0 | 0.00 | 0 | 5 | 55.56 | 9.07 | 9 | 5.72 |

The results from the HC seem to confirm the preliminary evidence on the evolution of *mortal* provided by the historical dictionaries (cf. Section 6.1.3), even though, it should be remembered, there are no tokens of the adverb *mortal* in the corpus. The first occurrences of the adjective date to the third subperiod of ME (1350–420), which coincides with the very first quotations in both the MED and the OED. In the HC the first examples of *mortal* are descriptive, corresponding to the collocations *mortal man*, *mortal folk* and *mortal thing*. As shown in Section 6.1.3, when *mortal* was borrowed from Anglo-Norman and Middle French at the close of the fourteenth century, it could occur not only with descriptive meanings, but also in combination with nouns referring to feelings such as hatred or fear, hence showing incipient subjectivity. In the case of the HC, subjective meanings of *mortal* do not appear until the last subperiod of the corpus (1420–500), though only in one collocation: *mortal enemy*. In the EModE period, however, such meanings become more frequent, accounting for 80% of the total of subjective readings in the corpus. By contrast, intensifying meanings are not attested in the HC, although, as suggested by the OED, these were possible from the eighteenth century. In sum, then, the adjective *mortal* seems to have developed more subjective readings over time, and to co-occur predominantly with elements which have either neutral or negative semantic prosody, hence retaining traces of its original negative meaning.

As regards the data from ARCHER, the adjective *mortal* is attested in thirty-three examples, which are distributed along the seventeenth (21%), eighteenth (39%), nineteenth (28%) and twentieth centuries (12%). The difference in the absolute frequencies among these periods is, however, not statistically significant, according to the values resulting from Fisher's exact test and the chi-square test.[31]

Further to the collocations, their token frequency is actually very low, with only four collocations attested a minimum of three times in the data: *mortal enemy* (four tokens), *mortal life* (three tokens), *mortal majesty* (three tokens) and *mortal man* (three tokens). The occurrence of the collocations over the different centuries (cf. Table 6.86) is, however, not systematic, since some of them are not attested at a given century, which makes it impossible to track the development of any specific collocation.

Even so, those collocations which are recorded in the corpus with a threshold frequency of three or more have been tested to determine their collocational strength in the light of four different values, as was done for the different intensifiers in the HC. The results of the Mutual Information (*MI*), the log-likelihood test (*LL*), the *z*-score and the *MI* formula taken to the power of three (*MI3*) indicate that the co-occurrence of *mortal* with the nouns *majesty*, *man*, *enemy* and *life* is in fact highly significant and not to be attributed to chance (cf. Table 6.87 for the different values).

In regard to the types of meanings, about 79% of the total of the occurrences of *mortal* in ARCHER evince a descriptive or literal meaning, while the remaining 21% show subjective readings of the adjective. There are, therefore, no instances of intensifying *mortal* in the data. The distribution of the different meaning types of the adjective over the centuries is shown in Table 6.88. The difference in the number of tokens for each of these meanings in the four periods turned out not to be statistically significant, in the light of the values from the chi-square test and Fisher's exact test.[32]

Example (6.152) shows a descriptive reading of the adjective, *mortal* meaning in this case 'subject to death', which thus contrasts with the divine. Conversely, (6.153) and (6.154) illustrate subjective readings of *mortal*, for the adjective in this case is not interpreted literally, referring instead to

31 **17th > 18th c.:** $\chi^2$ (1) = 0.03; $p$ = 0.86249023; **18th > 19th c.:** $\chi^2$ (1) = 0.448; $p$ = 0.50328626; **19th > 20th c.:** Fisher's exact test = 0.267216.

32 *Descriptive meanings*: 17th > 18th c. $\chi^2$ (1) = 0; $p$ = 1; 18th > 19th c. $\chi^2$ (1) = 0.001; $p$ = 0.97477288; 19th > 20th c. Fisher's exact test = 0.146281; *subjective meanings*: 17th > 18th c. Fisher's exact test = 0.41373; 18th > 20th c. Fisher's exact test = 0.218779.

Table 6.86. The collocations of *mortal* (adj.) in ARCHER

| | Collocation | Abs. Freq. | % | NF | Total in ARCHER |
|---|---|---|---|---|---|
| **17th c.** | *mortal battle* | 1 | 100.00 | 2.87 | 1 |
| | *mortal breeding* | 1 | 100.00 | 2.87 | 1 |
| | *mortal frailty* | 1 | 100.00 | 2.87 | 1 |
| | *mortal hatred* | 1 | 50.00 | 2.87 | 2 |
| | *mortal mould* | 1 | 50.00 | 2.87 | 2 |
| | *mortal parent* | 1 | 50.00 | 2.87 | 2 |
| | *mortal syncope* | 1 | 100.00 | 2.87 | 1 |
| | **Total** | 7 | **21.21** | **20.09** | **33** |
| **18th c.** | *mortal blackness* | 1 | 100.00 | 1.87 | 1 |
| | *mortal enemy* | 3 | 75.00 | 5.60 | 4 |
| | *mortal hatred* | 1 | 50.00 | 1.87 | 2 |
| | *mortal life* | 3 | 100.00 | 5.60 | 3 |
| | *mortal majesty* | 3 | 100.00 | 5.60 | 3 |
| | *mortal man* | 1 | 33.33 | 1.87 | 3 |
| | *mortal poison* | 1 | 100.00 | 1.87 | 1 |
| | **Total** | **13** | **39.39** | **24.26** | **33** |
| **19th c.** | *mortal eye* | 1 | 100.00 | 1.84 | 1 |
| | *mortal inquietude* | 1 | 100.00 | 1.84 | 1 |
| | *mortal loss* | 1 | 100.00 | 1.84 | 1 |
| | *mortal mould* | 1 | 50.00 | 1.84 | 2 |
| | *mortal parent* | 1 | 50.00 | 1.84 | 2 |
| | *mortal part* | 1 | 100.00 | 1.84 | 1 |
| | *mortal sole* | 1 | 100.00 | 1.84 | 1 |
| | *mortal state* | 1 | 100.00 | 1.84 | 1 |
| | *mortal tongue* | 1 | 100.00 | 1.84 | 1 |
| | **Total** | **9** | **27.27** | **16.59** | **33** |

(*continued*)

Table 6.86. Continued

| | Collocation | Abs. Freq. | % | NF | Total in ARCHER |
|---|---|---|---|---|---|
| 20th c. | *mortal enemy* | 1 | 25.00 | 1.88 | 4 |
| | *mortal man* | 2 | 66.67 | 3.77 | 3 |
| | *mortal sin* | 1 | 100.00 | 1.88 | 1 |
| | **Total** | **4** | **12.12** | **7.54** | **33** |

Table 6.87. Standardised scores for *mortal* (adj.) in ARCHER

| Collocation | *z*-score | *MI* | *MI3* | *LL*-value |
|---|---|---|---|---|
| *mortal enemy* | 39.810 | 8.637 | 12.637 | 39.959 |
| *mortal life* | 14.378 | 6.148 | 9.317 | 19.657 |
| *mortal majesty* | 30.416 | 8.278 | 11.448 | 28.471 |
| *mortal man* | 8.912 | 4.830 | 8.000 | 14.300 |

Table 6.88. Meaning types for *mortal* (adj.) in ARCHER

| | | D | S | Total |
|---|---|---|---|---|
| 17th c. | # | 6 | 1 | 7 |
| | % | 23.08 | 14.29 | 21.22 |
| | NF | 17.22 | 2.87 | 20.09 |
| 18th c. | # | 8 | 5 | 13 |
| | % | 30.76 | 71.43 | 39.39 |
| | NF | 14.93 | 9.33 | 24.26 |
| 19th c. | # | 9 | 0 | 9 |
| | % | 34.62 | 0.00 | 27.27 |
| | NF | 16.59 | 0 | 16.59 |
| 20th c. | # | 3 | 1 | 4 |
| | % | 11.54 | 14.28 | 12.12 |
| | NF | 5.65 | 1.88 | 7.54 |
| **Total (#)** | | **26** | **7** | **33** |

qualities which are commonly related to death. In (6.153), for instance, Lord Lyttleton is described as a mortal enemy, that is, a person who is much hated by this character and with whom the character has argued, perhaps even fought to death. The same idea is present in example (6.154), since bearing a mortal hatred to someone is equivalent to being his/her mortal enemy.

(6.152) *He shewed me here two or three Turkish Emperors, to whom his most* ***mortal*** *Majesty seemed to express much Civility*. (1743fiel_f3b. Henry Fielding. *A journey from this world to the next*)

(6.153) *He says, that I am in a close Confederacy with Lord Lyttleton, his* ***mortal*** *Enemy*, (1766hume_x4b. 1766. David Hume. *New letters of David Hume*)

(6.154) *But from that time Lyndaraxa bore me a* ***mortal*** *hatred, and solemnly swore to Sabina to be revenged of me the first opportunity she could find*. (1702anon_f3b. 1702. Anonymous. *The adventures of Lindamira, a lady of quality*)

Concerning semantic prosody (cf. Table 6.89), 40% of the occurrences of *mortal* in the corpus have negative semantic prosody, and 60% show neutral semantic prosody. The difference in the absolute frequencies for both the negative and the neutral semantic prosodies between the four centuries was not found to be statistically significant, in view of the results from Fisher's exact test and the chi-square test.[33]

The last variable considered in the data was the category of word modified by the adjective. Considering that *mortal* is an adjective and that adjectives chiefly denote qualities of nouns, it comes as no surprise that *mortal* is found as a modifier of nouns in all its occurrences in the corpus, as shown in Table 6.90.

The evidence for the adverb *mortal* in ARCHER is extremely scarce, since only one token is attested in the data, specifically in the twentieth century. In this example, (6.155), *mortal* functions as an intensifier and modifies the adjective *hard*, which has negative semantic prosody. On the basis of the data available, therefore, nothing can be concluded in regard to the evolution of this adverb over time.

(6.155) *It's* ***mortal*** *'ard, sir, that a man o' my years should be tole, 'e in liquor twice in one evenin'*! (1911besi_d7b. 1911. Rudolf Besier. *Lady Patricia Clare*)

33 *Negative semantic prosody*: 17th c. > 18th c. Fisher's exact test = 0.745562; 18th c. > 19th c. Fisher's exact test = 0.286034; 19th c. > 20th c. Fisher's exact test = 1; *neutral semantic prosody*: 17th c. > 18th c. Fisher's exact test = 0.544067; 18th c. > 19th c. $\chi^2(1) = 0.001$; $p = 0.97477288$; 19th c. > 20th c. Fisher's exact test = 0.17992.

Table 6.89. The semantic prosody of *mortal* (adj.) in ARCHER

| | | D | S | Total |
|---|---|---|---|---|
| **17th c.** | # | 4 | 3 | 7 |
| | % | 30.77 | 15.00 | 21.21 |
| | **NF** | 11.48 | 8.61 | 20.09 |
| **18th c.** | # | 5 | 8 | 13 |
| | % | 38.46 | 40.00 | 39.39 |
| | **NF** | 9.33 | 14.93 | 24.26 |
| **19th c.** | # | 2 | 7 | 9 |
| | % | 15.38 | 35.00 | 27.27 |
| | **NF** | 3.69 | 12.90 | 16.59 |
| **20th c.** | # | 2 | 2 | 4 |
| | % | 15.38 | 10.00 | 12.12 |
| | **NF** | 3.77 | 3.77 | 7.54 |
| **Total (#)** | | **13** | **20** | **33** |

Table 6.90. Categories modified by *mortal* (adj.)

| **Period** | **N** | | **NF** |
|---|---|---|---|
| | **Abs. Freq.** | % | |
| **17th c.** | 7 | 21.21 | 20.09 |
| **18th c.** | 13 | 39.39 | 24.26 |
| **19th c.** | 9 | 27.27 | 16.59 |
| **20th c.** | 4 | 12.12 | 7.54 |

The EEBOCorp 1.0 data record a total of 20,697 analysable tokens of *mortal* (adj.), in a total of 728 collocations. As shown in Table 6.91, the absolute frequencies for the adjective increase exponentially over time. This rise in the number of tokens of the adjective is significant for all the periods, except for the difference between P. I and P. II.[34]

34 **P. II > P. III** $\chi^2$ (1) = 55.606; $p$ = 0; **P. III > P. IV** $\chi^2$ (1) = 347.862; $p$ = 0; **P. IV > P. V** $\chi^2$ (1) = 683.554; $p$ = 0.

Table 6.91. *Mortal* (adj.) in EEBOCorp 1.0

| Period | Abs. Freq. | % | NF | Total |
|---|---|---|---|---|
| I (1470s–90s) | 204 | 0.99 | 6.97 | 20,697 |
| II (1500s–40s) | 853 | 4.12 | 83.30 | |
| III (1550s–90s) | 4,628 | 22.36 | 63.10 | |
| IV (1600s–40s) | 6,707 | 32.41 | 44.26 | |
| V (1650s–90s) | 8,305 | 40.12 | 28.90 | |

Considering the total number of collocations, it would be impractical to provide all of them on a table. Hence, Table 6.92 lists the most frequent collocations in the data, in particular those which are attested at least 100 times in the corpus. Table 6.93, in turn, provides their standardised scores. In the light of these values, all the collocations are significant, even though there are negative significance values for *mortal nature*, *mortal part*, *mortal state* and *mortal thing* according to the *MI*, and *mortal part* in regard to the *z*-score. Nonetheless, these figures must be interpreted cautiously, for certain collocates pose the same problem as with the adjective *deadly* (cf. Section 6.2.3). Thus, *battle*, *blow*, *disease*, *hate*, *sin*, *war* and *wound* can be both nouns and verbs and are in fact highly frequent forms in EEBOCorp 1.0. To calculate the standardised values, it should be recalled, we need not only the raw frequencies of these forms and of the adjective *mortal* in isolation: we also need their token frequencies in combination with *deadly*. However, filtering out the verbal from the nominal occurrences of these forms would be impractical given their high token frequency in the corpus. Even so, I have decided to include the standardised values to illustrate the significance of these collocations, for the values themselves would probably not differ too much after a manual pruning, considering the high frequency of these words.

As can be gathered from the list of collocates in Table 6.92, the adjective *mortal* modifies nouns in all the occurrences in the corpus, as we would expect considering its adjectival nature.

As far as the types of meanings are concerned, descriptive senses of adjectival *mortal* clearly prevail in the corpus, accounting for 83.28% of the

Table 6.92. Absolute and normalised frequencies for the most frequent collocates of *mortal* (adj.) in EEBOCorp 1.0

| **Collocation** | **Abs. Freq.** | **NF** |
|---|---|---|
| *mortal battle* | 121 | 0.22 |
| *mortal blow* | 165 | 0.31 |
| *mortal body* | 1,554 | 0.00 |
| *mortal creature* | 561 | 1.07 |
| *mortal disease* | 226 | 0.43 |
| *mortal enemy* | 1,799 | 0.00 |
| *mortal eye* | 592 | 1.13 |
| *mortal flesh* | 247 | 0.47 |
| *mortal foe* | 340 | 0.65 |
| *mortal hate* | 115 | 0.22 |
| *mortal hatred* | 269 | 0.51 |
| *mortal life* | 1,255 | 0.00 |
| *mortal man* | 4,567 | 0.01 |
| *mortal nature* | 151 | 0.29 |
| *mortal part* | 102 | 0.19 |
| *mortal sickness* | 109 | 0.21 |
| *mortal sin* | 2,153 | 4.10 |
| *mortal state* | 244 | 0.46 |
| *mortal thing* | 381 | 0.73 |
| *mortal war* | 241 | 0.46 |
| *mortal wight* | 237 | 0.45 |
| *mortal wound* | 693 | 1.32 |

occurrences, followed by subjective readings (14.82%), those occurrences which could be described as either descriptive or subjective (1.78%) and, finally, those which admit both a subjective and an intensifying reading (0.12%). The raw frequencies for each of the meanings of the adjective generally increase over time (cf. Table 6.94). However, this tendency is disrupted

Table 6.93. Standardised scores for *mortal* (adj.) in EEBOCorp 1.0

| **Collocation** | ***z*-score** | ***MI*** | ***MI3*** | ***LL*-value** |
|---|---|---|---|---|
| *mortal battle* | 85.360 | 5.959 | 19.797 | 763.219 (p < 0.0001) |
| *mortal blow* | 89.784 | 5.668 | 20.400 | 973.885 (p < 0.0001) |
| *mortal body* | 149.462 | 4.028 | 25.232 | 5,765.515 (p < 0.0001) |
| *mortal creature* | 102.412 | 4.368 | 22.632 | 2,331.830 (p < 0.0001) |
| *mortal disease* | 83.913 | 5.050 | 20.690 | 1,144.626 (p < 0.0001) |
| *mortal enemy* | 389.440 | 6.431 | 28.057 | 12,500.699 (p < 0.0001) |
| *mortal eye* | 77.174 | 3.582 | 22.001 | 1,856.163 (p < 0.0001) |
| *mortal flesh* | 39.050 | 3.009 | 18.906 | 598.022 (p < 0.0001) |
| *mortal foe* | 203.059 | 6.946 | 23.764 | 2,604.181 (p < 0.0001) |
| *mortal hate* | 55.928 | 4.866 | 18.557 | 554.039 (p < 0.0001) |
| *mortal hatred* | 159.700 | 6.597 | 22.740 | 1,930.682 (p < 0.0001) |
| *mortal life* | 113.963 | 3.617 | 24.204 | 3,990.130 (p < 0.0001) |
| *mortal man* | 195.884 | 3.365 | 27.680 | 13,068.975 (p < 0.0001) |
| *mortal nature* | 7.863 | 0.908 | 15.385 | 49.035 (p < 0.0001) |
| *mortal part* | -2.755 | -0.392 | 12.953 | 8.277 (p < 0.01) |
| *mortal sickness* | 42.819 | 4.230 | 17.767 | 433.263 (p < 0.0001) |
| *mortal sin* | 196.110 | 4.308 | 26.453 | 8,779.760 (p < 0.0001) |
| *mortal state* | 28.043 | 2.329 | 18.190 | 397.061 (p < 0.0001) |
| *mortal thing* | 8.626 | 0.632 | 17.780 | 63.617 (p < 0.0001) |
| *mortal war* | 46.131 | 3.425 | 19.250 | 707.537 (p < 0.0001) |
| *mortal wight* | 213.433 | 7.601 | 23.379 | 2,037.119 (p < 0.0001) |
| *mortal wound* | 266.014 | 6.702 | 25.575 | 5,083.099 (p < 0.0001) |

from P. I to P. II in regard to those instances which could be categorised as ambiguous between descriptive and subjective, and also from P. III to P. IV in regard to those meanings which are indeterminate between subjective and intensifying. The variation in the number of occurrences between the different periods was found to be statistically significant for descriptive

Table 6.94. Meaning types for *mortal* (adj.) in EEBOCorp 1.0

| | | D | D/S | S | S/I | Total |
|---|---|---|---|---|---|---|
| **1470–99** | **#** | 130 | 17 | 56 | 1 | 204 |
| | **%** | 0.76 | 4.62 | 1.83 | 3.85 | 0.99 |
| | **NF** | 44.42 | 5.81 | 19.13 | 0.34 | 69.70 |
| **1500–49** | **#** | 745 | 9 | 98 | 1 | 853 |
| | **%** | 4.32 | 2.44 | 3.20 | 3.85 | 4.12 |
| | **NF** | 72.75 | 0.88 | 9.57 | 0.10 | 83.30 |
| **1550–99** | **#** | 3,744 | 90 | 791 | 3 | 4,628 |
| | **%** | 21.72 | 24.46 | 25.79 | 11.54 | 22.36 |
| | **NF** | 51.05 | 1.23 | 10.78 | 0.04 | 63.10 |
| **1600–49** | **#** | 5,727 | 122 | 856 | 2 | 6,707 |
| | **%** | 33.23 | 33.15 | 27.90 | 7.69 | 32.41 |
| | **NF** | 37.79 | 0.81 | 5.65 | 0.01 | 44.26 |
| **1650–99** | **#** | 6,890 | 130 | 1,266 | 19 | 8,305 |
| | **%** | 39.97 | 35.33 | 41.28 | 73.08 | 40.13 |
| | **NF** | 23.98 | 0.45 | 4.41 | 0.07 | 28.90 |
| **Total (#)** | | **17,236** | **368** | **3,067** | **26** | **20,697** |

meanings.[35] The rise in frequency was only significant in the transition from P. I to P. II and from P. IV to P. V concerning those cases which were classified as ambiguous between descriptive and subjective ($\chi^2$ (1) = 25.568; $p$ = 0.00000043 for P. I and P. II; $\chi^2$ (1) = 20.88; $p$ = 0.00000489 for P. IV and P. V). As far as subjective meanings are concerned, the variation is only not significant if we compare the frequencies of P. II and P. III.[36] Finally, the different frequencies for those meanings which can be rated as ambiguous between subjective and intensifying are only significant at $p < 0.05$ if we compare P. IV and P. V (Fisher's exact test = 0.019152).

35 **P. I > P. II** ($\chi^2$ (1) = 27.08; $p$ = 0.0000002; **P. II > P. III** $\chi^2$ (1) = 78.42; $p$ = 0; **P. III > P. IV** $\chi^2$ (1) = 205.987; $p$ = 0; **P. IV > P. V** $\chi^2$ (1) = 658.08; $p$ = 0.

36 **P.I > P. II** ($\chi^2$ (1) = 16.99; $p$ = 0.00003762322; **P. III >P. IV** $\chi^2$ (1) = 177.37; $p$ = 0; **P. IV > P. V** $\chi^2$ (1) = 31.44; $p$ = 0.00000002.

Illustrations of the different types of meanings of the adjective *mortal* are provided in examples (6.156)–(6.161). *Mortal vapour* in (6.156) denotes the contaminated air which has caused the death of many people in the city of Troy, bringing about a fatal epidemic disease. It is, therefore, an example of a descriptive meaning of the adjective, being here a synonym of *fatal, deadly*.

(6.156) *Wherof roos a corrupte and a* ***mortall*** *vapour that Infectid alle the Cyte* [...]. (D00000998449480000. 1473. Raoul Lefèvre. *The recuyell of the historyes of Troye*).

Conversely, examples (6.157)–(6.158) show subjective meanings of *mortal*. A mortal distress is a feeling of extreme anxiety and sorrow, which may as well be accompanied by physical discomfort, even if in principle it is not deadly. The collocation *mortal anger* in (6.158) refers to the rage felt by Bradaman Campeon, known as a fierce warrior. His mortal anger, however, is not lethal. What is deadly in this case is the power of the weapons used by this person, since we know that, as a matter of fact, blood 'flowed with great aboundance'.

(6.157) *And then~e ought not I to haue the vysage banisshid fro alle consolacion and Ioye & ought not my herte to lye on the bedde of tribulacion vnder the couertour of right* ***mortal*** *distresse & betwene the shetes of bewaylinges*; (D00000998546500000. 1477. Raoul Lefèvre. [...] *The historie of Iason*)

(6.158) *This daye was the death of the Gran Campion* [...] *for that his sonne for to make cruell reuengement for the same, with furious wrath and* ***mortall*** *anger, doth destroy & ouerthrow all that commeth before him*, (D00000998488760000. 1586. Diego Ortúñez de Calahorra. *The third part of the first booke, of the Mirrour of knighthood*)

Finally, the corpus also records some cases of collocations which pave the way for the later emergence of unambiguously intensifying meanings. This is the case of *mortal envy, mortal hatred* and *mortal displeasure* in (6.159) – (6.161), which have been classified as intermediate between subjective and intensifying. Feeling envy for someone does not automatically imply hating him/her or bearing him/her any ill will and instead a mortal envy could simply be read as an extreme or huge envy, as in (6.159), which allows both a subjective and an intensifying reading. The same applies to the collocation *mortal hatred and displeasure* in example (6.160) and to *mortal displeasure* in (6.161). Example (6.160), for instance, mentions specifically a prince's servant who lost the prince's favour after offending him. In this context, we might interpret that the prince might feel infuriated and consequently take revenge on the servant, so the collocations are more likely to have a subjective reading. Example (6.161), though showing the same collocation, presents a different context. The mortal displeasure here is not caused by anyone in particular, but it is rather a specific situation which is annoying, in this case for a citizen from Rouen to be deprived of his children and give them a pension. The mortal displeasure in this example is thus more likely to be interpreted as having an intensifying reading. Examples such as this one might in fact favour unequivocally intensifying readings of the adjective later on.

(6.159) *If two Sunnes cannot shine within one spheare, Then why should two arch-villaines? thou hast discouered Projects almost beyond me, and for which I haue ingrost a* ***mortall*** *enuy here, I will be sole, or none.* (D00000998397890000. 1632. Thomas Heywood. *The iron age* [...])

(6.160) *Which, how great a losse it is, we may esteeme in part, by the state of a worldly princes seruant and fauorite, who being in highe grace and credit with his Soueraine, should by some one great offence lose al his fauour at one instant, and incurre his* ***mortal*** *hatred and displeasure.* (D00000998493970000. 1585. Robert Parsons. *A Christian directorie guiding men to their saluation*)

(6.161) *where is there a father that can digest the* ***mortal*** *displeasure to see himself bereaved of the fruits of his Marriage, and to be condemned afterwards to pay them a Pension,* (D00000135340670000. 1681. Edmund Everard. *The great pressures and grievances of the Protestants in France* [...])

Concerning the variable semantic prosody, the results from EEBOCorp 1.0 indicate that *mortal* occurs in 59.60% of the cases in combination with neutral elements, followed by negative (39.09%) and positive ones (1.31%). Table 6.95 displays the total number of tokens of the adjective per period for each of the three prosodies. Although the individual frequencies increase over time, these results are not statistically significant for positive semantic prosody. It is only the increase in the number of occurrences with neutral semantic prosody that is considered statistically significant in all periods.[37]

37 **P. I > P. II** $\chi^2$ (1) = 16.903; $p$ = 0.00003142; **P. II > P. III** $\chi^2$ (1) = 11.17; $p$ = 0.00075489; **P. III > P. IV** $\chi^2$ (1) = 170.091; $p$ = 0; **P. IV > P. V** $\chi^2$ (1) = 575.09; $p$ = 0.

Table 6.95. Semantic prosody for *mortal* (adj.) in EEBOCorp 1.0

| | | Neg | Neu | Pos | Total |
|---|---|---|---|---|---|
| **1470–99** | # | 123 | 80 | 1 | 204 |
| | % | 1.52 | 0.65 | 0.37 | 0.99 |
| | **NF** | 42.02 | 27.33 | 0.34 | 69.70 |
| **1500–49** | # | 386 | 461 | 6 | 853 |
| | % | 4.77 | 3.74 | 2.21 | 4.12 |
| | **NF** | 37.70 | 45.02 | 0.59 | 83.30 |
| **1550–99** | # | 1,798 | 2,788 | 42 | 4,628 |
| | % | 22.22 | 22.60 | 15.50 | 22.36 |
| | **NF** | 24.51 | 38.01 | 0.57 | 63.10 |
| **1600–49** | # | 2,440 | 4,193 | 74 | 6,707 |
| | % | 30.16 | 33.99 | 27.31 | 32.41 |
| | **NF** | 16.10 | 27.67 | 0.49 | 44.26 |
| **1650–99** | # | 3,344 | 4,813 | 148 | 8,305 |
| | % | 41.33 | 39.02 | 54.61 | 40.13 |
| | **NF** | 11.64 | 16.75 | 0.52 | 28.90 |
| **Total (#)** | | **8,091** | **12,335** | **271** | **20,697** |

Likewise, the results for negative semantic prosody indicate that it is statistically significant in all periods except for the transition from P. I to P. II.[38]

Examples of the collocates in the data with neutral semantic prosody include *folk* and *vapour*, but also collocations such as *mortal judgement*, *mortal thing*, *mortal name*, *mortal engine*, *mortal life* and *mortal body*, among many others. It is clear that these nouns cannot per se be neither negative nor positive, and have hence been marked as neutral. Instances of inherently negative nouns collocating with the adjective *mortal* are also numerous in the corpus data, including, by way of illustration, *encumbrance*, *adversary*, *battle*, *peril*, *sorrow*, *danger*, *pain*, *wretchedness*, *heaviness*, *pestilence*, etc.

38 **P. II > P. III** $\chi^2$ (1) = 59.24; $p$ = 0; **P. III > P. IV** $\chi^2$ (1) = 185.26; $p$ = 0; **P. IV > P. V** $\chi^2$ (1) = 149.67; $p$ = 0.

Conversely, the collocates of *mortal* which are positive in meaning are relatively few, and include, among others, *pleasure*, *amity*, *delight*, *fame*, *reward*, *love*, *majesty* and *hope*.

In contrast to the adjectival form, EEBOCorp 1.0 hardly yields any evidence of the adverb *mortal*, since there are only four analysable tokens over three different periods, as shown in Table 6.96. The increase in one example from P. IV to P. V is not considered statistically significant (Fisher's exact test = 0.999999).

As regards its collocates, *mortal* (adv.) is attested in the data in combination with the participial element *wounded* (example (6.162) and the adjectives *sick* and *pale* ((6.163) and (6.164)).

(6.162) *Terry with louing thankes, his loue requites, And brings him to his foe, whom he defies: And valiant with the aduerse Champion fights, Till* ***mortall*** *wounded,* (D00000255958460000. 1620. Samuel Rowlands. *The famous history, of Guy Earle of Warwicke*)

(6.163) *A sottell Snack of laet, with sopple sugred words Haeth sleely crept in brestes of men* [...] *And drawn the marchant from his traed, and plowman from the ploughe Disenshon is his name* [...] *And maks them* ***mortall*** *sick, and sway somtims a sied* [...] (D00000998407130000. 1575. Thomas Churchyard. *The firste parte of Churchyardes chippes*)

(6.164) *His Blood, which rather you'd believe were hers, So* ***mortal*** *pale her lovely Face appears*: (D00000172430770000. 1693. Samuel Wesley. *The life of our blessed Lord & Saviour*)

The collocations *mortal wounded* and *mortal sick* are considered as descriptive, for they describe a literal meaning of the adverb. In (6.162) a character named Terry is wounded and dies as a consequence, while (6.163) mentions a snake which creeps in the breasts of men and, as a consequence, they fall ill. By contrast, in (6.164) the collocation *mortal pale* is regarded as subjective.

Table 6.96. *Mortal* (adv.) in EEBOCorp 1.0

| Period | Abs. Freq. | % | NF | Total |
|---|---|---|---|---|
| III (1550s–90s) | 1 | 25.00 | 0.01 | 4 |
| IV (1600s–40s) | 1 | 25.00 | 0.01 | |
| V (1650s–90s) | 2 | 50.00 | 0.01 | |

Being pale or pallid does not imply by any means being dead, although the connections with death itself are self-evident: the woman resembles a corpse on account of her paleness. Descriptive meanings, therefore, account for the majority of the examples of the adverb *mortal* in the corpus (75%), whereas subjective meanings, represented only by this collocation, amount to 25% of the total (cf. Table 6.97).

The three different collocations of *mortal* in the data, namely *mortal wounded*, *mortal sick* and *mortal pale*, also throw light on the semantic prosody of the adverb. Thus, *mortal* is mostly attested with negative semantic prosody (hence *mortal wounded* and *mortal sick*), which accounts for 75% of the total, while neutral semantic prosody (*mortal pale*) represents 25% of the total, as shown in Table 6.98 for the different periods.

In regard to the types of words modified by the adverb, and despite the overall low frequencies, *mortal* likewise modifies adjectives (*sick*, *pale*) and participial items (*wounded*), as shown in Table 6.99.

Therefore, although the EModE data for the adverb *mortal* is very scarce, the evidence suggests that it functions as a modifier of both participial forms and adjectives, and that it is attested mainly with negative semantic prosody. Descriptive readings represent the majority in the data,

Table 6.97. Meaning types for *mortal* (adv.) in EEBOCorp 1.0

| | | D | S | Total |
|---|---|---|---|---|
| **1550–99** | # | 1 | 0 | 1 |
| | % | 33.33 | 0.00 | 25.00 |
| | NF | 0.01 | 0 | 0.01 |
| **1600–49** | # | 1 | 0 | 1 |
| | % | 33.33 | 0.00 | 25.00 |
| | NF | 0.01 | 0 | 0.01 |
| **1650–99** | # | 1 | 1 | 2 |
| | % | 33.33 | 100.00 | 50.00 |
| | NF | 0 | 0 | 0.01 |
| **Total (#)** | | **3** | **1** | **4** |

Table 6.98. Semantic prosody for *mortal* (adv.) in EEBOCorp 1.0

| | | Neg | Neu | Total |
|---|---|---|---|---|
| **1550–99** | # | 1 | 0 | 1 |
| | % | 33.00 | 0.00 | 25.00 |
| | **NF** | 0.01 | 0 | 0.01 |
| **1600–49** | # | 1 | 0 | 1 |
| | % | 33.33 | 0.00 | 25.00 |
| | **NF** | 0.01 | 0 | 0.01 |
| **1650–99** | # | 1 | 1 | 2 |
| | % | 33.33 | 100.00 | 50.00 |
| | **NF** | 0 | 0 | 0.01 |
| **Total (#)** | | **3** | **1** | **4** |

Table 6.99. Categories modified by *mortal* (adv.) in EEBOCorp 1.0

| | | Adj | Part | Total |
|---|---|---|---|---|
| **1550–99** | # | 1 | 0 | 1 |
| | % | 50.00 | 0.00 | 25.00 |
| | **NF** | 0.01 | 0 | 0.01 |
| **1600–49** | # | 0 | 1 | 1 |
| | % | 0.00 | 50.00 | 25.00 |
| | **NF** | 0 | 0.01 | 0.01 |
| **1650–99** | # | 1 | 1 | 2 |
| | % | 50.00 | 50.00 | 50.00 |
| | **NF** | 0 | 0 | 0.01 |
| **Total (#)** | | **2** | **2** | **4** |

since there are no intensifying examples of the adverb and subjective interpretations account only for 25% of the total.

The eighteenth-century evidence from ECF records a total of 286 tokens of *mortal* (adj.) in 106 collocations. For convenience, and in view of the impracticality of displaying all these collocates of *mortal* on a table, only those which are attested at least ten times are given in Table 6.100. Table 6.101 additionally gives the standardised scores for these collocates, so as to determine their degree of collocational strength with the node *mortal*. As suggested by these scores, the five most frequent collocations, namely *mortal man*, *mortal enemy*, *mortal life*, *mortal wound* and *mortal offence*, are all highly statistically significant. There is, therefore, a close link between the adjective and its collocates. Moreover, in line with the results for the adjective *mortal* in the other sources consulted, and as was the case with the adjectives *dead* or *deadly*, *mortal* is only recorded as a modifier of nouns.

Table 6.100. Absolute and normalised frequencies for the most frequent collocations of *mortal* (adj.) in ECF

| **Collocation** | **Abs. Freq.** | **NF** |
|---|---|---|
| *mortal enemy* | 17 | 1.75 |
| *mortal life* | 16 | 1.65 |
| *mortal man* | 37 | 3.81 |
| *mortal offence* | 11 | 1.13 |
| *mortal wound* | 15 | 1.55 |

Table 6.101. Standardised scores for *mortal* (adj.) in ECF

| **Collocation** | ***z*-score** | ***MI*** | ***MI3*** | ***LL*-value** |
|---|---|---|---|---|
| *mortal enemy* | 33.876 | 6.119 | 14.294 | 110.827 ($p < 0.0001$) |
| *mortal life* | 13.276 | 3.694 | 11.694 | 52.422 ($p < 0.0001$) |
| *mortal man* | 17.493 | 3.347 | 13.765 | 104.963 ($p < 0.0001$) |
| *mortal offence* | 33.429 | 6.695 | 13.613 | 80.433 ($p < 0.0001$) |
| *mortal wound* | 46.123 | 7.168 | 14.982 | 119.518 ($p < 0.0001$) |

Table 6.102. Meaning types for *mortal* (adj.) in ECF

| | **Abs. Freq.** | **%** | **NF** |
|---|---|---|---|
| **D** | 207 | 72.38 | 21.33 |
| **D/S** | 7 | 2.45 | 0.72 |
| **S** | 69 | 24.12 | 7.11 |
| **S/I** | 3 | 1.05 | 0.31 |
| **Total** | **286** | **100.00** | **29.48** |

In what concerns the types of meanings of the adjective (cf. Table 6.102), *mortal* is documented in the majority of the cases in ECF with descriptive meanings (72.38%), followed by subjective ones (24.12%). To a lesser extent, *mortal* is also found with readings which are ambiguous between descriptive and subjective (2.45%) and with those between subjective and intensifying (1.05%). Purely intensifying instances of the adjective are not attested in the data.

A selection of the different types of meanings in ECF is provided in (6.165)–(6.169). Example (6.165) presents a descriptive or literal meaning, as it can be paraphrased with 'human understanding'. By contrast, the collocation *mortal danger* in (6.166) was marked as ambiguous between descriptive and subjective, for it is not completely literal, as is the case of a disease or a wound. Something may be dangerous and imply a certain risk, but it may not necessarily have a fatal result. In turn, *mortal agony* in (6.167) and *mortal inquietude* in (6.168) were regarded as subjective, since being in a state of restlessness or anguish can make one feel in such a poor general condition, both physically and psychologically, as to think himself or herself on the verge of dying. However, these collocations are not considered as descriptive, as feeling distressed or sorrowful does not mean that one is going to perish. *Mortal displeasure* in (6.169) is instead regarded as a meaning which is ambiguous between subjective and intensifying. In this case, the female protagonist of the story has been offended and is angry with the male protagonist. Considering that she is now angry and displeased with the male character, she might decide to take some kind of revenge on him. However, given the context, it is also likely to interpret the collocation *mortal displeasure* here as 'great displeasure', being therefore closer to an intensifying reading. Both interpretations seem to be possible here.

(6.165) [...] *I concluded there was a mystery in religion above* ***mortal*** *comprehension, or at least that it was perfectly incommunicable to another.* (1754. Sarah Fielding. *The cry*)

(6.166) [...] *a judicious physician shall be able, at any time, to persuade them that they are in* ***mortal*** *danger.* (1770. Frances Chamberlaine Sheridan. *Conclusion of the Memoirs of Miss Sidney Bidulph*)

(6.167) *She seem'd surpriz'd at seeing me so early, and with her wonted good Humour, asking me the reason of it, put me into a* ***mortal*** *Agony how to answer her;* (1725. Eliza Fowler Haywood. *Love in excess*)

(6.168) *How strange, then, is it, that the letter in which she tells me she is the happiest of human beings, should give me the most* ***mortal*** *inquietude*! (1778–1788. Fanny Burney. *Evelina*)

(6.169) *To this was owing the ready offence you took at my four friends; and at the unavailing attempt I made to see a dropt Letter; little imagining from what two such Ladies could write to each other, that there could be room for* ***mortal*** *displeasure.* (1748. Samuel Richardson. *Clarissa*)

As for semantic prosody, *mortal* is found in the data mainly with neutral (48.60%) or negative (46.15%) elements, while positive collocates are much more rarely attested, accounting only for 5.25% of the total (cf. Table 6.103).

Among the collocates with neutral semantic prosody we find the nouns *man, body, race, nature, mould* and *state*, and among the negative collocates *enemy, hate, envy, aversion, suffering, wound* and *inquietude*. Collocates such as *fame, majesty, courage, perfection, charm* and *beauty* are instead considered positive.

Table 6.103. Semantic prosody for *mortal* (adj.) in ECF

| | **Abs. Freq.** | % | **NF** |
|---|---|---|---|
| **neg** | 132 | 46.15 | 13.60 |
| **neu** | 139 | 48.60 | 14.33 |
| **pos** | 15 | 5.25 | 1.55 |
| **Total** | **286** | **100.00** | **29.48** |

In contrast to the adjective, the evidence for *mortal* (adv.) in ECF is more limited, with a total of seven examples and five different collocations. Moreover, since their individual frequency is extremely low, occurring a maximum of two times, I will not measure the degree of collocational strength between the node and its collocates by means of statistical tests, but just provide the absolute and normalised frequencies of such collocates (cf. Table 6.104). Furthermore, although its adverbial nature would in principle allow for a wide range of collocate types, the adverb *mortal* is only found as a modifier of adjectives in ECF. It should be recalled, however, that the adverb was attested as a modifier of both participial elements and adjectives with very similar low frequencies in the EModE data from EEBOCorp 1.0 (cf. supra).

Unlike the EModE data from EEBOCorp 1.0, in which descriptive meanings prevailed, in ECF those meanings which are ambiguous between descriptive and subjective are the most frequent (42.86%), followed by those which are ambiguous between subjective and intensifying (28.57%) and by intensifying readings of the adverb (28.57%) (cf. Table 6.105).

Example (6.170) is taken to be ambiguous between descriptive and subjective. In this case, the protagonist has overindulged in drink and, as a result, he suffered from colic and thought he was going to die, until he was afterwards given some *higry-pigry*[39] or laxative and recovered from the

Table 6.104. Absolute and normalised frequencies for the collocations of *mortal* (adv.) in ECF

| **Collocation** | **Abs. Freq.** | **NF** |
|---|---|---|
| *mortal dear* | 1 | 0.10 |
| *mortal good* | 1 | 0.10 |
| *mortal ill* | 2 | 0.21 |
| *mortal jealous* | 2 | 0.21 |
| *mortal sick* | 1 | 0.10 |

39 Vulgar perversion of *hiera picra* (n.) 'A purgative drug composed of aloes and canella bark, sometimes mixed with honey and other ingredients'. Also corruptly *hickery-pickery*, *hicra picra*, *higry-pigry* (OED, s.v. *hiera picra* n.).

Table 6.105. Meaning types for *mortal* (adv.) in ECF

| | Abs. Freq. | % | NF |
|---|---|---|---|
| D/S | 3 | 42.86 | 0.31 |
| S/I | 2 | 28.57 | 0.21 |
| I | 2 | 28.57 | 0.21 |
| Total | 7 | 100.00 | 0.72 |

intoxicating effects of cider. The mortal sickness cannot be taken literally in this particular example, for it just means that the person is indisposed, although he may feel so unwell that he thinks he is going to pass away. Example (6.171), in turn, was counted as ambiguous between a subjective and a purely intensifying reading. In (6.171) *mortal jealous* can be regarded as subjective, since the woman who is distrustful of her husband might eventually decide to wreak revenge on him or damage him in some way. On the other hand, *mortal* can also be considered to have an intensifying meaning here, simply meaning 'very, extremely jealous'. The latter seems to be the most likely interpretation. By contrast, in the examples presented in (6.172) and (6.173) *mortal* clearly functions as an intensifier, boosting the adjectives *good* and *dear*. The former instance mentions a character who is very skilled or has a very good hand at reprimanding people. *Mortal* here does not modify the noun *hand*, but is instead a modifier of the adjective *good*, which has positive semantic prosody. This, therefore, rules out the possibility of a literal interpretation of the adverb. The same applies in (6.173), in which *mortal* modifies the adjective *dear*, which is also positive 'precious, valuable', and for which a literal reading is not possible either.

(6.170) *It is no longer ago than last October, we had been* [...] *making cyder* [...] ; *and all the next day I was* ***mortal*** *sick, and troubled with the gripes and the belly-ach*; (1773. Richard Graves. *The spiritual Quixote*)

(6.171) *Will told them, before I came, 'That his lady was but lately married to one of the finest gentlemen in the world. But that, he being very gay and lively, she was* ***mortal*** *jealous of him; and in a fit of that sort, had eloped from him.* (1748. Samuel Richarson. *Clarissa*)

(6.172) *'Aye, aye, (answered Timothy) your honour has a* ***mortal*** *good hand at giving a slap with a fox's tail*; (1748. Samuel Richardson. *Clarissa*)

(6.173) *'They'd need be goddesses with a vengeance', said the Captain, 'for they're* ***mortal*** *dear to look at'.* (1778–1788. Fanny Burney. *Evelina*)

As for the semantic prosody of the adverb (cf. Table 6.106), *mortal* modifies mostly inherently negative elements (71.43%), as is the case of the adjectives *sick*, *ill* and *jealous*. However, it is also attested as a modifier of collocates which are positive in meaning, such as the adjectives *dear* and *good*, although to a much lesser extent (28.57%).

The last of the sources consulted was NCF, which yielded 1,009 tokens of the adjective *mortal* in a total of 342 collocations. In all these occurrences *mortal* is found as a modifier of nouns. Given the large number of collocates, Table 6.107 only shows the absolute and normalised frequencies for those which occurred at least five times in the data. Table 6.108 additionally provides their standardised scores.

As indicated by the standardised scores, the association between the node *mortal* and the accompanying nouns turned out to be highly statistically significant for the overwhelming majority of the collocations. The only differences found concerned the *MI* value for the collocations *mortal being*, *mortal hand*, *mortal nature*, *mortal power*, *mortal thing* and *mortal woman*, which have low *MI* scores. This owes to the fact that the nouns *being*, *hand*, *nature*, *power*, *thing* and *woman* are highly frequent items on their own in the database, and the *MI* test tends to give much less weight to high-frequency items. However, the cubed version of the *MI* test, *MI3*, indicates that the association between *mortal* and these nouns is to be taken as significant. The other values also confirm the significance of this connection between the node and these collocates, although in the case of the log-likelihood value, the level of significance for *mortal being*, *mortal nature* and *mortal hand* decreases in comparison with all the other collocations

Table 6.106. Semantic prosody for *mortal* (adv.) in ECF

| | **Abs. Freq.** | % | **NF** |
|---|---|---|---|
| **neg** | 4 | 71.43 | 0.52 |
| **pos** | 2 | 28.57 | 0.21 |
| **Total** | 7 | 100.00 | 0.72 |

Table 6.107. Absolute and normalised frequencies for the most frequent collocations of *mortal* (adj.) in NCF

| Collocation | Abs. Freq. | NF |
|---|---|---|
| *mortal agony* | 17 | 0.45 |
| *mortal anguish* | 6 | 0.16 |
| *mortal being* | 10 | 0.27 |
| *mortal blow* | 15 | 0.40 |
| *mortal combat* | 17 | 0.45 |
| *mortal creature* | 17 | 0.45 |
| *mortal danger* | 6 | 0.16 |
| *mortal disease* | 19 | 0.51 |
| *mortal dread* | 5 | 0.13 |
| *mortal ear* | 14 | 0.37 |
| *mortal enemy* | 37 | 0.98 |
| *mortal existence* | 11 | 0.29 |
| *mortal eye* | 29 | 0.77 |
| *mortal fear* | 20 | 0.53 |
| *mortal foe* | 11 | 0.29 |
| *mortal frame* | 14 | 0.37 |
| *mortal hand* | 10 | 0.27 |
| *mortal illness* | 5 | 0.13 |
| *mortal injury* | 10 | 0.27 |
| *mortal life* | 28 | 0.74 |
| *mortal man* | 96 | 2.55 |
| *mortal nature* | 5 | 0.13 |
| *mortal offence* | 17 | 0.45 |
| *mortal paleness* | 5 | 0.13 |
| *mortal peril* | 5 | 0.13 |
| *mortal power* | 7 | 0.19 |
| *mortal quarrel* | 5 | 0.13 |

(*continued*)

Table 6.107. Continued

| Collocation | Abs. Freq. | NF |
|---|---|---|
| *mortal remains* | 17 | 0.45 |
| *mortal sin* | 12 | 0.32 |
| *mortal soul* | 8 | 0.21 |
| *mortal struggle* | 9 | 0.24 |
| *mortal terror* | 11 | 0.29 |
| *mortal thing* | 13 | 0.35 |
| *mortal woman* | 22 | 0.59 |
| *mortal wound* | 18 | 0.48 |

Table 6.108. Standardised scores for the most frequent collocations of *mortal* (adj.) in NCF

| Collocation | *z*-score | *MI* | *MI3* | *LL*-value |
|---|---|---|---|---|
| *mortal agony* | 37.514 | 6.406 | 14.580 | 117.479 (p < 0.0001) |
| *mortal anguish* | 15.777 | 5.442 | 10.612 | 33.559 (p < 0.0001) |
| *mortal being* | 3.946 | 1.700 | 8.344 | 9.727 (p < 0.01) |
| *mortal blow* | 2.7223 | 5.683 | 13.497 | 88.828 (p < 0.0001) |
| *mortal combat* | 70.811 | 8.214 | 16.389 | 160.123 (p < 0.0001) |
| *mortal creature* | 21.034 | 4.807 | 12.982 | 80.535 (p < 0.0001) |
| *mortal danger* | 7.874 | 3.615 | 8.785 | 19.052 (p < 0.0001) |
| *mortal disease* | 65.830 | 7.846 | 16.342 | 169.194 (p < 0.0001) |
| *mortal dread* | 10.844 | 4.671 | 9.315 | 22.781 (p < 0.0001) |
| *mortal ear* | 17.046 | 4.505 | 12.120 | 60.696 (p < 0.0001) |
| *mortal enemy* | 57.506 | 6.514 | 16.932 | 261.191 (p < 0.0001) |
| *mortal existence* | 20.141 | 5.280 | 12.199 | 59.116 (p < 0.0001) |
| *mortal eye* | 13.519 | 3.032 | 12.748 | 71.002 (p < 0.0001) |
| *mortal fear* | 18.393 | 4.237 | 12.881 | 79.634 (p < 0.0001) |
| *mortal foe* | 42.386 | 7.369 | 14.288 | 90.659 (p < 0.0001) |
| *mortal frame* | 31.626 | 6.198 | 13.813 | 92.763 (p < 0.0001) |
| *mortal hand* | 2.582 | 1.148 | 7.791 | 4.937 (p < 0.05) |

Table 6.108. Continued

| **Collocation** | ***z*-score** | ***MI*** | ***MI3*** | ***LL*-value** |
|---|---|---|---|---|
| *mortal illness* | 12.870 | 5.133 | 9.777 | 25.881 ($p < 0.0001$) |
| *mortal injury* | 26.728 | 6.198 | 12.842 | 66.257 ($p < 0.0001$) |
| *mortal life* | 14.568 | 3.244 | 12.859 | 75.850 ($p < 0.0001$) |
| *mortal man* | 29.530 | 3.458 | 16.628 | 285.807 ($p < 0.0001$) |
| *mortal nature* | 3.898 | 2.273 | 6.916 | 7.823 ($p < 0.01$) |
| *mortal offence* | 42.385 | 6.750 | 14.925 | 125.554 ($p < 0.0001$) |
| *mortal paleness* | 32.481 | 7.735 | 12.379 | 43.750 ($p < 0.0001$) |
| *mortal peril* | 15.878 | 5.712 | 10.355 | 29.802 ($p < 0.0001$) |
| *mortal power* | 5.669 | 2.686 | 8.301 | 14.243 ($p < 0.001$) |
| *mortal quarrel* | 10.325 | 4.541 | 9.185 | 21.913 ($p < 0.0001$) |
| *mortal remains* | 4.9136 | 7.170 | 15.345 | 135.418 ($p < 0.0001$) |
| *mortal sin* | 24.669 | 5.720 | 12.890 | 71.655 ($p < 0.0001$) |
| *mortal soul* | 7.506 | 3.159 | 9.159 | 20.827 ($p < 0.0001$) |
| *mortal struggle* | 18.560 | 5.331 | 11.671 | 48.989 ($p < 0.0001$) |
| *mortal terror* | 19.069 | 5.130 | 12.049 | 56.895 ($p < 0.0001$) |
| *mortal thing* | 4.917 | 1.840 | 9.241 | 14.429 ($p < 0.001$) |
| *mortal woman* | 11.335 | 2.947 | 11.866 | 51.590 ($p < 0.0001$) |
| *mortal wound* | 3.7660 | 6.336 | 14.676 | 122.667 ($p < 0.0001$) |

(from $p < 0.0001$ to $p < 0.01$ for *mortal being* and *mortal nature*, and to $p < 0.05$ for *mortal hand*).

In what concerns the types of meanings of the adjective in NCF (see Table 6.109), *mortal* seems to be still relatively attached to its original sense, since 77.11% of the examples in the data correspond to descriptive or literal readings of the adjective. Those occurrences which show incipient subjectivity, that is, subjective meanings, represent 17.15% of the total, and those uses of the adjective in which *mortal* is taken to be a grammaticalised intensifier account for 2.58%. Ambiguous examples which can be graded as either descriptive or subjective (2.96%) and those which can be considered both as subjective or intensifying (0.20%) are also attested in the data.

Table 6.109. Meaning types for *mortal* (adj.) in NCF

| | Abs. Freq. | % | NF |
|---|---|---|---|
| D | 778 | 77.11 | 20.70 |
| D/S | 30 | 2.96 | 0.80 |
| S | 173 | 17.15 | 4.60 |
| S/I | 2 | 0.20 | 0.05 |
| I | 26 | 2.58 | 0.69 |
| **Total** | **1,009** | **100.00** | **26.84** |

A selection of the different readings of the adjective in NCF is provided in (6.174)–(6.180). Example (6.174) shows a descriptive or literal meaning of *mortal*, referring to worldly existence, which is temporary and ephemeral.

(6.174) *He could no longer doubt that she had reached the last stage of* ***mortal*** *existence.* (1836. Catherine Grace Frances. *Mrs Armytage; or, Female Domination*)

*Mortal peril* in (6.175) was considered indeterminate between descriptive and subjective. This example refers to the danger for one of the characters of being recognised by another. Regardless of whether the character eventually passed away or not, for which outcome we would need to read on, a risk or danger per se does not kill anyone, as it may well be the case that a person is in serious danger and (s)he does not die in the end. On this account, the collocation was not marked as purely descriptive or literal.

(6.175) *If I could get speech of him that night, if I could show him that I, too, knew of the* ***mortal*** *peril in which he stood, what result would follow?* (1860. Wilkie Collins. *The woman in white*)

In turn, (6.176) and (6.177) are considered subjective, given that they refer to qualities which are negatively construed and may somehow recall death. Bearing deep resentment against someone, as is the case between the two characters mentioned in (6.176), may also imply hurting each other, perhaps even to death. Suffering from a phobia about beetles and cockroaches, which is the case of the protagonist in (6.177), may also trigger a panic attack, as a result of which the character might have breathing difficulties and feel faint. In sum, (s)he might feel in a state which is relatively close to death.

(6.176) *There were stronger differences between him and her, than there had been between him and his father, and it is suspected that he cherished a deep and* ***mortal*** *grudge against her,* (1861. Charles Dickens. *Great Expectations*)

(6.177) [...] *and being seated, commenced the acquisition of my task; while I learned, not forgetting to keep a sharp look-out on the black beetles and cockroaches, of which, more even, I believe, than of the rats, I sat in* ***mortal*** *dread.* (1853. Charlotte Brontë. *Vilette*)

The collocation *mortal daring* in (6.178) was classified as intermediate between subjective and intensifying. On the one hand, the context clearly indicates the determination of the character, hence the *resolute ferocity* of his expression, and in this light *mortal* could be considered an intensifier; *mortal daring* could then be paraphrased as *extreme boldness* or *extreme courage*. On the other hand, a subjective reading cannot be totally discarded here, since we do not exactly know the consequences of the character's boldness, mainly because there is a fight.

(6.178) *'What is it you intend, my lord?' cried Halbert, viewing with increased alarm the resolute ferocity which now blazed from every part of his countenance, and seemed to dilate his figure with more than* ***mortal*** *daring, 'what can you do?'* (1810. Jane Porter. *The Scottish chiefs*)'

Finally, in (6.179) and (6.180) *mortal* has an unequivocal intensifying or degree value. The mortal aversion referred to in (6.179) is not towards a person, but towards a thing, in particular to the word *business*, which Mrs Skewton is said to hate in the extreme. The degree interpretation also applies to (6.180), which describes a gentleman in a terrible haste to find somebody to take care of his companion's luggage, and for which a literal interpretation or a subjective reading of the adjective *mortal* is not possible.

(6.179) *Mrs. Skewton reposing on her sofa, and sipping her chocolate, had heard nothing but the low word business, for which she had a* ***mortal*** *aversion,* [...] (1848. Charles Dickens. *Dombey and son*)

(6.180) *The gentleman was in a* ***mortal*** *hurry about the lady's luggage;* (1860. Wilkie Collins. *The woman in white*)

Table 6.110. Semantic prosody for *mortal* (adj.) in NCF

| | **Abs. Freq.** | **%** | **NF** |
|---|---|---|---|
| **neg** | 394 | 39.05 | 10.48 |
| **neu** | 584 | 57.88 | 15.54 |
| **pos** | 31 | 3.07 | 0.82 |
| **Total** | **1,009** | **100.00** | **26.84** |

As far as semantic prosody is concerned (cf. Table 6.110), *mortal* is mainly attested with neutral and negative nouns (57.88% and 39.05% of the cases, respectively), though it also occurs as a modifier of inherently positive nouns (3.07%). By way of illustration, *mortal* modifies neutral nouns such as *(wo)man*, *creature*, *comprehension*, *body*, *thing* and *condition*. Negative collocates of *mortal* in the data include, among others, *enemy*, *wound*, *vanity*, *combat*, *pang* and *depravity*. Finally, *happiness*, *fortitude*, *harmony*, *beauty*, *magnificence*, *excellence* and *love* feature among the positive collocates of the adjective in NCF.

As regards the adverbial form, NCF returned a total of forty-one tokens of *mortal* (adv.), in combination with thirty-two different collocates. Nevertheless, only the collocations *mortal angry*, *mortal cold*, *mortal hard*, *mortal high*, *mortal hungry*, *mortal long* and *mortal still* occur two or three times in NCF. Owing to these low frequencies, Table 6.111 provides the absolute and normalised frequencies for these collocations, and Table 6.112 gives the standardised scores only for those which are attested a minimum of three times. Except for the *MI* test, all the values indicate that both *mortal angry* and *mortal cold* are statistically significant, although in the case of the latter collocation the log-likelihood test also shows that it is only significant at $p < 0.05$.

In regard to the types of meanings of *mortal* (adv.) (cf. Table 6.113), it occurs mostly with intensifying meanings (68.29% of the cases) and with meanings which are ambiguous between subjective and intensifying (19.51%). Subjective and descriptive meanings are, by contrast, far less numerous (7.32% and 4.88% each).

Table 6.111. Absolute and normalised frequencies for the most frequent collocations of *mortal* (adv.) in NCF

| Collocation | Abs. Freq. | NF |
|---|---|---|
| *mortal angry* | 3 | 0.08 |
| *mortal cold* | 3 | 0.08 |
| *mortal hard* | 2 | 0.05 |
| *mortal high* | 2 | 0.05 |
| *mortal hungry* | 2 | 0.05 |
| *mortal long* | 2 | 0.05 |
| *mortal still* | 2 | 0.05 |

Table 6.112. Standardised scores for the most frequent collocations of *mortal* (adv.) in NCF

| Collocation | *z*-score | *MI* | *MI3* | *LL*-value |
|---|---|---|---|---|
| *mortal angry* | 4.246 | 2.979 | 6.149 | 7.151 ($p < 0.01$) |
| *mortal cold* | 3.036 | 2.283 | 5.453 | 4.728 ($p < 0.05$) |

Table 6.113. Meaning types for *mortal* (adv.)

| | Abs. Freq. | % | NF |
|---|---|---|---|
| **D** | 2 | 4.88 | 0.05 |
| **S** | 3 | 7.32 | 0.08 |
| **S/I** | 8 | 19.51 | 0.21 |
| **I** | 28 | 68.29 | 0.74 |
| **Total** | **41** | **100.00** | **1.09** |

Examples (6.181)–(6.186) serve to illustrate the different meanings of the adverb in the data. *Mortal sick* in (6.181) is a literal or descriptive meaning, alluding to a person who is seriously ill and will presumably die as a consequence. *Mortal still* in (6.182), on the other hand, represents a subjective reading, for quietness and peacefulness may foretell and be figuratively linked to death. (6.183) is on the borderline between subjective and intensifying, although in this case *mortal* is most likely closer to the intensifying function. Being angry with somebody may imply taking revenge on him/her, and it could therefore be argued to be subjective rather than purely intensifying. Even so, *mortal angry* here could also be taken to be a synonym of *terribly, extremely angry*. Finally, *mortal* in (6.184)–(6.186) has a purely intensifying meaning. The floor in (6.184) is said to be extremely cold and the character is accordingly recommended to wear an apron on the head. In (6.185) and (6.186) *mortal* modifies adjectives which have positive semantic prosody: *fond* (*of something*) and *fine*, which is clearly incompatible with its original meaning and therefore clearly has an intensifying or degree meaning.

(6.181) *As he came nearer, queering me pretty curious* […], *I saw he looked* ***mortal*** *sick, for the truth was he had a fever on, and had just had a chill in the boat.* (1893. Robert Louis Stevenson. *The beach of Falesa*)

(6.182) *It was* ***mortal*** *still and solemn and chilly, and the light of the dawn on the lagoon was like the shining of a fire.* (1893. Robert Louis Stevenson. *The beach of Falesa*)

(6.183) […] *that morning Mary took you out and left you; for which I was* ***mortal*** *angry with her, for my mind misgave me that some mischief would come of it.* (1810. Mary Brunton. *Self-control*)

(6.184) '*We are coming to the Banketing Hall, now. The floor's* ***mortal*** *cold, and the damp sticks to the place like cockroaches to a collier.*' (1862. Wilkie Collins. *No name*)

(6.185) '*And she's* ***mortal*** *fond of him, that's true,*' (1796. Fanny Burney. *Camilla*)

(6.186) '*La, sir, how can you? why, like our squire, Sir John, who rides in such a* ***mortal*** *fine gold coach*"; (1839. William Makepeace Thackeray. *Catherine*)

As for the semantic prosody of the adverb, *mortal* occurs mostly with neutral and negative elements (41.46% each), although it is also recorded as a modifier of elements with positive semantic prosody (17.08%), as shown in Table 6.114. The adjectives *long, cold, high, still* or *stout* feature among

Table 6.114. Semantic prosody for *mortal* (adv.)

| | Abs. Freq. | % | NF |
|---|---|---|---|
| **neg** | 17 | 41.46 | 0.45 |
| **neu** | 17 | 41.46 | 0.45 |
| **pos** | 7 | 17.08 | 0.19 |
| **Total** | **41** | **100.00** | **1.09** |

the neutral collocates of *mortal*; *angry*, *spiteful*, *bad*, *sick* and *inconvenient* count as negative collocates, while the collocations *mortal passionate*, *mortal good*, *mortal kind* and *mortal fine* were marked as illustrative of positive semantic prosody.

Unlike other adverbs such as *dead* (cf. Section 6.2.2), *mortal* does not modify a wide variety of categories. In fact, in NCF it is only recorded as a modifier of adjectives and participial items, as indicated in Table 6.115, showing a clear strong preference for the former category.

### 6.2.4.1. *Mortal* (adj. and adv.) across time

As shown by the individual figures in Table 6.116 and also by the graph in Figure 6.6, the adjective *mortal* is clearly most frequent with descriptive meanings in the overall data.

The normalised frequencies evince a dramatic rise in the number of descriptive uses of *mortal* from the HC to EEBOCorp 1.0 (HC: 10 exx.; NF pmw 16.43 > EEBOCorp 1.0: 17,236 exx.; NF pmw 32.80), which was not found to be statistically significant ($\chi^2$ (1) = 4.483; $p$ = 0.03423358). After EModE, however, the frequency of descriptive examples of the adjective

Table 6.115. Categories modified by *mortal* (adv.) in NCF

| | Abs. Freq. | % | NF |
|---|---|---|---|
| **Adj.** | 39 | 95.12 | 1.04 |
| **Part.** | 2 | 4.88 | 0.05 |
| **Total** | **41** | **100.00** | **1.09** |

Table 6.116. Types of meanings for *mortal* (adj.) in the data (absolute/normalised frequencies)

| | HC (ME) | EEBOCorp 1.0 | ECF | NCF | ARCHER (20th c.) |
|---|---|---|---|---|---|
| **D** | 10/16.43 | 17,236/32.80 | 207/21.33 | 778/20.7 | 3/5.65 |
| **D/S** | 0 | 368/0.70 | 7/0.72 | 30/0.8 | 0 |
| **S** | 1/1.64 | 3,067/5.84 | 69/7.11 | 174/4.63 | 1/1.88 |
| **S/I** | 0 | 26/0.05 | 3/0.31 | 2/0.05 | 0 |
| **I** | 0 | 0 | 0 | 26/0.69 | 0 |
| **N. of words** | 608,570 | 525,432,293 | 9,702,699 | 37,589,837 | 530,832 |

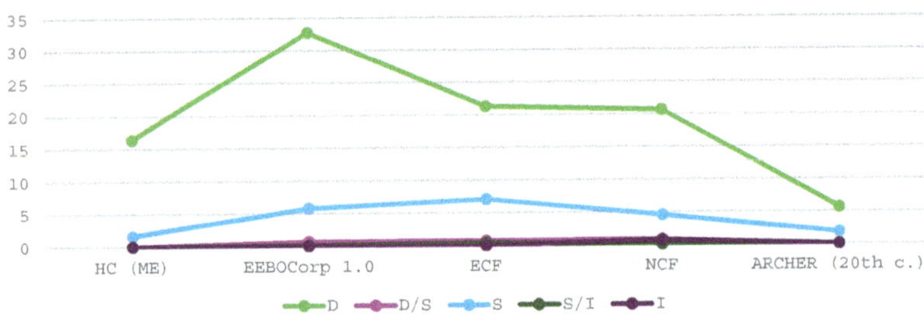


Figure 6.6. Types of meanings for *mortal* (adj.)

is considerably reduced, most conspicuously from EEBOCorp 1.0 to ECF (EEBOCorp 1.0: 17,236 exx.; NF pmw 32.80 > ECF: 20 exx.; NF pmw 21.33) and then again from NCF to ARCHER (NCF: 778 exx.; NF pmw 20.7 > ARCHER: 3 exx.; NF pmw 5.65). The difference between EModE and the eighteenth century, as well as that between the eighteenth and nineteenth centuries, is not statistically significant either ($\chi^2(1) = 38.094$; $p = 0.03423358$ and $\chi^2\,(1) = 0.121$; $p = 0.72795243$, respectively). By contrast, the drastic reduction in the frequency of *mortal* from NCF to ARCHER is statistically significant at $p < 0.01$ (Fisher's exact test = 0.009042). The normalised frequencies for those readings of the adjective which are indeterminate between descriptive and subjective indicate that these instances of *mortal*, though not frequent, remain relatively constant over time. A statistical comparison of these values yielded negative significance results.[40] In turn, subjective meanings of *mortal* increase substantially from the HC to EEBOCorp 1.0 (HC: 1 ex.; NF pmw 1.64 > EEBOCorp 1.0: 3,067 exx.; NF pmw 5.84) and less pronouncedly from EEBOCorp 1.0 to ECF (ECF: 69 exx.; NF pmw 7.11). From the eighteenth century onwards, the frequency of subjective *mortal* decreases (NCF: 174 exx.; NF pmw 4.63 > ARCHER: 1 ex.; NF pmw 1.88). These results, however, are only statistically significant when the eighteenth- and nineteenth-century data are contrasted ($\chi^2$ (1) = 8.773; $p$ = 0.00305722). For the remaining periods, however, these figures are not significant.[41] Those readings which are ambiguous between subjective and intensifying also remain relatively stable over time, as shown by the normalised figures, and the results from the statistical tests indicate negative significance values.[42]

In regard to semantic prosody (cf. Table 6.117 and Figure 6.7), the adjective *mortal* is attested mainly with nouns which have neutral prosody (e.g. *man, thing, life, creature*), although it also occurs as a modifier of

Table 6.117. Semantic prosody for *mortal* (adj.) in the data (absolute/normalised frequencies)

| | HC (ME) | EEBOCorp 1.0 | ECF | NCF | ARCHER (20th c.) |
|---|---|---|---|---|---|
| **neg** | 2/3.29 | 8,091/15.40 | 132/13.6 | 394/10.48 | 2/3.77 |
| **neu** | 9/14.79 | 12,335/23.48 | 139/14.33 | 585/15.56 | 2/3.77 |
| **pos** | 0 | 271/0.51 | 15/1.55 | 31/0.82 | 0 |
| **N. of words** | 608,570 | 525,432,293 | 9,702,699 | 37,589,837 | 530,832 |

40 **EEBOCorp 1.0 > ECF:** $\chi^2$ (1) = 0.013; $p$ = 0.90922389; **ECF > NCF:** $\chi^2$ (1) = 0.001; $p$ = 0.97477288.

41 **HC > EEBOCorp 1.0:** Fisher's exact test = 0.279476; **EEBOCorp 1.0 > ECF:** $\chi^2$ (1) =2.427; $p$ = 0.11926094; **NCF> ARCHER:** Fisher's exact test = 0.526532.

42 **EEBOCorp 1.0 > ECF:** Fisher's exact test = 0.11926094; **ECF > NCF:** Fisher's exact test = 0.061962.

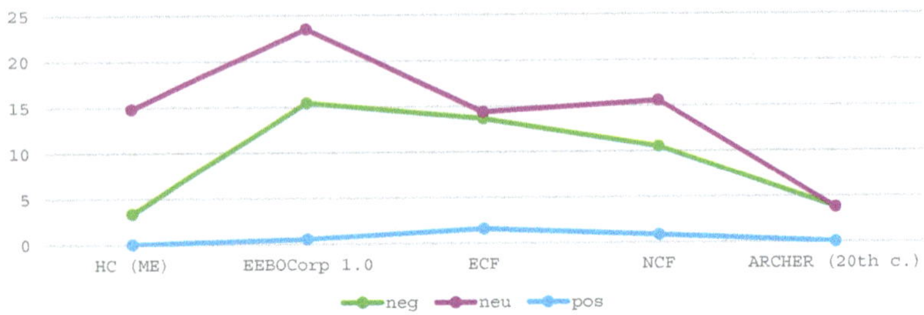


Figure 6.7. Semantic prosody for *mortal* (adj.)

inherently negative (e.g. *accident*, *battle*, *detestation*) and positive (e.g. *glory*, *joy*, *fame*) nouns. The frequency of *mortal* with neutral collocates grows substantially from ME to EModE (HC: 9 exx.; NF pmw 14.79 > EEBOCorp 1.0: 12,335 exx.; NF pmw 23.48), to be dropped from EEBOCorp 1.0 to ECF (ECF: 139 exx.; NF pmw 14.33). There is then a slight increase in the normalised figures from ECF to NCF (NCF: 585 exx.; NF pmw 15.56) and again a rapid decrease at the turn of the twentieth century (2 exx; NF pmw 3.77). Despite these differences, the only value which is statistically significant is that between EModE and the eighteenth-century data ($\chi^2$ (1) =33.825; $p$ = 0.00000001).[43] Combinations of *mortal* with negative collocates proliferate in the transition of ME to EModE (HC: 2 exx.; NF pmw 3.29 > EEBOCorp 1.0: 8,091 exx.; NF pmw 15.40), a growth which is statistically significant (Fisher's exact test = 0.008301). However, from EModE onwards, the uses of *mortal* with negative elements decrease, most notably from the nineteenth to the twentieth century (NCF: 394 exx.; NF pmw 10.48 > ARCHER: 2 exx.; NF pmw 3.77), although this difference is not statistically significant.[44] Instances of the adjective *mortal* as a modifier of positive nouns are not frequent in the data in comparison with the other types of prosody and the normalised frequencies remain low over time. Nevertheless, the increase from EEBOCorp 1.0 to ECF (EEBOCorp

43 **HC > EEBOCorp 1.0:** $\chi^2$ (1) = 1.602; $p$ = 0.20562001; **ECF > NCF:** $\chi^2$ (1) = 0.692; $p$ = 0.40548494; **NCF > ARCHER:** Fisher's exact test = 0.021032.

44 **EEBOCorp 1.0 > ECF:** $\chi^2$ (1) =1.881; $p$ = 0.17022053); **ECF > NCF:** $\chi^2$ (1) = 6.484; $p$ = 0.01088498; **NCF > ARCHER:** Fisher's exact test = 0.191363.

1.0: 271 exx.; NF pmw 0.51 > ECF: 15 exx.; NF pmw 1.55) was found to be highly statistically significant ($\chi^2$ (1) = 17.04; $p$= 0.0000366), while the difference is not significant when the eighteenth and the nineteenth-century data (ECF: 15 exx.; NF pmw 1.55 > NCF: 31 exx.; NF pmw 0.82) are compared ($\chi^2$ (1) = 3.417; $p$ = 0.06452818).

In view of the results from the types of meanings and semantic prosody discussed in the preceding paragraphs, the adjective *mortal* seems to behave much alike its Germanic counterpart *deadly* (cf. Section 6.2.3.1). In this case, too, the percentage of intensifying uses of *mortal* does not reach 1% either and combinations of *mortal* with positive nouns are also scarcely attested (1.44% of the total). As mentioned in Section 6.1.3, the OED describes the adjective *mortal* as a borrowing from Anglo-Norman, dating to the late fourteenth century. Subjective readings are recorded in the data from EModE onwards, thus bearing out the information provided by the OED, where *mortal* is shown to have subjective meanings from the very beginning. Intensifying uses of *mortal* emerged, according to the OED, in the eighteenth century. The first attestations of intensifying *mortal* in the corpora and databases consulted are found in NCF, a century later than the first records claimed by the OED (cf. Section 6.1.3). Prior to these intensifying uses, however, there are some eighteenth-century instances of the adjective which are indeterminate between subjective and intensifying. As was the case for *deadly* (cf. Section 6.2.3.1), these examples may well have favoured a subsequent degree reading for the adjective *mortal*. Also in line with the results of the adjective *deadly*, these contexts implied situations of annoyance, anger and envy. One such example is the collocation *mortal displeasure* in (6.169), where the circumstances described resemble closely those involved in the instances of *deadly*. In this particular case, although a degree reading can be argued for *mortal* ('extreme displeasure'), there are also signs in the preceding and following context that Clarissa may seek some form of vengeance and hence the intention of harming, whether physically or psychologically, is still in the background. For this reason, a subjective account of *mortal* here cannot be completely ruled out.

Even though the intensifying meanings of *mortal* are rare in the data (26 exx., 0.12%, all of them recorded in NCF), the adjective has developed an increasingly abstract meaning over time, until its eventual grammaticalisation as an intensifier. Collocations such as *mortal certainty*, *mortal disappointment*, *mortal degree* or *mortal hurry* effectively attest to the intensifying uses of the adjective. The cline of evolution argued above (cf. Section 4.1.2) for the adjective *deadly* (descriptive > subjective > intensifying), however, does not fully apply in this case, since, as suggested before, the adjective *mortal* could already occur from its first records with subjective meanings. As was the case with *deadly*, the paucity of intensifying uses suggests that the degree of grammaticalisation of this adjective is not very advanced. Moreover, the intensifying uses of *mortal* do not correlate with positive semantic prosody in any of the materials analysed. Nevertheless, along the lines of adjectival *deadly* (cf. Section 6.2.3), *mortal* (adj.) also serves to illustrate some of Hopper's grammaticalisation principles (see Section 3.2). In the nineteenth-century data, for instance, *mortal* is attested with the five different meanings (D, D/S, S, S/I and I). In other words, these different meanings or 'layers' of the adjective coexist synchronically and though *mortal* had a new, grammaticalised meaning by the nineteenth century, it was still possible to find it with its original, literal sense. These features are characteristic of the principles of layering and divergence (cf. Section 3.2). In addition, the adjective *mortal* shows signs of persistence by collocating with negative nouns. Nonetheless, unlike the adjective *deadly* (cf. Section 6.2.3.1), *mortal* is more frequent with neutral collocates (59.39%), followed by negative (39.17%) and positive ones (1.44%).

In comparison with its adjectival counterpart, the adverb *mortal* is hardly attested in the different sources consulted (only fifty-two examples). Interestingly, most of these occurrences correspond to intensifying meanings (59.61%), as shown in Table 6.118 and Figure 6.8. These readings, in fact, grow moderately from the eighteenth to the twentieth century (ECF: 2 exx.; NF pmw 0.21 > NCF: 28 exx.; NF pmw 0.74 > ARCHER: 1 ex.; NF pmw 1.88). Even so, none of these values is judged as statistically significant at $p < 0.01$.[45] As for the meanings of *mortal* which are ambiguous between subjective and intensifying, there is no variation in the normalised frequencies from ECF to NCF (NF pmw 0.21). The results from Fisher's exact test also reveal that the difference in frequency between the two collections is not statistically significant at $p < 0.01$ (Fisher's exact test = 0.334133).

45 **ECF > NCF**: Fisher's exact test = 0.068971; **NCF > ARCHER**: Fisher's exact test = 0.334133.

Table 6.118. Types of meanings for *mortal* (adv.) in the data (absolute/normalised frequencies)

| | HC (ME) | EEBOCorp 1.0 | ECF | NCF | ARCHER (20th c.) |
|---|---|---|---|---|---|
| D | 0 | 3/0.01 | 0 | 2/0.05 | 0 |
| D/S | 0 | 0 | 3/0.31 | 0 | 0 |
| S | 0 | 1/0.002 | 0 | 2/0.05 | 0 |
| S/I | 0 | 0 | 2/0.21 | 8/0.21 | 0 |
| I | 0 | 0 | 2/0.21 | 28/0.74 | 1/1.88 |
| N. of words | 608,570 | 525,432,293 | 9,702,699 | 37,589,837 | 530,832 |

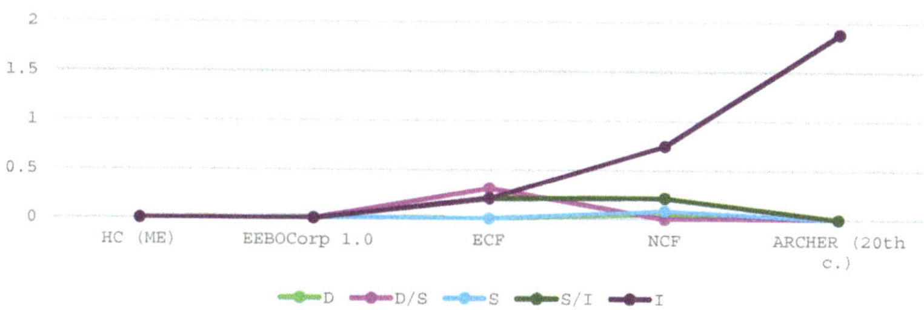


Figure 6.8. Types of meanings for *mortal* (adv.)

In regard to semantic prosody (see Table 6.119), *mortal* is attested mainly with negative (e.g. *sick*, *dull*, *bad*) and neutral elements (e.g. *pale*, *high*, *long*), although positive collocates of *mortal* are also found (e.g. *kind*, *passionate*, *good*). In what concerns negative semantic prosody, the biggest growth is seen from the nineteenth- to the twentieth-century data (NCF: 17 exx.; NF pmw 0.45 > ARCHER: 1 ex.; NF pmw 1.88), as shown in Figure 6.9.

However, this increase in the normalised frequency of *mortal* (adv.) from NCF to ARCHER cannot be regarded as statistically significant at $p < 0.01$ (Fisher's exact test = 0.223076). The difference in frequency between

Table 6.119. Semantic prosody for *mortal* (adv.) in the data (absolute/normalised frequencies)

| | HC (ME) | EEBOCorp 1.0 | ECF | NCF | ARCHER (20th c.) |
|---|---|---|---|---|---|
| **neg** | 0 | 3/0.01 | 5/0.52 | 17/0.45 | 1/1.88 |
| **neu** | 0 | 1/0.002 | 0 | 16/0.43 | 0 |
| **pos** | 0 | 0 | 2/0.21 | 7/0.19 | 0 |
| **N. of words** | 608,570 | 525,432,293 | 9,702,699 | 37,589,837 | 530,832 |

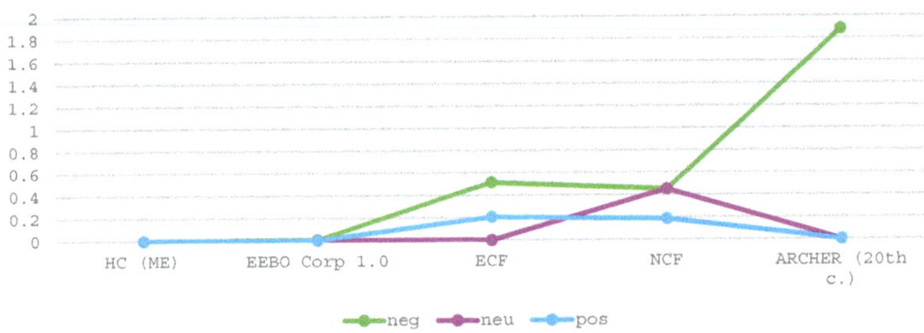


Figure 6.9. Semantic prosody for *mortal* (adv.)

ECF and NCF is not significant either (Fisher's exact test = 0.792214). In turn, the difference between the EEBOCorp 1.0 data and ECF is statistically significant (Fisher's exact test = 0). The values for neutral semantic prosody could not be statistically tested, since there are zero values in the pairs which should be considered for analysis. Finally, the frequency of *mortal* in combination with positive elements decreases slightly from the eighteenth to the nineteenth century (ECF: 2 exx.; NF pmw 0.21 > NCF: 7 exx.; NF pmw 0.19), but this difference is not statistically significant either (Fisher's exact test = 1).

Being an adverb, *mortal* can in principle modify a wider range of words than the homonymous adjective. In practice, however, it is only found in the data as a modifier of adjectives and participial forms, showing a much stronger preference for the former (see Table 6.120). This tendency

Table 6.120. Categories modified by *mortal* (adv.) in the data (absolute/normalised frequencies)

| | HC (ME) | EEBOCorp 1.0 | ECF | NCF | ARCHER (20th c.) |
|---|---|---|---|---|---|
| **Adj.** | 0 | 2/0.004 | 7/0.72 | 38/1.01 | 1/1.88 |
| **Part.** | 0 | 2/0.004 | 0 | 2/0.05 | 0 |
| **N. of words** | 608,570 | 525,432,293 | 9,702,699 | 37,589,837 | 530,832 |

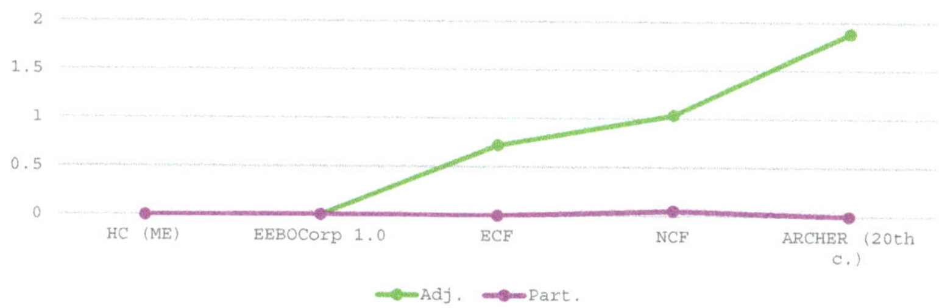


Figure 6.10. Categories modified by *mortal* (adv.)

is confirmed by the graph in Figure 6.10, which clearly shows that the combinations of *mortal* with adjectives gradually increase over time. Despite the tendency for *mortal* to be on the rise with adjectives, these values are only statistically significant if we consider the EModE and eighteenth-century data (Fisher's exact test = 0).[46]

In view of the data presented in this section, the adverb *mortal* occurs mostly with intensifying readings (59.61%), followed by descriptive uses (9.62%), those which are indeterminate between descriptive and subjective (5.77%), subjective uses (5.77%) and those instances of the adverb which allow a double interpretation, either as subjective or as intensifying (19.23%). Positive semantic prosody, though the least common, amounts to 17.31% of the total, which clearly outnumbers the percentages obtained for negative

46 **ECF > NCF:** $\chi^2$ (1) =0.409; $p$ = 0.5224775; **NCF > ARCHER:** Fisher's exact test = 0.421256.

prosody for the adjective and adverb *deadly* (cf. Section 6.2.3.1) as well as for the adjective *mortal* (cf. supra).

Despite the overall low figures for the adverb, the data provide convincing evidence for the intensifying readings of *mortal*, attested with such meanings in both NCF and ARCHER. As in the case of the adjectives *deadly* (cf. Section 6.2.3.1) and *mortal* discussed above, some earlier examples could have worked as bridging contexts (cf. Section 3.2), facilitating its eventual reinterpretation as a marker of degree, in collocations such as *mortal unconvenient*, *mortal cunning*, *mortal passionate* and *mortal good*. One of such potential bridging contexts is illustrated in (6.171), which features the collocation *mortal jealous*. Consequences of jealousy and resentment are again far from clear in this context, so that *mortal* can be read either as an intensifier or as having a subjective meaning.

However, the earliest examples which were marked as indeterminate between subjective and intensifying in the data date back to the 1750s, more precisely to Richardson's novel *Clarissa*, which is also the source of (6.171). In turn, the first documented instances of intensifying *mortal* in my data are from the 1760s and 1780s. Attributing a clear influence to these ambiguous occurrences of *mortal* is therefore too speculative, in view of the co-occurrence of these alleged bridging examples and the first unequivocal intensifying meanings of the adverb. However, given that most occurrences of intensifying *mortal* are attested in the nineteenth century, contexts such as the ones provided by these 'bridging contexts' may have contributed to the reinforcement of a degree interpretation of the adverb.

Adamson's (2000) cline for the evolution of intensifiers, which was taken as a model in this work, does not fully apply to the development of the adverb *mortal*. As explained above, *mortal* could be found with subjective meanings already from the moment in which it was borrowed, at the end of the fourteenth century, so that the first step in Adamson's descriptive > subjective > intensifying cline cannot be tested. Furthermore, the low number of examples in the sources consulted is clearly insufficient to draw any tentative conclusions on the diachronic development of the adverb *mortal*. By contrast, it can safely be claimed that it has developed increasingly grammaticalised meanings over time, being semantically reanalysed as an intensifier equivalent to *very* or *terribly*. Furthermore, the data examined have also provided some interesting examples which could, in principle, prove the relationship between the intensifying function and the left periphery, as in example (6.172), which involved the collocation *mortal good hand*. However, as in the case of *deadly* (adj. and adv.), the development of the intensifying function of the adverb *mortal* is independent to that of its homonymous adjective, as suggested in Sections 6.1.3 and 6.2.4 in the light of the dictionary and corpus evidence, respectively. Therefore, as an adverb modifying in this case the adjective *good*, *mortal* has to occur in the leftmost position. In this example *mortal* is clearly not an adjective describing the fatal power of a hand: *mortal* is instead an adverb which reinforces the adjective *good* ('very good').

In spite of the limited number of examples, and as was the case for *deadly* (cf. Section 6.2.3.1), it can also be argued that the different meanings of the adverb *mortal* (descriptive, subjective and intensifying) coexist at a given point in time, as shown in Table 6.118. This, together with the fact that each of these senses of the adverb can be used independently of each other, proves Hopper's principles of layering and divergence (see Section 3.2). Moreover, *mortal* modifies negative elements in half of its occurrences in the data, while neutral and positive semantic prosody account for 32.69% and 17.31%, respectively. The predisposition of the adverb towards combinations with negative elements is, therefore, in keeping with the principle of persistence. Moreover, the collocations of *mortal* which are marked as positive show in all cases an intensifying meaning.

### 6.2.5. *The long diachrony of* mortally

Like the form *mortal* (cf. Section 6.1.3), the adverb *mortally* also dates from the late fourteenth century. Nonetheless, in the corpus data there are no examples of the adverb until the EModE period. Even so, the total number of occurrences in the corpus amounts to three. The corpus evidence, therefore, is not very conclusive.

Being an adverb, *mortally* admits a certain degree of variation in regard to the type of words modified. In the corpus it is found as a modifier of verbs (*hate* and *malign* 'to injure, wrong', 'to feel malice or ill will') and of participial forms (*wounded*), as shown in Table 6.121. Furthermore, *mortally* was only found with negative semantic prosody (cf. Table 6.122).

Of the three examples recorded in the HC, two of them show subjective readings (66%, NF 3.63) and one is descriptive (33%, NF 1.81), as Table 6.123 shows.

The collocation *mortally wounded* is counted as descriptive, as it indicates that the person is injured to death and will die as a result. Conversely, *mortally hate* and *mortally malign* are considered subjective collocations (cf. examples (6.187)–(6.188)). *Mortally hate* in (6.187) constitutes an interesting example, since the hatred in this case can also apply to things and not only to people, a change which might have later triggered an interpretation of

Table 6.121. Categories modified by *mortally* in the HC

| **Period** | **P** | | | **V** | | | **Total** | **NF** |
|---|---|---|---|---|---|---|---|---|
| | **Abs. Freq.** | % | **NF** | **Abs. Freq.** | % | **NF** | | |
| **EModE** | 1 | 33.33 | 1.81 | 2 | 66.67 | 3.63 | 3 | 5.44 |

Table 6.122. The semantic prosody of *mortally* in the HC

| **Period** | **Neg** | | | **Pos** | | | **Neu** | | | **Total** | **NF** |
|---|---|---|---|---|---|---|---|---|---|---|---|
| | **Abs. Freq.** | % | **NF** | **Abs. Freq.** | % | **NF** | **Abs. Freq.** | % | **NF** | | |
| **EModE** | 3 | 100.00 | 5.44 | 0 | 0.00 | 0 | 0 | 0.00 | 0 | 3 | 5.44 |

Table 6.123. Meaning types for *mortally* in the HC

| **Period** | **D** | | | **S** | | | **I** | | | **Total** | **NF** |
|---|---|---|---|---|---|---|---|---|---|---|---|
| | **Abs. Freq.** | % | **NF** | **Abs. Freq.** | % | **NF** | **Abs. Freq.** | % | **NF** | | |
| **EModE** | 1 | 33.33 | 1.81 | 2 | 66.67 | 3.63 | 0 | 0.00 | 0 | 3 | 5.44 |

*mortally* as a degree modifier.[47] Thus, hating a person might imply hurting him/her, whereas hating something *mortally* might already hint an extreme degree. For this reason, *hate mortally* is considered as subjective, for death is still in the background and can still be easily evoked. Likewise, *mortally malign* in (6.188) is considered subjective, as *malign* in this example means rather 'to bear ill will, to be hostile', although it could also mean 'to attack (somebody or something), to injure' (MED, s.v. *malignen* v. 1). This latter meaning is the least likely in this context, however, which alludes to Cardinal Wolsey's anger when Charles V proposed Cardinal Adrian for next pope of Rome. Wolsey is said to have been so 'wood ['angry'] therwith, that he studied to invent all waies of reuengment of his grief ['anger, spite'] against the Emperour [Charles V]'.[48] Therefore, considering Wolsey's failure to the see of Rome and his hatred of the emperor for having put forward another candidate, it is more likely that the meaning of *malign* in this particular case is simply 'to bear ill will'. There is no mention, at least in this text, to the fact that Cardinal Wolsey was planning to physically attack Charles and wound him to death. On this account, *mortally* is considered to illustrate a subjective rather than a descriptive reading of the adverb here.

(6.187) [...] *yet he confessed they cared not for it* [*morality*], *further than the reputation of it was necessary for their credit, and affairs*: *of which he gave me many Instances, as their professing and swearing Friendship, where they hated* ***mortally***; (CEBIO3. 1680. Gilbert Burnet. *Some passages of the life and death of the right honourable John, Earl of Rochester*)

(6.188) *This Cardinall therefore* [...] *devised to allure the kinge* [...] *to cast fantasy to one of the Frenche kings Sisters*: *which thing, because of the Enmity and warre that was at that tyme betweene the French king and the Emperour* (*whom, for the cause afore remembred, he* ***mortally*** *maligned*) *he was* [{*very*{] *desirouse to procure*; (CEBIO1. 1500–1570. William Roper. *The lyfe of Sir Thomas Moore, Knighte*)

As was the case with the adverb *deadly*, the results for *mortally* in the HC are also insufficient to provide firm evidence of the behaviour of this

47 The use of the verb *hate* here is absolute, and the relativiser *where* refers back to the noun *instances*: 'instances in which they hated mortally'. Therefore, the absolute use of *hate* in this case allows for both a human and a non-human referent.

48 HC. William Roper. 1500–70. *The lyfe of Sir Thomas Moore, Knighte*. CEBIO1, p. 31.

Table 6.124. The collocations of *mortally* in ARCHER

| | Collocation | Abs. Freq. | % | NF | Total in ARCHER |
|---|---|---|---|---|---|
| **17th c.** | *mortally wounded* | 1 | 25.00 | 2.87 | 4 |
| | **Total** | **1** | **16.67** | **2.87** | **6** |
| **18th c.** | *mortally wound* | 1 | 100.00 | 1.87 | 1 |
| | *mortally wounded* | 1 | 25.00 | 1.87 | 4 |
| | **Total** | **2** | **33.33** | **3.73** | **6** |
| **19th c.** | *mortally wounded* | 2 | 50.00 | 3.69 | 4 |
| | **Total** | **2** | **33.33** | **3.69** | **6** |
| **20th c.** | *mortally offend* | 1 | 100.00 | 1.88 | 1 |
| | **Total** | **1** | **16.67** | **1.88** | **6** |

adverb and its development over time. It was recorded in the data as a modifier of verbs (two tokens) and participial items (only one occurrence), with both descriptive and subjective meanings (one and two tokens, respectively) and with negative semantic prosody exclusively.

In the case of the ARCHER material, the adverb *mortally* is firstly attested in the seventeenth century, as shown in example (6.189). Table 6.124 provides the absolute, relative and normalised frequencies of *mortally* over the different periods. The difference is, however, not statistically significant, as indicated by Fisher's exact test values.[49]

Concerning the collocations of *mortally* in ARCHER, the frequencies are very low to be able to make any conclusive remarks on their evolution over time. Moreover, only *mortally wounded* is recorded in the seventeenth, eighteenth and nineteenth centuries. The remaining collocations, namely *mortally wound* and *mortally offend*, are documented only in one century, the eighteenth and the twentieth century, respectively. The only collocation which is recorded more than once is *mortally wounded*, which appears four times in ARCHER and which is, according to the different statistical measures, highly statistically significant (refer to the different values in Table 6.125).

49 **17th c. > 18th c.:** = 1; **18th c.> 19th c.:** = 1; **19th c. > 20th c.:** = 1.

Table 6.125. Standardised scores for *mortally* in ARCHER

| Collocation | *z*-score | *MI* | *MI3* | *LL*-value |
|---|---|---|---|---|
| *mortally wounded* | 222.949 | 13.601 | 17.601 | 67.577 |

Table 6.126. Meaning types for *mortally* in ARCHER

| | | D | I | Total |
|---|---|---|---|---|
| **17th c.** | # | 1 | 0 | 1 |
| | % | 20.00 | 0.00 | 16.67 |
| | **NF** | 2.87 | 0 | 2.87 |
| **18th c.** | # | 2 | 0 | 2 |
| | % | 40.00 | 0.00 | 33.33 |
| | **NF** | 3.73 | 0 | 3.73 |
| **19th c.** | # | 2 | 0 | 2 |
| | % | 40.00 | 0.00 | 33.33 |
| | **NF** | 3.69 | 0 | 3.73 |
| **20th c.** | # | 0 | 1 | 1 |
| | % | 0.00 | 100.00 | 16.67 |
| | **NF** | 0 | 1.88 | 1.88 |
| **Total (#)** | | 5 | 1 | 6 |

As for the types of meaning (see Table 6.126), *mortally* is not attested with subjective readings in the data. Approximately 83% of the meanings in ARCHER are descriptive or literal, while the remaining 17% correspond to intensifying readings of the adverb. The low absolute frequencies also indicate that the results for each of these meanings comparing the different centuries are not statistically significant.[50] Example (6.189), for instance, shows a descriptive meaning of *mortally*, in particular its co-occurrence

50 *Descriptive meanings*: 17th c. > 18th c. Fisher's exact test = 1; 18th c. > 19th c.: Fisher's exact test = 1.

with the participial item *wounded*, which shows a literal interpretation, alluding to the deadly wounds of one of the characters. Example (6.190), by contrast, illustrates an intensifying meaning of the adverb, for its original meaning is no longer retrievable in this context. Instead, what is meant here is that the publication of an article has greatly offended or irritated two characters. *Mortally* in this context is therefore interpreted as a synonym for *immensely* or *greatly*.

(6.189) *It fell out that shortly after, one of the Murderers was upon a party* ***mortally*** *wounded,* [...] *and then died imediatly*. (1653merc_n2b. 1653. Anonymous. *Mercurius Politicus*)

(6.190) *Am afraid the article* ***mortally*** *offended both of them*. (1933agat_y7b. 1933. James Agate. *The autobiography of James Agate*)

The semantic prosody of *mortally* in ARCHER is invariably negative, as indicated in Table 6.127, since it is only attested with the verbs *wound* and *offend*, which are indubitably negative in meaning, and with the participial element *wounded*, which is negative as well. There are therefore no occurrences of *mortally* in combination with neutral or positive elements in the data.

Finally, in regard to the type of word modified by the adverb, *mortally* is found as a modifier of participial forms in 66.67% of the cases, and as a modifier of verbs in 33.33% of the occurrences (see Table 6.128 for the distribution of the figures over the different centuries). The individual frequencies of *mortally*, however, make it impossible to establish a diachronic comparison of this distribution, given the low rate of occurrence of the

Table 6.127. The semantic prosody of *mortally* in ARCHER

| **Period** | **Neg.** | | **NF** |
|---|---|---|---|
| | **Abs. Freq.** | **%** | |
| **17th c.** | 1 | 16.67 | 2.87 |
| **18th c.** | 2 | 33.33 | 3.73 |
| **19th c.** | 2 | 33.33 | 3.69 |
| **20th c.** | 1 | 16.67 | 1.88 |

Table 6.128. Categories modified by *mortally* in ARCHER

| | | P | Vb | Total |
|---|---|---|---|---|
| **17th c.** | # | 1 | 0 | 1 |
| | % | 25.00 | 0.00 | 16.67 |
| | **NF** | 2.87 | 0 | 2.87 |
| **18th c.** | # | 1 | 1 | 2 |
| | % | 25.00 | 50.00 | 33.33 |
| | **NF** | 1.87 | 1.87 | 3.73 |
| **19th c.** | # | 2 | 0 | 2 |
| | % | 50.00 | 0.00 | 33.33 |
| | **NF** | 3.69 | 0 | 3.73 |
| **20th c.** | # | 0 | 1 | 1 |
| | % | 0.00 | 50.00 | 16.67 |
| | **NF** | 0 | 1.88 | 1.88 |
| **Total (#)** | | 4 | 2 | 6 |

adverb. Even so, the difference in the number of tokens for each of these categories is not statistically significant.[51]

In the EModE data from EEBOCorp 1.0 the adverb *mortally* occurred in a total of 1,413 examples and in 95 different collocations. The majority of the attestations of the adverb are dated to the last period (55.34%), followed by the remaining periods in decreasing order (30.71% for P. IV, 7.22% for P. III, 5.59% for P. II and, finally, 1.13% corresponding to P. I). Despite the rise in the absolute number of occurrences of the adverb over time (cf. Table 6.129), this increase was only found to be significant from P. II to P. III ($\chi^2$ (1) = 163.05; $p$ = 0) and from P. III to P. IV ($\chi^2$ (1) =44.38; $p$ = 0). Table 6.130 shows the most frequent collocates of *mortally* in the corpus, those occurring at least ten times. The combination of the adverb with these collocates cannot be attributed to mere chance, but is statistically significant, as reflected by the different values given in Table 6.131.

51 **Verbs: 17th c. > 18th c.**= 1; **18th c. > 19th c.**= 1.

Table 6.129. *Mortally* in EEBOCorp 1.0

| Period | Abs. Freq. | % | NF | Total |
|---|---|---|---|---|
| I (1470s–90s) | 16 | 1.13 | 5.47 | 1,413 |
| II (1500s–40s) | 79 | 5.59 | 7.71 | |
| III (1550s–90s) | 102 | 7.22 | 1.39 | |
| IV (1600s–40s) | 434 | 30.71 | 2.86 | |
| V (1650s–90s) | 782 | 55.34 | 2.72 | |

Table 6.130. Absolute and normalised frequencies for the most frequent collocates of *mortally* in EEBOCorp 1.0

| Collocation | Abs. Freq. | NF |
|---|---|---|
| *mortally dangerous* | 19 | 0.04 |
| *mortally hate* | 292 | 0.56 |
| *mortally hated* | 24 | 0.05 |
| *mortally hurt* | 34 | 0.06 |
| *mortally offend* | 32 | 0.06 |
| *mortally offended* | 12 | 0.02 |
| *mortally sick* | 45 | 0.09 |
| *mortally sin* | 220 | 0.42 |
| *mortally wound* | 146 | 0.28 |
| *mortally wounded* | 412 | 0.78 |

As for the types of meanings (cf. Table 6.132), the overwhelming majority of the examples present descriptive meanings of *mortally* (72.89%), while subjective examples amount to 23.64%. Those readings which are ambiguous between subjective and intensifying and those between descriptive and subjective are much less numerous, accounting for 1.48% and 1.42% of the total, respectively. Intensifying meanings of *mortally* are, in turn, scarcely found in the corpus (0.57%). As for the significance of these results, both the chi-square test and Fisher's exact test indicate that the scores are

Table 6.131. Standardised scores for *mortally* in EEBOCorp 1.0

| Collocation | *z*-score | *MI* | *MI3* | *LL*-value |
|---|---|---|---|---|
| *mortally dangerous* | 35.022 | 6.056 | 14.552 | 122.094 ($p < 0.0001$) |
| *mortally hate* | 574.914 | 10.147 | 26.527 | 3,526.170 ($p < 0.0001$) |
| *mortally hated* | 83.281 | 8.185 | 17.355 | 224.526 ($p < 0.0001$) |
| *mortally hurt* (vb.) | 8.873 | 4.145 | 8.789 | 19.296 ($p < 0.0001$) |
| *mortally hurt* (pp.) | 54.359 | 6.699 | 16.415 | 211.888 ($p < 0.0001$) |
| *mortally offend* | 84.663 | 7.820 | 17.820 | 283.241 ($p < 0.0001$) |
| *mortally offended* | 30.912 | 6.351 | 13.521 | 81.949 ($p < 0.0001$) |
| *mortally sick* | 86.579 | 7.397 | 18.381 | 372.045 ($p < 0.0001$) |
| *mortally sin* | 163.200 | 6.943 | 22.506 | 1,681.310 ($p < 0.0001$) |
| *mortally wound* | 277.777 | 9.051 | 23.431 | 1,540.995 ($p < 0.0001$) |
| *mortally wounded* | 1,097.586 | 11.515 | 28.888 | 5,760.706 ($p < 0.0001$) |

Table 6.132. Meaning types for *mortally* in EEBOCorp 1.0

| | | D | D/S | S | S/I | I | Total |
|---|---|---|---|---|---|---|---|
| **1470–99** | # | 16 | 0 | 0 | 0 | 0 | 16 |
| | % | 1.55 | 0.00 | 0.00 | 0.00 | 0.00 | 1.13 |
| | **NF** | 5.47 | 0 | 0 | 0 | 0 | 5.47 |
| **1500–49** | # | 76 | 0 | 3 | 0 | 0 | 79 |
| | % | 7.38 | 0.00 | 0.90 | 0.00 | 0.00 | 5.59 |
| | **NF** | 7.42 | 0 | 0.29 | 0 | 0 | 7.71 |
| **1550–99** | # | 68 | 0 | 31 | 3 | 0 | 102 |
| | % | 6.60 | 0.00 | 9.28 | 14.29 | 0.00 | 7.22 |
| | **NF** | 0.93 | 0 | 0.42 | 0.04 | 0 | 1.39 |
| **1600–49** | # | 345 | 9 | 75 | 1 | 4 | 434 |
| | % | 33.50 | 45.00 | 22.46 | 4.76 | 50.00 | 30.71 |
| | **NF** | 2.28 | 0.06 | 0.49 | 0.01 | 0.03 | 2.86 |
| **1650–99** | # | 525 | 11 | 225 | 17 | 4 | 782 |
| | % | 50.97 | 55.00 | 67.36 | 80.95 | 50.00 | 55.34 |
| | **NF** | 1.83 | 0.04 | 0.78 | 0.06 | 0.01 | 2.72 |
| **Total (#)** | | **1,030** | **20** | **334** | **21** | **8** | **1,413** |

statistically significant only for descriptive, subjective and meanings which are ambiguous between subjective and intensifying in certain periods.[52]

A selection of the different types of meanings of *mortally* is provided in (6.191)–(6.196). The combination of *mortally* with the verb *smite* in (6.191) is taken to be descriptive, as beating or striking someone mortally implies wounding him/her to death.

(6.191) *and there smote hem doun with his clubbe so* ***mortally*** *that he maad hit reed with their blood and slewe hem all* (D00000998449480000. 1473. Raoul Lefèvre. [...] *The recuyell of the historyes of Troye*)

In (6.192) *mortally* modifies the adjective *dangerous* and is considered to be halfway between descriptive and subjective. This example relates how risky it is to enter a house in which a person is infected with the plague. Going into a house is not itself fatal, but the risk of contracting the disease is greatest when in contact with someone infected with the virus. On this account, this example was not counted as properly descriptive, but as intermediate between descriptive and subjective, although it is ultimately referring to a highly infectious disease, and, therefore, closer to a literal meaning.

(6.192) *imagine with your selves, how* ***mortally*** *dangerous it is to enter an infected house*; (D00000998403690000. 1630. Richard Brathwaite. *The English gentleman* [...])

Examples (6.193)–(6.195) present the same collocation, *hate mortally*, but differ slightly. Thus, while (6.193) was marked as subjective, (6.194) and (6.195) were considered ambiguous between subjective and intensifying. Example (6.193) presents the case of a person who hates another, and dislikes him so much as to treat him worse than he would treat a serpent or a dog. That does not mean necessarily that this person wishes his actual death or that he intends to kill him. For this reason *hate mortally* is regarded here as subjective rather than as literal or descriptive. Examples (6.194) and (6.195) differ from (6.193) in that what is hated is not a person, but a thing, and this

52 *Descriptive meanings*: P. II > P. III $\chi^2$ (1) = 216.25; $p = 0$; P. III > P. IV $\chi^2$ (1) = 48.27; $p = 0$; P. IV > P. V $\chi^2$ (1) =9.89; $p = 0.00147067$; *subjective meanings*: P. IV > P. V $\chi^2$ (1) = 11.63; $p = 0.00051848$; *subjective/intensifying meanings*: P. IV > P. V Fisher's exact test = 0.01057 (significant at $p < 0.05$).

paves the way for a subsequent degree or intensifying reading. In (6.194) what is hated is rebellion or the suspicion of it, which is said to be avoided at all costs. Similarly, the quotation in (6.195) describes Queen Christina Alessandra of Sweden, who was said to be an extremely educated woman that devoted her time to the study of books and slept only for a few hours. Christina hence hated inactivity and laziness, as suggested in this excerpt. Therefore, the meaning of the adverb *mortally* here seems to be closer to that of an intensifier ('extremely, very') and in this precise context it is the most likely interpretation, although the combination of *mortally* with the verb *hate* can still easily evoke death. Example (6.196) presents the same context although with a different collocate, namely the verb *dislike*. One may feel hostility towards a particular person and hence dislike him/her, which would be considered subjective, for there is always the possibility of damaging him/her or of bearing him/her ill will. However, disliking something is different, so the meaning of the adverb is here closer to that of an intensifier: 'very much'.

(6.193) *He hatethe him wars than a dogge or a serpente: as who sayth,* ***mortally*** *without hope of reconcylynge*. (D00000998468240000. 1538. Sir Thomas Eliot. *The dictionary of syr Thomas Eliot knight*).

(6.194) *Neuertheles we haue thought good* [...] *to put away all suspicion of rebellion, which we haue fled, &* ***mortally*** *hated all the dayes of our life.* (D00000998376540000. 1568. William I, Prince of Orange. *A declaration and publication of the most worthy Prince of Orange*)

(6.195) *She hates* ***mortally*** *idleness, and is adorned with so many vertues, that every Queen may easily envie her* [...]. (D00000998719860000. 1658. Gualdo Priorato. *The history of* [...] *Christina Alessandra Queen of Swedland*)

(6.196) *I* ***Mortally*** *dislike a damning Face: Pleas'd or displeas'd; no matter now, 'tis past.* (D00000135065200000. 1696. George Granville Lansdowne. *The she-gallants, a comedy*)

Finally, examples (6.197)–(6.198) show purely intensifying meanings of *mortally*. More conspicuously, *mortally* is found in these examples as a modifier of positive items: the *–ed* form *enamoured* and the prepositional phrase *in love*. A descriptive or literal meaning here is completely ruled out, and the only possible interpretation is that of an intensifier: 'totally enamoured' and 'totally in love', respectively. The adverb *mortally* is also found as an intensifier in combination with elements which are inherently negative, as the adjective *tedious* in (6.199). In this example, a character is describing a tempest and the description is said to be very boring, but the fact that something is uninteresting does not imply in any case that it can be fatal. Again, *mortally tedious* here can only be read as an intensifier: 'extremely tedious'.

(6.197) *For Brohars became* ***mortally*** *inamored with Basina, the wife of Croisant,* [...] (D00000998478650000. 1612. Gervase Markham. *The most famous and renowned historie, of that woorthie and illustrous knight Meruine* [...])

(6.198) *I can endure no more, Diablo, he is* ***mortally*** *in love With Catalina.* (D00000998524600000. 1640. James Shirley. *The maides revenge A tragedy*)

(6.199) *But Mr. Blackmore, after he has wearied us with the Description of a Tempest, which is* ***mortally*** *tedious, gives us the solemn Entertainment of a sententious Harangue,* [...]. (D00000155097250000. 1696. John Dennis. *Remarks on a book entituled Prince Arthur*)

The adverb *mortally* occurs in the corpus in the overwhelming majority of the cases with elements which are inherently negative (99.65%). Those elements modified by *mortally* with positive semantic prosody only amount to 0.28% of the total and those with neutral semantic prosody represent 0.07% of the total of examples, as shown in Table 6.133.

Thus, only the collocates *enamoured* and *in love* in examples (6.197) and (6.198), in addition to the adjective *happy* and the participial form *surprised*, were classified as representing positive semantic prosody. The adjective *strong* was the only collocate of *mortally* which was tagged as having neutral semantic prosody, for *strong* can be regarded as both a positive and a negative quality. The remaining collocates of the adverb all had negative semantic prosody, including, among many others, *wounded*, *afflicted*, *torment*, *sin*, *sick*, *pursue*, *stab* and *infect*. Moreover, although the absolute frequencies for negative semantic prosody rise exponentially over time, the results from the chi-square test show that these figures can only be considered as statistically significant if we compare P. II and P. III ($\chi^2$ (1) = 163.046; $p$ = 0) and P. III and P. IV ($\chi^2$ (1) = 43.744; $p$= 0).

Given its adverbial nature, *mortally* can modify a relatively wide variety of word classes, although it shows a strong preference for verbs (55.70%) and participial items (38.36%). Even so, it was also found as a modifier of adjectives (5.87%) and of prepositional phrases (0.07%). The individual

Table 6.133. Semantic prosody for *mortally* in EEBOCorp 1.0

| | | Neg | Neu | Pos | Total |
|---|---|---|---|---|---|
| 1470–99 | # | 16 | 0 | 0 | 16 |
| | % | 1.14 | 0.00 | 0.00 | 1.13 |
| | NF | 5.47 | 0 | 0 | 5.47 |
| 1500–49 | # | 79 | 0 | 0 | 79 |
| | % | 5.61 | 0.00 | 0.00 | 5.59 |
| | NF | 7.71 | 0 | 0 | 7.71 |
| 1550–99 | # | 102 | 0 | 0 | 102 |
| | % | 7.24 | 0.00 | 0.00 | 7.22 |
| | NF | 1.39 | 0 | 0 | 1.39 |
| 1600–49 | # | 432 | 0 | 2 | 434 |
| | % | 30.68 | 0.00 | 50.00 | 30.71 |
| | NF | 2.85 | 0 | 0.01 | 2.86 |
| 1650–99 | # | 779 | 1 | 2 | 782 |
| | % | 55.33 | 100.00 | 50.00 | 55.34 |
| | NF | 2.71 | 0 | 0.01 | 2.72 |
| Total (#) | | 1,408 | 1 | 4 | 1,413 |

distribution as a modifier of each of these categories over the different periods in the corpus is given in Table 6.134.

The statistical tests show that the variation over the different periods is only significant in regard to verbs and participial elements. As for verbs, the difference was found to be slightly significant if we compare P. I with P. II ($\chi^2$ (1) = 9.96; $p$ = 0.00160587) and highly significant in the transition from P. II to P. III ($\chi^2$ (1) = 205.006; $p$ = 0). As for participial items, the difference is significant from P. I to P. II (Fisher's exact test = 0.000012) and from P. III to P. IV ($\chi^2$ (1) = 37.212; $p$ = 0).

In the eighteenth-century data, the adverb *mortally* occurred in a total of 73 tokens and 18 different collocations (cf. Table 6.135), only three of which occur over ten times in the database and were therefore considered for statistical testing. The results from the different tests show that in fact

Table 6.134. Categories modified by *mortally* in EEBOCorp 1.0

| | | Adj | Part | PP | Vb | Total |
|---|---|---|---|---|---|---|
| **1470–99** | # | 0 | 10 | 0 | 6 | 16 |
| | % | 0.00 | 1.84 | 0.00 | 0.76 | 1.13 |
| | **NF** | 0 | 3.42 | 0 | 2.05 | 5.47 |
| **1500–49** | # | 0 | 2 | 0 | 77 | 79 |
| | % | 0.00 | 0.37 | 0.00 | 9.78 | 5.59 |
| | **NF** | 0 | 0.20 | 0 | 7.52 | 7.71 |
| **1550–99** | # | 0 | 27 | 0 | 75 | 102 |
| | % | 0.00 | 4.98 | 0.00 | 9.53 | 7.22 |
| | **NF** | 0 | 0.37 | 0 | 1.02 | 1.39 |
| **1600–49** | # | 31 | 185 | 1 | 217 | 434 |
| | % | 37.35 | 34.13 | 100.00 | 27.57 | 30.71 |
| | **NF** | 0.20 | 1.22 | 0.01 | 1.43 | 2.86 |
| **1650–99** | # | 52 | 318 | 0 | 412 | 782 |
| | % | 62.65 | 58.68 | 0.00 | 52.36 | 55.34 |
| | **NF** | 0.18 | 1.11 | 0 | 1.43 | 2.72 |
| **Total (#)** | | **83** | **542** | **1** | **787** | **1,413** |

Table 6.135. Absolute and normalised frequencies for the most frequent collocations of *mortally* in ECF

| **Collocation** | **Abs. Freq.** | **NF** |
|---|---|---|
| *mortally hate* | 14 | 1.44 |
| *mortally offend* | 15 | 1.55 |
| *mortally wounded* | 17 | 1.75 |

the association of *mortally* with its most frequent collocates, the verbs *hate* and *offend*, and the participial form *wounded*, is to be considered highly statistically significant (cf. Table 6.136).

Concerning the types of meanings of *mortally* in ECF (see Table 6.137), the adverb seems to favour those readings which are ambiguous between

Table 6.136. Standardised scores for *mortally* in ECF

| Collocation | *z*-score | *MI* | *MI3* | *LL*-value |
|---|---|---|---|---|
| *mortally hate* | 91.670 | 9.234 | 16.849 | 151.394 ($p < 0.0001$) |
| *mortally offend* | 119.198 | 9.891 | 17.704 | 175.918 ($p < 0.0001$) |
| *mortally wounded* | 184.010 | 10.961 | 19.136 | 224.863 ($p < 0.0001$) |

Table 6.137. Meaning types for *mortally* in ECF

| | Abs. Freq. | % | NF |
|---|---|---|---|
| **D** | 22 | 30.14 | 2.27 |
| **S** | 13 | 17.80 | 1.34 |
| **S/I** | 34 | 46.58 | 3.50 |
| **I** | 4 | 5.48 | 0.41 |
| **Total** | 73 | 100.00 | 7.52 |

subjective and intensifying (46.58%), as well as descriptive readings, which make up 30.14% of the total. Much less frequently, however, *mortally* is also attested with subjective (17.80%) and with intensifying meanings (5.48%).

*Mortally wounded* in (6.200) is a clear example of a descriptive or literal meaning, for the character, a captain, has been injured to death.

(6.200) *The Evening before the Day appointed for our Marriage, the Captain of the Guard, our Roman Friend, sent one to let me know, that he was* ***mortally*** *wounded in a Rencounter, and desir'd to speak with me speedily.* (1719. Jane Barker. *Exilius*)

Example (6.201), in turn, illustrates a subjective meaning of the adverb, specifically its use with the adjective *afraid*. When somebody feels frightened or terrified due to a specific situation, (s)he may have the feeling that his/her heart is racing, and may even experience other physical symptoms such as shortness of breath and sweating. That discomfort may make this person think that (s)he is at death's door. The connections of the collocation *mortally afraid* with death, and, hence, with its original meaning, seem logical, and for this reason *mortally* is considered here as subjective rather than as purely intensifying.

(6.201) *I retired to mine [bed], where I found Strap* ***mortally*** *afraid, he having got away in the dark, while the captain and his lady were at logger-heads.* (1748. Tobias George Smollett. *Roderick Random*)

Examples (6.202)–(6.203) involve the collocates *hate* and *detest*, respectively:

(6.202) *Hating, as I* ***mortally*** *do, all long unnecessary prefaces, I shall give you good quarter in this,* [...] (1749. John Cleland. *Memoirs of a Woman of Pleasure*)
(6.203) *'I have scarce seen my Children Today,' answered Amelia. 'Besides, I* ***mortally*** *detest Cards.'* (1752. Henry Fielding. *Amelia*)

As was the case with the collocation *mortally hate* in EEBOCorp 1.0 in (6.194) and (6.195), in this example the object of hatred is not a person, but a thing. This leaves room for the interpretation of *mortally* as a degree adverb, 'very much, extremely'. This is also the case of *mortally detest* in example (6.203), which could also contextually allow for a degree reading. Nonetheless, as *hate* and *detest* can still be linked to death when the referent is human, I have marked these collocates as intermediate between subjective and intensifying, even though the latter interpretation is the most likely.

Conversely, *mortally* in examples (6.204)–(6.205) has an intensifying meaning. *Chagrined* in (6.204) means 'disappointed' and feeling disenchanted with something does not relate any longer to the original meaning of *mortally*, but *mortally chagrined* here means rather 'terribly disappointed'. In a similar fashion, *mortally obstropolous* in (6.205) is also detached from the earliest literal meaning of the adverb; *obstropolous* means 'noisy' and refers to a patient who is in hospital and who has been rather noisy. As a result, the meaning of *mortally* here can only be taken as that of an intensifier.

(6.204) *I am* ***mortally*** *chagrin'd at the triumph you have furnished to that rascally citizen.* (1753. Tobias George Smollett. *Ferdinand Count Fathom*)
(6.205) *Good lack! A' has been* ***mortally*** *obstropolous, and out of his senses all this blessed day.* (1762. Tobias George Smollett. *Sir Launcelot Greaves*)

In the ECF data *mortally* is attested with verbal collocates (54.79%), as well as with participial (38.36%) and, less frequently, with adjectival

Table 6.138. Categories modified by *mortally* in ECF

| | Abs. Freq. | % | NF |
|---|---|---|---|
| **Adj.** | 5 | 6.85 | 0.52 |
| **Part.** | 28 | 38.36 | 2.89 |
| **Vb.** | 40 | 54.79 | 4.12 |
| **Total** | 73 | 100.00 | 7.52 |

elements (6.85%) (cf. Table 6.138). Unlike the EModE material from EEBOCorp 1.0 (cf. supra), in the eighteenth-century data *mortally* does not modify prepositional phrases.

As for the other variable considered in the collocational analysis, namely semantic prosody, while in the EModE data from EEBOCorp 1.0 *mortally* was attested with neutral, negative and even positive semantic prosody (cf. supra), in ECF the adverb is only recorded as a modifier of elements which are inherently negative.

Finally, NCF records 122 instances of the adverb *mortally* in a total of 42 different collocations. Table 6.139 provides the most frequent collocations, while Table 6.140 records the standardised scores for the most common combinations, that is, those occurring at least five times in the data. As these scores reveal, all these collocations are highly statistically significant.

Table 6.139. Absolute and normalised frequencies for the most frequent collocations of *mortally* in NCF

| Collocation | Abs. Freq. | NF |
|---|---|---|
| *mortally afraid* | 5 | 0.13 |
| *mortally hate* | 6 | 0.16 |
| *mortally offend* | 20 | 0.53 |
| *mortally offended* | 12 | 0.32 |
| *mortally wound* | 9 | 0.24 |
| *mortally wounded* | 24 | 0.64 |

Table 6.140. Standardised scores for the most frequent collocations of *mortally* in NCF

| Collocation | *z*-score | *MI* | *MI3* | *LL*-value |
|---|---|---|---|---|
| *mortally afraid* | 23.727 | 6.840 | 11.484 | 37.504 ($p < 0.0001$) |
| *mortally hate* | 35.314 | 7.713 | 12.883 | 52.221 ($p < 0.0001$) |
| *mortally offend* | 249.993 | 11.684 | 20.180 | 270.190 ($p < 0.0001$) |
| *mortally offended* | 119.929 | 10.230 | 17.399 | 146.288 ($p < 0.0001$) |
| *mortally wound* | 66.682 | 8.954 | 15.294 | 93.786 ($p < 0.0001$) |
| *mortally wounded* | 215.271 | 10.917 | 20.086 | 315.537 ($p < 0.0001$) |

In the data, *mortally* occurs mostly with descriptive and intensifying meanings (40.98% and 42.62%, respectively), even though subjective examples are also attested (11.48% of the total), as well as readings which are ambiguous between descriptive and subjective and between subjective and intensifying (2.46% each) (cf. Table 6.141).

Examples (6.206)–(6.211) serve to illustrate the different meanings of the adverb *mortally* present in the NCF data. *Mortally hurt* in (6.206) conveys a literal meaning. *Mortally quarrelled* in (6.207) is ambiguous between descriptive and subjective, for it is unclear whether the women mentioned in the passage simply had a row or whether they ended up fighting and injuring each other. In turn, *mortally apprehensive* in (6.208) is considered to be subjective, since when someone is afraid of something,

Table 6.141. Meaning types for *mortally*

| | Abs. Freq. | % | NF |
|---|---|---|---|
| D | 50 | 40.98 | 1.33 |
| D/S | 3 | 2.46 | 0.08 |
| S | 14 | 11.48 | 0.37 |
| S/I | 3 | 2.46 | 0.08 |
| I | 52 | 42.62 | 1.38 |
| **Total** | **122** | **100.00** | **3.25** |

physical symptoms, such as anxiety, panic attacks or breathing difficulties may arise and, for this reason, (s)he may feel in a state which is relatively close to death, even if that is not eventually the case. As regards *mortally envious* in (6.209), this was marked as indeterminate between subjective and intensifying. On the one hand, *mortal* may function here as a mere intensifier, 'exceedingly envious, envious to the extreme'. On the other hand, the fact of being jealous might also imply further consequences, in the sense that the teachers who are reported to envy Miss Monflathers may have a desire for vengeance, and we do not know the far-reaching implications of their envy. By contrast, (6.210) and (6.211) present two unambiguously intensifying examples, where *mortally* can only be interpreted as expressive of high or utmost degree: 'extremely or very changed' and 'extremely or very unpleasant'.

(6.206) *The Regent,* [...] *saw with satisfaction* [...] *that none were* ***mortally*** *hurt.* (1810. Jane Porter. *The Scottish chiefs*)

(6.207) *Mrs. Glenarm and Lady Lundie looked at each other in mute amazement. Here was a difference about which two women would have* ***mortally*** *quarrelled;* (1870. Wilkie Collins. *Man and wife*)

(6.208) *Here I walked about for a long time, feeling very strange, and* ***mortally*** *apprehensive of some one coming in and kidnapping me*: (1847. Charlote Brontë. *Jane Eyre*)

(6.209) *And last of the goodly procession came Miss Monflathers, bearing herself a parasol of lilac silk, and supported by two smiling teachers, each* ***mortally*** *envious of the other,* (1840. Charles Dickens. *The old curiosity shop*)

(6.210) *I found her so* ***mortally*** *changed, that I took her for her own mother*! (1814. Fanny Burney. The wanderer)

(6.211) *'I've been to I-don't-know-where ---No man's land---and a* ***mortally*** *unpleasant country it is.'* (1876. George Eliot. *Daniel Deronda*)

As for semantic prosody (see Table 6.142), the results from NCF reveal that *mortally* is still considerably attached to its original meaning in the nineteenth century, given that in the overwhelming majority of the examples (94.26%) it is found as a modifier of inherently negative elements, such as *apprehensive*, *fear* and *offended*. There are, however, occasional examples in the data in which *mortally* modifies items which have neutral (e.g. *changed*, *sensible* and *certain*) or positive (e.g. *beautiful*) semantic prosody.

Table 6.142. Semantic prosody for *mortally* in NCF

| | Abs. Freq. | % | NF |
|---|---|---|---|
| **neg** | 115 | 94.26 | 3.06 |
| **neu** | 6 | 4.92 | 0.16 |
| **pos** | 1 | 0.82 | 0.03 |
| **Total** | **122** | **100.00** | **3.25** |

As regards its collocates, *mortally* allows for modification of a wide variety of word types, not just adjectives and participial forms, as was the case of the adverb *mortal*, but also of verbs (*offend*, *strike*, *wound*, etc.) and prepositional phrases (*at feud*). Table 6.143 shows the distribution for each of these categories in NCF. It seems that *mortally* shows a clear preference for verbs and participial elements, with about 40% each, next to adjectives, which approximately account for the remaining 20%. There is only one example in which *mortally* modifies a prepositional phrase, namely *at feud*.

Table 6.143. Categories modified by *mortally* in NCF

| | Abs. Freq. | % | NF |
|---|---|---|---|
| **Adj.** | 21 | 17.22 | 0.56 |
| **Part.** | 51 | 41.80 | 1.36 |
| **PP** | 1 | 0.82 | 0.03 |
| **Vb.** | 49 | 40.16 | 1.30 |
| **Total** | **122** | **100.00** | **3.25** |

#### 6.2.5.1. *Mortally* across time

As shown in Table 6.144, the first examples of the adverb *mortally* in the different sources consulted date from EModE, which is attested mainly with descriptive and subjective meanings. The evolution for each of the readings of the adverb is illustrated in Figure 6.11.

Descriptive uses of *mortally*, amounting to 68.57%, increase slightly from EModE to the eighteenth century (EEBOCorp 1.0: 1,030 exx.; NF

Table 6.144. Types of meanings for *mortally* in the data (absolute/normalised frequencies)

| | HC (ME) | EEBOCorp 1.0 | ECF | NCF | ARCHER (20th c.) |
|---|---|---|---|---|---|
| **D** | 0 | 1,030/1.96 | 22/2.27 | 50/1.33 | 0 |
| **D/S** | 0 | 20/0.04 | 0 | 3/0.08 | 0 |
| **S** | 0 | 334/0.64 | 13/1.34 | 14/0.37 | 0 |
| **S/I** | 0 | 21/0.04 | 34/3.50 | 3/0.08 | 0 |
| **I** | 0 | 8/0.02 | 4/0.41 | 50/1.33 | 1/1.88 |
| **N. of words** | 608,570 | 525,432,293 | 9,702,699 | 37,589,837 | 530,832 |

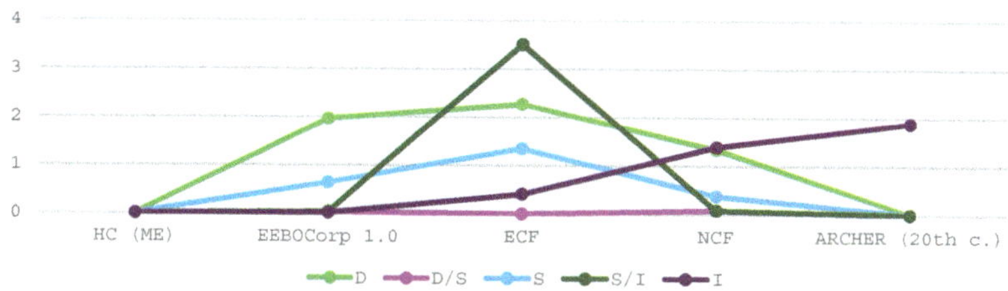


Figure 6.11. Types of meanings for *mortally*

pmw 1.96 > ECF: 22 exx.; NF pmw 2.27) and are since then reduced again (NCF: 50 exx.; NF pmw 1.33). These differences are, however, not statistically significant.[53] Subjective examples of *mortally*, the second most common after the descriptive uses (22.46%), are also more frequent in ECF than in EEBOCorp 1.0 (13 exx.; NF pmw 1.34 vs 334 exx.; NF pmw 0.64), but then drop again in the transition to the nineteenth century (from NF pmw 1.34 to NF pmw 0.37). The only difference which was found to be statistically significant is the one which concerns ECF and NCF ($\chi^2$ (1) =11.004; $p$ = 0.00090915).[54] The normalised frequencies for

53 **EEBO > ECF:** $\chi^2$ (1) = 0.314; $p$ = 0.57523594; **ECF > NCF:** $\chi^2$ (1) =3.856; $p$ = 0.04956837.

54 **EEBO > ECF:** $\chi^2$ (1) = 6.24; $p$ = 0.01248965.

those meanings of *mortally* which are ambiguous between subjective and intensifying increase considerably from EEBOCorp 1.0 to the ECF data (EEBOCorp 1.0: 21 exx.; NF pmw 0.04 > ECF: 34 exx.; NF pmw 3.50), to fall then substantially from the eighteenth to the nineteenth century (NCF: 3 exx.; NF pmw 0.08). The difference for both periods is in fact statistically significant.[55] Further to the intensifying uses of *mortally*, although the normalised frequencies of the adverb actually increase over time, the only difference which is considered statistically significant is that between EModE and the eighteenth century (Fisher's exact test = 0.000048).[56]

The corpus evidence also reveals the tendency for *mortally* to occur with inherently negative elements (see Table 6.145 and Figure 6.12), which account

Table 6.145. Semantic prosody for *mortally* (absolute/normalised frequencies)

| | HC (ME) | EEBOCorp 1.0 | ECF | NCF | ARCHER (20th c.) |
|---|---|---|---|---|---|
| **neg** | 0 | 1,408/2.68 | 73/7.52 | 113/3.01 | 1/1.88 |
| **neu** | 0 | 1/0.002 | 0 | 6/0.16 | 0 |
| **pos** | 0 | 4/0.01 | 0 | 1/0.03 | 0 |
| **N. of words** | 608,570 | 525,432,293 | 9,702,699 | 37,589,837 | 530,832 |

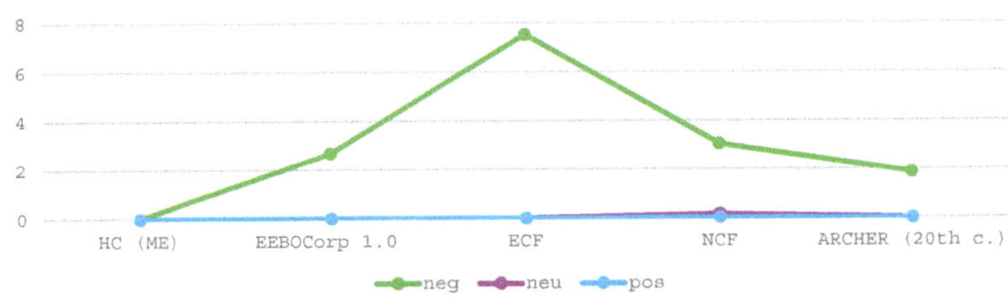


Figure 6.12. Semantic prosody for *mortally*

55 **EEBO > ECF:** $\chi^2$ (1) = 1078.932; $p$ = 0; **ECF > NCF:** Fisher's value = 0.

56 **ECF > NCF:** Fishers's exact test = 0.016853; **NCF > ARCHER:** Fisher's exact test = 0.510891.

for 99.25% of the examples. The normalised frequencies show a sharp rise in the combinations of *mortally* with negative elements from EModE to the eighteenth century (EEBOCorp 1.0: 1,408 exx.; NF pmw 2.68 > ECF: 73 exx.; NF pmw 7.52), when these uses start to decrease. Moreover, while the growth in frequency from EEBOCorp 1.0 to ECF and the subsequent decline from ECF to NCF are statistically significant, the drop in the number of attestations of *mortally* with negative items from NCF to ARCHER was not found to be statistically significant (Fisher's exact test = 1).[57]

The results from the individual frequencies of *mortally* in the data suggest that the adverb occurs mainly as a modifier of verbal (54.57%) and participial elements (38.39%) (see Table 6.146). An overall picture for each of the categories over time is provided in Figure 6.13.

Table 6.146. Categories modified by *mortally* in the data (absolute/normalised frequencies)

| | HC (ME) | EEBOCorp 1.0 | ECF | NCF | ARCHER (20th c.) |
|---|---|---|---|---|---|
| **Adj.** | 0 | 83/0.16 | 5/0.52 | 23/0.61 | 0 |
| **Part.** | 0 | 542/1.03 | 28/2.89 | 47/1.25 | 0 |
| **PP** | 0 | 1/0.002 | 0 | 1/0.03 | 0 |
| **Vb.** | 0 | 787/1.50 | 40/4.12 | 49/1.30 | 1/1.88 |
| **N. of Words** | 608,570 | 525,432,293 | 9,702,699 | 37,589,837 | 530,832 |

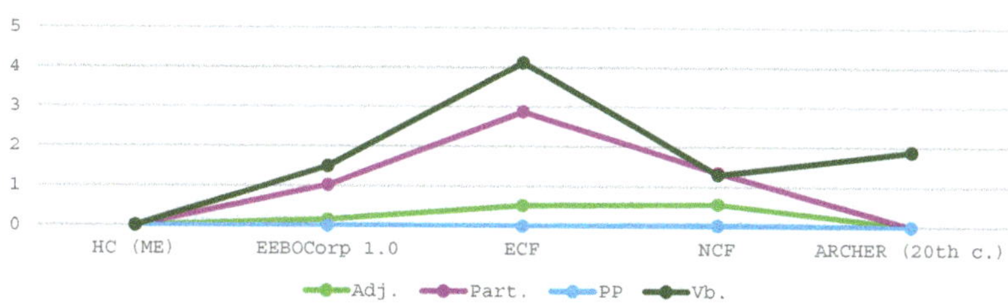


Figure 6.13. Categories modified by *mortally*

57 **EEBO > ECF:** $\chi^2$ (1) = 79.03; $p$ = 0; **ECF > NCF:** $\chi^2$ (1) = 38.877; $p$ = 0.

With regard to verbal elements, the normalised frequencies clearly increase from EModE to the eighteenth century (EEBOCorp 1.0: 787 exx; NF pmw 1.50 > ECF: 40 exx.; NF pmw 4.12). There is then a drop in the transition from the eighteenth to the nineteenth century (NCF: 49 exx.; NF pmw 1.30), followed by another rise in the twentieth century (1 ex.; NF pmw 1.88). However, the only differences which can be regarded as significant are that between EModE and the eighteenth-century data ($\chi^2$ (1) = 40.788; $p = 0$) and that between the eighteenth- and nineteenth-century data ($\chi^2$ (1) = 31.086; $p = 0.00000002$). The difference between the nineteenth and the twentieth century is, by contrast, not statistically significant at $p < 0.01$ (Fisher's exact test = 0.503984). The combinations of *mortally* with participial elements in the data follow the same trend as those with verbs, gradually increasing until the eighteenth century (EEBOCorp 1.0: 542 exx.; NF pmw 1.03> ECF: 28 exx.; NF pmw 2.89) and decreasing again in the nineteenth century (47 exx.; NF pmw 1.25). The difference between the periods is significant in all cases.[58] Finally, in regard to the modification of adjectives the variation over time by *mortally* was not found to be statistically significant in any case.[59]

Unlike its zero counterpart *mortal*, for which intensifying meanings prevailed (cf. Section 6.2.4.1), *mortally* is most often found with descriptive readings in my data. According to the OED (cf. Section 6.1.4), *mortally* first developed an intensifying function in the eighteenth century. The corpus evidence, however, provided earlier occurrences, as in the case of the collocations *mortally in love*, *mortally tedious* and *mortally desperate* in EEBOCorp 1.0, all dating to the seventeenth century. Furthermore, as in the case of the forms *deadly* and *mortal*, some collocations of *mortally* such as *hate mortally* or *dislike mortally*, when referring to things rather than to people, could have contributed to the development of unequivocal

58 **EEBOCorp 1.0 > ECF**: $\chi^2$ (1) = 29.036; $p = 0.00000008$; **ECF > NCF**: $\chi^2$ (1) = 11.996; $p = 0.00053315$.

59 **EEBOCorp 1.0 > ECF**: Fisher's exact test = 0.021286; **ECF > NCF**: Fisher's exact test = 1.

intensifying readings, as in *mortally changed*, *mortally obstropolous* and *mortally unpleasant*. This is the case, for instance, of (6.194), which dates from the sixteenth century. In this passage William I was said to detest rebellions, rather than someone in particular.

In view of the data discussed in this section, *mortally* has come to acquire intensifying meanings over time. In line with its zero counterpart, which was borrowed from Anglo-Norman, *mortally* was also attested with subjective meanings from its first records. For this reason, Adamson's (2000) cline of evolution descriptive > subjective > intensifying cannot be fully applied in this case either. Nonetheless, *mortally* was semantically reanalysed as an intensifier, acquiring a more grammaticalised status over time. The degree of grammaticalisation of *mortally*, however, is not very advanced, considering that intensifying *mortally* amounts to just 3.92% of the total of occurrences and that it is found with negative items in 99.25% of the cases. Even so, positive collocates are also documented, as is the case of *enamoured*, *in love* or *happy*, which are consistent with an intensifying reading of the adverb. The predisposition of *mortally* towards negative collocates is, however, closely related to Hopper's principle of persistence (see Section 3.2), which was also applicable to the adjectival and adverbial forms *deadly* and *mortal* discussed above (cf. Sections 6.2.3.1 and 6.2.4.1). The data analysis has also shown that the different readings of the adverb coexisted synchronically. This, again, illustrates Hopper's principles of layering and divergence (cf. Section 3.2).

### *6.2.6. The long diachrony of* to death

As indicated in Section 6.1.5, the prepositional phrase *to death* dates to the OE period, in which it could occur as a modifier of verbs which indicate a violent action, such as *beat*. The HC provides only six occurrences of *to death*, all of them dated to EModE, which actually makes it impossible to trace its diachrony.

As a prepositional phrase, *to death* was also more versatile than adjectives and behaved similarly to adverbs, modifying participial (*bewitched* and *witched*) and verbal elements (*bleed*, *condemn*, *perish* and *pinch*), as shown in Table 6.147.

Table 6.147. Categories modified by *to death* in the HC

| Period | P | | | V | | | Total | NF |
|---|---|---|---|---|---|---|---|---|
| | Abs. Freq. | % | NF | Abs. Freq. | % | NF | | |
| EModE | 4 | 66.67 | 7.26 | 2 | 33.33 | 3.63 | 6 | 10.89 |

As far as semantic prosody is concerned, it seems that *to death* invariably occurs in the HC in combination with elements which have negative semantic prosody (Table 6.148). Likewise, in the corpus data *to death* is not attested with intensifying meanings, although this could have been possible, given that such uses emerged in the course of the sixteenth century (cf. Section 6.1.5). Instead, in roughly 67% of the occurrences, *to death* is found with descriptive meanings (four tokens, NF 7.26), while two tokens are ambiguous between descriptive and subjective interpretations (33%, NF 3.63) (cf. Table 6.149).

Examples (6.212)–(6.213) exemplify some of the uses of *to death* in the HC. In (6.212) *to death* modifies the verb *perish*, reinforcing the end point or final result which is already present in the verb. This passage criticises the practice of some surgeons, who often left sick people to die, as they would not be able to afford the large sums which these physicians claimed. Example (6.213) shows the collocation *witched to death*, whose

Table 6.148. The semantic prosody of *to death* in the HC

| Period | | Neg | | | Pos | | | Neu | | Total | NF |
|---|---|---|---|---|---|---|---|---|---|---|---|
| | Abs. Freq. | % | NF | Abs. Freq. | % | NF | Abs. Freq. | % | NF | | |
| EModE | 6 | 100.00 | 10.89 | 0 | 0.00 | 0 | 0 | 0.00 | 0 | 6 | 10.89 |

Table 6.149. Meaning types for *to death* in the HC

| Period | | D | | | D/S | | | I | | Total | NF |
|---|---|---|---|---|---|---|---|---|---|---|---|
| | Abs. Freq. | % | NF | Abs. Freq. | % | NF | Abs. Freq. | % | NF | | |
| EModE | 4 | 66.67 | 7.26 | 2 | 33.33 | 3.63 | 0 | 0.00 | 0 | 6 | 10.89 |

reading is ambiguous between descriptive and subjective. In principle, being witched or bewitched to death has no fatal consequences, and means being affected by witchcraft or magic instead (see the OED, s. v. *bewitch*, v. 1). Nonetheless, in this specific context the situation describes a man who is now dead, presumably killed by witchery. His widow was told by a cunning man ['witch, wizard, conjurer'] that the devil, reincarnating in the form of the witch's cat, killed her husband, acting pretty much in the same guise as a mortal disease. This could therefore be taken as a descriptive reading of the prepositional phrase. However, if we consider that being witched is just being affected by witchcraft or magic, generally injuriously, as defined in the OED, then it is not entirely clear how this collocation can be read descriptively, for the mere fact of being bewitched would not necessarily result in someone's death. The other collocation which has been classified as ambiguous between descriptive and subjective is *bewitched to death*, which is in fact featured in the same text, and which poses exactly the same problem when it comes to classifying its meaning.

(6.212) *and it is nowe well knowen that the surgeons admytted wooll doo no cure to any p~sone, for in cace they wolde mynistre theyre coonning to sore people unrewarded, there shoulde not so manye rotte and perishe* ***to deathe*** *for lacke of helpe of Surgerye*, (CELAW1. 1500–1570. *The Statutes of the realm*).

(6.213) *The Deuill can turne himselfe into the likenes of an Angell of light.* [...] *Satan saith, the man was witched* ***to death***. (CEHAND2A. 1593. George Gifford. *A handbook of witches and witchcraft*)

As far as the uses of *to death* are concerned, ARCHER yields a total of eighteen occurrences of this prepositional phrase, 16.67% of which are attested in the seventeenth century, 44.44% in the eighteenth century, 22.22% in the nineteenth century and 16.67% in the twentieth century. The difference in the number of tokens between the four centuries is not statistically significant, considering the values of Fisher's exact test.[60]

As was the case for *mortally*, the results for the different collocations of *to death* in ARCHER do not favour a diachronic collocational analysis, since the absolute frequencies for each of the collocates are very low. In fact, the only collocates which are recorded in two different periods are the

60 **17th c. > 18th c.** = 0.544067; **18th c. > 19th c.** = 0.263918; **19th c. > 20th c.** = 1.

infinitival and participial forms *condemn* and *condemned* and the adjective *tired*, each of which is recorded two times (cf. Tables 6.150–6.153 for the distribution of the collocations over the centuries). Given the low token frequencies of these forms, I will not test the different collocations statistically, since, as was mentioned earlier (cf. Section 5.3.2), I have established a minimum threshold frequency of three, and this is not the case with any of the collocates of *to death*.

As regards the types of meanings, 61.11% of the occurrences in the corpus correspond to literal or descriptive readings of *to death*, followed by subjective readings, which make up 27.78%, and by intensifying readings, amounting to 11.11% of the total. The individual figures for each of

Table 6.150. The collocations of *to death* in the 17th c. in ARCHER

| **Collocation** | **Abs. Freq.** | **%** | **NF** | **Total in ARCHER** |
|---|---|---|---|---|
| *bite to death* | 1 | 100.00 | 2.87 | 1 |
| *jostle to death* | 1 | 100.00 | 2.87 | 1 |
| *sting to death* | 1 | 100.00 | 2.87 | 1 |
| **Total** | **3** | **16.67** | **8.61** | **18** |

Table 6.151. The collocations of *to death* in the 18th c. in ARCHER

| **Collocation** | **Abs. Freq.** | **%** | **NF** | **Total in ARCHER** |
|---|---|---|---|---|
| *condemned to death* | 1 | 50.00 | 1.87 | 2 |
| *frozen to death* | 2 | 100.00 | 3.73 | 2 |
| *hurried to death* | 1 | 100.00 | 1.87 | 1 |
| *squeeze to death* | 1 | 100.00 | 1.87 | 1 |
| *starve to death* | 1 | 100.00 | 1.87 | 1 |
| *tickled to death* | 1 | 100.00 | 1.87 | 1 |
| *tired to death* | 1 | 50.00 | 1.87 | 2 |
| **Total** | **8** | **44.44** | **14.93** | **18** |

Table 6.152. The collocations of *to death* in the 19th c. in ARCHER

| Collocation | Abs. Freq. | % | NF | Total in ARCHER |
|---|---|---|---|---|
| *chloroform to death* | 1 | 100.00 | 1.84 | 1 |
| *condemned to death* | 1 | 50.00 | 1.84 | 2 |
| *sick to death* | 1 | 100.00 | 1.84 | 1 |
| *tired to death* | 1 | 50.00 | 1.84 | 2 |
| **Total** | **4** | **22.22** | **7.37** | **18** |

Table 6.153. The collocations of *to death* in the 20th c. in ARCHER

| Collocation | Abs. Freq. | % | NF | Total in ARCHER |
|---|---|---|---|---|
| *burned to death* | 1 | 100.00 | 1.88 | 1 |
| *condemn to death* | 1 | 100.00 | 1.88 | 1 |
| *worried to death* | 1 | 100.00 | 1.88 | 1 |
| **Total** | **3** | **16.67** | **5.65** | **18** |

the centuries are provided in Table 6.154. The difference in the types of meanings across the four centuries is not statistically significant, according to the values of Fisher's exact test.[61]

Examples (6.214)–(6.216) illustrate the different meanings of *to death* in the corpus. Example (6.214), for instance, shows the collocation *condemned to death*, which is a literal or descriptive meaning, since the three men mentioned in the example have been sentenced to death as a punishment for the crime they have committed. In (6.215) the character is complaining for having walked too much since breakfast and is now overtired as a result of the physical effort. Although he is not going to die as a consequence of the effort, the physical weariness and exhaustion are certainly

61 *Descriptive meanings*: 17th c. > 18th c. = 0.711292; 18th c. > 19th c. = 0.286034; 19th c. > 20th c. = 1; *subjective meanings*: 17th c. > 18th c. = 1; 18th c. > 19th c. = 1; 19th c. > 20th c. = 1.

Table 6.154. Meaning types for *to death* in ARCHER

| | | D | S | I | Total in ARCHER |
|---|---|---|---|---|---|
| **17th c.** | # | 2 | 1 | 0 | 3 |
| | % | 18.18 | 20.00 | 0.00 | 16.67 |
| | **NF** | 5.74 | 2.87 | 0 | 8.61 |
| **18th c.** | # | 5 | 1 | 2 | 8 |
| | % | 45.46 | 20.00 | 100.00 | 44.44 |
| | **NF** | 9.33 | 1.87 | 3.73 | 14.93 |
| **19th c.** | # | 2 | 2 | 0 | 4 |
| | % | 18.18 | 40.00 | 0.00 | 22.22 |
| | **NF** | 3.69 | 3.69 | 0 | 7.37 |
| **20th c.** | # | 2 | 1 | 0 | 3 |
| | % | 18.18 | 20.00 | 0.00 | 16.67 |
| | **NF** | 3.77 | 1.88 | 0 | 5.65 |
| **Total (#)** | | **11** | **5** | **2** | **18** |

reminiscent of death. Given that death is still in the background and can be recalled relatively easily, I consider this collocation to be illustrative of a subjective meaning. Finally, (6.216) is said to represent an intensifying meaning, for being in a hurry has no relationship at all with death. Instead, *to death* here simply emphasises the idea of rapidity and speed present in the context. *I am hurried to death* could thus be paraphrased as *I am in a terrible haste.*

(6.214) *Three men, condemned* ***to death*** *at the last sessions, were sent from here under escort to a village near Gongudgh, where the execution was to have taken place.* (1872glai_n6b. 1872. Anonymous. *Glasgow Sentinel* 1/27/1872)

(6.215) *Well, I must sit down, at all events, for I'm tired* ***to death***! (1839plan_d5b. 1839. James Planche. *The garrick fever*)

(6.216) *I propose setting out soon from this place, so that you are to expect no more letters from this side of the water; besides I am hurried* ***to death***, [...] (1718mmon_x3b. 1718. Mary Montagu, Lady Wortley. *The correspondence of Alexander Pope*)

*To death* in ARCHER is attested with negative, neutral and positive semantic prosody, although the overwhelming majority of the examples (88.90%) correspond to negative semantic prosody. The occurrences of *to death* with neutral (*hurried to death*) and positive semantic prosody (*tickled to death*) account for 5.55% each. The difference in the absolute frequencies for each of the centuries was not found to be statistically significant in the light of Fisher's exact test.[62] The distribution per centuries is given in Table 6.155.

The data from ARCHER also reveal that *to death* is attested mostly as a modifier of participial forms, in 72.23% of the occurrences. Next to participial elements, this prepositional phrase can equally function as a modifier of verbs (22.22% of the cases) and of adjectives (5.55%), as shown

Table 6.155. The semantic prosody of *to death* in ARCHER

| | | **Neg** | **Neu** | **Pos** | **Total in ARCHER** |
|---|---|---|---|---|---|
| **17th c.** | # | 3 | 0 | 0 | 3 |
| | % | 18.75 | 0.00 | 0.00 | 16.67 |
| | **NF** | 8.61 | 0 | 0 | 8.61 |
| **18th c.** | # | 6 | 1 | 1 | 8 |
| | % | 37.50 | 100.00 | 100.00 | 44.44 |
| | **NF** | 11.20 | 1.87 | 1.87 | 14.93 |
| **19th c.** | # | 4 | 0 | 0 | 4 |
| | % | 25.00 | 0.00 | 0.00 | 22.22 |
| | **NF** | 7.37 | 0 | 0 | 7.37 |
| **20th c.** | # | 3 | 0 | 0 | 3 |
| | % | 18.75 | 0.00 | 0.00 | 16.67 |
| | **NF** | 5.65 | 0 | 0 | 5.65 |
| **Total (#)** | | **16** | **1** | **1** | **18** |

62 *Negative semantic prosody*: 17th c. > 18th c. = 1; 18th c. > 19th c. = 0.546328; 19th c. > 20th c. = 1.

Table 6.156. Categories modified by *to death* in ARCHER

| | | A | P | V | Total in ARCHER |
|---|---|---|---|---|---|
| **17th c.** | **#** | 0 | 1 | 2 | 3 |
| | **%** | 0.00 | 7.69 | 50.00 | 16.67 |
| | **NF** | 0 | 2.87 | 5.74 | 8.61 |
| **18th c.** | **#** | 0 | 8 | 0 | 8 |
| | **%** | 0.00 | 61.55 | 0.00 | 44.44 |
| | **NF** | 0 | 14.93 | 0 | 14.93 |
| **19th c.** | **#** | 1 | 2 | 1 | 4 |
| | **%** | 100.00 | 15.38 | 25.00 | 22.22 |
| | **NF** | 1.84 | 3.69 | 1.84 | 7.37 |
| **20th c.** | **#** | 0 | 2 | 1 | 3 |
| | **%** | 0.00 | 15.38 | 25.00 | 16.67 |
| | **NF** | 0 | 3.77 | 1.88 | 5.65 |
| **Total (#)** | | **1** | **13** | **4** | **18** |

in Table 6.156 for each of the centuries. However, the rise in both the absolute and normalised frequencies of *to death* as a modifier of participial items is not statistically significant, in the light of Fisher's exact test.[63]

In the EModE data from EEBOCorp 1.0, the prepositional phrase *to death* is attested in a total of 8,500 examples and 341 different collocations. As shown in Table 6.157, there are no instances of *to death* in the late fifteenth century, and the first attestations in the corpus date to the early sixteenth century. From that time onwards, the frequency of *to death* increases dramatically from P. II to P. III and then it is doubled from P. III to P. IV and also from P. IV to P. V. This overall increase is considered as statistically significant only from the P. II to P. III ($\chi^2$ (1) = 43.07; $p$ = 0) and from P. IV to P. V ($\chi^2$ (1) = 131.86; $p$ = 0).

63 *Participial items*: 17th c. > 18th c. = 0.098386; 18th c. > 19th c. = 0.063823; 19th c. > 20th c. = 1.

Table 6.157. *To death* in EEBOCorp 1.0

| Period | Abs. Freq. | % | NF | Total |
|---|---|---|---|---|
| I (1470s–90s) | 0 | 0.00 | 0 | 8,500 |
| II (1500s–40s) | 97 | 1.15 | 9.47 | |
| III (1550s–90s) | 1,372 | 16.14 | 18.71 | |
| IV (1600s–40s) | 2,886 | 33.95 | 19.04 | |
| V (1650s–90s) | 4,145 | 48.76 | 14.42 | |

Given the high number of collocations of *to death*, it would be impractical to provide a comprehensive list of these on a table. Hence, Table 6.158 records only the most frequent collocates in the data, in this case, those which were attested at least 100 times in the corpus. Table 6.159 provides the standardised scores for the same collocates. If we consider the different values, the association of all these collocates with *to death* is significant in all cases. However, these figures must be interpreted cautiously, for certain collocates pose the same problem as with *deadly* and *mortal* (cf. Sections 6.2.3 and 6.2.4). *Sentence*, *shot*, *stone* and *wound*, in addition to being highly frequent forms, can be both verbs and nouns, and in the case of *stone*, we would have to discard the nominal occurrences, as there are no stones to death, though it is possible to stone somebody to death. Even so, I have decided to include these values to illustrate the significance of these collocations.

Turning now to the types of meanings of *to death* in the corpus (cf. Table 6.160), descriptive readings clearly prevail in the data, accounting for 93.39% of the cases, followed by subjective interpretations (2.98%), those instances which have been marked as ambiguous between descriptive and subjective (2.08%), the intensifying attestations of *to death* (1.44%), and, finally, those meanings which are intermediate between subjective and intensifying (0.11%). Although the individual token frequencies rise for all types of meanings over the different periods, this increase is more conspicuous for descriptive readings. However, these frequencies are only statistically significant for descriptive interpretations if we compare P. II to P. III ($\chi^2$ (1) = 36.59; $p$ = 0) and P. IV to P. V ($\chi^2$ (1) = 146.80; $p$ = 0). The

Table 6.158. Absolute and normalised frequencies for the most frequent collocates of *to death* in EEBOCorp 1.0

| Collocation | Abs. Freq. | NF |
|---|---|---|
| *adjudge to death* | 109 | 0.21 |
| *adjudged to death* | 113 | 0.22 |
| *bleed to death* | 235 | 0.45 |
| *burnt to death* | 168 | 0.32 |
| *condemn to death* | 541 | 1.03 |
| *condemned to death* | 588 | 1.12 |
| *frozen to death* | 135 | 0.26 |
| *persecute to death* | 136 | 0.26 |
| *pressed to death* | 172 | 0.33 |
| *sentence to death* | 116 | 0.22 |
| *sentenced to death* | 144 | 0.27 |
| *shot to death* | 252 | 0.48 |
| *sick to death* | 143 | 0.27 |
| *starve to death* | 146 | 0.28 |
| *starved to death* | 197 | 0.37 |
| *sting to death* | 156 | 0.30 |
| *stone to death* | 288 | 0.55 |
| *stoned to death* | 656 | 1.25 |
| *trodden to death* | 109 | 0.21 |
| *wound to death* | 161 | 0.31 |
| *wounded to death* | 292 | 0.56 |

increase from P. III to P. IV was also found to be statistically significant at $p < 0.05$ in relation to those examples which are ambiguous between subjective and intensifying (Fisher's exact test = 0), while the results for the other meanings of *to death* are not statistically significant.

Examples (6.217)–(6.225) illustrate the different types of meanings for *to death* found in the corpus. Example (6.217) corresponds to a descriptive or literal reading, as the collocation *stone to death* refers to a common type

Table 6.159. Standardised scores for *to death* in EEBOCorp 1.0

| Collocation | *z*-score | *MI* | *MI3* | *LL*-value |
|---|---|---|---|---|
| *adjudge to death* | 296.122 | 9.655 | 23.192 | 1,251.799 ($p < 0.0001$) |
| *adjudged to death* | 137.769 | 7.409 | 21.049 | 938.190 ($p < 0.0001$) |
| *bleed to death* | 208.409 | 7.546 | 23.299 | 1,995.772 ($p < 0.0001$) |
| *burnt to death* | 94.573 | 5.787 | 20.572 | 1,018.936 ($p < 0.0001$) |
| *condemn to death* | 337.132 | 7.728 | 25.887 | 4,732.678 ($p < 0.0001$) |
| *condemned to death* | 143.167 | 5.203 | 23.602 | 3,099.384 ($p < 0.0001$) |
| *frozen to death* | 209.124 | 8.348 | 22.502 | 1,298.392 ($p < 0.0001$) |
| *persecute to death* | 111.283 | 6.540 | 20.715 | 965.375 ($p < 0.0001$) |
| *pressed to death* | 152.330 | 7.097 | 21.950 | 1,353.450 ($p < 0.0001$) |
| *sentence to death* | 42.251 | 4.115 | 17.831 | 443.379 ($p < 0.0001$) |
| *sentenced to death* | 309.680 | 9.384 | 23.724 | 1,597.104 ($p < 0.0001$) |
| *shot to death* | 158.731 | 6.672 | 22.627 | 1,834.730 ($p < 0.0001$) |
| *sick to death* | 62.722 | 4.881 | 19.201 | 691.869 ($p < 0.0001$) |
| *starve to death* | 198.412 | 8.086 | 22.465 | 1,350.202 ($p < 0.0001$) |
| *starved to death* | 346.272 | 9.254 | 24.498 | 2,148.245 ($p < 0.0001$) |
| *sting to death* | 141.772 | 7.032 | 21.602 | 1,213.400 ($p < 0.0001$) |
| *stone to death* | 82.367 | 4.673 | 21.013 | 1,313.236 ($p < 0.0001$) |
| *stoned to death* | 1,195.857 | 11.091 | 29.807 | 8,957.612 ($p < 0.0001$) |
| *trodden to death* | 130.965 | 7.316 | 20.852 | 890.874 ($p < 0.0001$) |
| *wound to death* | 69.754 | 5.009 | 19.670 | 806.441 ($p < 0.0001$) |
| *wounded to death* | 180.940 | 6.834 | 23.214 | 2,191.453 ($p < 0.0001$) |

of punishment at this period, consisting in throwing stones at someone till (s)he died as a consequence.

(6.217) [...] *they violently thrust him out of the cytie, and then cruelly stoned him* ***to death***: (D00000998432980000. 1546. Polydore Vergil. *An abridgement of the notable woorke of Polidore Vergile*)

Table 6.160. Meaning types for *to death* in EEBOCorp 1.0

| | | D | D/S | S | S/I | I | Total |
|---|---|---|---|---|---|---|---|
| **1470–99** | **#** | 0 | 0 | 0 | 0 | 0 | 0 |
| | **%** | 0.00 | 0.00 | 0.00 | 0.00 | 0.00 | 0.00 |
| | **NF** | 0 | 0 | 0 | 0 | 0 | 0 |
| **1500–49** | **#** | 97 | 0 | 0 | 0 | 0 | 97 |
| | **%** | 1.22 | 0.00 | 0.00 | 0.00 | 0.00 | 1.14 |
| | **NF** | 9.47 | 0 | 0 | 0 | 0 | 9.47 |
| **1550–99** | **#** | 1,305 | 43 | 21 | 1 | 2 | 1,372 |
| | **%** | 16.44 | 24.16 | 8.30 | 11.11 | 1.64 | 16.14 |
| | **NF** | 17.79 | 0.59 | 0.29 | 0.01 | 0.03 | 18.71 |
| **1600–49** | **#** | 2,723 | 63 | 63 | 0 | 37 | 2,886 |
| | **%** | 34.30 | 35.39 | 24.90 | 0.00 | 30.33 | 33.95 |
| | **NF** | 17.97 | 0.42 | 0.42 | 0 | 0.24 | 19.04 |
| **1650–99** | **#** | 3,813 | 72 | 169 | 8 | 83 | 4,145 |
| | **%** | 48.04 | 40.45 | 66.80 | 88.89 | 68.03 | 48.76 |
| | **NF** | 13.27 | 0.25 | 0.59 | 0.03 | 0.29 | 14.42 |
| **Total (#)** | | **7,938** | **178** | **253** | **9** | **122** | **8,500** |

Example (6.218), in turn, is more ambiguous. Thus, the effects of being affected by witchcraft are less clear and it is not so evident that the person will suffer any physical damage and pass away as a result of sorcery. Much like this example, (6.219) was also tagged as intermediate between descriptive and subjective, since putting someone in a dangerous situation does not necessarily imply that (s)he is going to die eventually. Instead, this person may just be (slightly) injured or not injured at all, as is actually the case in many of the examples of the collocation *hazard to death* in the corpus.

(6.218) *Ursley Kempe alias Grey bewitched* ***to death*** *Kempes Wife.* (D00000998376240000. 1582. W. W. *A true and iust recorde, of the information, examination and confession of all the witches*)

(6.219) *So that it was a maruelous pleasure, & likewise a dredfull fight, to see the whole battell marche together in order, at the sound of the pipes, and neuer to breake their pace, [...] but to goe on quietly & ioyfully at the sounde of these pipes, to hazard themselues euen* ***to death***. (D00000202431840000. 1579. Plutarch. *The lives of the noble Grecians and Romanes*)

Examples (6.220) and (6.221), by contrast, illustrate subjective meanings of *to death*, its use with the participial form *afflicted* and the noun *sorrow*. In both cases, the general condition of someone who is suffering from mental distress, anguish and extreme sadness may be very poor and often accompanied by other physical symptoms, so that his/her general state of dispiritedness may as well make him/her think that (s)he is going to pass away. On this account, these examples are regarded as subjective.

(6.220) *Consider how the professors of the word of God els wher in Europe [...] be manaced, vexed, and persecuted, & [...] from time to time afflicted, euen* ***to death***: (D00000998486030000. 1589. Christopher Ocland. *The fountaine and vvelspring of all variance, sedition, and deadlie hate*)

(6.221) *For first these words, My soule is full of sorrowes euen* ***to death***, [...]. (D00000998427750000. 1604. Thomas Bilson. *The suruey of Christs sufferings*)

Example (6.222) represents a turning point before purely intensifying meanings (examples (6.223)–(6.225)). In this case, *to death* modifies the noun *jealousy*, and this collocation is ambiguous between a subjective and an intensifying meaning. It could be argued, on the one hand, that being jealous to death is a synonym of being extremely jealous of someone; on the other, when someone envies another person, it is possible, though not necessarily the case, that (s)he wishes (in)directly him/her some kind of damage. For this reason, this collocation is probably closer to a subjective meaning. Given this ambiguity, I have decided to mark it as ambiguous between subjective and intensifying.

(6.222) [...] *he no sooner was told the approaching of his fate, but he caused Hortensius to be call'd, who being come, jealousie remaining in his heart, even* ***to death***, *he constrained him to promise him, never to deliver the Prince of Cyparissa*, [...] (D00000120436130000. 1678. Madeleine de Scudéry. *Clelia*)

Finally, examples (6.223)–(6.225) show intensifying meanings of *to death*. The prepositional phrase in combination with the verbs *laugh* and *blush* and with the adjective *impatient* can no longer be interpreted literally, and the degree meaning is the only one possible in such cases. The degree reading of *to death* in (6.223) is reinforced by the adverb *exceedingly*. In other words, *laugh to death* in this example can only be read as 'laugh very much'. The degree reading is also applicable to (6.224) and (6.225), for *impatient to death* can only be read as 'extremely impatient' and *blush to death* in this context simply means 'to blush exceedingly'.

(6.223) [...] *it hath some time so mad a countenaunce, that it wyll make fooles to ioye and laugh so excéedinglie, as they laugh the~selues* ***to death***. (D00000998377480000. 1587. John Ryckes. *The true image of Christian love*)

(6.224) *MAdam, my evill Fortune gives one common beginning to all my Letters: I am impatient even* ***to death****, to have the honour to come and see you*: (D00000998680080000. 1654. Jean-Louis Guez, seigneur de Balzac. *Letters of Mounsieur de Balzac*)

(6.225) *I shall blush* ***to death****, if you speak thus again*. (D00000182081950000. 1665. William Killigrew. *Three playes written by Sir William Killigrew*)

Concerning semantic prosody, the corpus data (cf. Table 6.161) clearly reveal a preference for *to death* to be combined with elements which have inherently negative semantic prosodies. This accounts for 99.09% of the attestations of *to death* in EEBOCorp 1.0, while neutral semantic prosody is found in 0.11% of the examples, and positive semantic prosody represents only 0.8% of the total. Moreover, although there is an obvious increase in the absolute figures for all the different semantic prosodies, most conspicuously for negative semantic prosodies, the results were only statistically significant for negative and positive semantic prosody. Thus, for negative prosody we can only consider as statistically significant the rise in token frequency from P. II to P. III ($\chi^2$ (1) = 42.869; $p$ = 0) and the rise from P. IV to P. V ($\chi^2$ (1) = 130.328; $p$ = 0). For positive semantic prosody, it is only the rise in the number of attestations from P. III to P. IV which was found to be significant at $p < 0.05$ (Fisher's exact test value = 0.000631). Examples (6.217)–(6.225) all illustrate negative semantic prosodies, except for the collocation *laugh to death* in (6.223), which is positive. Further instances of *to death* combined with inherently positive elements are *tickled to death*, *in love to death*, *enamoured to death*, *defend to death*, *resolved to death* and *adore to death*. Examples of *to death* as a modifier of neutral elements, way less numerous in the corpus, are *amazed to death* and *drink to death*.

Table 6.161. Semantic prosody for *to death* in EEBOCorp 1.0

| | | Neg | Neu | Pos | Total |
|---|---|---|---|---|---|
| **1470–99** | # | 0 | 0 | 0 | 0 |
| | % | 0.00 | 0.00 | 0.00 | 0.00 |
| | **NF** | 0 | 0 | 0 | 0 |
| **1500–49** | # | 97 | 0 | 0 | 97 |
| | % | 1.15 | 0.00 | 0.00 | 1.14 |
| | **NF** | 9.47 | 0 | 0 | 9.47 |
| **1550–99** | # | 1,370 | 1 | 1 | 1,372 |
| | % | 16.26 | 11.11 | 1.47 | 16.14 |
| | **NF** | 18.68 | 0.01 | 0.01 | 18.71 |
| **1600–49** | # | 2,855 | 5 | 26 | 2,886 |
| | % | 33.90 | 55.26 | 38.24 | 33.95 |
| | **NF** | 18.84 | 0.03 | 0.17 | 19.04 |
| **1650–99** | # | 4,101 | 3 | 41 | 4,145 |
| | % | 48.69 | 33.33 | 60.29 | 48.76 |
| | **NF** | 14.27 | 0.01 | 0.14 | 14.42 |
| **Total (#)** | | **8,423** | **9** | **68** | **8,500** |

Finally, the last variable considered in the data is word class. As shown in Table 6.162, *to death* functions predominantly as a modifier of participial forms (50.69%) and of verbs (44.8%), although it is also found to a lesser extent as a modifier of nouns (2.61%), adjectives (1.88%) and prepositional phrases (0.02%). These figures, therefore, indicate the versatile nature of this prepositional modifier, in contrast to the limitations of other word categories, such as the adjectives *deadly* or *mortal*, which only modify nouns. If we consider the raw frequencies and their variation along the different periods, the results are statistically significant for the participial and the verbal forms, the two major categories modified by *to death*, but also for nouns if we consider P. IV and P. V ($\chi^2$ (1) = 15.584; $p$ = 0.00007892). As for participial elements, the increase in the number of instances was found to be significant from P. II to P. III ($\chi^2$ (1) = 13.169; $p$ = 0.00028462) and

Table 6.162. Categories modified by *to death* in EEBOCorp 1.0

| | | Adj | N | Part | PP | Vb | Total |
|---|---|---|---|---|---|---|---|
| **1470–99** | # | 0 | 0 | 0 | 0 | 0 | 0 |
| | % | 0.00 | 0.00 | 0.00 | 0.00 | 0.00 | 0.00 |
| | **NF** | 0 | 0 | 0 | 0 | 0 | 0 |
| **1500–49** | # | 0 | 4 | 59 | 0 | 34 | 97 |
| | % | 0.00 | 1.80 | 1.37 | 0.00 | 0.89 | 1.14 |
| | **NF** | 0 | 0.39 | 5.76 | 0 | 3.32 | 9.47 |
| **1550–99** | # | 11 | 52 | 693 | 0 | 616 | 1,372 |
| | % | 6.87 | 23.42 | 16.09 | 0.00 | 16.18 | 16.14 |
| | **NF** | 0.15 | 0.71 | 9.45 | 0 | 8.40 | 18.71 |
| **1600–49** | # | 51 | 82 | 1,456 | 0 | 1,297 | 2,886 |
| | % | 31.88 | 36.94 | 33.78 | 0.00 | 34.06 | 33.95 |
| | **NF** | 0.34 | 0.54 | 9.61 | 0 | 8.56 | 19.04 |
| **1650–99** | # | 98 | 84 | 2,101 | 1 | 1,861 | 4,145 |
| | % | 61.25 | 37.84 | 48.76 | 100.00 | 48.87 | 48.76 |
| | **NF** | 0.34 | 0.29 | 7.31 | 0 | 6.48 | 14.42 |
| **Total (#)** | | **160** | **222** | **4,309** | **1** | **3,808** | **8,500** |

also from P. IV to P. V ($\chi^2$ (1) = 64.266; $p$ = 0). The same periods were considered statistically significant for verbs: the transition from P. II to P. III ($\chi^2$ (1) = 29.15; $p$ = 0.00000007) and from P. IV to P. V ($\chi^2$ (1) = 39.496; $p$ = 0).

In the eighteenth-century data from ECF *to death* is attested in 249 examples, distributed across 86 different collocations. Considering the high number of collocations, Table 6.163 displays only the most frequent ones, in this case those which appear at least ten times in the database. As indicated by the various values in Table 6.164, *bleed to death*, *condemn to death*, *frighted to death* and *starve to death*, the most frequent collocations, are all highly statistically significant. Therefore, the association between *to death* and these collocates is very strong and in no way attributed to chance.

As for the types of meanings of *to death* in the data (cf. Table 6.165), this prepositional phrase occurs chiefly with descriptive and subjective

Table 6.163. Absolute and normalised frequencies for the most frequent collocations of *to death* in ECF

| Collocation | Abs. Freq. | NF |
|---|---|---|
| *bleed to death* | 11 | 1.13 |
| *condemn to death* | 10 | 1.03 |
| *frighted to death* | 21 | 2.16 |
| *starve to death* | 16 | 1.65 |

Table 6.164. Standardised scores for *to death* in ECF

| Collocation | *z*-score | *MI* | *MI3* | *LL*-value |
|---|---|---|---|---|
| *bleed to death* | 71.060 | 8.849 | 15.768 | 113.387 ($p < 0.0001$) |
| *condemn to death* | 46.743 | 7.785 | 14.428 | 88.180 ($p < 0.0001$) |
| *frighted to death* | 108.312 | 9.064 | 17.983 | 233.459 ($p < 0.0001$) |
| *starve to death* | 104.473 | 9.418 | 17.418 | 177.825 ($p < 0.0001$) |

Table 6.165. Meaning types for *to death* in ECF

| | Abs. Freq. | % | NF |
|---|---|---|---|
| **D** | 139 | 55.82 | 14.33 |
| **D/S** | 2 | 0.80 | 0.21 |
| **S** | 86 | 34.54 | 8.86 |
| **S/I** | 6 | 2.41 | 0.62 |
| **I** | 16 | 6.43 | 1.65 |
| **Total** | 249 | 100.00 | 25.66 |

meanings, which together account for about 90% of the total (55.82% and 34.54%, respectively). Nevertheless, *to death* is also attested with intensifying readings (6.43%) and with readings which are indeterminate between subjective and intensifying (2.41%) and between descriptive and subjective (0.80%).

Examples (6.226)–(6.232) show the different meanings of *to death* in ECF. The collocation *burn to death* in (6.226) clearly evinces a literal or descriptive reading: the excerpt thus recounts an episode of a character who had the plague and apparently committed suicide by burning himself.

(6.226) *There was also One Man in or about Whitecross-street, burnt himself* ***to Death*** *in his Bed*; (1722. Daniel Defoe. *A Journal of the Plague Year*)

In (6.227), the meaning of *to death* cannot be taken literally, and is hence considered as transitory to a subjective meaning, for the context does not specify if the nuns mentioned eventually died. They are said to suffer physical torture recurrently and to live in very poor conditions. As their suffering is not metaphorical but real, in this particular example *to death* is taken to be intermediate between descriptive and subjective, although the former reading is the most likely one.

(6.227) *The penitentiaries of the third order of saint Francis* [...] *were still in a worse condition* [...] *---by tumbling and tossing, and tossing and tumbling from one side of their beds to the other the whole night long---the several sisterhoods had scratch'd and mawl'd themselves all* ***to death***--- (1760. Laurence Sterne. *Tristram Shandy*)

By contrast, the collocations *tormented to death* and *frighted to death* in (6.228) and (6.229) are considered subjective. Feeling distressed or anguished and feeling scared are not fatal circumstances, although a mental situation of affliction and anguish may concur with physical discomfort. For this reason, these collocations are considered to represent a stage further ahead along the grammaticalisation cline of the prepositional phrase *to death*.

(6.228) '*You have tormented me* ***to death***; *you have forced me from my friends, and intruded yourself upon me, against my will, for a partner*.' (1778–1788. Fanny Burney. *Evelina*)

(6.229) *The poor fellow is frighted* ***to death*** *about him*, (1763. Frances Brooke. *Lady Julia Mandeville*)

The meaning of *to death* in (6.230) is taken to be between subjective and purely intensifying. Roxana, the protagonist, sorrows over the death of her lover, and her sadness makes her cry constantly. Sorrow, grief and mental distress are states which may recall death-related properties, since the person who suffers them may feel both physically and mentally in a state that approximates death itself. In this particular example, however, a degree reading would also be possible. In fact, the adverb *almost* and the prepositional phrase *to a degree inexpressible* seem to point to a degree interpretation of *to death* here. Hence, *cry to death* could also be contextually read as 'I cried a lot for him'. Owing to this ambiguity, I have classified this collocation as intermediate between a subjective and an intensifying reading.

(6.230) *I think I almost cry'd myself* ***to Death*** *for him; for I abandon'd myself to all the Excesses of Grief; and indeed, I lov'd him to a Degree inexpressible*; (1724. Daniel Defoe. *Roxana*)

In contrast, (6.231) and (6.232) can only be read as intensifiers. Blushing to death and puzzling to death mean here 'blush tremendously' and 'puzzle someone hugely'. In both cases, a literal interpretation of *to death* is utterly excluded.

(6.231) *'Thank Heaven I have no daughters, resumed he; formerly a young maid was ready to blush* ***to death*** *at being told a man was in love with her*; (1753. Eliza Fowler Haywood. *Jemmy and Jenny Jessamy*)

(6.232) *You puzzle me* ***to death****, cried my uncle Toby.* (1760. Laurence Sterne. *Tristram Shandy*)

As far as semantic prosody is concerned (cf. Table 6.166), *to death* is found in the overwhelming majority of the instances in ECF with negative semantic prosody (e.g. *wounded*, *torture* and *crush*), although there are also a few occurrences in which it appears with neutral elements (e.g. *blush* or *long*). There are no instances of *to death* with positive collocates, as was the case with the EModE data (cf. supra).

Finally, as for the types of words modified by *to death* in ECF, it shows a clear preference for verbal collocates (77.11%), although it also occurs as a modifier of participial forms (21.29%) and, to a much lesser extent, of adjectives such as *pale* or *sick* (1.20%) and of the noun *sickness* (0.40%), as shown in Table 6.167.

Table 6.166. Semantic prosody for *to death* in ECF

| | **Abs. Freq.** | **%** | **NF** |
|---|---|---|---|
| **neg** | 246 | 98.80 | 25.35 |
| **neu** | 3 | 1.20 | 0.31 |
| **Total** | **249** | **100.00** | **25.66** |

Table 6.167. Categories modified by *to death* in ECF

| | Abs. Freq. | % | NF |
|---|---|---|---|
| **Adj.** | 3 | 1.20 | 0.31 |
| **N.** | 1 | 0.40 | 0.10 |
| **Part.** | 53 | 21.29 | 5.46 |
| **Vb.** | 192 | 77.11 | 19.79 |
| **Total** | **249** | 100.00 | **25.66** |

In the last period examined, the nineteenth century, *to death* is recorded in a total of 536 examples and 137 collocations. The most frequent collocations of *to death* in NCF are provided in Table 6.168, and the normalised scores for the combinations of these collocates with *to death* are given in Table 6.169. These in fact reveal that all the combinations are to be considered as highly statistically significant.

As regards the types of meanings, descriptive readings account for half of the examples of *to death* (54.48%), followed by subjective and intensifying meanings (31.90% and 11.94%, respectively). Those readings which are ambiguous between descriptive and subjective and those between subjective and intensifying are far less numerous in the data, accounting for only 0.75% and 0.93% of the total, as shown in Table 6.170.

A selection of the different meanings of *to death* in NCF is given in (6.233)–(6.241). To start with, *burnt to death* in (6.233) is descriptive and refers to a torturous and painful type of death. By contrast, *sick to death* in (6.234) has been marked as indeterminate between descriptive and subjective, thus differing from other examples of the same collocation in the data, in which someone has a fatal disease. Here the meaning is not properly descriptive, but tends more towards a subjective reading: the character feels unwell and indisposed, as if she was going to die, but she does not pass away; it is simply a death-like feeling.

(6.233) [...] *in a given time a hundred thousand persons went to sea on long voyages, and only five hundred of them were drowned or burnt* ***to death***. (1854. Charles Dickens. *Hard times*)

(6.234) *Poor Miss Thorne. She heard all this and yet did not quite swoon. She made her way through the crowd as best she could, sick herself almost* ***to death***. (1857. Anthony Trollope. *Barchester Towers*)

Table 6.168. Absolute and normalised frequencies for the most frequent collocations of *to death* in NCF

| **Collocation** | **Abs. Freq.** | **NF** |
| --- | --- | --- |
| *beat to death* | 6 | 0.16 |
| *beaten to death* | 5 | 0.13 |
| *bleed to death* | 19 | 0.51 |
| *bored to death* | 10 | 0.27 |
| *burnt to death* | 10 | 0.27 |
| *condemn to death* | 12 | 0.32 |
| *condemned to death* | 22 | 0.59 |
| *crushed to death* | 9 | 0.24 |
| *doomed to death* | 8 | 0.21 |
| *drink to death* | 13 | 0.35 |
| *fret to death* | 5 | 0.13 |
| *frighten to death* | 17 | 0.45 |
| *frightened to death* | 13 | 0.35 |
| *frozen to death* | 5 | 0.13 |
| *hunt to death* | 5 | 0.13 |
| *moped to death* | 7 | 0.19 |
| *plague to death* | 5 | 0.13 |
| *press to death* | 6 | 0.16 |
| *sentenced to death* | 9 | 0.24 |
| *sick to death* | 18 | 0.48 |
| *starve to death* | 18 | 0.48 |
| *starved to death* | 28 | 0.74 |
| *terrified to death* | 9 | 0.24 |
| *terrify to death* | 6 | 0.16 |
| *tired to death* | 34 | 0.90 |
| *torture to death* | 5 | 0.13 |
| *trample to death* | 7 | 0.19 |

(*continued*)

Table 6.168. Continued

| Collocation | Abs. Freq. | NF |
|---|---|---|
| *wearied to death* | 6 | 0.16 |
| *weary to death* | 9 | 0.24 |
| *work to death* | 17 | 0.45 |
| *worked to death* | 6 | 0.16 |
| *worry to death* | 10 | 0.27 |
| *wounded to death* | 5 | 0.13 |

Table 6.169. Standardised scores for the most frequent collocations of *to death* in NCF

| Collocation | *z*-score | *MI* | *MI3* | *LL*-value |
|---|---|---|---|---|
| *beat to death* | 14.878 | 5.280 | 10.450 | 32.240 (p < 0.0001) |
| *beaten to death* | 23.050 | 6.758 | 11.402 | 36.962 (p < 0.0001) |
| *bleed to death* | 90.418 | 8.756 | 17.252 | 193.105 (p < 0.0001) |
| *bored to death* | 96.505 | 9.866 | 16.510 | 117.247 (p < 0.0001) |
| *burnt to death* | 46.803 | 7.788 | 14.432 | 88.163 (p < 0.0001) |
| *condemn to death* | 76.175 | 8.923 | 16.093 | 124.775 (p < 0.0001) |
| *condemned to death* | 114.328 | 9.219 | 18.138 | 237.882 (p < 0.0001) |
| *crushed to death* | 48.902 | 8.064 | 14.404 | 82.799 (p < 0.0001) |
| *doomed to death* | 46.769 | 8.105 | 14.105 | 74.055 (p < 0.0001) |
| *drink to death* | 25.490 | 5.699 | 13.100 | 77.244 (p < 0.0001) |
| *fret to death* | 35.299 | 7.973 | 12.617 | 45.362 (p < 0.0001) |
| *frighten to death* | 92.797 | 8.990 | 17.165 | 178.353 (p < 0.0001) |
| *frightened to death* | 38.805 | 6.880 | 14.281 | 98.292 (p < 0.0001) |
| *frozen to death* | 38.380 | 8.212 | 12.856 | 47.028 (p < 0.0001) |
| *hunt to death* | 14.701 | 5.498 | 10.142 | 28.343 (p < 0.0001) |
| *moped to death* | 169.024 | 11.996 | 17.610 | 103.867 (p < 0.0001) |
| *plague to death* | 29.436 | 7.454 | 12.097 | 41.763 (p < 0.0001) |
| *press to death* | 15.217 | 5.342 | 10.512 | 32.742 (p < 0.0001) |

Table 6.169. Continued

| Collocation | *z*-score | *MI* | *MI3* | *LL*-value |
|---|---|---|---|---|
| *sentenced to death* | 131.010 | 10.899 | 17.239 | 118.832 (p < 0.0001) |
| *sick to death* | 50.814 | 7.184 | 15.524 | 143.642 (p < 0.0001) |
| *starve to death* | 97.709 | 9.056 | 17.396 | 190.512 (p < 0.0001) |
| *starved to death* | 213.426 | 10.670 | 20.284 | 360.415 (p < 0.0001) |
| *terrified to death* | 42.192 | 7.642 | 13.982 | 77.526 (p < 0.0001) |
| *terrify to death* | 71.146 | 9.724 | 14.894 | 69.140 (p < 0.0001) |
| *tired to death* | 93.201 | 8.008 | 18.183 | 310.144 (p < 0.0001) |
| *torture to death* | 15.906 | 5.716 | 10.360 | 29.825 (p < 0.0001) |
| *trample to death* | 54.485 | 8.735 | 14.350 | 70.940 (p < 0.0001) |
| *wearied to death* | 35.447 | 7.724 | 12.894 | 52.362 (p < 0.0001) |
| *weary to death* | 27.579 | 6.435 | 12.774 | 62.527 (p < 0.0001) |
| *work to death* | 17.688 | 4.347 | 12.522 | 70.139 (p < 0.0001) |
| *worked to death* | 20.318 | 6.145 | 6.145 | 39.305 (p < 0.0001) |
| *worry to death* | 66.837 | 8.810 | 15.454 | 102.387 (p < 0.0001) |
| *wounded to death* | 16.403 | 5.802 | 10.446 | 30.408 (p < 0.0001) |

Table 6.170. Meaning types for *to death* in NCF

| | **Abs. Freq.** | **%** | **NF** |
|---|---|---|---|
| **D** | 292 | 54.48 | 7.77 |
| **D/S** | 4 | 0.75 | 0.11 |
| **S** | 171 | 31.90 | 4.55 |
| **S/I** | 5 | 0.93 | 0.13 |
| **I** | 64 | 11.94 | 1.70 |
| **Total** | **536** | **100.00** | **14.26** |

Examples (6.235) and (6.236), on the other hand, are regarded as subjective, for being scared and tired does not imply anybody's death. However, death-related properties can actually be recalled: when somebody is very scared of something, (s)he may feel symptoms similar to those of a heart attack, and extreme exhaustion and a poor physical condition may evoke illness symptoms.

(6.235) *'Miss Jane is just frightened* ***to death*** *by a monster above stairs,* [...]' (1813. Eaton Stannard Barrett. *The Heroine, Or Adventures Of Cherubina*)

(6.236) *We are sadly off in the country; not but what we have very good shops in Salisbury, but it is so far to go;* [...] *and it is such a fag---I come back tired* ***to death***. (1818. Jane Austen. *Northanger Abbey*)

In turn, the collocation *shocked to death* in (6.237) is ambiguous between subjective and intensifying. On the one hand, being shocked may be regarded as subjective, and although we ignore the consequences of that feeling of shock, it may be the case that the person mentioned in the example has suffered a nervous breakdown or some kind of crisis as a result. On the other hand, note that the *–ed* form *shocked* is repeated twice in the example, so *to death* in this context is more likely to play the role of an intensifier, used for emphatic purposes ('very, extremely shocked').

(6.237) *'And I trust lady Dashfort will reward me by the assurance, that* [...] *she seriously disapproves and is shocked." "Oh, shocked! shocked* ***to death***!' (1812. Maria Edgeworth. *The absentee*)

Finally, examples (6.238)–(6.241) all present clear intensifying meanings. Note in particular (6.238) and (6.239), featuring the collocations *tired to death* and *sick to death*. In previous occurrences of the same collocations in the earlier data, they were marked as subjective and descriptive, respectively. Nonetheless, in these specific examples I argue that they illustrate intensifying meanings. The reason for this is that here they refer to things rather than to people. *Tired to death* in this context means 'bored in extreme', in this case of the rooms, and *sick to death* means 'bored with or fed up with friends'. The collocation *bored to death* is also present in the data, as shown in (6.240). Finally, *ashamed to death* in (6.241) can also be paraphrased as *being extremely ashamed*. In all these cases, therefore, the degree or intensifying reading is the only possible interpretation for the prepositional phrase *to death*.

(6.238) *She immediately declared herself tired* ***to death*** *of the rooms*, [...] (1796. Fanny Burney. *Camilla*)

(6.239) *'O no! to be worn out by seeing always the same faces!---one is sick* ***to death*** *of friends; nothing makes one so melancholy.'* (1866. Wilkie Collins. *Armadale*)

(6.240) [...] *my Lady Dedlock has been bored* ***to death****. Concert, assembly, opera, theatre, drive, nothing is new to my Lady* [...] (1853. Charles Dickens. *Bleak House*)

(6.241) *Then she felt ashamed* ***to death*** *that she was crying, and for one long instant her happiness was all gone.* (1859. George Eliot. *Adam Bede*)

In regard to semantic prosody, the results from NCF reveal that in the overwhelming majority of the occurrences *to death* is recorded as a modifier of elements which are inherently negative, although it is also found as a modifier of items with either neutral or positive semantic prosody (cf. Table 6.171). *Tired*, *plague*, *terrify*, *frightened*, *fatigue* or *torture*, among many others, were considered to represent negative semantic prosody; *study*, *tinkle* and *yawn* were tagged as showing neutral semantic prosody and only *kiss* was marked as a positive collocate of *to death*.

Finally, in the light of the NCF data *to death* is attested with a variety of word types (cf. Table 6.172). It modifies verbs in half of the tokens in the data (50%), but it is also found as a modifier of participial forms (44.96%) and, to a much lesser extent, of adjectives (3.73%) and nouns (1.31%).

Table 6.171. Semantic prosody for *to death* in NCF

| | **Abs. Freq.** | **%** | **NF** |
|---|---|---|---|
| **neg** | 528 | 98.51 | 14.05 |
| **neu** | 7 | 1.31 | 0.19 |
| **pos** | 1 | 0.19 | 0.03 |
| **Total** | **536** | **100.00** | **14.26** |

Table 6.172. Categories modified by *to death* in NCF

| | Abs. Freq. | % | NF |
|---|---|---|---|
| **Adj.** | 20 | 3.73 | 0.53 |
| **N.** | 7 | 1.31 | 0.19 |
| **Part.** | 241 | 44.96 | 6.41 |
| **Vb.** | 268 | 50.00 | 7.13 |
| **Total** | **536** | **100.00** | **14.26** |

### 6.2.6.1. *To death* across time

As shown by the individual frequencies in Table 6.173, in my data *to death* is attested primarily with descriptive meanings, which appear for the first time in EEBOCorp 1.0. Figure 6.14, in turn, provides an overview of the evolution of the different types of meanings of *to death*.

Descriptive uses of *to death* experience a gradual decrease from EModE to the twentieth-century data, which is most pronounced from ECF to NCF (ECF: 139 exx.; NF pmw 14.33 > NCF: 292 exx.; NF pmw 7.77). This steep fall from the eighteenth to the nineteenth century is regarded as statistically significant ($\chi^2 = 35.676$; $p = 0$), while this is not the case

Table 6.173. Types of meanings for *to death* in the data (absolute/normalised frequencies)

| | HC (ME) | EEBOCorp 1.0 | ECF | NCF | ARCHER (20th c.) |
|---|---|---|---|---|---|
| **D** | 0 | 7,938/15.11 | 139/14.33 | 292/7.77 | 2/3.77 |
| **D/S** | 0 | 178/0.34 | 2/0.21 | 4/0.11 | 0 |
| **S** | 0 | 253/0.48 | 86/8.86 | 171/4.55 | 1/1.88 |
| **S/I** | 0 | 9/0.02 | 6/0.62 | 5/0.13 | 0 |
| **I** | 0 | 122/0.23 | 16/1.65 | 64/1.70 | 0 |
| **N. of words** | 608,570 | 525,432,293 | 9,702,699 | 37,589,837 | 530,832 |

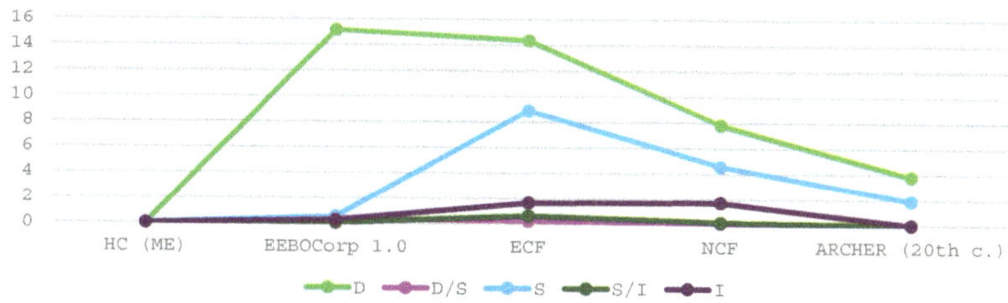


Figure 6.14. Types of meanings for *to death*

for the remaining periods.[64] The frequencies for those readings which were marked as ambiguous between descriptive and subjective remain low over time and the difference between the periods is not statistically significant.[65] In turn, subjective instances of *to death* experience a remarkable growth from EModE to the eighteenth century in the light of the normalised figures (EEBOCorp 1.0: 253 exx.; NF pmw 0.48 > ECF: 86 exx.; NF pmw 8.86) and then are progressively reduced until the twentieth century (NCF: 171 exx.; NF pmw 4.55 > ARCHER: 1 ex.; NF pmw 1.88). The difference between the periods is only significant in what concerns the EEBOCorp 1.0 and ECF data, on the one hand, and ECF and NCF, on the other ($\chi^2 = 1043.388$; $p = 0$, and $\chi^2=25.628$; $p = 0.00000041$, respectively).[66] Examples of *to death* which are indeterminate between subjective and intensifying have also remained rather stable over time. Nevertheless, the difference in regard to these uses from EModE to the eighteenth century is statistically significant ($\chi^2 = 102.353$; $p = 0$), whereas that between the eighteenth and the nineteenth century is not (Fisher's exact test = 0.013229). Finally, as regards the intensifying uses of *to death*, there is a gradual rise in frequency from EEBOCorp 1.0 to NCF (EEBOCorp 1.0: 122 exx.; NF pmw 0.23 > ECF: 16 exx.; NF pmw 1.65 > NCF: 64 exx.; NF pmw 1.70). The difference in frequency between EEBOCorp 1.0 and ECF was found

64 **EEBOCorp 1.0 > ECF** = $\chi^2 = 0.336$; $p = 0.56214725$; **NCF > ARCHER**: Fisher's exact test = 0.451307.

65 **EEBOCorp 1.0 > ECF:** Fisher's exact test = 0.776576; **ECF > NCF:** Fisher's exact test = 0.357328.

66 **NCF > ARCHER**: Fisher's exact test = 0.737108.

to be statistically significant ($\chi^2 = 68.767$; $p = 0$), while that between ECF and NCF is not ($\chi^2 = 0.001$; $p = 0.97477288$).

As shown in Table 6.174 and Figure 6.15, *to death* shows a strong preference for elements with inherently negative prosody, although it is also recorded with collocates which are neutral (e.g. *study*, *yawn*, *amazed*) and positive (e.g. *laugh*, *passionate*, *in love*).

The normalised figures reveal an exponential growth in the occurrences of *to death* with negative elements from EModE to the eighteenth century (EEBOCorp 1.0: 8,423 exx.; NF pmw 16.03 > ECF: 246 exx; NF pmw 25.35), which is statistically significant ($\chi^2 = 50.542$; $p = 0$). Combinations of *to death* with negative elements decline continually until the twentieth century (NCF: 528 exx.; NF pmw 14.05 > ARCHER: 3 exx.; NF pmw 5.65), although the variation is only significant when we compare the ECF

Table 6.174. Semantic prosody for *to death* (absolute/normalised frequencies)

| | HC (ME) | EEBOCorp 1.0 | ECF | NCF | ARCHER (20th c.) |
|---|---|---|---|---|---|
| **neg** | 0 | 8,423/16.03 | 246/25.35 | 528/14.05 | 3/5.65 |
| **neu** | 0 | 9/0.02 | 3/0.31 | 7/0.19 | 0 |
| **pos** | 0 | 68/0.13 | 0 | 1/0.03 | 0 |
| **N. of words** | 608,570 | 525,432,293 | 9,702,699 | 37,589,837 | 530,832 |

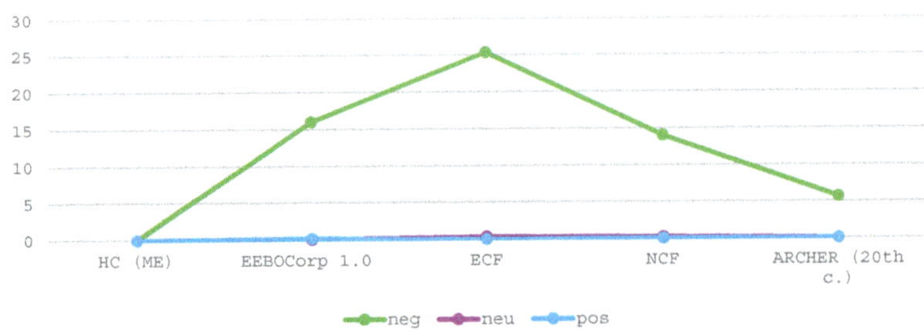


Figure 6.15. Semantic prosody for *to death*

with the NCF data ($\chi^2 = 59.559; p = 0$).[67] By contrast, the values for neutral semantic prosody remain rather low in the different sources and do not vary greatly from one to the other period, as suggested by the normalised figures. The difference between EEBOCorp 1.0 and ECF is, however, statistically significant (Fisher's exact test = 0.00116).[68]

With regard to the last variable considered, the type of element modified by *to death*, the data indicate that this prepositional phrase functions mainly as a modifier of participial and of verbal forms (49.58% and 45.96%, respectively), as shown in Table 6.175 and in Figure 6.16.

As indicated by the normalised frequencies, the uses of *to death* with participial items are reduced from EModE to the eighteenth century (EEBOCorp 1.0: 4,309 exx.; NF pmw 8.20 > ECF: 53 exx; NF pmw 5.46), as indicated by the normalised frequencies, although this difference is not statistically significant ($\chi^2 = 8.432; p = 0.00368675$). They then increase in the transition from the eighteenth to the nineteenth century (NCF: 241 exx.; NF pmw 6.41), to decrease again in the twentieth-century data from ARCHER (2 exx.; NF pmw 3.77). None of these results, however, turned

Table 6.175. Categories modified by *to death* (absolute/normalised frequencies)

| | HC (ME) | EEBOCorp 1.0 | ECF | NCF | ARCHER 20th c. |
|---|---|---|---|---|---|
| **Adj.** | 0 | 160/0.30 | 3/0.31 | 20/0.53 | 0 |
| **N.** | 0 | 222/0.42 | 1/0.10 | 7/0.19 | 0 |
| **Part.** | 0 | 4,309/8.20 | 53/5.46 | 241/6.41 | 2/3.77 |
| **PP** | 0 | 1/0.002 | 0 | 0 | 0 |
| **Vb.** | 0 | 3,808/7.25 | 192/19.79 | 268/7.13 | 1/1.88 |
| **N. of words** | 608,570 | 525,432,293 | 9,702,699 | 37,589,837 | 530,832 |

67 **NCF > ARCHER:** Fisher's exact test = 0.133919.

68 The difference between ECF and NCF, in turn, is not statistically significant (Fisher's exact test = 0.438482).

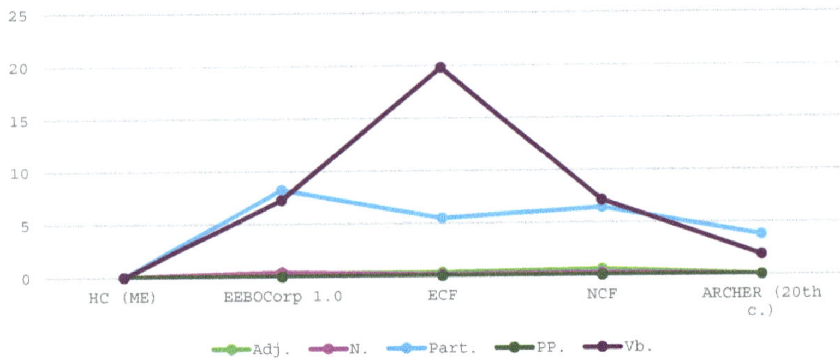


Figure 6.16. Categories modified by *to death*

out to be statistically significant.[69] The uses of *to death* with verbal elements, the second most common type after participial collocates, increase considerably from EEBOCorp 1.0 to ECF (from NF pmw 7.25 to NF pmw 19.79). From the eighteenth century onwards, the occurrences of *to death* as a modifier of verbal elements are progressively reduced (NCF: 268 exx.; NF pmw 7.13 > ARCHER: 1 ex.; NF pmw 1.88). These figures were found to be significant for the difference between EEBOCorp 1.0 and ECF, on the one hand, and for that between ECF and NCF, on the other.[70] Conversely, the drop in the number of occurrences from the nineteenth to the twentieth century is not statistically significant (Fisher's value = 0.194852). As regards those cases in which *to death* modifies adjectives in the data, the normalised values seem to remain rather constant over time until the nineteenth century, when there is a slight increase in frequency. The difference between the periods in regard to the adjectival collocates of *to death* is, however, not statistically significant in any of the cases.[71] Finally, with regard

69 **ECF > NCF:** $\chi^2 = 0.97$; $p = 0.32468018$; **NCF > ARCHER:** Fisher's exact test = 0.779676.

70 **EEBOCorp 1.0 > ECF:** $\chi^2 = 198.774$; $p = 0$; **ECF > NCF:** $\chi^2 = 125.753$; $p = 0$.

71 **EEBOCorp 1.0 > ECF:** Fisher's exact test = 0.771897; **ECF > NCF:** Fisher's exact test = 0.603977.

to the nominal collocates of *to death*, for which there is no conspicuous variation in frequency across the different periods, the figures show statistically negative results.[72]

Given the results from the type of meaning and semantic prosody discussed above, *to death* functions much alike the other forms examined in the previous sections, with a predominance of descriptive (90.13% of the total) over intensifying readings (2.17%) and of negative (99.05%) over positive collocates (0.74%). In addition, there is a correspondence in the data between these positive collocates and the intensifying uses of *to death*. According to the OED (cf. Section 6.1.5), the first intensifying examples of the prepositional phrase go back to the late sixteenth century and in fact EEBOCorp 1.0 provides evidence for these early uses, in collocations such as *laugh to death*, *amazed to death* or *resolute to death*. Moreover, in the light of the OED evidence, *to death* showed signs of incipient subjectivity since very early; some of the collocations in OE could already be counted as subjective (e.g. *afraid to death*). Unfortunately, the HC yields no examples of *to death*; there are, therefore, no records of subjective uses in my data until EModE. All the possible readings of *to death* are actually found in EEBOCorp 1.0, which makes it difficult to establish an actual cline of evolution in the light of these data. While descriptive and subjective meanings are attested in the first half of the sixteenth century, with the first records of *to death* in the corpus, those instances which were marked as either ambiguous between subjective and intensifying or as clearly intensifying partially coincide in time. In fact, there is only one occurrence in the 1590s which was counted as indeterminate and which predates most intensifying readings, mainly attested in the seventeenth century. On the basis of the EModE data, therefore, it cannot be argued that some kind of bridging context may have favoured a degree meaning of *to death*, although it could well have been the case. Despite this somehow limited information, *to death* has become increasingly grammaticalised over time, being reanalysed as an intensifier expressing high degree (cf. Section 3.3.2). The

72 **EEBOCorp 1.0 > ECF**: Fisher's exact test = 0.19981; **ECF > NCF**: Fisher's exact test = 1.

process of subjectification is assumed to have taken place earlier, but it cannot be confirmed with the corpus data. Like *dead(ly)* and *mortal(ly)*, *to death* is another paradigmatic case of Hopper's principle of persistence, since it occurs principally in combination with negative elements, as well as of the principles of layering and divergence (cf. Section 3.2). If we examine Table 6.173 again, the different types of meanings of *to death* coexist in time and these readings are completely independent of each other.

The data analysed in this chapter for *to death* only partially confirm Margerie's (2011) results for this prepositional phrase. As seen in Section 4.1.1, Margerie argues that the first occurrences of *to death* as a degree modifier date to the second half of the sixteenth century and are very scarce. These early examples involve the verb *hate* and apply to things rather than to people. Before developing its intensifying meaning, however, *to death* occurs in a number of transitional constructions which facilitate a degree interpretation. A construction which, according to Margerie, is crucial for the inference of a degree reading of *to death* also involves the verb *hate*, but applied to people rather than to things. This construction, which suggests an indirect relationship between death and the feeling of hating someone, represents a clear case of subjectification, and constitutes, in Margerie's view, a bridging context for the subsequent emergence of an unequivocal degree meaning of *to death*. However, as seen above, no evidence of such bridging contexts for the development of intensifying *to death* has been found in my data. In the sixteenth- and early seventeenth-century examples from EEBOCorp 1.0 *to death* is attested already with an intensifying meaning in collocations such as *laugh to death*, *tickle to death*, *impatient to death* and *enamoured to death*. These early intensifying occurrences coincide synchronically with those for the collocation *hate to death*, which is claimed by Margerie to have functioned as a trigger for the degree interpretation of the prepositional phrase. Therefore, this gradual cline of evolution cannot, unfortunately, be confirmed in the light of the data examined here.

## 6.3. Death-related intensifiers: Grammaticalisation and related processes

Sections 6.1–6.2 discussed the rise and development of the intensifiers *dead(ly)*, *mortal(ly)* and *to death* in the light of several sources of data, specifically historical dictionaries (6.1), corpora and electronic collections (Section 6.2). Section 6.3, by contrast, is intended to connect, in a more explicit way, the corpus-based study carried out in this section with the theorical discussion on intensifiers and grammaticalisation provided in Chapters 2–4, hence setting the current study within the specific theoretical framework of grammaticalisation.

The data analysis in the preceding sections has clearly shown that the forms under study in this piece of research, all of which belong to the semantic field of death and, therefore, refer to a crucial human experience, came to develop hyperbolic uses over time ('very, extremely'). As suggested in Chapter 2, intensification and exaggeration are prevalent in language, serving a crucial function, namely to highlight or maximise the relevance of our message. The remainder of this section thus looks into the rise of the degree meanings of *dead(ly)*, *mortal(ly)* and *to death*, which goes hand in hand with subjectification and grammaticalisation.

The evidence consulted revealed that subjective uses of the forms under analysis developed after originally literal or descriptive uses, and before their intensifying meanings, thereby conforming to the cline proposed by Adamson (2000: 55): descriptive > subjective > intensifying (cf. Section 4.1.2). An exception to this is *mortal(ly)*, which, being a borrowing from Anglo-Norman and Middle French, was adopted in English already with subjective readings from the start. The subjective meanings of the forms analysed implied a semantic transfer of death-related properties or qualities, thus involving the speaker's/writer's negative affect or appreciation of the situation. Death was metaphorically evoked by means of specific properties or circumstances, such as the paleness of a person, gloom and darkness, silence and quietness, etc., all of which recall death-related features. In addition to metaphor, their development involves metonymy, as there is an implied similarity between death and some of these states involved in the early subjective collocations, as in the case of being sick, pale or asleep. By metaphorical and metonymic extension, therefore, these subjective uses of *dead(ly)*, *mortal(ly)* and *to death* seemed to have paved the way for later unequivocal intensifying uses, since death actually marks the very end or extreme of our existence. In other words, a degree reading of extreme paleness or extreme silence was initially possible only as a pragmatic implicature in context, since 'pragmatic implicatures arising in context are crucial for interpreting how each new meaning comes into being' (Traugott 2006: 354). It was only later that such implicatures became conventionalised and that the new degree meaning was coded. These subjective meanings of the different death-related forms can be compared to what Traugott (1989) calls *weakly subjective uses*, that is, those which at a further stage prompt purely intensifying readings or *strongly subjective meanings* in Traugott's (1989) terms.

As explained in Section 5.4.2, with the aim of minimising the risk of a biased interpretation of dubious examples I added two further intermediate stages to Adamson's original cline: one for those meanings which are ambiguous between descriptive and subjective and another for those readings which are indeterminate between subjective and intensifying. The materials analysed yielded numerous cases of such ambiguous meanings. Some occurrences, for instance, showed contexts in which someone was sick, in agony or sharp physical pain, but his/her eventual death was not explicitly mentioned. Likewise, other instances involved cases which could be categorised as either subjective or intensifying, describing situations, among others, in which somebody was very angry or jealous. In such contexts it was unclear whether such feelings would have further consequences (e.g. a violent reaction of the character) or, by contrast, the form in question was simply emphasising the degree of the character's anger or jealousy. The addition of these two further stages to Adamson's cline to account for intermediate types of meanings, however, did not correlate in all cases with the long diachrony for these forms in my data. Thus, many of the examples of *dead(ly)*, *mortal(ly)* and *to death* which were marked as ambiguous between descriptive and subjective were documented at the same or at a later period than clearly subjective examples. Likewise, some occurrences which could be counted as both subjective and intensifying appeared later than the first intensifying attestations of some of the forms, except in the case of the adjectives *deadly* and *mortal* and of the adverb *mortally*. In other words, although the diachronic cline of evolution descriptive (D) > descriptive/subjective (D/S) > subjective (S) > subjective/intensifying (S/I) > intensifying (I) could have been possible and is certainly appealing, it cannot be effectively confirmed in the light of the materials analysed. This, however, may be a by-product of the data included in the materials analysed: for instance, the HC, which was used to obtain data for the ME period, yielded very few attestations of the forms at issue here, so that there is no corpus evidence for any descriptive/subjective use of *dead(ly)*, *mortal(ly)* and *to death*. Moreover, EEBOCorp 1.0 also recorded very few examples of these forms with meanings which are ambiguous between subjective and intensifying and which clearly antedate the first intensifying examples. In fact, this is only the case for *mortally*, *deadly* (adj.) and *mortal* (adj.). Whether ambiguous attestations could have predated intensifying occurrences of *to death* and of the adverbs *deadly* and *mortal*, therefore acting as triggers for a subsequent degree reading, is something which, unfortunately, cannot be empirically confirmed.

From the corpus-based analysis presented here, it can safely be concluded that all the death-related forms examined here have come to develop intensifying uses over time and show a number of features typically concomitant with grammaticalisation, specifically:

- *Semantic bleaching, attrition or desemanticisation*: the forms studied here evolved from literal or descriptive meanings, gradually increasing in subjectivity (subjective uses), and eventually becoming grammaticalised as intensifiers, hence the possibility for their co-occurrence with collocates which are inherently positive. Thus, from collocations such as *dead wounded*, *mortally sick* or *deadly sin*, via a process of grammaticalisation, we find, at a later stage, collocations such as *blush to death*, *mortal fine*, *dead sure* or *deadly determination*, among many others. This is related to the parameter of semantic attrition referred to by Lehmann (1985) (cf. Section 3.2), since these forms gradually lost semantic substance, developing a much more abstract degree meaning, from an originally concrete literal meaning. The only exception to the cline descriptive > subjective > intensifying is *mortal(ly)*, which was borrowed already with subjective uses. Attrition in these death-related items, however, applies only at the semantic level, as these forms have not undergone phonological reduction over time.

- *Subjectification*: the semantic development of these death-related intensifiers clearly indicates that their meanings came to be increasingly based in the speaker's subjective belief state/attitude towards the proposition (Traugott 1989: 35) (cf. Section 3.3.3). Death-related qualities such as paleness, silence, etc. implied in all cases the speaker's/writer's negative judgement of the situation and hence a subjective view of the situation. In that sense, being deadly pale could be read, for instance, as 'being pale to a degree that (s) he reminds me of a corpse'. Furthermore, it was also hypothesised that these subjective uses eventually favoured a contextualised reading of these forms as intensifiers. Although the intensifying meaning was only initially available as a contextualised pragmatic inference, these invited inferences (cf. Traugott and Dasher 2002) then turned into conventionalised degree meanings. Subjective meanings could therefore be argued to have functioned in the current data as bridging contexts (cf. Heine 2002: 84–5), eventually giving rise to intensifying readings. In sum, the development of these forms, which implied in all cases a gradual increase in subjectivity, can be summarised as follows: 'characteristic of death' > 'to a degree which I consider reminiscent of the negative aspects of death' > 'to a degree which I consider very/extremely high'. As they refer to the speaker's attitudes, they illustrate in particular semantic subjectivity, specifically ideational subjectivity, in De Smet and Verstraete's proposal (2006) (see also Section 3.3.3). The development of *dead(ly)*, *mortal(ly)* and *to death*, therefore, fits into the subjectivity cline non-/less subjective > subjective > intersubjective (cf. Traugott 2010: 34). In contrast to other intensifiers such as *absolutely* (Aijmer 2020) or *kind of* (Margerie 2010), however, these intensifiers have not developed intersubjective uses as discourse markers.

- *Reanalysis*: the semantic development of the death-related forms examined clearly shows that they all came to be semantically re-analysed as intensifiers over time. *Dead(ly)*, *mortal(ly)* and *to death* originally indicated a literal meaning ('fatal(ly)'), death being the ultimate consequence. Nonetheless, as explained above, they came to be used with meanings which gradually deviated from the originally literal reading, to later express meanings which implied more subjective views on the part of the speaker/writer, with an obvious increase in subjectivity. Finally, they were eventually reinterpreted as markers of degree. However, unlike the case of *lovely*, which implied a syntactic reanalysis of [adj.] + [adj.] into [adv.] + [adj.] and the reinterpretation of the leftmost adjective as an intensifying adverb in premodifier position (cf. Adamson 2000), *dead(ly)*, *mortal(ly)* and *to death* did not undergo the same syntactic reanalysis. Thus, as argued in Sections 6.1 and 6.2, the adjectives *mortal* and *deadly* and the homonymous adverbs developed independently. In fact, as evinced by the historical dictionaries, the adverb *deadly* developed intensifying uses considerably earlier than the adjective, as in the collocation *deadly dill* 'stupid' in example (6.35), whereas the adjective was not apparently used in such function until the second half of the seventeenth century, as reflected in the collocation *deadly drinker* in (6.29). On this account, for these death-related items one cannot claim that the adjective came to be reinterpreted as an intensifying adverb by reason of its co-occurrence in the leftmost position. In turn, the development of the adjective and the adverb in these cases is independent.
- *Decategorialisation*: the development of the adverbs *dead(ly)*, *mortal(ly)* and of the prepositional phrase *to death* suggests a categorial shift from manner adjunct to modifier uses with adjectival and participial elements, thereby expanding their syntactic potential. In the case of the adjectives *dead(ly)* and *mortal*, however, this shift is only semantic, from descriptive to intensifying meanings, as *dead(ly)* and *mortal* remain adjectives throughout and there is no shift from adjunct to modifier level in this case. Decategorialisation, it should be recalled, involved a shift from a major or lexically open

class to a minor or closed category (see Section 3.2). This also applies to the intensifiers at issue here, which belonged to a lexically open class in origin, but as intensifiers they belong to a much more restricted paradigm, namely that of intensifiers or degree words.

- *Condensation*: the evolution of the adverbial forms *deadly*, *mortally* and *to death* implies scope reduction: from adjunct uses having clausal scope, they occurred in premodifier function with phrasal scope over the adjacent word.
- *Fixation*: closely related to the parameter of condensation is fixation, as these intensifiers came to be increasingly used as premodifiers rather than as manner adjuncts, most conspicuously in the case of the adverb *deadly*.
- *Expansion*: in addition to scope reduction, the development of these forms is also compatible with host-class, syntactic and semantic-pragmatic expansion (Himmelmann 2004). As argued above, the different adverbial forms and *to death* have come to be used in various syntactic environments, both at clausal and phrasal level, which clearly implies an expansion of their syntactic potential. Likewise, *dead*(*ly*), *mortal*(*ly*) and *to death* have increased their contexts of use: from an initial use with negative collocates only, they came to accept neutral and even positive polarity items over time. This shows semantic-pragmatic expansion. Host-class expansion is also at issue in the case of the adverbs and *to death*, since they have also enlarged their range of collocates, which include verbal, adjectival, participial, nominal and prepositional elements. The adjectives, in turn, are more restricted in that sense, as they only allow nominal collocates.
- *Layering*: the synchronic coexistence of different types of meanings for these forms represents a clear case of layering, that is, the 'persistence of older forms and meanings alongside newer forms and meanings' (Hopper and Traugott 2003: 124) (cf. Section 3.2). Thus, *blush to death* or *mortal lazy*, clearly intensifying, coexisted in the data side by side with literal senses such as *press to death* or *mortal sick*. In other words, although descriptive readings were the

oldest ones recorded for these forms, they are still possible in the most recent stages of the language. Therefore, the emergence of a new layer, in this case a new meaning, did not automatically imply the disappearance of an older layer.

- *Divergence*: closely related to layering is the principle of divergence; that is, 'when a form undergoes grammaticalization and the original form continues to be used as an autonomous element so that the grammaticalised and the ungrammaticalised forms coexist side by side' (Heine 2003: 589) (cf. Section 3.2). The data show that, for instance, descriptive meanings for the adjective *dead* (e.g. *dead man*) were independent of intensifying uses of the adjective, although both descriptive and intensifying *dead* could actually co-occur in the data.
- *Persistence*: the death-related intensifiers examined tend to modify elements with inherently negative prosody, in line with their original negative meaning. Negative semantic prosody, therefore, is still well-entrenched for these forms. Nonetheless, the data also record ample evidence of semantically positive collocations, among others *deadly handsome*, *mortal good*, *dead sure*, *mortally enamoured* or *laugh to death*.

In view of the characteristics discussed in the preceding paragraphs, it can be concluded that *dead(ly)*, *mortal(ly)* and *to death* have developed increasingly abstract and grammatical meanings over time, as they came to be used hyperbolically as markers of degree or intensifiers. Their degree of grammaticalisation, however, differs considerably. Moreover, the different grammaticalisation features argued above suggest that the evolution of these forms can be considered both in terms of reduction and expansion, a development which may seem contradictory but which is clearly not incompatible.

Figure 6.17 illustrates a potential grammaticalisation cline (see Section 3.3.1) for these death-related intensifiers, considering the results of the corpus data for the variables 'type of meaning', 'semantic prosody' and 'type of word modified'.

\+ ⟵⟶ –

[*dead*$_{adv}$] *mortal*$_{adv}$ *deadly*$_{adv}$ [*dead*$_{adj}$] *mortally to death deadly*$_{adj}$ *mortal*$_{adj}$

Figure 6.17. The grammaticalisation cline of death-related intensifiers

Positive semantic prosody, as we have seen, is a clear indicator of a form becoming increasingly grammaticalised, but in some cases it was found to actually correlate with literal meanings. For instance, the adjective *mortal* modified the positive noun *love* in some occurrences, but this collocation in particular was counted as descriptive, since it referred to human love as opposed to divine love. However, the data analysis showed that except for the adjectival forms *deadly* and *mortal*, the association between positive semantic prosody and intensifying meanings is very strong.

Furthermore, the results for the adjective and adverb *dead* are an artefact of the methodology. In view of the data, none of the forms would be very advanced in the grammaticalisation cline, as they are not recorded with intensifying meanings until the eighteenth century, in the case of *dead* (adj.), and the nineteenth century in the case of *dead* (adv.). It should be recalled at this point that intensifying uses of the adverb *dead* are actually attested in EEBOCorp 1.0 (cf. Section 6.2.2), but for this corpus only a selection of collocations was analysed, so the results must be taken cautiously. In fact, if we consult the *British National Corpus* (BNC) for more recent data (cf. Claridge 2011; Blanco-Suárez 2014b), the picture turns out to be completely different, since the adverb *dead* would be the most advanced of all these forms in the grammaticalisation cline, given its occurrence as a modifier of relatively recent forms in the language, such as the adjectives *chuffed*, *sexy*, *naff*, *ace*, *spooky* and *choosy*.[73] This clearly shows an increasing productivity as an intensifier in the contemporary language.

As suggested by the cline in Figure 6.17, the adverbial forms are more advanced in the grammaticalisation process and are more widely used as intensifiers than the corresponding adjectival forms, which are found at

73 *Spooky* and *choosy* date to the nineteenth century. *Sexy*, with the meaning 'sexually attractive', *ace* 'very good, excellent' and *naff*, by contrast, were first recorded in the twentieth century, according to the OED.

the opposite end of the cline. In view of the data, therefore, adverbs tend to specialise in the intensifying function. Interestingly, zero forms outnumber *–ly* forms as intensifiers in the material analysed in this study. As noted by Nevalainen (1999: 429–30), zero forms were frequently employed as intensifiers in EModE, but towards the end of this period the suffixed counterparts were clearly on the rise. In the case of death-related intensifiers, however, zero adverbs such as *dead* and *mortal* are the preferred forms overall in the intensifying function. In the case of *dead* and *deadly*, it may have helped that they already had transferred uses in which death was no longer the end result, as in the collocations *dead sleep*, *dead oppressed* 'overcome' or *deadly hue* in examples (6.5), (6.13) and (6.25), respectively. These subjective uses, as argued above, may have later triggered their purely degree readings. *Mortal*(*ly*), as a loan, was borrowed in the late fourteenth century with both descriptive and subjective uses already. The model of *dead*(*ly*) may have reinforced the subjective and eventual rise of intensifying uses, even though their degree function is by far not the most common in the data, neither for the native form *dead*(*ly*) nor for the loanword *mortal*(*ly*).

To conclude, taking into account the results from all the sources consulted in the current piece of research, as well as the grammaticalisation cline suggested for these intensifiers in Figure 6.17, it can be argued that *dead*(*ly*), *mortal*(*ly*) and *to death* all show grammaticalised uses. Clear indicators of their oingoing grammaticalisation are their increasing subjectivity and semantic bleaching, their reanalysis as expressive of a high/extreme degree and their gradual semantic-pragmatic expansion to admit positive collocates. It was also shown that despite their high token frequency (consider the large number of examples yielded by the different corpora and electronic collections), the type frequency of these items as intensifiers is, by contrast, comparatively small. Their intensifying function is not, therefore, a high-frequency phenomenon. Moreover, as noted by Claridge (2011: 200) for *dead* in particular, the intensifying uses of these forms must have been overall too infrequent and colloquial to surface in the historical sources consulted. Finally, although *dead*(*ly*), *mortal*(*ly*) and *to death* do not illustrate other features often associated with grammaticalisation, such as phonological attrition or intersubjectification, the results presented in this chapter provide convincing evidence of their ongoing subjectification and grammaticalisation.

CHAPTER 7

# Concluding remarks and suggestions for future research

In view of the significance of an all-important experience such as death, this monograph explored its use for intensification purposes in language. Its overarching aim was to offer a comprehensive diachronic corpus-based analysis of the origin and development of several intensifiers from the semantic field of death in English, in particular *dead(ly)*, *mortal(ly)* and *to death*. Drawing on data from different historical dictionaries, corpora and electronic collections, the study covered from the ME period to the twentieth century, thereby filling a gap in the extensive literature on English intensifiers.

Chapter 1 served as an introduction to this piece of research, contextualising the topic, presenting its main aims and offering an outline of the different chapters and sections into which it is divided. The theoretical foundations of the research were then set forth in the literature review section, comprising Chapter 2 ('Intensification and intensifiers in language'), Chapter 3 ('Grammaticalisation') and Chapter 4 ('English intensifiers: A historical overview'). The methodology used in the study was the focus of Chapter 5, while Chapter 6, the core of the research, corresponded to the data analysis. A more detailed description of the contents of each chapter is provided in the following paragraphs.

Chapter 2 opened with some explanatory notes on intensification, a very successful strategy used for persuasive purposes. In fact, in a given speech event speakers do not only transmit content or information, but time and again intrude into that speech event to express opinions, attitudes, etc. Intensification can be achieved in language by means of several intensification strategies including, among others, the use of superlatives, figures of speech, word order, repetition and intonation. The second part of the chapter, Section 2.2, focused on the main features of intensifiers and outlined different proposals for their classification. It was suggested that the label *intensifier* was used here in a wide sense to refer to those items which can have either a lowering or a heightening effect (e.g. *scarcely* or *extremely*, respectively). This label was chosen at the expense of alternative denominations such as *degree words* or *degree modifiers*, since the term *intensifier* highlights the most immediate function of these forms, that is, that of giving prominence to a specific quality or feature, whether up or down on the degree scale. It must be remembered, however, that *dead(ly)*, *mortal(ly)* and *to death,* the intensifiers under analysis here, can only indicate a high or extreme degree on an imaginary degree scale. These preliminary terminological considerations were followed by a review of the different models which have been put forward in the literature for the classification of intensifiers. In general, these proposals can be classified into two main groups: on the one hand, those models which establish degree scales, among many others the proposals by Bolinger (1972) or Quirk et al. (1985) and, on the other, those which consider different semantic categories, including the models put forward by Spitzbardt (1965) or Suscinskij (1985). The classification chosen here was the one by Paradis (1997, 2008), as she takes into account not only the establishment of the relevant degree scales, but also the inherent relationship between the degree modifier and the word modified.

Chapter 3, the second of the literature review part, was concerned with the theory of grammaticalisation, since the analysis conducted here hinges precisely upon this approach. The chapter opened with some introductory comments on grammaticalisation and on its most basic features. Next, Section 3.2 was devoted to the parameters and principles of grammaticalisation, as defined by Lehmann (1985) and Hopper (1991), respectively. Lehmann thus postulated that the degree of grammaticalisation of an item can be measured against three different aspects: weight, cohesion and variability, which can be viewed both paradigmatically and syntagmatically, resulting in a set of parameters (cf. Table 3.1). If grammaticalisation is considered diachronically, a number of processes arise, namely (i) attrition, (ii) paradigmaticisation, (iii) obligatorification, (iv) condensation, (v) coalescence and (vi) fixation (see Table 3.2). Hopper also adduced a number of principles characteristic of grammaticalisation: (i) decategorialisation,

(ii) specialisation, (iii) layering, (iv) divergence and (v) persistence (Hopper 1991: 22–31). Unlike Lehmann's parameters, however, these principles apply at the early stages of grammaticalisation. A number of illustrative case studies from the literature on grammaticalisation were presented to account for these different processes, including, but not only, examples of intensifiers. Thus, intensifiers or degree words constitute paradigmatic cases of semantic attrition, since most of them originate in lexical material and develop increasingly grammatical or abstract meanings (e.g. *very*, originally meaning 'true'). Intensifiers also serve to illustrate further processes such as fixation and condensation or scope reduction: when they function as markers of degree, their scope is reduced to phrasal level and their position is fixed to the premodifier slot. Although intensifiers do not comply with all of Lehmann's and Hopper's parameters and principles, they are in fact illustrative of many of these processes fundamental to grammaticalisation research. For this reason, they were examined again in relation to the corpus data in Sections 6.2 and 6.3.

After presenting the parameters and principles of grammaticalisation in Section 3.2, Section 3.3 discussed some of the phenomena which are often related to this process of change, specifically (i) unidirectionality and grammaticalisation clines, (ii) reanalysis and (iii) (inter)subjectification. These phenomena are also crucial in the changes undergone by the death-related intensifiers examined, so they were tackled again in the discussion of the data in Chapter 6.

A controversial topic often discussed in relation to grammaticalisation is the issue of unidirectionality. As shown in Section 3.3.1, grammaticalisation is a cross-linguistic and widely attested phenomenon which typically proceeds in the direction from less to more grammatical. Some grammaticalisation clines often proposed in the literature were mentioned in this section, including, at the semantic level, the following: lexical > grammatical; less subjective > more subjective > intersubjective; and concrete > abstract and general meanings. Other clines commonly discussed in the literature operate at the syntactic (major > minor categories) and phonological levels (full > reduced phonological forms).

Another phenomenon related to grammaticalisation is reanalysis (cf. Section 3.3.2), which implies a redefinition of constituent boundaries, turning an original structure (A, B) C into a new one, reinterpreted as A (B, C) (cf. Heine et al. 1991). There are manifold examples of reanalysis understood in terms of grammaticalisation, including the reanalysis of the adjective *lovely* as a degree marker (cf. Adamson 2000) or the expression of the inflectional future in the Romance languages, going back to a construction in Latin with the verb *habeo* ('have to') postposed to an infinitive. However, reanalysis can also occur outside grammaticalisation.

The notion of subjectivity is also frequently mentioned in connection with grammaticalisation (cf. Section 3.3.3). This concept relates to the subjective component and the expressive function of language, since in every communicative act we are not only exchanging information, but we are also transmitting our beliefs, attitudes and points of view. Moreover, we pay attention to our interlocutor(s), both in regard to their possible reactions to the our message and with respect to their social stance, hence the use of forms of address such as *madam* and *sir* or of V-pronouns in the Romance languages. These meanings whereby speakers/writers show their attention to the addressee are known as intersubjective. The diachronic processes giving rise to these subjective and intersubjective meanings are known as subjectification and intersubjectification, both of which play a major role in semantic change. The approach to (inter)subjectivity adopted in the current study is the one proposed by Traugott (1989, 1995, 2003, 2007, 2010). In Traugott's theory of semantic change, in fact, meanings tend to be increasingly based in the speaker's subjective belief state/attitude toward the proposition (1989: 35), so that the following cline of evolution is cross-linguistically observed: propositional > (textual) > (expressive) (1989: 31). These expressive or subjective meanings may additionally be used to code the speaker's attention to the addressee, thereby resulting in the following cline of subjectivity: non-/less subjective > subjective > intersubjective (cf. Traugott and Dasher 2002: 225; Traugott 2003: 134). As has been shown both in this chapter and then in Chapter 6 in relation to the data analysis, this research has followed Traugott's model, which is crucial in the account of the semantic development of *dead(ly)*, *mortal(ly)* and *to death* (cf. Sections 6.2 and 6.3).

The last chapter in the literature review section, Chapter 4, provided an account of English intensifiers from the perspective of grammaticalisation.

Since *dead(ly)*, *mortal(ly)* and *to death* are all reinforcers, that is, they can only scale upwards on a degree scale, the chapter was only concerned with the history of English reinforcers, both with maximisers (Section 4.1.1) and boosters (Section 4.1.2). Attenuators, therefore, were not considered in this review. It was shown that most reinforcers originate in words and expressions with literal meanings (e.g. *really* and *very*), mainly manner adverbs, which came to develop intensifying or degree readings via a grammaticalisation process. Some other forms, such as *downright* or *utterly* (cf. Méndez-Naya 2014), however, derive from more abstract sources. The numerous studies revised in this section therefore support the fevered invention and competition of intensifiers noted by Bolinger (1972: 18), as well as their constant recycling (Tagliamonte 2008). Many PDE intensifiers, including *downright*, *right*, *utterly* or *very*, have a long history, going back to the ME period. Some other forms, by contrast, were rather short-lived, as is the case of *throughout* and *þwert-out*, and were soon ousted by other rival forms. The research presented in this section therefore presents a direct connection with the corpus-based analysis conducted in Chapter 6.

The methodology adopted in the present piece of research was the focus of Chapter 5, which opened with some preliminary remarks about Corpus Linguistics (Section 5.1), before actually looking into the sources of data consulted (Section 5.2), specifically dictionaries (Section 5.2.1), corpora (Section 5.2.2) and electronic collections (Section 5.2.3). The two historical dictionaries consulted, the OED and the MED, proved to be invaluable to trace a preliminary overview of the evolution of the death-related intensifiers under analysis. Thanks to them it was possible, for instance, to obtain an estimation of the first attestations of subjective and intensifying uses for these forms, as well as of their earliest collocations (cf. Section 6.1). This initial picture provided by the OED and MED was subsequently expanded in a more fine-grained analysis based on the evidence from the different corpora and collections (see Sections 6.2 and 6.3). Details about the compilation and composition of the different corpora and electronic collections were given in this chapter, as well as of their advantages and disadvantages in the searches conducted. The computer and statistical tools used were the focus of Section 5.3. Thus, the software chosen for the retrieval of examples from the different corpora was WordSmith 6.0

(cf. Section 5.3.1). This section additionally introduced the collocational analysis conducted in Chapter 6, presenting to this end the different tests used to measure the statistical significance of the results: the *z*-score, the *mutual information* (*MI*), the cubed version of the *mutual information* (*MI3*) and the *log-likelihood* test (Section 5.3.2). Finally, Section 5.4 was concerned with the database (Section 5.4.1) and variables considered for the analysis (Section 5.4.2).

The results of the corpus-based study were presented in Chapter 6, which first offered an overview of the evolution of *dead*(*ly*), *mortal*(*ly*) and *to death* in the light of the evidence from the historical dictionaries (Section 6.1). This was followed by a close examination of the data from the corpora and databases to trace their long diachrony (Section 6.2). Finally, in Section 6.3 the development of these death-related forms across time was presented in the light of grammaticalisation theory. What follows is a summary of the most relevant conclusions drawn from the analysis.

*Dead* (adj. and adv.) shows signs of incipient subjectivity already from the ME period, in collocations such as *dead slow* or *dead still*. However, purely intensifying meanings of *dead* are not attested until the close of the sixteenth century in the case of the adverb (e.g. *dead sure*) and the second half of the seventeenth century in that of the adjective (e.g. *dead ripeness*). Though the data from the HC and ARCHER for the intensifying adjective and adverb *dead* were very scarce (just one instance of the collocation *dead serious* in ARCHER), EEBOCorp 1.0 provided evidence of early intensifying readings of these forms, as shown by the collocations *dead sure* and *dead sober* for the adverb, and by *dead flat* for the adjective. The results from ECF and NCF served to throw more light on the degree function of *dead*, with collocations which were not attested in the earlier data, such as *dead loss*, *dead bargain*, *dead against*, *dead trivial* and *dead sick* (*of something*).

The results for *deadly* (adj. and adv.) went much along the same lines as for its zero counterpart. The OED and MED record the first subjective uses of *deadly* (adj. and adv.) in ME. Their intensifying function, however, was not attested until centuries later: in the fifteenth century in the case of the adverb (e.g. *deadly dill* 'stupid') and in the second half of the seventeenth century in that of the adjective (e.g. *deadly drinker*). The data from the HC and ARCHER for the long diachrony of *deadly* turned out to be very limited, with very few examples of subjective meanings for the adjective (e.g. *deadly feud*, *deadly enemy* or *deadly grief*) and no instances of intensifying *deadly* (adj. and adv.). Although EEBOCorp 1.0 recorded a vast number of examples of the adjectival and adverbial forms, the corpus actually yielded very few occurrences of the intensifying function, all of them corresponding to the adverb. Subjective collocations of the adjective *deadly* in EEBOCorp 1.0 include *deadly sorrow*, *deadly swoon* and *deadly darkness*. Some other collocations such as *deadly jealousy* and *deadly envy* were argued to allow both a subjective and an intensifying reading. Moreover, in the overwhelming majority of the examples in the corpus, adjectival *deadly* showed negative or neutral semantic prosody, although it occasionally modified positive nouns as well, such as *glory* or *charm*. Nonetheless, in all these examples *deadly* still had a descriptive or literal meaning. Therefore, positive semantic prosody did not correlate with intensifying meanings and, hence, with a high degree of grammaticalisation of the adjective *deadly* at this stage. In contrast to its adjectival counterpart, the adverb *deadly* showed a grammaticalised status in the EEBOCorp 1.0 data, as it was attested with readings which were intermediate between subjective and intensifying from the early sixteenth century (e.g. *envy deadly*) and with intensifying meanings from the late sixteenth century (e.g. *deadly set*). Most importantly, in its intensifying function it was found as a modifier of positive elements (e.g. in the collocations *deadly handsome*, *deadly witty*, *love deadly*), though not exclusively, as it also collocated with neutral (*set*, *sure*, *deep*) and negative items (e.g. *dull*, *lazy*, *unfortunate*). The adverb *deadly* could also modify a wider range of forms than its homonymous adjective, and although it functioned predominantly as a modifier of verbs, participles and adjectives, it was also attested with an intensifying meaning as a modifier of the adverb *near* (*deadly near*). The evidence from ECF and NCF served to confirm the results provided by the corpora, not only with examples of subjective collocations (e.g. *deadly pale* or *deadly still*), but also with further intensifying collocations such as *deadly comfortable*, *deadly long* or *deadly curious*.

The form *mortal* was borrowed from Anglo-Norman and Middle French, which conditioned its development, as it could be used both with literal and subjective uses from these very first attestations. It would take several centuries for *mortal* (adj. and adv.) to develop purely intensifying meanings. These in fact only arose in the eighteenth century in the collocation *mortal pains* for the adjective (e.g. *to take mortal pains to do something*) and *mortal fond* for the adverb. As far as the adjective *mortal* is concerned, the evidence consulted provided mostly occurrences of its descriptive function, hence collocations such as *mortal venom* or *mortal judgement*. Subjective uses were also occasionally found, as in *mortal enemy*, *mortal hate* and *mortal sorrow*. Neither the HC nor ARCHER or EEBOCorp 1.0 recorded purely intensifying readings of the adjective, although in EEBOCorp 1.0 some examples could allow both a subjective and an intensifying reading. This was the case of the collocations *mortal jealousy*, *mortal ire* and *mortal envy*, some of which dated to the late fifteenth century. *Mortal* could also occur with positive elements in these early data (*love*, *praise* and *honour*). Positive prosody, however, was not in harmony with a high degree of grammaticalisation, as most of these positive collocates had literal rather than intensifying meanings. The first unambiguous degree uses of the adjective are found in the LModE data from ECF and NCF, as in *mortal disappointment*, *mortal hurry*, *mortal speed*, *mortal certainty* and *mortal repugnance*, although intensifying readings were by no means the most frequent. In contrast to the adjective, the evidence provided by the different sources for *mortal* (adv.) was very scarce: no instances in the HC, just one occurrence in ARCHER (the intensifying collocation *mortal hard*, from the early twentieth century) and just four tokens in a megacorpus such as EEBOCorp 1.0, in the collocations *mortal wounded*, *mortal sick* and *mortal pale*. In contrast, ECF and NCF provided a larger number of tokens. What is more, the overwhelming majority of the attestations of the adverb in these collections corresponded to intensifying meanings (e.g. *mortal cunning*, *mortal fond*, *mortal inconvenient*, *mortal sorry* and *mortal fine*), which suggests that its intensifying function must have been in vogue at that time. In addition, positive semantic prosody (as in the combination of the adverb with adjectives such as *good* or *passionate*) matched an intensifying function, which indicates a higher degree of grammaticalisation. The adverb also showed a strong preference for adjectival collocates, although it could also modify participial items.

Just like *mortal*, its *–ly* counterpart *mortally* was attested from the very beginning with both literal and subjective uses and its intensifying function also arose in the eighteenth century (e.g. *mortally ugly*) (cf. Section 6.1.4). The HC and ARCHER provided limited examples of this adverb, with both descriptive (e.g. *mortally wounded*) and subjective collocations (e.g. *mortally hate* or *mortally malign* 'feel malice or ill will against someone'). In turn, EEBOCorp 1.0 returned a considerable number of tokens (1,413 in total), most of which corresponded to literal readings, although subjective examples were also found (e.g. *mortally afflicted* or *mortally grieved*). Interestingly, intensifying uses also occurred (e.g. *mortally in love*, *mortally tedious*, *mortally surprised*), as well occurrences which were counted as ambiguous between subjective and intensifying (e.g. *mortally perplexed*, *mortally displeased*). Moreover, although negative semantic prosody prevailed, instances of *mortally* as a modifier of positive elements were also recorded in EEBOCorp 1.0 (e.g. *in love*, *happy* and *enamoured*), which correlate with an intensifying function. The LModE data from ECF and NCF served to expand the data on the intensifying uses of *mortally*, with collocations such as *mortally changed*, *mortally surprised*, *mortally certain* and *mortally unpleasant*. Furthermore, in line with its source meaning, *mortally* was mostly attested with negative semantic prosody in the data. *Mortally* may modify various word categories, including verbs, participles, adjectives and prepositional phrases (*at feud*), yet it showed a clear tendency to modify verbal and participial forms.

Finally, the prepositional phrase *to death* could already occur in OE with non-literal meanings, hence showing incipient subjectivity, as in the collocation *to deaðe afærede* ('troubled to death'). Intensifying readings emerged relatively early, as shown by the collocation *enamoured to death*, recorded from the sixteenth century. As was the case with the other intensifiers, the HC and ARCHER returned few occurrences of *to death*, mostly corresponding to descriptive uses (e.g. *condemned* or *pinched to death*) and some sporadic occurrences of collocations whose meaning was unclear between descriptive and subjective (e.g. *bewitched to death*). In contrast, the much larger EEBOCorp 1.0 corpus recorded ample evidence of subjective (*languish to death*, *afraid to death* or *sorrow to death*) and intensifying (*tickle to death*, *laugh to death* or *blush to death*) uses, in addition to examples in which it could be interpreted as either subjective or intensifying (e.g. *angry to death* or *oppose to death*). Interestingly, the overwhelming majority of the occurrences in which *to death* modified items with positive semantic prosody (e.g. *laugh*, *tickle*, *adore* or *enamoured*) showed intensifying meanings, so that positive prosody can be said to correlate with more grammaticalised meanings of the form. ECF and NCF also provided additional examples of intensifying *to death*, hence collocations such as *blush to death*, *mortify to death*, *tease to death*, *bored to death* or *ashamed to death*. In these collections, however, intensifying uses did not correlate with positive meanings, as *to death* collocated instead with negative or neutral elements. As was the case with *mortally* (see above), *to death* mostly modified participles and verbs, but could additionally occur in the data as a modifier of nouns, adjectives and prepositional phrases (e.g. *in love*).

Chapter 6 closed with a discussion on the semantic evolution of the selected death-related intensifiers from the perspective of grammaticalisation (Section 6.3). The results from the variety of materials consulted indicate that the intensifying meanings of *dead*(*ly*), *mortal*(*ly*) and *to death* did not emerge instantaneously. On the contrary, their grammaticalisation as intensifiers was a gradual process. The cline proposed by Adamson (2000: 55) for the semantic evolution of intensifiers, descriptive > affective (subjective) > intensifying meanings, seemed to be suitable to describe the development of the death-related intensifiers examined in the current piece of research. Even so, I decided to adapt it by adding two intermediate stages: one between descriptive and affective (subjective), for those cases which could be ambiguous between these two meanings, and a further stage between affective (subjective) and intensifying, for those occurrences which could be read in either way. This addition was intended to minimise a biased interpretation of the data. Despite the prodigious amount of occurrences of the death-related forms at issue in the different sources (241,875 in total, of which 40,976 were eventually considered for analysis), and hence the serious challenges posed by a corpus-based semantic analysis of this kind, this cline of evolution proved to be extremely valuable to account for their semantic development over the history of English. The analysis carried out in Chapter 6 also showed that, notwithstanding the vast number of tokens considered, their type frequency as intensifiers was not particularly high.

Furthermore, their relatively low productivity as intensifiers adds value to the type of analysis conducted here, since opting for a random sample of these forms in the data sources would return very few hits, if any, of intensifying *dead(ly)*, *mortal(ly)* and *to death*, and would clearly not allow to draw many firm conclusions on how these meanings emerged and which contexts may have favoured a potential degree reading for these forms.

This study has proved that *dead(ly)*, *mortal(ly)* and *to death* illustrate a number of features typically associated with grammaticalisation (cf. Section 6.3). For example, it was shown that these forms evince semantic bleaching or desemanticisation, progressively developing more grammatical and abstract meanings, in the light of collocations such as *dead sure*, *dead right*, *deadly determination*, *deadly lazy*, *mortal hurry*, *mortal fine*, *mortally ugly* and *blush to death*. In such cases they can no longer be considered literally and a degree meaning is the only possible interpretation.

In addition to semantic bleaching or attrition, the data analysis also revealed a progressive increase in subjectivity for these forms. In some examples a literal reading was not completely straightforward, especially in those cases in which a character was described as being very ill or in terrible pain. In all likelihood these unclear instances favoured the emergence of subsequent subjective and more metonymic and metaphorical uses of the forms, implying the semantic transfer of death-related properties such as paleness or tranquillity, for example. These uses involved the speaker's/writer's subjective assessment of the situation (for instance, referring to an ominous silence, as if death or a fatal outcome was being presaged). Moreover, these more subjective meanings, typically denoting paleness, enmity, silence, etc., contextually invited a degree inference, and thus acted as bridging contexts for the later emergence and eventual conventionalisation of unambiguously intensifying meanings. Therefore, what first arose as a pragmatic inference in context was finally reanalysed as a conventionalised degree meaning ('very, extremely'). In fact, contexts which implied semantic fields such as anger, hatred or enmity seemed to allow potential degree readings in context, and these may have eventually paved the way for subsequent unambiguous degree uses.

*Dead(ly)*, *mortal(ly)* and *to death* were also claimed to illustrate layering, which implies that descriptive, subjective and intensifying meanings (e.g.

*wounded to death*, *terrified to death* and *enamoured to death*, respectively) may coexist synchronically. This is closely related to the principle of divergence: the different meanings are autonomous and may occur independently and synchronically. The collocational analysis conducted also revealed that despite the ample evidence of death-related intensifiers in combination with positive collocates, they exhibited a clear preference to modify elements with negative semantic prosody, which is undoubtedly in keeping with their original death-related meaning. This shows another grammaticalisation feature, namely persistence. Moreover, the development of these forms is compatible with grammaticalisation understood in terms of both reduction and expansion in Lehmann's (1985) and Himmelmann's terms (2004), respectively (cf. Section 6.3), since they underwent scope reduction, yet at the same time they increased their range of collocates. In view of these features, therefore, we might assume that *dead*(*ly*), *mortal*(*ly*) and *to death* have undergone grammaticalisation, becoming increasingly schematic and abstract over time, notwithstanding their low token and type frequency as intensifiers (see Section 6.3 for a more comprehensive account of their grammaticalisation).

The study of death-related intensifiers presented in this monograph hence fills a gap in the literature on English intensifiers, covering a semantic field which had hitherto not been extensively explored (see, however, the case study on *die*, *dead* and *to death* by Claridge 2011 (197–207) and Margerie 2011 on *to death*). The results of this corpus-based analysis could, however, be complemented with further work on intensifiers originating in the same semantic domain. Some suggestions on possible future lines of research could include:

- to examine other constructions from the semantic field of death, such as *fatal* (e.g. *fatal experience*), *die for* (e.g. *I'm dying for a cuppa*) and *die to* (e.g. *I was dying to see her*), which have been left out from the present analysis. It would be worth exploring whether these forms have also undergone parallel developments and show traces of ongoing grammaticalisation;
- to expand the analysis of these forms to the more recent history of English, so as to gain an understanding of their behaviour

and degree of (un)productivity in the contemporary language. It should be recalled at this point that the twentieth-century evidence presented here was restricted to ARCHER, which proved to be insufficient in view of the low token frequency of these forms in the corpus;

- to consider the behaviour and rates of use of all these forms in different varieties of English worldwide;
- to explore the uses of the suffixed *–ly* forms as opposed to their zero counterparts, as well as the factors which may lie behind the more apparent productivity of zero forms as intensifiers;
- to look into the evolution of death-related intensifiers from the perspective of Construction Grammar, which could reveal in which ways these forms and their collocational profiles are interconnected and compete with or reinforce the different members of the constructional network;
- to carry out a cross-linguistic diachronic corpus-based study of death-related intensifiers in order to identify potential trends and possible semantic fields which are emphasised across languages, such as basic needs like hunger or thirst, and common feelings or states, including tiredness, fright, drunkenness, coldness or paleness (see Claridge 2011 for some parallels of *dead*, *die* and *to death* in German and French).

All of these issues remain, however, to be discussed in future works.

# Bibliography


Adamson, Sylvia. 1995. From empathetic deixis to empathetic narrative: Stylisation and (de)subjectivisation as processes of language change. In Dieter Stein and Susan Wright (eds), *Subjectivity and subjectivisation: Linguistic perspectives*. Cambridge: Cambridge University Press, 195–224.

Adamson, Sylvia. 2000. A lovely little example: Word order options and category shift in the premodifying string. In Olga Fischer, Anette Rosenbach and Dieter Stein (eds), *Pathways of change: Grammaticalization in English*. Amsterdam: John Benjamins, 39–66.

Aijmer, Karin. 2020. *That's absolutely fine*: An investigation of *absolutely* in the spoken BNC2014. In Paula Rautionaho, Arja Nurmi and Juhani Klemola (eds), *Corpora and the changing society: Studies in the evolution of English*. Amsterdam: John Benjamins, 143–68.

Aijmer, Karin. 2021. 'That's well good': A re-emergent intensifier in current British English. *Journal of English Linguistics* 49(1): 18–38.

Allan, Kathryn. 2012. Using OED data as evidence for researching semantic change. In Kathryn Allan and Justyna A. Robinson (eds), *Current methods in historical semantics*. Berlin: Mouton de Gruyter, 17–39.

Allerton, David J. 1987. English intensifiers and their idiosyncrasies. In Ross Steele and Terry Threadgold (eds), *Language topics: Essays in honour of Michael Halliday*. 2 vols. Amsterdam: John Benjamins, 15–31.

Athanasiadou, Angeliki. 2007. On the subjectivity of intensifiers. *Language Sciences* 29(4): 554–65.

Bäcklund, Ulf. 1973. *The collocations of adverbs of degree*. Uppsala: Uppsala Reprotryck.

Barnfield, Kate and Isabelle Buchstaller. 2010. Intensifiers on Tyneside: Longitudinal developments and new trends. *English World-Wide* 31(3): 252–87.

Baugh, Albert Croll and Thomas Cable. 2002. *A history of the English language*. 2nd edn. London: Routledge.

Benveniste, Émile. 1966 [1958]. *Problèmes de linguistique générale*. Paris: Éditions Gallimard.

Biber, Douglas, Stig Johansson, Geoffrey Leech, Susan Conrad and Edward Finegan. 1999. *The Longman grammar of spoken and written English*. Essex: Longman.

Biedermann, Reinhard. 1969. *Die deutsche Gradadverbien in synchronischer und diachronischer Hinsicht*. Heidelberg: Dissertation.

Biscetti, Stefania. 2008. The diachronic development of the intensifier *bloody*: A case study in historical pragmatics. In Richard Dury, Maurizio Gotti and Marina

Dossena (eds), *English Historical Linguistics 2006: Selected papers from the fourteenth International Conference on English Historical Linguistics* (ICEHL 14). *Volume II: Lexical and semantic change*. Amsterdam: John Benjamins, 53–74.

Blanco-Suárez, Zeltia. 2013. The competition between the intensifiers *dead* and *deadly*: Some diachronic considerations. In Hilde Hasselgård, Jarle Ebeling and Signe Oksefjell Ebeling (eds), *Corpus perspectives on patterns of lexis*. Amsterdam: John Benjamins, 71–90.

Blanco-Suárez, Zeltia. 2014a. *Oh he is olde dogge at expounding, and* deade *sure at a Catechisme*: Some considerations on the history of the intensifying adverb *dead* in English. *Acta Linguistica Hafniensia* 46(1): 117–36.

Blanco-Suárez, Zeltia. 2014b. '*Ma daddy wis* dead *chuffed*: On the dialectal distribution of the intensifier *dead* in contemporary English'. In Kristin Davidse, Caroline Gentens, Lobke Ghesquière and Lieven Vandelanotte (eds), *Corpus interrogation and grammatical patterns*. Amsterdam: John Benjamins, 151–72.

Bolinger, Dwight. 1972. *Degree words*. The Hague: Mouton.

Borst, Eugene. 1902. *Die Gradadverbien im Englischen* (Anglistische Forschungen 10). Heidelberg: Winter.

Boye, Kasper and Peter Harder. 2014. (Inter)subjectification in a functional theory of grammaticalization. *Acta Linguistica Hafniensia : International Journal of Linguistics* 46(1): 7–24.

Bréal, Michel. 2005 [1897]. *Essai de sémantique : Science des significations*. 3rd edn. Limoges: Editions Lambert-Lucas.

Breban, Tine and Kristin Davidse. 2016. The history of *very*: The directionality of functional shift and (inter)subjectification. *English Language and Linguistics* 20(2): 221–49.

Brezina, Vaclav. 2014. Statistics in corpus linguistics: Web resource. Available from <http://corpora.lancs.ac.uk/stats>.

Brezina, Vaclav, Tony McEnery and Stephen Wattam. 2015. Collocations in context: A new perspective on collocation networks. *International Journal of Corpus Linguistics* 20(2): 139–73.

Brinton, Laurel J. 1996. *Pragmatic markers in English: Grammaticalization and discourse functions*. Berlin: Mouton de Gruyter.

Brinton, Laurel J. 2017. *The evolution of pragmatic markers in English: Pathways of change*. Cambridge: Cambridge University Press.

Brinton, Laurel J. and Elizabeth Closs Traugott. 2005. *Lexicalization and language change*. Cambridge: Cambridge University Press.

Buchstaller, Isabelle and Elizabeth Closs Traugott. 2006. *The lady was al demonyak*: Historical aspects of Adverb *all*. *English Language and Linguistics* 10(2): 345–70.

Bühler, Karl. 1990 [1934]. *Theory of language: The representational function of language*. Amsterdam: John Benjamins.

Burridge, Kate. 1998. From modal auxiliary to lexical verb: The curious case of Pennsylvania German *wotte*. In Richard M. Hogg and Linda van Bergen (eds), *Historical linguistics 1995: Selected papers from the 12th International conference on historical linguistics*. Volume 2: *Germanic linguistics*. Amsterdam: John Benjamins, 19–33.

Bybee, Joan L. 2003. Mechanisms of change in grammaticization: The role of frequency. In Brian D. Joseph and Richard D. Janda (eds), *The handbook of historical linguistics*. Oxford: Blackwell, 602–23.

Bybee, Joan L. 2006. From usage to grammar: The mind's response to repetition. *Language* 82(4): 711–33.

Bybee, Joan L. and Sandra A. Thompson. 1997. Three frequency effects in syntax. *Berkeley Linguistics Society* 23: 378–88.

Calle-Martín, Javier. 2014. On the history of the intensifier *Wonder* in English. *Australian Journal of Linguistics* 34(3): 399–419.

Cantos-Gómez, Pascual. 2013. *Statistical methods in language and linguistic research*. Sheffield: Equinox.

Claridge, Claudia. 2011. *Hyperbole in English: A corpus-based study of exaggeration*. Cambridge: Cambridge University Press.

Claridge, Claudia, Ewa Jonsson and Merja Kytö. 2019. *Entirely innocent*: A historical sociopragmatic analysis of maximizers in the Old Bailey Corpus. *English Language and Linguistics* 24(4): 855–74.

Cornillie, Bert. 2008. On the grammaticalization and (inter)subjectivity of evidential (semi-)auxiliaries in Spanish. In Elena Seoane and María José López-Couso (eds), *Theoretical and empirical issues in grammaticalization*. Amsterdam: John Benjamins, 55–76.

Couper-Kuhlen, Elizabeth. 2011. Grammaticalization and conversation. In Heiko Narrog and Bernd Heine (eds), *The Oxford handbook of grammaticalization*. Oxford: Oxford University Press, 424–37.

Cruzeiro, Maria Eduarda. 1973. *Processos de intensificaçao no português dos séculos XIII a XV*. Lisboa: Centro de Estudos Filológicos.

Crystal, David. 2003. *A dictionary of linguistics and phonetics*. 5th edn. Oxford: Blackwell.

Curzan, Anne. 2009. Historical corpus linguistics and evidence of language change. In Anke Lüdeling and Merja Kytö (eds), *Corpus linguistics: An international handbook*. Vol. 2. Berlin: Mouton de Gruyter, 1091–109.

Cuyckens, Hubert. 2018. Reconciling older and newer approaches to grammaticalization. *Yearbook of the German Cognitive Linguistics Association* 6: 183–96.

Cuyckens, Hubert, Kristin Davidse and Lieven Vandelanotte. 2010. Introduction. In Kristin Davidse, Lieven Vandelanotte and Hubert Cuyckens (eds), *Subjectification, intersubjectification and grammaticalization*. Berlin: Mouton de Gruyter, 1–25.

D'Hondt, Ulrike and Tine Defour. 2012. At the crossroads of grammaticalization and pragmaticalization: A diachronic cross-linguistic case study on *vraiment* and *really*. *Neuphilologische Mitteilungen* 113(2): 169–90.

Davidse, Kristin. 2009. *Complete* and *sort of*: From identifying to intensifying? *Transactions of the Philological Society* 107(3): 262–92.

De Smet, Hendrik and Jean Christophe Verstraete. 2006. Coming to terms with subjectivity. *Cognitive Linguistics* 17(3): 365–92.

Defour, Tine. 2012. The pragmaticalization and intensification of *verily*, *truly* and *really*: A corpus-based study on the developments of three truth-identifying adverbs. In Manfred Markus, Yoko Iyeiri, Reinhard Heuberger and Emil Chamson (eds), *Middle and Modern English corpus linguistics: A multi-dimensional approach*. Amsterdam: John Benjamins, 75–92.

Degand, Liesbeth and Anne-Marie Simon-Vandenbergen. 2011. Introduction: Grammaticalization and (inter)subjectification of discourse markers. *Linguistics* 49(2): 287–94.

Diewald, Gabriele. 2011a. Pragmaticalization (defined) as grammaticalization of discourse functions. *Linguistics* 49(2): 365–90.

Diewald, Gabriele. 2011b. Grammaticalization and pragmaticalization. In Heiko Narrog and Bernd Heine (eds), *The Oxford handbook of grammaticalization*. Oxford: Oxford University Press, 450–61.

Dixon, Robert M. W. 1977. Where have all the adjectives gone? *Studies in Language* 1(1): 19–80.

Dixon, Robert M. W. 2004. Adjective classes in typological perspective. In Robert M. W. Dixon and Alexandra Y. Aikhenvald (eds), *Adjective classes: A cross-linguistic typology*. Oxford: Oxford University Press, 1–49.

Dostie, Gaétane. 2004. *Pragmaticalisation et marqueurs discursifs : Analyse sémantique et traitement lexicographique*. Brussels: De Boeck.

Fillmore, Charles. 1992. 'Corpus linguistics' or 'Computer-aided armchair linguistics'. In Jan Svartvik (ed.), *Directions in corpus linguistics: Proceedings of Nobel symposium, 4–8 August 1991*. Berlin: Mouton de Gruyter, 35–60.

Finegan, Edward. 1995. Subjectivity and subjectivisation: An introduction. In Dieter Stein and Susan Wright (eds), *Subjectivity and subjectivisation: Linguistic perspectives*. Cambridge: Cambridge University Press, 1–15.

Fischer, Andreas. 1997. The *Oxford English Dictionary* on CD-ROM as a historical corpus: *To wed* and *to marry* revisited. In Udo Fries, Viviane Müller and Peter Schneider (eds), *From Aelfric to the New York Times: Studies in English corpus linguistics*. Amsterdam: Rodopi, 161–72.

Fischer, Olga. 2000. Grammaticalisation: Unidirectional, non-reversable? The case of *to* before the infinitive in English. In Olga Fischer, Anette Rosenbach and Dieter Stein (eds), *Pathways of change: Grammaticalization in English*. Amsterdam: John Benjamins, 149–69.

Fischer, Olga and Anette Rosenbach. 2000. Introduction. In Olga Fischer, Anette Rosenbach and Dieter Stein (eds), *Pathways of change: Grammaticalization in English*. Amsterdam: John Benjamins, 1–38.

Fitzmaurice, Susan. 2004. Subjectivity, intersubjectivity and the historical construction of interlocutor stance: From stance markers to discourse markers. *Discourse Studies* 6(4): 427–48.

Flores, Cristina Maria Moreira. 2004. *Zum Ausdruck des höchsten Grades im Deutschen und im Portugiesischen*. Unpublished MA thesis, Universidade do Minho.

Ghesquière, Lobke. 2014. *The directionality of (inter)subjectification in the English noun phrase: Pathways of change*. Berlin: Mouton de Gruyter.

Ghesquière, Lobke and Kristin Davidse. 2011. The development of intensification scales in noun-intensifying uses of adjectives: Sources, paths and mechanisms of change. *English Language and Linguistics* 15(2): 251–77.

Ghesquière, Lobke, Lieselotte Brems and Freek Van de Velde. 2014. Intersubjectivity and intersubjectification: Typology and operationalization. In Lieselotte Brems, Lobke Ghesquière and Freek van de Velde (eds), *Intersubjectivity and intersubjectification in grammar and discourse: Theoretical and descriptive advances*. Amsterdam: John Benjamins, 129–53.

González-Díaz, Victorina. 2008. Recent developments in English intensifiers: The case of *very much*. *English Language and Linguistics* 12(2): 221–43.

Halliday, Michael Alexander Kirkwood. 1973. *Explorations in the functions of language*. London: Edward Arnold.

Haspelmath, Martin. 1999. Why is grammaticalization irreversible? *Linguistics* 37(6): 1043–68.

Haspelmath, Martin. 2004. On directionality in language change with particular reference to grammaticalization. In Olga Fischer, Muriel Norde and Harry Perridon (eds), *Up and down the cline – The nature of grammaticalization*. Amsterdam: John Benjamins, 17–44.

Heine, Bernd. 1992. Grammaticalization chains. *Studies in Language* 16(2): 335–68.

Heine, Bernd. 2002. On the role of context in grammaticalization. In Ilse Wischer and Gabriele Diewald (eds), *New reflections on grammaticalization*. Amsterdam: John Benjamins, 83–101.

Heine, Bernd. 2003. Grammaticalization. In Brian D. Joseph and Richard D. Janda (eds), *The handbook of historical linguistics*. Oxford: Blackwell, 575–601.

Heine, Bernd, Ulrike Claudi and Friederike Hünnemeyer. 1991. *Grammaticalization: A conceptual framework*. Chicago: University of Chicago Press.

Heine, Bernd and Tania Kuteva. 2002. *World lexicon of grammaticalization*. Cambridge: Cambridge University Press.

Heine, Bernd and Mechthild Reh. 1984. *Grammaticalization and reanalysis in African languages*. Hamburg: Helmut Buske Verlag.

Hickey, Raymond (ed.). 2003. *Corpus presenter: Software language analysis with a manual and a corpus of Irish English as a sample data.* Amsterdam: John Benjamins.

Hilpert, Martin. 2013. Corpus-based approaches to constructional change. In Thomas Hoffmann and Graeme Trousdale (eds), *The Oxford handbook of construction grammar.* Oxford: Oxford University Press, 458–77.

Himmelmann, Nikolaus P. 2004. Lexicalization and grammaticization: Opposite or orthogonal? In Walter Bisang, Nikolaus P. Himmelmann and Björn Wiemer (eds), *What makes grammaticalization: A look from its fringes and its components.* Berlin: Mouton de Gruyter, 21–42.

Hoffmann, Sebastian. 2004. Using the *OED* quotations database as a corpus – a linguistic appraisal. *ICAME Journal* 28: 17–30.

Hoffmann, Thomas and Graeme Trousdale (eds). 2013. *The Oxford handbook of construction grammar.* Oxford: Oxford University Press.

Hopper, Paul J. 1991. On some principles of grammaticization. In Elizabeth Closs Traugott and Bernd Heine (eds), *Approaches to grammaticalization.* Vol. I. Amsterdam: John Benjamins, 17–35.

Hopper, Paul J. and Elizabeth Closs Traugott. 2003. *Grammaticalization.* 2nd edn. Cambridge: Cambridge University Press.

Huddleston, Rodney and Geoffrey K. Pullum et al. 2002. *The Cambridge grammar of the English language.* Cambridge: Cambridge University Press.

Jakobson, Roman. 1960. Linguistics and poetics. In Thomas A. Sebeok (ed.), *Style in language.* Cambridge, MA: Massachusetts Institute of Technology, 349–77.

Jespersen, Otto. 1972. *Growth and structure of the English language.* 9th edn. Oxford: Blackwell.

Kastovsky, Dieter. 2006. Typological changes in derivational morphology. In Ans van Kemenade and Bettelou Los (eds), *The handbook of the history of English.* Oxford: Blackwell, 151–76.

Kennedy, Christopher and Louise McNally. 2005. Scale structure, degree modification, and the semantics of gradable predicates. *Language* 81(2): 345–81.

Kirchner, Gustav. 1955. *Gradadverbien: Restriktiva und Verwandtes im heutigen Englisch (britisch und amerikanisch).* Halle (Saale): Niemeyer.

Krug, Manfred. 2003. Frequency as a determinant in grammatical variation and change. In Günter Rohdenburg and Britta Mondorf (eds), *Determinants of grammatical variation in English.* Berlin: Mouton de Gruyter, 7–67.

Kuryłowicz, Jerzy. 1965. The evolution of grammatical categories. *Diogenes* 13(51): 55–71.

Kytö, Merja. 1996. *Manual to the diachronic part of the Helsinki Corpus of English Texts: coding conventions and lists of source texts.* 3rd edn. Helsinki: University of Helsinki, Department of English.

Labov, William. 1984. Intensity. In Deborah Schiffrin (ed.), *Meaning, form, and use in context: Linguistic applications*. Washington, DC: Georgetown University Press, 43–70.

Langacker, Ronald W. 1990. *Concept, image, and symbol: The cognitive basis of grammar*. Berlin: Mouton de Gruyter.

Larreya, Paul. 2009. Towards a typology of modality in language. In Raphael Salkie, Pierre Busuttil and Johan van der Auwera (eds), *Modality in English: Theory and description*. Berlin: Mouton de Gruyter, 9–30.

Lass, Roger. 2000. Remarks on (uni)directionality. In Olga Ficher, Anette Rosenbach and Dieter Stein (eds), *Pathways of change: Grammaticalization in English*. Amsterdam: John Benjamins, 207–27.

Lehmann, Christian. 1985. Grammaticalization: Synchronic variation and diachronic change. *Lingua e Stile* XX(3): 303–18.

Lehmann, Christian. 1995. *Thoughts on grammaticalization*. Munich: Lincom Europa.

Lewis, Robert E. (ed.). 2007. *Middle English dictionary: Plan and bibliography*. 2nd edn. Ann Arbor: The University of Michigan Press.

Lightfoot, Douglas. 2011. Grammaticalization and lexicalization. In Heiko Narrog and Bernd Heine (eds), *The Oxford handbook of grammaticalization*. Oxford: Oxford University Press, 438–49.

López-Couso, María José. 2010. Subjectification and intersubjectification. In Andreas H. Jucker and Irma Taavitsainen (eds), *Historical pragmatics*. Berlin: Mouton de Gruyter, 127–63.

López-Couso, María José. 2016. Corpora and online resources in English historical linguistics. In Merja Kytö and Päivi Pahta (eds), *The Cambridge handbook of English historical linguistics*. Cambridge: Cambridge University Press, 127–45.

Lorenz, Gunter R. 1999. *Adjective intensification, learners versus native speakers: A corpus study of argumentative writing*. Amsterdam: Rodopi.

Lorenz, Gunter R. 2002. Adjective intensification, learners versus native speakers: A corpus study of argumentative writing. In Ilse Wischer and Gabriele Diewald (eds), *New reflections on grammaticalization*. Amsterdam: John Benjamins, 143–61.

Louw, Bill. 2000. Contextual prosodic theory: Bring semantic prosodies to life. In Chris Heffer and Helen Saunston (eds), *Words in context: A tribute to John Sinclair on his retirement*. Birmingham: University of Birmingham, 48–94.

Lyons, John. 1982. Deixis and subjectivity: Loquor, ergo sum? In Robert J. Jarvella and Wolfgang Klein (eds), *Speech, place, and action: Studies in deixis and related topics*. New York: Wiley, 101–24.

Macaulay, Ronald. 2006. Pure grammaticalization: The development of a teenage intensifier. *Language Variation and Change* 18(3): 267–83.

Mair, Christian. 2004. Corpus linguistics and grammaticalization theory: Statistics, frequencies, and beyond. In Hans Lindquist and Christian Mair (eds), *Corpus approaches to grammaticalization in English*. Amsterdam: John Benjamins, 121–50.

Marchello-Nizia, Christiane. 2006. *Grammaticalisation et changement linguistique*. Brussels: De Boeck.

Margerie, Hélène. 2010. On the rise of (inter)subjective meaning in the grammaticalization of *kind of/kinda*. In Kristin Davidse, Lieven Vandelanotte and Hubert Cuyckens (eds), *Subjectification, intersubjectification and grammaticalization*. Berlin: Mouton de Gruyter, 315–48.

Margerie, Hélène. 2011. Grammaticalising constructions: *To death* as a peripheral degree modifier. *Folia Linguistica Historica* 32: 115–47.

Mathesius, Vilém. 1939. Verstärkung und Emphase. In *Mélanges de linguistique offerts à Charles Bally*: 407–13.

Matisoff, James A. 1991. Areal and universal dimensions of grammatization in Lahu. In Elizabeth Closs Traugott and Bernd Heine (eds), *Approaches to Grammaticalization: Types of grammatical markers*. Vol. II. Amsterdam: John Benjamins, 383–53.

McEnery, Tony and Andrew Hardie. 2012. *Corpus linguistics: Method, theory and practice*. Cambridge: Cambridge University Press.

McEnery, Tony and Andrew Wilson. 2001. *Corpus linguistics: An introduction*. Edinburgh: Edinburgh University Press.

McMahon, April M. S. 1994. *Understanding language change*. Cambridge: Cambridge University Press.

McManus, Jennifer. 2012. English degree modifiers: A diachronic corpus-based study of the maximizer class. Doctoral dissertation: University of Liverpool. Available at: <https://livrepository.liverpool.ac.uk/9757/1/McManusJen_Sept2012_9757.pdf.pdf>

Meillet, Antoine. 1912. L'évolution des formes grammaticales. Reprinted in Meillet, Antoine. 1926. *Linguistique historique et linguistique générale*. 2nd edn. Paris: Honoré Champion, 131–48.

Méndez-Naya, Belén. 2003. On intensifiers and grammaticalization: The case of *swiþe*. *English Studies* 84(4): 372–91.

Méndez-Naya, Belén. 2006. Adjunct, modifier, discourse marker: On the various functions of *right* in the history of English. *Folia Linguistica Historica* 27: 141–69.

Méndez-Naya, Belén. 2007. *He nas nat right fat*: On the origin and development of the intensifier *right*. In Gabriella Mazzon (ed.), *Studies in Middle English forms and meanings*. Frankfurt am Main: Peter Lang, 191–207.

Méndez-Naya, Belén. 2008a. On the history of *downright*. *English Language and Linguistics* 12(2): 267–87.

Méndez-Naya, Belén. 2008b. 'The which is most and right harde to answere': Intensifying *right* and *most* in earlier English. In Richard Dury, Maurizio Gotti and Marina Dossena (eds), *English Historical Linguistics 2006: Selected papers from the fourteenth International Conference on English Historical Linguistics* (ICEHL 14). *Volume II: Lexical and semantic change*. Amsterdam: John Benjamins, 31–51.

Méndez-Naya, Belén. 2014. Out of the spatial domain: 'Out'-intensifiers in the history of English. *Folia Linguistica Historica* 35: 241–74.

Méndez-Naya, Belén. 2017. Co-occurrence and iteration of intensifiers in Early English. *English Text Construction* 10(2): 249–73.

Méndez-Naya, Belén. 2019. The intensifier system of the *Ormulum* and the interplay of micro-level and macro-level contexts in linguistic change. In Kristin Bech and Ruth Moehlig-Falke (eds), *Grammar – discourse – context*. Berlin: Mouton de Gruyter, 67–91.

Méndez-Naya, Belén. 2021. Synthetic intensification devices in Old English. *Journal of English Linguistics* 49(2): 208–27.

Meyer, Charles F. 2008. Pre-electronic corpora. In Anke Lüdeling and Merja Kytö (eds), *Corpus linguistics: An international handbook*. Vol. 1. Berlin: Mouton de Gruyter, 1–14.

Moreno de Oliveira, María Manuela. 1962. *Processos de intensificaçao no português contemporâneo: A entoaçao, processos morfológicos e sintácticos*. Lisboa: Centro de Estudos Filológicos.

Nevalainen, Terttu. 1999. Early Modern English lexis and semantics. In Roger Lass (ed.), *The Cambridge history of the English language*. Vol. 3. Cambridge: Cambridge University Press, 332–458.

Newmeyer, Frederick J. 2001. Deconstructing degrammaticalization. *Language Sciences* 23(2–3): 187–229.

Nicolle, Steve. 2011. Pragmatic aspects of grammaticalization. In Heiko Narrog and Bernd Heine (eds), *The Oxford handbook of grammaticalization*. Oxford: Oxford University Press, 401–12.

Norde, Muriel. 2001. Deflexion as a counterdirectional factor in grammatical change. *Language Sciences* 23(2–3): 231–64.

Norde, Muriel. 2009. *Degrammaticalization*. Oxford: Oxford University Press.

Núñez-Pertejo, Paloma. 2013. From degree adverb to response token: *Absolutely* in Late Modern and Contemporary British and American English. *Neuphilologische Mitteilungen* 114(2): 245–73.

Núñez-Pertejo, Paloma and Ignacio Palacios-Martínez. 2018. Intensifiers in Multicultural London English: New trends and developments. *Nordic Journal of English Studies* 17(2): 116–55.

Nuyts, Jan. 2001. Subjectivity as an evidential dimension in epistemic modal expressions. *Journal of Pragmatics* 33(3): 383–400.

O'Keeffe, Anne and Michael McCarthy. 2010. *The Routledge handbook of corpus linguistics*. London: Routledge.

Onodera, Noriko O. 2011. The grammaticalization of discourse markers. In Heiko Narrog and Bernd Heine (eds), *The Oxford handbook of grammaticalization*. Oxford: Oxford University Press, 614–24.

Paradis, Carita. 1997. *Degree modifiers of adjectives in spoken British English*. Lund: Lund University Press.

Paradis, Carita. 2001. Adjectives and boundedness. *Cognitive Linguistics* 12(1): 47–65.

Paradis, Carita. 2008. Configurations, construals and change: Expressions of degree. *English Language and Linguistics* 12(2): 317–43.

Partington, Alan. 1993. Corpus evidence of language change: The case of the intensifier. In Mona Baker, Gill Francis and Elena Tognini-Bonelli (eds), *Text and technology: In honour of John Sinclair*. Amsterdam: John Benjamins, 172–92.

Partington, Alan. 2004. 'Utterly content in each other's company': Semantic prosody and semantic preference. *International Journal of Corpus Linguistics* 9(1): 131–56.

Peters, Hans. 1992. English boosters: Some synchronic and diachronic aspects. In Günter Kellermann and Michael D. Morrissey (eds), *Diachrony within synchrony: Language history and cognition*. Frankfurt: Peter Lang, 529–45.

Peters, Hans. 1993. *Die englischen Gradadverbien der Kategorie booster*. Tübingen: Gunter Narr Verlag.

Peters, Hans. 1994. Degree adverbs in Early Modern English. In Dieter Kastovsky (ed.), *Studies in Early Modern English*. Berlin: Mouton de Gruyter, 269–88.

Quirk, Randolph, Sidney Greenbaum, Geoffrey Leech and Jan Svartvik. 1985. *A comprehensive grammar of the English language*. London: Longman.

Renkema, Jan. 1997. Geïntensiveerd taalgebruik: Een analyseschema. In Huub van den Bergh, Daniel Janssen, N. Bertens and M. Damen (eds), *Taalgebruik ontrafeld*. Dordrecht: Foris Publications, 495–504.

Rohdenburg, Günter. 2013. Using the OED quotations database as a diachronic corpus. In Manfred Krug and Julia Schlüter (eds), *Research methods in language variation and change*. Cambridge: Cambridge University Press, 136–57.

Scheibman, Joanne. 2002. *Point of view and grammar: Structural patterns of subjectivity in American English conversation*. Amsterdam: John Benjamins.

Schlüter, Julia. 2013. Using historical literature databases as corpora. In Manfred Krug and Julia Schlüter (eds), *Research methods in language variation and change*. Cambridge: Cambridge University Press, 119–35.

Sinclair, John McHardy. 1996. The search for the units of meaning. *Textus: English Studies in Italy* 9: 75–106.

Smith, K. Aaron and Dawn Nordquist. 2012. A critical and historical investigation into semantic prosody. *Journal of Historical Pragmatics* 13(2): 291–312.

Spitzbardt, Harry. 1965. English adverbs of degree and their semantic fields. *Philologia Pragensia* 8: 349–59.

Stenström, Anna-Brita. 1999. He was really gormless – She's bloody crap: Girls, boys and intensifiers. In Hilde Hasselgård and Signe Oksefjell (eds), *Out of corpora: Studies in honour of Stig Johansson*. Amsterdam: Rodopi, 69–78.

Stenström, Anna-Brita. 2000. *It's enough funny, man*: Intensifiers in teenage talk. In John M. Kirk (ed.), *Corpora galore: Analyses and techniques in describing English*. Amsterdam: Rodopi, 177–90.

Stoffel, Cornelis. 1901. *Intensives and downtoners: A study in English adverbs*. Heidelberg: Winter.

Stratton, James M. 2022. Old English intensifiers: The beginnings of the English intensifier system. *Journal of Historical Linguistics* 12(1): 31–69.

Stubbs, Michael. 1995. Collocations and semantic profiles: On the cause of the trouble with quantitative studies. *Functions of Language* 2(1): 23–55.

Suscinskij, Iossif I. 1985. Die Steigerungsmittel im Deutschen. *Deutsch als Fremdsprache (DaF)* 22: 95–100.

Svartvik, Jan. 1992. Corpus linguistics comes of age. In Jan Svartvik (ed.), *Directions in corpus linguistics: Proceedings of Nobel symposium 82 Stockholm, 4–8 August 1991*. Berlin: Mouton de Gruyter, 7–14.

Tagliamonte, Sali A. 2008. So different and pretty cool! Recycling intensifiers in Toronto, Canada. *English Language and Linguistics* 12(2): 361–94.

Tagliamonte, Sali A. and Chris Roberts. 2005. So weird, so cool, so innovative: The use of intensifiers in the television series *Friends*. *American Speech* 80(3): 280–300.

Traugott, Elizabeth Closs. 1982. From propositional to textual and expressive meanings: Some semantic-pragmatic aspects of grammaticalization. In Winfred P. Lehmann and Yakov Malkiel (eds), *Perspectives on historical linguistics*. Amsterdam: John Benjamins, 245–71.

Traugott, Elizabeth Closs. 1989. On the rise of epistemic meanings in English: An example of subjectification in semantic change. *Language* 65(1): 31–55.

Traugott, Elizabeth Closs. 1995. Subjectification in grammaticalisation. In Dieter Stein and Susan Wright (eds), *Subjectivity and subjectivisation: Linguistic perspectives*. Cambridge: Cambridge University Press, 31–54.

Traugott, Elizabeth Closs. 2003. From subjectification to intersubjectification. In Raymond Hickey (ed.), *Motives for language change*. Cambridge: Cambridge University Press, 124–39.

Traugott, Elizabeth Closs. 2006. The semantic development of scalar focus modifiers. In Ans van Kemenade and Bettelou Los (eds), *The handbook of the history of English*. Oxford: Blackwell, 335–59.

Traugott, Elizabeth Closs. 2007. (Inter)subjectification and unidirectionality. *Journal of Historical Pragmatics* 8(2): 295–309.

Traugott, Elizabeth Closs. 2010. (Inter)subjectivity and (inter)subjectification: A reassessment. In Kristin Davidse, Lieven Vandelanotte and Hubert Cuyckens (eds), *Subjectification, intersubjectification and grammaticalization*. Berlin: Mouton de Gruyter, 29–71.

Traugott, Elizabeth Closs. 2014. On the function of the epistemic adverbs *surely* and *no doubt* at the left and right peripheries of the clause. In Kate Beeching and Ulrike Detges (eds), *Discourse functions at the left and right periphery: Crosslinguistic investigations of language use and language change*. Leiden: Brill, 72–91.

Traugott, Elizabeth Closs and Richard B. Dasher. 2002. *Regularity in semantic change*. Cambridge: Cambridge University Press.

Traugott, Elizabeth Closs and Ekkehard König. 1991. The semantics-pragmatics of grammaticalization revisited. In Elizabeth Closs Traugott and Bernd Heine (eds), *Approaches to grammaticalization: Theoretical and methodological issues*. Vol. I. Amsterdam: John Benjamins, 189–218.

Traugott, Elizabeth Closs and Graeme Trousdale. 2013. *Constructionalization and constructional changes*. Cambridge: Cambridge University Press.

Trousdale, Graeme. 2010. Issues in constructional approaches to grammaticalization in English. In Katerina Stathi, Elke Gehweiler and Ekkehard König (eds), *Grammaticalization: Current views and issues*. Amsterdam: John Benjamins, 51–72.

Van Os, Charles. 1989. *Aspekte der Intensivierung im Deutschen*. Tübingen: Gunter Narr Verlag.

Vermeire, Antoine. 1979. *Intensifying adverbs: A syntactic, semantic and lexical study of fifteen degree intensifiers, based on an analysis of two computer corpuses of modern English*. Boston Spa: The British Library, Document Supply Centre.

Visconti, Jacqueline. 2013. Facets of subjectification. *Language Sciences* 36(1): 7–17.

Waltereit, Richard. 2002. Imperatives, interruption in conversation, and the rise of discourse markers: A study of Italian *guarda*. *Linguistics* 40(5): 987–1010.

Willis, David. 2007. Syntactic lexicalization as a new type of degrammaticalization. *Linguistics* 45(2): 271–310.

Yáñez-Bouza, Nuria. 2011. ARCHER: Past and present (1990–2010). *ICAME Journal* 35: 205–36.

# Sources

## *Primary sources*


ARCHER-3.2 = *A Representative Corpus of Historical English Registers* version 3.2. 1990–3/2002/2007/2010/2013. Originally compiled under the supervision of Douglas Biber and Edward Finegan at Northern Arizona University and University of Southern California; modified and expanded by subsequent members of a consortium of universities. Current member universities are Bamberg, Freiburg, Heidelberg, Helsinki, Lancaster, Leicester, Manchester, Michigan, Northern Arizona, Santiago de Compostela, Southern California, Trier, Uppsala, Zurich.

ECF = *Nineteenth Century Fiction*. Chadwyck Healey. 1996–2024. Available at: <http://collections.chadwyck.co.uk/home/home_c19f.jsp>.

EEBOCorp1.0: = *Early English Books Online Corpus* 1.0, compiled by Peter Petré. 2013. Available at <https://perswww.kuleuven.be/~u0050685/EEBOcorp1_0.zip>.

HC = The Helsinki Corpus of English Texts. 1991. Department of Modern Languages, University of Helsinki. Compiled by Matti Rissanen (Project leader), Merja Kytö (Project secretary); Leena Kahlas-Tarkka, Matti Kilpiö (Old English); Saara Nevanlinna, Irma Taavitsainen (Middle English); Terttu Nevalainen, Helena Raumolin-Brunberg (Early Modern English).

*MED* = *Middle English Dictionary*. Hans Kurath et al. (eds). 1952–2001. Ann Arbor, MI: University of Michigan Press. Available at: <http://quod.lib.umich.edu/m/med/>.

NCF = *Nineteenth Century Fiction*. Chadwyck Healey. 2000–24. Available at: <http://collections.chadwyck.co.uk/home/home_c19f.jsp>.

*OED* = *Oxford English Dictionary Online*. Oxford University Press. Available at <http://www.oed.com/>.


## *Secondary sources*


BYU-BNC = *Brigham Young University-British National Corpus* (Based on the British National Corpus from Oxford University Press), compiled by Mark Davies. 2004–24. Available at: <http://corpus.byu.edu/bnc/>.

COHA = *Corpus of Historical American English*, compiled by M. Davies. 2010–24. Available at: <http://corpus.byu.edu/coha/>.

WordSmith 6.0 = WordSmith 6.0 for Windows. 1996–2024. Lexical Analysis Software and Oxford University Press. Available at: <http://lexically.net/wordsmith/>.

# Index

# ENGLISH CORPUS LINGUISTICS

Series Editors: Graeme Davis and Damian Byrne

*English Corpus Linguistics* comprises studies that use a corpus-based methodology for the linguistic analysis of English-language real-world texts. The corpus methodology permits both synchronic and diachronic research. The outcomes may be primary linguistics research, or studies utilising concordancing tools to advance lexicographic, morphological or syntactic analyses. The series additionally supports academic study of the corpus methodology and the implementation of corpora in language teaching.

www.ingramcontent.com/pod-product-compliance
Ingram Content Group UK Ltd.
Pitfield, Milton Keynes, MK11 3LW, UK
UKHW020658041026
15590UKWH00001B/348

9 781803 745145